The Languages of Logic

For Helen and Jennifer

The Languages of Logic

An Introduction to Formal Logic

Second edition

Samuel Guttenplan

Blackwell
Publishing

© 1986, 1997 by Samuel Guttenplan

BLACKWELL PUBLISHING
350 Main Street, Malden, MA 02148-5020, USA
9600 Garsington Road, Oxford OX4 2DQ, UK
550 Swanston Street, Carlton, Victoria 3053, Australia

First published 1986
First published in USA 1987
Second edition published 1997

13   2006

Library of Congress Cataloging-in-Publication Data

Guttenplan, Samuel D.
   The languages of logic : an introduction to formal logic / Samuel
Guttenplan. — 2nd ed.
      p.   cm.
   Includes bibliographical references and index.
   ISBN 1-55786-988-X
   1. Logic. I. Title.
BC71.G88   1997
160 — dc20   96–38818
                                                           CIP

ISBN-13: 978-1-55786-988-3 (paperback)

A catalogue record for this title is available from the British Library.

Set in 10 on 12.5pt Sabon
by Wearset, Boldon, Tyne & Wear

For further information on
Blackwell Publishing, visit our website:
www.blackwellpublishing.com

Contents

Preface to the Second Edition

This second edition is best described as an enlargement of the first. There are many changes, and, where necessary, corrections, but the content of the original seventeen chapters has not been radically revised. Comments that I have received from many students, teachers and reviewers have encouraged me to think that the first edition achieved my original aim of making the subject matter of logic natural and accessible. However, having become convinced that clarity in exposition must be supplemented by more focused, exercise-based, material, I have added an appendix consisting of fourteen lessons devoted to central skills in logic. By providing more directed guidance in logical techniques, Appendix 1 should make it easier for students to supplement their understanding of logical concepts with the more practical capacity to solve logical problems. Further to this aim, I have included answers to most of the exercises in the main body of the book as well as to those in the lessons of Appendix 1.*

In addition, I have included (in Appendix 2) an account of truth trees (semantic tableaux). Some teachers find this method more congenial than truth tables or natural deduction, and it is sometimes seen as more accessible than deduction in application to predicate logic. Finally, there is a short account (Appendix 3) of alternative notations, both in respect of logical vocabulary and grouping. The use either of the dot system or Polish notation in place of parenthetical bracketing is no longer commonplace, but, as students will come across them, a brief account seemed apposite.

It is not possible to thank individually those who have given me useful comments about the book over the years. But I have taken note of them, and am especially grateful to students at Birkbeck who have been free (and fair) in offering me advice. Special thanks are owed to my wife Jennifer whose help included inspiration with the otherwise dire task of thinking up exercises.

S.G.

Answers are given to Exercises marked '' in Chapters 1–17 and Lessons 1–14.

Preface to the First Edition

I came to write this book in an attempt to solve a long-standing problem. Students of philosophy are usually given instruction in formal logic in the first year of their course. The rationale for this is the wholly laudable one that logic plays an important part in the further intricacies of philosophy and should be mastered as early in the course as possible. (Similar considerations operate in connection with many undergraduate courses in linguistics and in computer science.) However, when students come to use the formal logic they have learned in later parts of the course, the majority of them are simply not comfortable with any but the more introductory elements of the logic syllabus. They have mastered truth tables and proof procedures for sentential logic, but are far from easy with the structure and interpretations of predicate logic. And it is precisely the latter that is crucial for aspiring philosophers.

What puzzled me about this was not that there are elements of logic to which many students are resistant. Formal logic is notoriously lacking in appeal for some students, and while this is an unhappy state of affairs (about which more will be said shortly), it is hardly surprising. Rather, I found it puzzling there should be a particular problem with aspects of predicate logic. It seemed to me that dispassionate consideration would show that, if anything, there is more coherence, and indeed elegant simplicity, to the ideas behind predicate logic than there is to its precursor. Sentential logic is of necessity acquired first, but it doesn't seem to me simpler in any important sense. Stubbornly convinced that I was right about the simplicity of predicate logic, I set out to convince my students. My aim was to produce a set of notes which came as close as I could manage to making the ideas behind predicate logic so perspicuous as to be almost tangible.

One thing was clear from the start: sentential logic is more accessible to students because it is generally taught as item-by-item related to natural language. Many students come away thinking of the symbols of sentential logic as rather like an abbreviated code for sentences and connectives in natural language. This has unfortunate consequences:

1   It promotes a philosophically suspect view of logical languages.
2   It leads students to be deeply suspicious of their teachers (whether as textbooks or embodied) because of the plain fact that the connectives in sentential logic do not behave like those in natural language.
3   It encourages the student to expect something like the same relationship between predicate logic and natural language.

My initial interest was in 3. Predicate languages are structurally different from natural languages in all sorts of ways. Any attempt to understand them in a straightforward symbol-to-word way is bound to be frustrating. It struck me as no less difficult to learn predicate logic in this way than it would be to learn French by learning how individual French expressions mapped onto those in English. This, in turn, led me to think about how second languages are actually taught.

Even my casual encounters with 'foreign' language instruction convinced me of this much: they are taught, whenever possible, by the 'direct' method. This method consists in getting the student to use the new language directly in application to non-linguistic circumstances. (Typically included here are such things as ordering meals, booking rooms, meeting people, etc.) In this way, it is possible to become proficient in using the new language without having to consider at each stage how that language relates to one's native tongue. Thinking that this might work for logic, I wrote some notes which incorporated a version of the direct method in the teaching of predicate logic. The 'foreign' language was called 'Predicate' and the non-linguistic medium of communication was the Situation. A Situation was some simple arrangement of items which could be taken in at a glance, and whose portrayal did not strain my limited drawing ability. The idea was to get the student to apply the elements of Predicate to different Situations, and to do so without worrying about the connection between Predicate and natural language. (Incidentally, my use of Situations owes nothing to situation semantics though this latter subject can be introduced using the materials in this book.)

The result was, if I say so myself, impressive. Students found it easy and natural to use the resources of Predicate to describe Situations. This confirmed my original feeling that predicate logic has an elegance and simplicity that positively invite understanding. Also, I found that discussion in class tended to focus more on the 'right' questions about logic. Rather than worrying about the adequacy of Predicate as a symbolic code for English, there was genuine interest in the relationship between the resources of Predicate and those of English.

It was at this point that I was invited to turn my set of informal notes on predicate logic into a book. This presented further problems. First, it is easier to portray predicate logic as a self-contained language; sentential logic does not as naturally lend itself to this treatment. Second, as was clear from the start, neither of these is a language in the fullest sense. Sentential and Predicate are languages of structure ('languages of logic', as I came to call to them). Many of their components do not have the fixed meanings that one finds in natural languages. Neither of these problems was insuperable. What they require, as you will see, is some imagination on the part of the reader.

The reaction of my students to early drafts of this book encouraged me to think that I was right to persevere. Although my original interest was in predicate logic and in overcoming the obstacle mentioned in point 3 above, I have come to think that the approach to this book helps with points 1 and 2 and with the difficulties which logic presents to some students. There is less resistance to logic when there is an attempt to show the whole of the subject developing in an intellectually coherent way from concerns with languages and thought. As important, there is less suspicion of the subject (and its teachers) when the languages of logic are introduced independently of natural language. It gave me a certain satisfaction to realize that in this book the initial question is not: is the material conditional a good translation for 'if ... then'? Rather, it is: is 'if ... then' a good translation for the material conditional?

I have included chapters on modal logic and on truth definition because these are so central to further work in philosophy and linguistics. In the case of modal logic, I have tried to provide a way into this topic which would both interest the reader and form a framework onto which detail could be added. The chapter on truth was included to provide a background for the study of semantics and the philosophy of language.

I have more than once in this preface mentioned the help that I have received from students. It is with pleasure that I acknowledge this in a general way; and, more particularly, I would like to thank Alex Byrne, Kevan Norris, Siobhan Dowd, David Carter, Philippa Grindal, Kirstie Morrison, Protoklis Nicola, Erik Podgorski, Neil Ryder, Wendy Thomas and Aileen White. Also, for the enormously useful comments that I received from colleagues, I would like to thank Martin Davies, Ian McFetridge, Richard Spencer-Smith, Penelope Mackie and Dorothy Edgington. Finally, for the sort of help which cannot be sufficiently acknowledged, I would nonetheless like to thank Sally Barrett-Williams.

S.G.

Chapter one

Thinking

Logic can be described as a way of thinking about thinking; it is the study of certain specific features of thought. This needs explaining, so we will begin with some examples.

1.0   Movements of Thought

Example 1

Smith finds that her car won't start. She remembers that when Jones's car failed to start, it was because the distributor was wet. She also recalls reading that distributor problems are common in the sort of car she has. She is aware of how damp it is today. She concludes, therefore, that a wet distributor is the cause of the trouble.

Example 2

Brown is sitting at his desk gazing out of the window. He notices that the buds are just beginning to open on the trees. This reminds him of the unusually warm weather which was experienced last year at this time. That thought prompts the further thought that he must have his central heating boiler seen to as soon as possible.

Example 3

Green is planning his summer holiday. He knows that he can go by aeroplane or car. If he goes by aeroplane, he will get there faster, but will be unable to take much luggage. If he goes by car, he can take much more. He recognizes that the success of his holiday depends on his having the right sort of clothing for the unpredictable weather. He could not take the needed clothing on the aeroplane. He concludes that if the holiday is to be successful, he will have to go by car.

Each of these is a description of an episode of thinking – we all experience such episodes. One could characterize them as movements of thought. The subject in each case has one, and then other thoughts, which together form a series through which there is a kind of motion. Logic could be seen as containing laws of this sort of motion. However, not all movements of thought are the concern of logic, so we must first try to spell out precisely what sorts of movement are the proper subject matter of logic. This requires further characterization of the examples.

1.1   The First Example: Smith's Thoughts

There are many ways in which we could describe the series of thoughts in each case, but a particularly useful way is by giving two *inventories* of the subject's thoughts. Below is an illustration of what I mean using the first example.

The inventory of Smith's thoughts *just before* her final thought was:

1   My car doesn't start.
2   When Jones's car didn't start, the trouble was a wet distributor.
3   Cars like mine have this as a common problem.
4   It is very damp today.

I will label this INVENTORY$_1$. The inventory of Smith's thoughts at the end of the series was:

1   My car doesn't start.
2   When Jones's car didn't start, the trouble was a wet distributor.
3   Cars like mine have this as a common problem.
4   It is very damp today.
5   The fault of my car is a wet distributor.

I will label this INVENTORY$_2$. Notice that the inventories are the same except for the addition of 5 to INVENTORY$_2$.

The transition from INVENTORY$_1$ to INVENTORY$_2$ is what I want you to focus on. What you should note is that this transition is marked in the description of Smith's episode of thinking by the phrase 'she concludes, therefore'. This phrase invites us to recognize that INVENTORY$_2$ has some special relation to INVENTORY$_1$ of which it is an expansion. A look at the second example will bring out more clearly what this relation is like.

1.2   The Second Example: Brown's Thoughts

The inventories of Brown's thoughts are as follows:

INVENTORY$_1$

1   The buds are just beginning to open on the trees.
2   It was unusually warm this time last year.

INVENTORY$_2$

1   The buds are just beginning to open on the trees.
2   It was unusually warm this time last year.
3   The central heating boiler must be seen to.

In the original description, the transition from the first two thoughts to the third was marked by the phrase 'prompts the further thought'. We have now to investigate the difference between this and the transition in Example 1.

A first thing one might say is this: Smith's inventory of thoughts expanded because her final thought *followed* from the others, whereas this is not true in the case of Brown's final thought. This is not wrong, but it is not as helpful as it could be. After all, there is a perfectly good sense in which Brown's thought about his central heating boiler followed from the other thoughts that he had: it was prompted by them.

In using the notion of 'following from', what one wants to say is that there is a *logical* relation between Smith's thoughts, whereas Brown's thoughts merely come one after the other. This is true, but we ought to be able to say something which doesn't use 'logical', since the subject matter of logic is what is at issue. We cannot take for granted in this discussion that we know what logic is.

What makes the transition in Smith's case different from that in Brown's is that we think Smith could *defend* the movement of her thoughts in a way that Brown couldn't. Smith could say something like this: in so far as anyone has the thoughts in INVENTORY$_1$, and makes the transition to INVENTORY$_2$, then the move is *justified*. Such a defence would be wholly out of place for Brown. His thoughts were connected, but the connection was idiosyncratic to Brown. He can explain why INVENTORY$_2$ came after INVENTORY$_1$, but he couldn't justify it, nor would we expect him to. There is more to be said about this, but let us first look at Example 3.

1.3   The Third Example: Green's Thoughts

Here are the two inventories of Green's thoughts:

INVENTORY₁

1   I can go on holiday by aeroplane or car.
2   If I go on holiday by aeroplane, then I shall get there faster, but cannot take much luggage.
3   If I go by car, I can take more luggage.
4   A successful holiday requires that I take the right clothing.
5   I couldn't take the right clothing on the aeroplane.

INVENTORY₂

1   I can go on holiday by aeroplane or car.
2   If I go on holiday by aeroplane, then I shall get there faster, but cannot take much luggage.
3   If I go by car, I can take more luggage.
4   A successful holiday requires that I take the right clothing.
5   I couldn't take the right clothing on the aeroplane.
6   If my holiday is to be a success, I must go by car.

The transition between these two states of Green's mind is effected by 'concludes'. This is some evidence that the transition is more like that in Smith's than in Brown's thinking. Also, Green would be ready to defend the addition to INVENTORY₁ that led to INVENTORY₂ in this way: anyone who had the thoughts in INVENTORY₁ would be justified in making the transition to INVENTORY₂.

Exercise 1

(a)   Write out three examples of movements of thought from your own experience.
(b)   What words other than 'therefore' are used to indicate defensible transitions among thoughts?

1.4   Three Types of Movement of Thought

It is clear that the movement of thought in Brown's case is radically different from that in either of the other two cases. This is not to say that it is defective in any way. Our thinking is very often arranged in ways that are simply not suitable for the kind of defence described in connection with Smith and Green. There are many times when our thoughts move from one to another in a connected way, but not in a way that we would consider as needing justification of any kind.

The subject matter of logic, however, is precisely those movements of thought which are defensible in somewhat the way described in the cases of Smith and Green. *Logic studies the transitions in our states of mind which we are prepared to defend as justifiable.* There is, though, more to be said about such transitions.

Both Smith's and Green's thoughts involved transitions which could be defended in the way described above. Yet there is a very important difference between these two cases: there are *grounds* for the defence in the case of Green which do not carry over to the case of Smith. To understand these grounds ask yourself whether someone who thought as Smith (or Green) did initially (INVENTORY$_1$), would also think it possible that they were wrong about the additional thought which results in INVENTORY$_2$. That is, could their first thoughts be *true* and their final thought be *false*? We shall examine each case.

Smith employed her thinking to discover why her car didn't start. At the end of her thought episode, she held the view that a wet distributor was the fault. Moreover, she came to this view by a route that she would defend as justified. What would you say of all this if it turned out that the fault in the car was *not* a wet distributor? Would Smith be forced to admit that some item in INVENTORY$_1$ was false? The answer to this last question is surely 'No'. All the things that Smith thought initially could be true, and, yet, it could turn out that the concluding thought she had was mistaken.

Does this mean that there was something wrong with the way in which she arrived at her final thought? The answer here is again 'No'. Smith's method of getting to INVENTORY$_2$ was perfectly reasonable, given what she believed in the first place. It is simply a feature of this sort of movement of thought that, on the one hand, we think it justifiable or reasonable; and, on the other hand, we are prepared to admit that the truth of the initial thoughts does not guarantee the truth of the concluding thought. In short, there can be movements of thought which are defensible but which do not necessarily lead *from* true thoughts *to* true thoughts.

This is in contrast to the case of Green. Suppose it turned out that Green took the aeroplane, and had a successful holiday. This is as much as to say that his final thought was false. What would this result lead us to say about Green's original inventory of thoughts? Here we would say that he must have been mistaken about one of the thoughts in INVENTORY$_1$. *If they were all true, then this would have guaranteed the truth of his final thought.* Since his final thought turned out to be false, one of those in the initial inventory must have been false. (For the present, I expect that you can convince yourself of this by carefully comparing Smith's and Green's inventories. There will be more said about this shortly.)

Given this, it should be clear why I said that Smith's defence of her thinking would differ from Green's. Both sorts of thinking are defensible, but Green can offer a special ground for his defence. He can say: anyone's thoughts ought to move in the way that mine did because such movement guarantees the truth of the final thought given that the initial thoughts are true. Smith cannot say this – though, in contrast to Brown, she can insist that the movement of her thought was defensible in some other way.

NOTE   In each example, the final inventory was seen as an expansion of the initial one. This makes it seem as if our thinking always consists in adding new thoughts to those we have already, and this cannot be completely correct. An important feature of our thinking, and especially of our logical thinking, is that it sometimes leads us to eliminate thoughts we had previously accepted. In the rest of the book, we will explore this and other sorts of thinking. The examples in this chapter are merely intended to get you to distinguish between certain movements of thought. They should not be taken as an exhaustive classification of such movements.

1.5   Arguments

The three examples illustrate different ways in which thoughts can move. Two of these were singled out because they involved a movement signalled by words such as 'therefore' or 'concluded'. We shall call these sorts of movement *arguments*. An argument can be understood as a series of thoughts, the final one of which is set off by some such word as 'therefore'. The series of thoughts which precede the 'therefore' are called *premises*, and the final thought is called the *conclusion*. The Smith and Green examples contained arguments; the Brown example did not. Here are the arguments contained in the Smith and Green examples:

SMITH

Premises	(1)	My car doesn't start.
	(2)	When Jones's car didn't start, the trouble was a wet distributor.
	(3)	Cars like mine have this as a common problem.
	(4)	It is very damp today.
		Therefore
Conclusion	(5)	The fault in the car is a wet distributor.

GREEN

Premises   (1)   I can go on holiday by car or aeroplane.

              (2)   If I go on holiday by aeroplane, then I shall get there faster, but cannot take much luggage.

              (3)   If I go by car, I can take more luggage.

              (4)   A successful holiday requires that I take the right clothing.

              (5)   I couldn't take the right clothing on the aeroplane.

                    Therefore

Conclusion (6)   If my holiday is to be a success, I must go by car.

In saying that a movement of thought contains an argument, we are saying that the movement is of the sort for which a defence is appropriate. Of course, it can happen that our thoughts move in ways that *seem* defensible when they are not. Not all arguments are good ones. That is not our present concern. What is at issue here is how the movement of thought illustrated by Smith and Green differs from that illustrated by Brown. Smith's and Green's thoughts contained arguments, Brown's did not.

The subject matter of logic is movements of thought that contain arguments. (Or, we could say that the subject matter of logic is argument.) However, the logic to be studied is not about just any sort of argument. The difference between the arguments of Smith and Green is crucial to understanding the subject matter of this book.

Smith's argument has these features: the reasoning from premises to conclusion can be defended, yet, it could happen that her premises were all true, and her conclusion turned out to be false. This sort of argument is called *inductive* or *probabilistic*. We very often employ such arguments in our thinking.

Green's argument can be defended too, but its defence has this feature: *if all the premises are true, then the conclusion is bound to be true.* It could not turn out that the premises were true and the conclusion was false. Arguments that are intended to have this feature are called *deductive*. The subject matter of this book is deductive arguments. But why did I say arguments that are *intended* to have this feature?

1.6 Good and Bad Arguments

It would be wonderful if all the deductive arguments that we used in our thinking were like Green's: given that the premises of the argument are true, its conclusion is bound to be true. Unfortunately, this is not the case. It can, and often does, happen that we employ arguments which are intended to have this feature even though they don't. Here is an example:

> Wilson thinks to himself: If Jones died of natural causes and he had been to the doctor recently, the doctor was negligent in the way that he treated patients. In fact the doctor has been found guilty of negligent malpractice, and Jones had been to see that particular doctor recently. Therefore, Jones died of natural causes.

Let us write Wilson's argument this way:

(1) If Jones died of natural causes and he had been to the doctor recently, then that doctor was negligent.
(2) Jones had been to that doctor.
(3) That doctor was found guilty of negligence.
___
(4) Jones died of natural causes.

What we have done is to drop the labels 'premises' and 'conclusion' and the word 'therefore' which indicates the transition from premises to conclusion. Instead, we merely list the premises and use a line to set them off from the conclusion. From now on we will write arguments in this compact way.

There certainly seems to be something wrong with this argument, and it is not hard to put your finger on it. For all that Wilson thought (as represented in 1–3), it could have been the case that Jones met with some other end than a natural one. For example, nothing in the premises forces us to rule out the possibility that Jones was a murder victim, or that he died in an aeroplane crash.

I do not want to suggest that any of your thought episodes would be quite as obviously faulty as Wilson's, but we very often do think in ways that are more like Wilson's than like Green's. What this means is that there are times when we *intend* our thinking to terminate in conclusions reached by defensible deductive arguments, but that, through faults in the arguments, we are disappointed in these intentions. In short, we sometimes use bad arguments.

Using a bad deductive argument in one's thinking should be distinguished from the case of using an inductive argument. Remember Smith. She was trying to work out what was wrong with her car, and she ended up with the view that a wet distributor was responsible. Her argument seemed justifiable, even though she would have readily admitted that her premises could be true and her conclusion false. She didn't expect the sort of argument she used to *guarantee* the truth of the conclusion. On the other hand, Wilson's thinking seems quite clearly to be of the deductive sort – only faulty. Strictly speaking, all inductive arguments are defective by the standards of deductive reasoning. It's just that genuine inductive arguments do not even pretend to meet those standards.

It is no easy matter to spell out precisely what makes an argument inductive, as opposed to deductive and faulty. Nor is it easy to set out the grounds on which to justify inductive arguments. However, these won't be problems for us, interesting as they are. We will be dealing exclusively with arguments that are to be understood as deductive.

It is obviously of some importance to be able to tell whether an argument is good or not. (From here on I will use 'argument' meaning thereby 'deductive argument'.) In fact, much of this book will be taken up with just this issue. Of course, saying that some arguments are good, and some bad, is imprecise. This will be improved on in the next chapter. For the present, we can summarize the discussion so far this way:

> The logic to be studied in this book is the study of those movements of thought which are representable as deductive arguments. Most importantly, it is the study of the ways in which we distinguish between good and bad arguments. (From now on, when I say 'logic', I intend the study of deductive arguments.)

Exercise 2

Write out two examples of good arguments and two examples of bad arguments.

1.7 Logic as Morality

Human beings sometimes employ good arguments in their thinking, and sometimes bad arguments. In those cases where their arguments go wrong, there can be any number of explanations, some more interesting than others. Lack of care, insufficient memory, misunderstanding and wishful thinking are just some of the factors responsible.

From what I have said so far, you might now have the impression that logic consists in the study of how human beings actually think – how they are successful, when they are, and why they go wrong, when they do. Seen this way, logic would be descriptive of human reasoning. Its goal would be to provide laws of motion for thoughts in somewhat the way that astronomers provide laws of motion for planets and stars.

In spite of appearances, however, this descriptive view of logical laws is misleading. You can see this by focusing on the analogy with astronomical laws.

The laws that astronomers accept are intended to describe the motions of the heavenly bodies. What would they say about their laws if one of the planets were observed to move in a way that violated one or more of them? Quite obviously, if the observations were certified as correct, they would say that the law or laws needed to be revised. The laws are supposed to fit the motion of the planets; if they fail to do so, the defect is in the laws. Matters are very different with logic.

The laws of logic – laws which have yet to be discussed in any detail – are intended to characterize arguments as good or bad. Could it ever happen that human beings used forms of argument that were classified as bad? The answer here is obviously 'Yes'. For any of the reasons mentioned above, a particular individual might well use a bad argument in his thinking. More interestingly, could it be the case that human reasoners *generally* used a bad form of argument? Be careful with your answer here.

If the laws of logic are as descriptive as the laws of planetary motion, then it would seem to be impossible for this to happen. On this analogy, if human beings generally used a form of argument, this form would have to be accommodated by the laws of logic. After all, we don't criticize the planets for not moving according to the laws; we criticize and reformulate the laws. Yet, it does seem perfectly possible that human beings generally violate some law of logic. At least we ought to allow this as a possibility. However, it can only be a possibility if we give up thinking of the laws of logic as being like the laws of planetary motion. Logic must be seen as more than merely descriptive of human reasoning.

In place of the analogy with physical laws, we would do better to think of logic as a morality of thought. We think it a moral law (or rule) that we should not murder. Would it count against this law that murder occurs all too commonly on this planet? Of course not. The moral law which forbids murder is not meant to be descriptive of human behaviour; it is intended to set a standard or norm for such behaviour. Violations of a moral law are grounds for regret, remorse and punishment; they are certainly not, by themselves, grounds for changing the moral law which was violated. The laws of thought which show us how to distinguish good from bad arguments are much more like moral laws than they are like physical laws. They set a standard or norm of what constitutes good reasoning and it is with respect to this norm that we can see our reasoning as sometimes faulty. This point is sometimes expressed this way: the laws of logic are *normative* rather than merely descriptive. Hence, it is an exaggeration, though true, to say that using a faulty argument is something like sinning.

1.8   On Not Keeping Our Thoughts to Ourselves

I have so far represented logic as the study of certain forms of thinking. Arguments have been treated as special sorts of movement in our thought episodes. While this is a good place to begin our understanding of what logic is about, it is by no means the whole of the story. We do not keep all our thoughts to ourselves, and a crucial fact about arguments is that they can be used to influence other people's thinking as well as our own. When arguments go public, two important new factors must be considered.

A.   Language

First, the thoughts which form the premises and conclusion of arguments must be expressed in some language or other. That is, if I want to convey some argument that I use in my thinking, then I have to construct sentences in some language that you understand in order to get my argument across. This was obvious even in connection with the examples that were used above. The thoughts of Smith, Brown, Green and Wilson were brought to your attention using sentences of English.

This factor might seem quite straightforward, but it is fraught with important and interesting difficulties. Being able to understand fully the thought expressed by a sentence of a natural (i.e. actually used) language such as English, is not as simple as it sometimes seems. It seems easy because we all learned our native languages a long time ago, and we use them unreflectively – almost automatically. In laying out arguments and assessing them, you will be forced to reflect on language in a more thorough way. This will not be as easy as using the language in everyday interchanges but, then, that is why most of this book lies ahead.

Note   I seem to be claiming here that we have episodes of thought that take place in a private medium of thinking which is only sometimes dressed in a public language. This is a picturesque way of putting the matter, and is harmless, so long as you realize that things are, in fact, much more complicated. Some have argued that there can be no such wholly private medium. Also, and connectedly, some have argued that possession of a public language is a necessary condition for thinking anything at all. These questions about the nature of thought are very interesting, but we can proceed without settling them.

B.   Persuasion

The second factor brought into play by the public face of arguments revolves around the uses to which they are put. In thought, arguments help us to move from one series of thoughts to others in a defensible way. If our arguments are good ones, then we can be sure that we will *end up* with true thoughts, in so far as we *began* with true ones. This is clearly very useful. However, when arguments are communicated, when we want to use them to influence other people's thinking, we must take care to choose the arguments carefully. It can happen that an argument which we use is a good one in one sense, but is not good as an instrument of persuasion. For example, consider the following argument which John accepts:

(1)   By their very nature, jury trials sometimes allow the guilty to go free.
(2)   We must take steps to prevent this ever happening.

The jury system should be dropped.

In so far as John's thinking is concerned, this seems a perfectly good argument: if its premises are true, then its conclusion is bound to be true. However, it wouldn't be much use as an instrument to persuade Harriet, since she doesn't accept John's premises. She thinks that jury trials are an important part of the just administration of law, even if they sometimes allow the guilty to go free. That is, she doesn't accept the second premise. If we ask ourselves whether this is *really* a good argument, then it is unclear what the proper response should be. It is good when viewed as the pattern by which John's thoughts move, but it is not at all good as a way of convincing Harriet – and convincing is one of the main functions of arguments when they go public.

   In the next chapter, we will discuss the whole question of good and bad arguments. For the present, it is sufficient if you recognize that arguments can be seen as features both of the movement of thought and of communicative interchange.

The Main Points of Chapter 1

1   Our thoughts move from one to another in all sorts of ways. One of these ways is the subject matter of deductive logic. As a first approximation, we may say that a deductive movement of thought is one which is defensible on the following grounds: if the thoughts we begin with are all true, then the thought that we end up with is bound to be true. In describing a deductive movement of thought, we separate the resultant thought from the others by words such as 'therefore' or 'so'. This is not to say that these words *always* signal the presence of deductive thinking.

2   We can describe deductive thinking using the notion of *argument*. An argument is a listing of the thoughts that take place in an episode of deductive thinking. The initial thoughts are the *premises* and the final thought is the *conclusion*. To begin with, we will adopt the convention that arguments are written in the following format:

> Premises (numbered in a list).
> _____
> Conclusion.

3   Not all our deductive thinking goes as we would like. Sometimes we employ arguments which do not lead from true premises to true conclusions, even though it is our intention that they do so. In short, there are good and bad arguments. Logic is, in large part, a systematic study of the rules or laws of good arguments and ways of distinguishing them from bad arguments.

4   The rules or laws of thought which logic uncovers are not merely *descriptive* of human thinking. They tell us how we ought to think. This is why I described logic as a morality of thought, and why the laws of logic are often called *normative*.

5   Arguments have a public face. They figure in our (deductive) thinking, but they are also part of our talking to one another. When they figure in conversations, it is often because we are trying to influence other people's thinking. This use of arguments introduces two complications: (i) the thoughts which form the premises and conclusions have to be expressed in sentences of some language; and (ii) there could be a conflict between what counts as a good deductive argument and what counts as a good argument for persuading others.

Chapter two

Arguments

In the last chapter we said very roughly what made arguments good or bad. We must improve on that. We must also consider how we can tell whether any particular argument is good or bad. This is no easy matter. Most people are competent to tell whether fairly simple arguments are acceptable, but, perhaps surprisingly, there does not seem to be anything that deserves to be called a *method* behind that skill. That is, if you ask people whether simple arguments such as those used in the previous chapter are good, they can usually give the correct answer without much difficulty. I depended on that when I asked you to decide whether those arguments were good. However, if you ask people how they arrived at their answer, the chances are that they would be at a loss to say. The main business of this chapter will be to look more deeply into the nature of arguments. The ultimate goal (realized in the next chapter) will be to draw up a strategy for *testing* whether any argument is good or bad. But first things first. What precisely is a good argument and how is it different from a bad one?

2.0 Validity

Two things were said about what makes an argument good:

(a) if its premises are true, then its conclusion is bound to be true;

(b) it is suitable as a means of persuading someone of the truth of its conclusion.

Let us concentrate first on (a). An argument which is good in this sense will be called *valid*. In order to see precisely what makes an argument valid we have to look more deeply into the form of words used in (a).

What does it mean to say that the conclusion of an argument is *bound to be true*, when its premises are true? Substituting for the phrase 'bound to be true' we could define validity this way:

(N)   It is necessarily the case that if all the premises of an argument are true then so is the conclusion.

The notion of necessity here is something like that in:

Anything which is red is necessarily coloured.
Bachelors are necessarily unmarried.
Nine is necessarily greater than five.

Defining validity in terms of necessity doesn't take us very far from talk of a conclusion as 'bound to be true' if the premises are. However, there is another formulation which is fully equivalent to (N), though it is easier to work with. Validity can be defined in terms of possibility as follows:

(P)   It is not possible for all the premises of an argument to be true and the conclusion false.

In spite of its apparent simplicity, (P) can give rise to misunderstandings. To prevent this, it is best if we see how (P) is applied to specific examples.

Example 1

(1)   All oak trees have roots.
(2)   All the trees that grow in England have roots.

Some oak trees grow in England.

Is this a valid argument? One's immediate reaction is to deny that it is – to say that it is *invalid*. But we have to try to understand why. We begin by seeing whether the premises and conclusion of the argument are, in fact, true.

It doesn't require a great deal of knowledge of botany and geography to see that they are indeed all true. However, (P) requires that, for an argument to be valid, it is not *possible* for the premises to be true and the conclusion false. Merely knowing that the premises and conclusion are *actually* true does not tell us that. What is required is some thought about the possibilities in this case.

The world is such that all oak trees have roots, all trees that grow in England have roots, and some oak trees grow in England. That much we know. But the world could have been different. It could have been the case that the world was created in such a way that all oak trees have roots and all the trees that grow in England have roots, but that there were no oak trees in England. Things are not that way but *it is possible for them to have been that way*. That is, it is possible for the world to be such that the premises are true and the conclusion of the argument is false. It is this possibility which makes Example 1 invalid, even though its premises and conclusion are actually true.

Many people have very little patience with mere possibilities. Why, they would ask, do we bother with the possibility that the world might have been created with an England devoid of oak trees? England does have oak trees, so that's that.

The reply to this goes right back to our original discussion of arguments in chapter 1. An argument is a particular way in which our thoughts move. If it is a good argument, then it can be justified. What better way could there be of justifying an argument than by showing that it could not happen that its premises are true and its conclusion false? And here talk of what 'could be' the case is talk of possibilities. If an argument has the sort of goodness we have called *validity*, it offers a guarantee that the conclusion is true if the premises are. This is a very good reason for being interested in the sort of possibility we need for validity.

Example 2

(1) Oak trees grow only in places where it rains with some degree of regularity.
(2) It does not rain in the Sahara with any degree of regularity.

Oak trees do not grow in the Sahara.

By now you should anticipate the inevitable questions: are the premises and conclusion true? Is the argument valid? Interestingly, in this case, the answer to both questions is 'Yes'. Here we have a case where an argument is valid and has true premises and conclusion. It is not possible for (1) and (2) to be true and the conclusion false, *and*, as a matter of fact, all three thoughts are true.

Is it the truth values of the premises and conclusion which leads you to say that this is a valid argument? Of course not! Remember, Example 1 had true premises and conclusion. In that respect, it is just like Example 2. Nonetheless, Example 1 is invalid and Example 2 is valid. This difference between them does not turn on the actual truth or falsity of their premises and conclusions, but on certain possibilities. What is important is not that the premises and conclusion of Example 2 are actually true, but that it is not possible for its premises to be true and its conclusion false. It is this fact about possibility which leads us to say that Example 2 is valid.

How does one decide these possibilities? This question will occupy us more fully in the next chapter. There we will begin to work out a strategy for enabling us to tell whether any given argument is valid. Our present concern is with what it means to say that an argument is valid, rather than with working out whether this is so. For that reason, I have chosen examples which you can easily classify as valid or invalid.

Example 3

    (1)   All fish swim.
    (2)   All whales swim.

    All whales are fish.

The premises of this argument are true and its conclusion is false, so we do not have to look deeply into possibilities to tell that it is invalid. Validity requires that it not be possible for the premises to be true and the conclusion false. Since the premises are actually true and the conclusion false, we know straightaway that the argument is invalid. After all, what is actually the case surely counts as a possibility.

However, you should be careful here. In most cases, we have to think about non-actual possibilities in order to tell whether an argument is valid. Here, it suffices to know the actual truth values of the premises and conclusion. In this respect, Example 3 seems to contrast with Examples 1 and 2, but do not let this mislead you. The invalidity of Example 3 is as much connected with possibility as, for instance, Example 1. It is just that, as I noted above, the way things actually are counts as a way things could be, as a possibility.

Example 4

    (1)   If the Earth is round, then many things would just fall off it.
    (2)   Things do not just fall off the Earth.

    The Earth is not round.

This is a valid argument, but its conclusion is certainly false. How can this happen? Validity requires that it not be possible for the premises to be true and the conclusion false. It does not require that the premises and conclusion actually be true. In this case, since the conclusion is false and the argument is valid, at least one of the premises must be false. The culprit is quite clearly premise (1).

Exercise 1

Write out an argument in which:

(i)   All the premises are false, the conclusion is true, the argument is *valid*.
(ii) All the premises are false, the conclusion is true, the argument is *invalid*.
(iii) All of the premises are false, the conclusion is false, the argument is *valid*.
(iv) All of the premises are false, the conclusion is false, the argument is *invalid*.

If you followed the Examples and did the EXERCISE, you should understand the relationship between validity, possibility and truth. We now turn to consider two interesting features of validity.

2.1   Validity and True Thoughts

In order to tell whether an argument is valid, you do not have to know whether the premises and conclusion of the argument are true. It isn't even required that they be true, whether or not you know it. Of course, if you happen to know that the premises are true and the conclusion is false, then you know the argument is invalid. But, this is a special case – one in which the counter-example is actual. Validity turns on what is possibly the case rather than what is actually the case, but in saying this we are not ruling out the actual. What is actually the case counts as one of the possibilities. All of this is familiar from our previous discussion. What I want to point out here is something about the relationship between truth and validity which is both puzzling and important.

Our thoughts are true, when they are, in virtue of their subject matter. If I think that trees have roots, then my thought is true because of 'how it is' with trees. It would be useful if my thoughts could be made true merely in virtue of my thinking them, but this just isn't so. In order to tell whether a thought is true, I have to go and see whether the world is as it is held to be by my thought. Or so it would seem. Let's look more closely at validity.

Here is an example of an argument that was used in the earlier discussion of validity:

(1) Oak trees only grow in places where it rains with some degree of regularity.

(2) It does not rain in the Sahara with any degree of regularity.

Oak trees do not grow in the Sahara.

In that earlier discussion, I asked you to examine the argument and say whether it was valid. I had very little doubt that you could see that it was, even though you as yet have not been taught any procedures for testing validity. Try to remember what your examination of this argument involved. Did you have to ask yourself whether each of the premises and conclusion were true? Did you have to consult encyclopedias or try to imagine what the Sahara is like? Certainly not. Very likely it was a matter of just reading through the argument and seeing how it struck you. Notice that in doing this, you were in effect examining the thoughts in the argument; you were not consulting the world to see whether the thoughts were true of it.

However, in so far as the argument did strike you as valid, your inspection showed you that:

Oak trees do not grow in the Sahara,

could be checked for being true by checking the truth of:

Oak trees only grow where it rains with some degree of regularity,

AND

It doesn't rain in the Sahara with any degree of regularity.

This is because, since the argument is valid, the truth of the conclusion is a necessary consequence of the truth of the two premises. But this is really quite amazing. The standard way of checking whether oak trees grow somewhere is by looking in that place for oak trees. The existence of the above valid argument gives us a different way of checking: just do whatever looking is needed to tell whether the premises are true. It is surprising that, by examining the argumentative relationship between certain thoughts, we can come up with ways of checking the truth of some thought in other than the standard way. That is, we can check the truth of the conclusion of a valid argument by checking the truth of its premises.

How can this happen? That very deep question is certainly beyond the scope of this chapter, and is one for which there is nothing like an agreed answer. This is a question for discussion in the branch of philosophy called the 'philosophy of logic'. I have raised it to give you both some idea of the importance of the notion of validity and an inkling of the deeper issues that lie behind this notion.

2.2   Validity and Other-Than-True Thoughts

I said earlier that the definition of validity raised two issues. It is time to consider the second of them. Here is an argument:

(1)   If you go out, you'll get wet.
(2)   You do not want to get wet.

_____

Do not go out!

Is it valid? Be careful here. There is certainly something natural about this progression of thoughts. (1) and (2) seem to offer a very good *reason* for the conclusion. Nonetheless, given our definition of validity, we cannot really say that this argument is either valid or invalid. To see why, remind yourself what validity is, and take a closer look at the conclusion.

To say that an argument is valid is to say that it is not possible for the premises to be true and the conclusion false. The trouble is that the conclusion of this argument isn't the sort of thought that is either true or false. I would expect you to be puzzled if someone were to ask you if the advice:

Do not go out!

were true. As advice, it could be described as 'useful' but not as 'true', or 'unhelpful' but not as 'false'. Because of this, the notion of validity simply doesn't apply to the above argument. Here we have hit on a feature of our understanding of validity which makes it somewhat restrictive. *An argument is a candidate for validity only if its premises and conclusion are the sort of thing which it makes sense to describe using the words 'true' and 'false'.* The following are a few examples of thoughts that might figure in arguments but which would not be described using these words:

Where shall I go on holiday?
Pass the sugar!
Would that I were happy.

Many people dislike restrictions. Why not define validity so that it does not impose this restriction on possible premises and conclusions of valid arguments? The short answer is that it is very difficult to see how to go about it. The long answer – and it is the one I prefer – comes roughly to this. By defining validity the way we have, we end up with a clear notion which can be studied further. When we are able to understand arguments valid in this sense, we will be better placed to understand more general forms of argument. In other words, our definition of validity is best viewed not so much as restrictive, but as a way of not biting off more than we can chew.

Exercise 2

Arrange each of the arguments below in the standard way and say whether they are valid. (Try to keep track of how you decide whether each one is valid.)

   (i)   If you exercise regularly and do not smoke, then you will be healthy. John doesn't smoke and he's healthy, so he must exercise regularly.

   (ii) Every number is either odd or even. The number of planets is odd, so it is not even.

*(iii) If God is omnipotent, there is nothing he cannot do. He can build a mountain so large that he cannot move it, or he cannot build such a mountain. Either way there is something he cannot do. Therefore, God is not omnipotent.

   (iv) The TV has no picture either because of a fault in the transmitter, or because it is not plugged in. There is a fault in the transmitter. So, it is plugged in.

2.3   Arguments and Persuasion

Being valid is one way in which an argument could be said to be good. We are now ready to consider the other way. Here is the formulation given earlier:

> An argument is good when it is suitable as a means of persuading someone of the truth of its conclusion.

It doesn't take much of an argument to convince some people of things they are predisposed to believe, and we can hardly allow gullibility to feature in our understanding of what makes an argument good. It might help a bit if we changed 'someone' to 'anyone', but the benefit would be very limited. On the one hand, it might be the case that some form of argument *seemed* convincing to all of us, even though it was defective. On the other hand, we would hardly want to reject an argument as good simply because some exceedingly stubborn individual refused to be convinced by it.

The first of these possibilities can be illustrated by an analogy. Suppose we defined two lines to be of equal length just in case everyone would perceive that they were. Are the *horizontal* lines in the following drawing of equal length?

I have no doubt that you perceive them as unequal. So do I, even though I know, and perhaps you do too, that they are equal. It seems to be a fact about our perceptual system that it unavoidably misleads us about these lines. But is it really a mistake? It wouldn't be if we stuck to the definition of equal length proposed above, and this shows that there is something wrong with the definition. The same could be the case about the convincingness of arguments. There might be an argument which convinced everyone who came across it, even though it might be one which we came to think of as a bad argument. However, if we *defined* a good argument as one which convinced everyone, then we would have defined out of existence the very real possibility that we could be systematically mistaken. This won't do.

One thing we might do is revise our definition of a good argument so it reads:

> An argument is good just in case it could be used to persuade any rational thinker of the truth of its conclusion.

This certainly avoids all the problems raised above. We can stipulate that a rational thinker is one who is not gullible, not prone to systematic errors, and not given to insupportable stubbornness. The trouble with this new definition is that, while it is correct, it isn't very helpful. We are trying to understand what connection there is between goodness and persuasiveness in arguments. Introducing the rational thinker helps only if we can say what such a thinker would be like. Saying that a rational thinker is one who is persuaded only by good arguments is true, but it doesn't tell us what makes an argument good.

Why not use 'good argument' in the sense described earlier? We would expect a rational thinker to be one who wouldn't allow himself to be persuaded by any but valid arguments. So, why not equate persuasiveness with validity? If this were accepted, we would have shown that the two senses of 'good argument' come to pretty much the same.

We certainly do not want to allow that the rational thinker can be persuaded by an invalid argument: a thinker would not be rational if he could be convinced of the truth of a conclusion by an invalid argument. However, we cannot directly define a convincing argument as one which is valid because there are many cases in which it would not be at all rational to accept as true the conclusion of a valid argument. Here is one:

(1)   Unicorns have been depicted in tapestries.
(2)   If something has been depicted, then that thing exists.

Unicorns exist.

Remember that a valid argument might very well have false premises and a false conclusion. The conclusion of this argument is almost certainly false and, since it is valid, it must have at least one false premise – in this case, premise (2). It would hardly do for a rational thinker to be convinced that there are unicorns by this valid argument. Here is another example:

(1)   There has never been an authenticated sighting of a unicorn.
(2)   Unless something has been authentically sighted, it doesn't exist.

Unicorns do not exist.

If you accepted that the conclusion of the previous argument were false, then you certainly accept that the conclusion of this argument is true. However, even though it is true and the argument is valid, it would not be rational to accept it on the basis of this argument. Premise (2) here is certainly false; there are any number of things of which no one has yet had an authenticated sighting, but which nonetheless exist.

These examples simply reiterate the point made earlier: validity is a way of guaranteeing that the conclusion is true *if the premises are*. It is in no way a guarantee that either the conclusion or the premises are actually true. If an argument is to convince the rational thinker then we want that argument to have features in addition to validity.

2.4   Persuasion and Truth

Why not take the hint of these examples and define an argument as good just in case it is valid *and* has premises that are actually true? Surely, this would do the trick since these two properties together guarantee that the conclusion is actually true. Even this, though, will not do.

An argument that is valid and has true premises is called *sound*. This is a very important combination of features for an argument, and it is to be aimed at in our thinking. A sound argument, as opposed to a merely valid one, is certainly closer to what is intended when we think of an argument as persuasive. However, ask yourself is the following valid? Sound? Persuasive?

(1) Money cannot guarantee happiness.

Money cannot guarantee happiness.

This argument is certainly valid. How could it fail to be, since the premise and conclusion are one and the same? Also, in so far as you accept the received wisdom of the premise, you will regard it as sound. (If you dissent from this, then it is easy to see how to construct your own example.) Finally, is it persuasive? Would it be a good way to convince a rational thinker that money cannot guarantee happiness? Obviously not. Of course, if the person to whom you addressed the argument agreed that it was sound, he would thereby be accepting the truth of the conclusion. But, since the conclusion and the premise are the same, the acceptance could hardly be seen as the result of the *argument*. A rational thinker will require that a conclusion be supported by a valid argument with true premises, but he will also require that the premises be sufficiently different from the conclusion. That is, the premises must be distinct enough from the conclusion for us to see the movement from premises to conclusion as a genuine movement of thought.

This is admittedly very vague, but it is not easy to improve on it. It might be tempting to require that an argument is persuasive only if the conclusion is not already contained in the premises. This is a little less vague but it gets us into a different sort of trouble. There is a sense in which the conclusion of any valid argument is 'contained' in the premises. At this stage of discussion, I do not expect you to fully understand this; we are at this point getting into very deep philosophical waters. However, compare the above unconvincing argument with this one:

(1) Happiness requires self-fulfilment.
(2) Money cannot guarantee self-fulfilment.

Money cannot guarantee happiness.

This argument is valid and is, I think, sound. It is also plausible to see it as persuasive. Yet, there is a clear sense in which (1) and (2) already contain the conclusion; embracing these premises is embracing the conclusion, or it certainly would be for an ideally rational thinker. Saying this seems no more than saying that the argument is valid.

There is a tension between requiring that a convincing argument is valid, and requiring that its conclusion is other than a repetition of the premises. Validity seems to demand that the conclusion not stray too far from the premises, while persuasiveness demands that it be some distance away.

Exercise 3

Arrange each of the arguments below in standard form. Is each of them valid? Sound? Persuasive?

(i) If there isn't an after-life, then death is just an indefinite absence of consciousness – it is a long, deep sleep. If there is an after-life, then death will be just a different sort of existence. A rational person should fear neither the state of being asleep, nor a different sort of existence. Therefore, it is not rational to fear the state of death.

(ii) Aristotle died in 322 BC. So, Plato either married or he didn't.

(iii) If God doesn't exist and you believe in him, then you are apt to waste some time in worship. But, if God does exist and you don't believe, then you will be eternally damned. It is more reasonable to risk wasting some time during your life, than to risk eternal damnation. Thus, it is reasonable to believe that God exists.

2.5   The Subject Matter of Logic Reconsidered

Our discussion of good and bad arguments has uncovered three possible distinctions. Arguments can be:

(i)   valid or invalid,
(ii)   sound or unsound,
(iii)   persuasive or unpersuasive.

The study of logic in this book is the study of (i). The reason for the restriction follows.

In order for an argument to be either persuasive (to a rational thinker) or sound, it must at least be valid. This certainly gives us the best possible reason for studying validity. Additionally, there are grounds for thinking that our study cannot sensibly go beyond the study of validity.

We never did discover any criterion for distinguishing persuasive from unpersuasive arguments, but that by itself is no reason for abandoning the search. What is more to the point are the difficulties with the notion of soundness. Persuasive arguments have to be sound whatever else they are. Remember, we discussed persuasiveness in connection with the ideal of the rational thinker, and such a thinker could only be persuaded by arguments which were at least sound. A sound argument is defined as a valid argument which has true premises. The study of soundness is therefore clearer than the study of persuasiveness, but it has one very great disadvantage. To decide whether an argument is sound, we have to decide whether the premises are true. Since premises can be about anything that we happen to be thinking of, the study of soundness would be the study of every subject matter – and even that would not be enough. After all, there are no doubt many truths which are at present unknown to us. There may even be truths we will never know. All of this means that the study of soundness within the bounds of one book is simply not a real option.

Validity can be investigated without our having to bother unduly as to whether any given specific thought is true. This is just as well since logicians can lay no claim to being omniscient.

The Main Points of Chapter 2

1 Arguments can be *valid, sound* or *persuasive*. These are three related sorts of goodness in arguments.

2 An argument is valid just in case it meets the following condition:

(N) It is necessarily the case that if the premises are all true, then so is the conclusion.

This condition is equivalent to one that can be stated using the notion of possibility:

(P) It is not possible for all the premises of the argument to be true, and the conclusion false.

3 The following two important observations about validity were made:

(i) A valid argument for a conclusion provides a way of telling whether the conclusion is true which can differ from the usual direct way. Normally, we tell whether a thought is true by comparing it with how things are in the world. However, if the thought is the conclusion of a valid argument, we can determine its truth by finding out whether the premises of the argument are true.

(ii) Validity as defined only applies to arguments whose premises and conclusions are thoughts that can be true or false.

4 An argument is sound just in case it is *both* valid *and* its premises are all true. Given this, it is clear that sound arguments are more likely to be persuasive than merely valid ones.

5   It is very difficult to spell out just what is required of an argument if it is to be persuasive. Part of the trouble is that it is unclear *who* is the intended object of the persuasion. Also, there seems to be no way to spell out what features, in addition to soundness, are needed for persuasiveness.

6   The subject matter of the remainder of the book is the validity of deductive arguments.

Chapter three

Strategy

We now have to plan a strategy for working out whether any given argument is valid. This is not to say that you now lack all ability to tell whether an argument is valid. I depended on your views about typical cases of valid and invalid arguments in my discussion of these notions, and this discussion would not have served its purpose unless you already had some skill in telling whether arguments are valid. Our first task will be to take a closer look at this skill.

3.0   Validity in Everyday Life

Below is a sample argument. I want you to say whether it is valid *and* ask yourself how you arrived at your answer:

SAMPLE   (1)   Cats have backbones.
         (2)   Most pets have backbones.
         _____
              Most pets are cats.

The argument is transparently invalid. What is more interesting is the question of how we come to know this. There seem to be two ways in which we manage the task. One can be called *Visualizing*, and the other *Analogizing*.

NOTE   There is considerable interest among psychologists in the question of how we actually decide that certain arguments are valid. For more on this see the Reading List. My remarks are, in effect, an attempt to spell out ways which seem plausible candidates for explaining how we perform this task. I think that you will recognize some of your own thinking in these ways, but I do not claim that we always use them – that they fully characterize the actual working of the human mind. Nor would you expect me to be able to do this without detailed experimental investigation.

A. Visualizing

The Visualizing method works like this: you imagine what it would be like for the premises of an argument to be true and, at the same time, you try to imagine that the conclusion is false. Applied to the above argument, the method might come out as follows.

I picture cats as having backbones. This is easy since they do have backbones. I next picture various pets – goldfish, dogs, cats, etc. as having backbones and I try not to picture too many pets as lacking backbones. This is also fairly easy since it is likely that most pets do have backbones. The truth is often, but not always, easier to picture. Finally, I picture cats as very rare pets. They are, of course, not rare at all, but I find that I can picture them this way without upsetting my previous efforts to picture the premises of the argument. It is this that convinces me that the argument is invalid – that the premises can be true and the conclusion false.

The method is called 'Visualizing' and I used the word 'picture' in applying it, but it is not strictly and literally visual. It is more a method based on our sensitivity to possibilities. My justification for the use of the visual metaphor is that such words as 'see' and 'picture' are not solely visual: I can *see* a reason as well as a landscape.

B. Analogizing

When required to say why they think the SAMPLE argument is invalid, many people are apt to say something like this: if the SAMPLE argument were valid, then I could just as well argue in the following way:

(1) People have fathers.
(2) Most frogs have fathers.

Most frogs are people.

But, it is as plain as can be that the premises of this argument are true and its conclusion is false – it is blatantly invalid. Since the argument about frogs is just like the argument about cats, the invalidity of the frog argument shows the invalidity of the original one.

NOTE   By the way, not all frogs have fathers. Consult a zoology text for confirmation of this – look under 'parthenogenesis'. I mention this because some people may think that if all frogs have fathers, then (2) is false. I think that they would be wrong, but there is no need to argue about it here, given the biological facts.

Crucial to this procedure is the idea of certain arguments being *just like* or *analogous* to one another. For anyone who is excessively literal-minded, the argument about cats is not just like the one about frogs. After all, one is about cats and the other is about frogs. However, I suspect that most of us would understand what is meant by the claim that the two arguments are alike, and would agree. What the arguments share is not a content, but a *form* or *structure*. Implicit in Analogizing is the idea that what makes the above arguments invalid is that they are of the same structure, and that this structure is in some way defective.

We can spell out what goes on in Analogizing as follows. First, a structure for the argument is isolated. In the SAMPLE argument case, this structure can be displayed as follows:

(1) As have Bs.
(2) Most Cs have Bs.

Most Cs are As.

Next, there is a search for an argument which has just this structure, but which has true premises and a clearly false conclusion. This is where the argument about frogs came in. It is analogous in structure to the SAMPLE argument, but it doesn't require any effort to see that its premises are true and its conclusion is false.

C.   Comparison

Visualizing and Analogizing are alike in two important respects. First, imagination plays a key role in their operation; and second, validity is demonstrated in both of them by a certain sort of failure. Let me expand on these points.

In Visualizing, you keep fixed the thoughts expressed by the premises and conclusion, while you use your imagination to vary the way the world is, to think of it as how it might have been. If this exercise of the imagination convinces you that the world could have been such as to make the premises true and the conclusion false, you will judge the argument invalid. The world in which the premises are true and the conclusion false constitutes a *counter-example* to the argument.

In Analogizing, you do not keep the thoughts expressed by the premises and conclusion fixed, but you do keep fixed a structure which you discern in those thoughts. You then exercise your imagination in a search for an argument which shares that structure, but whose premises are true and conclusion false. If this search is successful, then you have found in the new argument a counter-example to the original one.

In both cases, the judgement that an argument is *valid* depends upon a *failure* to find a counter-example. This is a weakness of everyday methods which I shall discuss shortly. Before that, I want to highlight a difference between the two methods.

The method of Visualizing comes directly from the definition of validity. An argument is valid when it is not possible for its premises to be true and its conclusion false. Visualizing is the exercise of imagination to see whether this is so of particular arguments. In contrast, the method of Analogy introduces a new and important idea – structure.

It seems obvious that the arguments we have discussed so far in the book have structure – logical structure – and that their validity (or invalidity) is closely tied to this. What could be more natural than the way in which the SAMPLE argument was shown to have a logical structure that rendered it invalid? Yet, there is no mention of logical structure in the definition of validity itself. The definition speaks only of possibility and truth.

We have here the beginnings of what will grow into the governing idea of this book. It can be expressed as follows: one way to tell whether an argument is valid is to discern in it a logical structure which can then be assessed. The method of Analogy works by employing imagination in this assessment, and this has many disadvantages. It shares these disadvantages with the method of Visualizing. Nonetheless, once we have discussed the failings of both everyday methods, the way will be clear to explore the connection between logical structure and validity. The aim will be to develop a method for isolating and assessing logical structure which does not suffer from the disadvantages imposed by our reliance on imagination.

3.1 Not Good Enough?

Some of you might be thinking: if what he calls Visualizing and Analogizing have served us in our assessment of arguments up to this point in our lives, why do we need to acquire further ways of assessing arguments? This seems to me a question worth answering. In fact, it seems worth two different answers.

The first answer comes roughly to this: everyday methods have practical and theoretical limitations which the methods of logic overcome. The second answer will have to wait until the next section. You will be better placed to understand it when you have considered the first answer in more detail.

A. Practical Limitations

Everyday methods are limited by these three facts:

(i)   Our memories are very limited.

(ii)   We sometimes lack imagination.

(iii) Structure is sometimes hard to discern.

All three merit discussion.

(i)   Visualizing requires memory: you have to see each premise as true, and keep that in mind, while imagining the conclusion is false. An argument with a number of premises, and/or complex premises, is going to exhaust most people's memory capacity. Here is a fairly simple argument – as arguments go. Can you decide its validity by Visualizing? By any method you now know?

(1)   If unemployment keeps on increasing and investment declines, then interest rates will go up.

(2)   Either productivity will go down or unemployment will keep on increasing.

(3)   If interest rates go up, then investment will decline.

(4)   Productivity will go down unless investment increases.

If investment declines, then unemployment will keep on increasing.

I suspect that by the time you go to premise (3) you had already lost your grip on (1) and (2): it is very difficult to picture simultaneously such thoughts as true. The problem is one of memory.

Does Analogizing fare any better? I won't try to guess what sort of device you might use to describe a structure for this argument. I will simply assume that you have worked out that structure for yourself. However, even if you have managed to do this satisfactorily, you still face the formidable task of searching for an argument with the same structure, but with true premises and a false conclusion. The burden which this places on your memory is no less prodigious than it was for Visualizing.

(ii)   Not everyone is blessed with a powerful imagination. Even if you had unlimited memory, if you lacked the requisite imagination, you would be unable to assess many arguments for validity using the everyday methods. This is obviously true for Visualizing, but it applies to Analogizing as well. Even after you isolate a logical structure in an argument, you still must use your imagination to search for a counterexample.

(iii) We are all sensitive to the structure of thoughts: the thoughts of others, and arguably our own, are expressed in the medium of language and we are quite good at producing and understanding sentences of our native language. However, it is one thing to understand a sentence as expressing a thought, and another to specify the features of that sentence which are relevant to the validity of an argument. To see this, reconsider the argument about employment given earlier.

Each premise and the conclusion are expressed in sentences of English. Anyone who understands English should have no difficulty in understanding each of these sentences. Yet, it is not always clear which features of these sentences contribute to the structure of the *argument*. In the simpler example:

(1) Cats have backbones.
(2) Most pets have backbones.
_____

Most pets are cats.

it was fairly obvious how to isolate the structure of the argument; that is what makes it a simple example. In more complex cases, it is not obvious. We have all learned ways in which to see structure in sentences. Sentences have words and these can be described by grammatical terms such as 'noun', 'verb', 'adjective', etc. Most of us learned about this when we learned English. However, the sort of structure we need in making decisions about validity is the *logical* structure of whole arguments, and this is not something that is explicit in our linguistic training.

So even if our imagination was up to the task, it is not always easy to say what the task is. For our imagination can only provide counter-examples to arguments whose structure we have laid out.

B.   A Theoretical Limitation

Things are even worse. Let us suppose that our memory and imagination are no hindrance, and our ability to discern logical structure is keen. What if the argument we are trying to evaluate is valid? Notice that I never did say whether the long argument about unemployment is valid. If it is valid, then no counter-example can be constructed, all your attempts would fail. Yet, can we really think we are justified in moving from:

(1)   I have not been able to construct a counter-example,

to:

(2)   no counter-example can be constructed?

There is a world of difference between failing to construct a counter-example, and knowing that one cannot be constructed.

Of course, we do quite confidently claim that certain arguments are valid. No doubt we are able to do this for these arguments because, having discerned a logical form in them, we are able to assess it directly as one which would never allow the construction of a counter-example. But this reliance on our intuitions is not much of a method, and is liable to lead us astray in more difficult cases.

3.2 Deeper Reasons

At this point, I have probably said enough to convince you of the severe limitations of everyday methods. By itself, that might be enough to get you interested in the less limited methods offered by logic. Logic would be like a new car which a salesman has talked you into buying by pointing out all the defects of your present car. There are, however, more profound reasons for interest in the methods of logic.

In order to replace the everyday methods we use for testing arguments we will have to develop systematic ways of displaying the logical structures of arguments. When I asked you about this argument:

> (i) Cats have backbones.
> Most pets have backbones.
> ———————————————
> Most pets are cats.

I depended on your sensitivity to linguistic and logical structure to convince you that such structure could be (partly) revealed in this way:

> (ii) As have Bs.
> Most Cs have Bs.
> ———————————————
> Most Cs are As.

However, (ii) is only really of use if it engages with a *method* of showing something about the validity of (i). Unless it does so, there can be no reason to think that (ii) does genuinely exhibit the appropriate logical structure of the original argument. The imagination gets to work on the basis of structures such as (ii), but it does not offer any guarantee that (ii) really does give the correct logical structure of (i). Also, any way of revealing logical structure must be general: it must show us logical structure in a whole range of arguments. It was noted earlier that the structural proposals in (ii) do not carry over to more complex arguments such as the one about unemployment. So, what we need is a way of displaying logical structure which is both general and goes hand in hand with a method for deciding whether a given structure is valid.

The interest of such a general way of displaying logical structure goes much deeper than its connection with testing for validity. Understanding the structure of arguments is an ability very closely connected with the ability to understand and use language. The development of methods of logic will give us insights into the nature of language, and through this, into the nature of thought. This is a second, and more important, reason for pursuing logic.

3.3   Language and Structure

Language has figured prominently in our discussion of arguments and validity in two ways:

1   The thoughts which make up an argument have to be expressed in sentences of a language if the argument is used in a public way, for example to influence someone else. It may also be true that our thoughts are dependent on language, even in cases where we are not making our arguments public. Perhaps there cannot even be thought without language.
2   Our sensitivity to the structure of arguments which is used to assess validity is something like, and may be part of, our sensitivity to linguistic structure.

Let us consider each of these in a bit more detail.

A.   Sentences and Thoughts

To be confronted by an argument is to be confronted by sentences. (We can rule out telepathy here since even its most enthusiastic supporters do not claim that it can be used to 'transmit' complex arguments.) This means that we need to understand sentences in order to so much as understand what argument is being offered.

The arguments used so far in this book were expressed using sentences chosen for ease of comprehension. Because of this, you may now think that there is no real problem in moving from sentences to the thoughts expressed by them. This would be a mistake. There are many intricacies in our use of language, and these intricacies often make it difficult to tell what is being expressed in a sentence, and how it is related to what is expressed in other sentences. For example, suppose you are told:

(1)   John saw an old friend on his bicycle.

Which of the following are plausible interpretations of (1)?

(2a)   John saw his friend Ralph who at 80 was still riding around on his bicycle.

(2b)   John saw Michael, his childhood friend, sitting on John's bicycle.

(2c)   John saw Michael, his childhood friend, riding John's bicycle.

(2d)   John saw his 80-year old friend, Alice, riding his bicycle.

(2e)   John saw his 80-year old friend, Ralph, sitting on John's bicycle.

All of these *might* serve to capture (1), and this list is only partial.

This is an extreme case. Most of the sentences we use are not open to quite so many interpretations. However, (1) illustrates very clearly just how careful one has to be about moving from sentences to thoughts. Moreover, it illustrates how ambiguity can infect the study of arguments and validity. Unless you know what thought is expressed by a sentence, you will be at a loss to say whether an argument using the sentence is valid.

B.   Linguistic and Logical Structure

How did you know that 'John saw an old friend on his bicycle' could be used to express the very different thoughts which (2a)–(2e) suggested? In outline, I suspect the answer is this: in learning English, you acquired a sensitivity to the linguistic forms used in (1), and this sensitivity makes it possible for you to understand the different interpretations that are indicated by (2a)–(2e). For example, the word 'old' in the phrase 'old friend' can be understood either as an adjective describing the person in question, or as an adjective describing the nature of the friendship. Either someone is said to be old and a friend, or someone is said to have been a friend for some time.

Sensitivity to linguistic structure does not require that you have mastered all sorts of grammatical terms: you could perfectly well see what is going on in (1) without even knowing what an adjective is. However, grammar does provide us with a way of describing and explaining such cases. Knowing a grammar for a language enables you to explain why certain sentences express certain thoughts, and to chart the relationships between different sentences.

The logical structure of arguments depends upon, and is closely related to, linguistic structure. As you have seen, you need to have some idea of linguistic structure in order to be able to identify arguments. However, it should be clear that linguistic and logical structure are not the same.

The linguistic structure of a given sentence is describable by a grammar for a specific language. Sentences are in English, French, Italian, etc., and the grammars of all these languages are different. The logical structure of an argument, however, is largely independent of the grammatical quirks of particular natural languages. If you translate a valid argument from English to French, you would expect the translation also to be valid. If it was, so to speak, valid in English then it should remain so when translated into any language. If this were not so in a given case, you should suspect the translation.

This means that any attempt to display the logical structure of an argument must be independent of many of the grammatical features of the language in which the argument is couched. This is not to deny that we have to have a command of the grammars of specific languages in order to discern logical structure. It is just that logical structure should not depend on the individual differences between languages.

3.4 The Strategy

Ideally, what we want is a very general language – a language of logical structure. This *language of logic* would have its own grammar and would be independent of any particular natural language. The idea would be this: we could use our knowledge of natural language to translate arguments from, say English, into the language of logic. Once this is done, we could apply the yet-to-be-described methods of logic to the result to test for validity. In fact, this is such a good idea that it is worth spelling it out very carefully. Here are the elements of what I will distinguish (in italic) as the Strategy:

1   *Construct a structural language – a language of logic.*

    This language will have its own grammar and you should be able to master it regardless of which natural language you use.

2   *Work out a method or methods of testing the validity of arguments which are expressed in the language of logic.*

    Unlike Analogizing, these methods should not depend on memory and imagination. They should allow us to tell directly whether a given structure makes for validity.

3   *Describe how to translate arguments from a natural language into the language of logic.*

    Translation depends on the understanding of both languages. It is here that logic gives us a great deal of insight into some of the mysteries of language.

Given what the Strategy is a strategy *for*, we must then satisfy ourselves that:

4   *An argument formulated in the language of logic is valid if and only if its translation into natural language is valid.*

That is, given an argument in natural language, you can test it for validity by *first* translating it into the language of logic, and *second* applying the methods of logic.

The major aim of the rest of this book will be to carry out steps (1)–(3) in an effort to achieve (4). Along the way, more will be said about language, translation and validity.

I hope that you understand how we arrived at the Strategy, but most important is that you understand what it now requires us to do. In the next chapter we will begin to construct a language of logic.

The Main Points of Chapter 3

1   Everyday methods for testing the validity of arguments include *Visualizing* and *Analogizing*. Both of these methods depend on our imaginative ability with respect to possibility.

(a)   In Visualizing, we try to construct a counter-example by imagining that the world is such that the premises of the argument are true and the conclusion is false.

(b)   In Analogizing, we try to construct a counter-example by imagining a different argument which has the same structure as the original, but which has true premises and a false conclusion.

(c)   An argument is said to be valid if there is no counter-example.

2   Everyday methods are defective in various ways. They depend too much on our memory and imagination and, most importantly, they let us down when an argument is valid. Such an argument does not allow for the construction of a counter-example, yet we can never be sure, in the specific case, that the failure to find a counter-example is due more to our lack of memory or imagination than to the validity of the argument.

3   The methods of logic aim to provide more efficient procedures for testing validity. This is valuable in itself. However, a deeper reason for interest in logic comes from the insight that the investigation of logical structure gives us into language and thought.

4   The Strategy which governs the remainder of the book is, in outline, as follows:

   (i)   CONSTRUCTION
         A language of logic will be constructed. Such a language is a language of logical structure.
         (Before we are finished, we will construct two languages of logic.)
   (ii) DECISION
         Methods will be developed to test the arguments formulated in the language of logic.
   (iii) TRANSLATION
         Ways of translating natural language arguments into the language of logic will be given.

In so far as (i)–(iii) are successful, we should be able to test an argument for validity by simply translating it into the language of logic, and then applying the methods of logic.

Chapter four

Primitive

The Strategy outlined in the last chapter requires us to construct a language that has the following features:

(i) Natural language arguments can be translated into it so as to reveal their logical structure.

(ii) We can test arguments formulated in it by procedures which do not rely on memory or imagination.

This chapter takes a *step* towards constructing such a language. For the present, do not worry about either procedures for testing validity or translation. The language about to be discussed is one of the simplest you are ever likely to come across, but it will serve as the basis for a language that will genuinely help us to realize our goal. Since it is useful to have a name for this language, I will call it 'Primitive'.

4.0   The Basic Sentences of Primitive

Primitive has four sentences which form the basis for the whole language. Each of these is completely unstructured. That is, these sentences do not contain what we would recognize as words or other 'sub-sentential' components. They are written like this:

P
Q
R
S.

Each of them says something about the weather, and, for our purposes, it will be sufficient if we concentrate on the first two. Speakers of Primitive use 'P' to describe the weather when it is like this:

but not when it is like this:

They use 'Q' to describe the weather when it is like this:

but not when it is like this:

Given this, it is reasonable to think of 'P' as meaning that it is raining, and 'Q' as meaning that it is windy.

(Indulging in the fantasy which this language conjures up, we may imagine that speakers of this language have an obsessive interest in the weather – perhaps because it interferes with their most cherished outdoor activities. As to why their language contains only four basic sentences, we may speculate that they are so reserved they have never had the need for a language which allows more than these comments on the weather.)

4.1   Another Sort of Sentence in Primitive

Primitive contains only four *basic* sentences, but these can be used in combination to make more complicated, *non-basic* sentences. These combinations are best explained one at a time.

Conjoining

Speakers of Primitive sometimes use sentences like:

P & Q,

which is made by using the '&' symbol and two basic sentences. The symbol is called *conjunction*. Perhaps the best way to understand what this sentence asserts is to consider those circumstances in which speakers think it applies, and those in which it does not. It applies in this case:

but not in any of these:

This range of application of 'P & Q' makes it seem reasonable to regard the '&' as functioning something like the word 'and', though we will not pause to speculate further about this. Our concern here is, above all, with the Primitive language, not with its relation to natural languages. It is worth considering, though, precisely how it is that the above pictures work to provide an explanation of 'P & Q'.

If you know the circumstances in which 'P' applies, and the circumstances in which 'Q' applies, then you understand these sentences; you can use them in the same way as a native speaker of Primitive. The pictures I gave you earlier were intended to provide you with a (somewhat crude) idea of these circumstances. Exactly the same thing carries over to non-basic sentences such as 'P & Q'. The pictures provide you with an idea of the circumstances in which this sentence could be correctly used, and an idea of those in which it would be incorrect.

> Why did I use four different pictures when I introduced the sentence 'P & Q' above?

The answer to this may seem obvious, but the question is not a trivial one, and it is worth pausing over.

4.2 Possible Circumstances

Four pictures were used to represent the possibilities relevant to 'P & Q' because, given what 'P' and 'Q' say, the applicability (or not) of each of these sentences determines four states that the weather might be in. These four ways are depicted below and, underneath each picture, is the information appropriate to each picture. (I have included approximate translation of the Primitive sentences in brackets.)

(1)

'P' applies (it is raining). 'Q' applies (it is windy).

(2)

'P' applies (it is raining). 'Q' does not apply (it is not windy).

(3)

'P' does not apply (it is not raining). 'Q' applies (it is windy).

(4)

'P' does not apply (it is not raining). 'Q' does not apply (it is not windy).

Given these four possibilities, we can tell what 'P & Q' says by noting whether it applies (or not) in each of the four cases. In fact, it applies in circumstance (1), but does not apply in (2), (3) or (4). This way of looking at 'P & Q' is merely an application of the common-sense idea that you know what a sentence asserts when you know, in any possible circumstance, whether the sentence applies. The pictures (1)–(4) depict those circumstances.

But do (1)–(4) show *all the possibilities* relevant to 'P & Q'?

Behind this question are two real worries.

First, couldn't there be cases in which it is indeterminate whether or not 'P' (or 'Q') applies? If there are such cases, these are not shown by the four scenes above, and yet they might be relevant to the applicability of 'P & Q'. For example, what would we say about 'P & Q' in a case where 'P' applies, but it is not clear whether 'Q' applies?

Second, couldn't the function of '&' be more complicated than we have so far recognized? It allows the construction of a sentence which applies to the circumstances shown, but it might have a meaning which is not fully expressed by this range of application. Suppose, for example, that it meant (roughly) 'and, curse the gods'. Since it is still used for conjoining, speakers of Primitive could apply 'P & Q' to (1) and not to (2), (3) or (4). However, under the hypothesis being considered, '&' is a sort of editorialized form of conjunction: it is used when both 'P' and 'Q' are appropriate, but it also carries overtones of mild blasphemy. Since '&' has this extra, emotive kind of meaning, there may be cases where Primitive speakers refrain from saying 'P & Q', not because of the weather, but because they don't want to anger the gods. (There is a further discussion of this shortly.)

The answers to these questions are as follows.

As to the first question, when speakers use any of their basic sentences, they use them in a way which does not allow any indeterminacy of application. For them, for example, all circumstances are divided into those to which 'P' applies, and those to which it does not; there is no middle ground. Many speakers of English would be less firm about our sentence: 'it is raining'. That is why I said that the English sentence was only an approximate translation of the sentence 'P'.

As to the second question, the speakers of Primitive use the '&' in such a way that its meaning is fully specified by its effect on the applicability of non-basic sentences in which it occurs. In other words, there is no extra ingredient to the meaning of '&'.

These answers make Primitive a very simple language indeed.

(a) The language contains only four basic sentences.
(b) Each sentence is itself understood as definitely applying or definitely not applying.
(c) A non-basic sentence made with '&' says no more than that it applies in certain cases, and doesn't apply in the others.

4.3 True and False

Everyone knows that a picture is worth a thousand words, but, as with most clichés, there are times when they fail to hold. Indeed, as you'll come to appreciate, this is a time when a word is worth more than a thousand pictures. That word is 'true'.

In explaining what 'P', 'Q' and 'P & Q' assert, I drew a rough sketch of a circumstance, and indicated whether or not the sentence applied. Thus, you learned that 'P & Q' applies to

but does not apply to these:

Instead of drawing such pictures, I could convey the same information by saying:

> 'P & Q' is true when 'P' is true and 'Q' is true,

and

> 'P & Q' is false when 'P' is false and 'Q' is true
> and when 'P' is true and 'Q' is false
> and when 'P' is false and 'Q' is false.

Given that you understand what each basic sentence says, you know precisely what circumstances must be like when someone asserts that one or other of them is either true or false. The pictures were helpful for getting started. They can now be replaced by the use of the words 'true' and 'false'. Aside from saving me a lot of space, this change removes some of the artificiality that my pictures imposed. After all, there are very many subtly different pictures that I could draw to represent how things are asserted to be by a basic sentence. Using the words 'true' and 'false' of sentences you understand is a way of telling you what is asserted without having to choose from among these different pictures.

For example, if I now tell you that 'P' is true, you know I have said that it is raining. No pictures are required to convey this to you. So, a word (or two if we count 'false') really is worth at least a thousand pictures.

Let us rewrite the explanation of 'P & Q' without pictures:

1   When 'P' is true, and 'Q' is true, then 'P & Q' is true.
2   When 'P' is true, and 'Q' is false, then 'P & Q' is false.
3   When 'P' is false, and 'Q' is true, then 'P & Q' is false.
4   When 'P' is false, and 'Q' is false, then 'P & Q' is false.

I have used the same numbers here as I did in the explanation given earlier with pictures so that you can compare the two, line by line. (Do that now.)

We can improve this explanation still further by writing it in table form as follows:

	'P'	'Q'	'P & Q'
(1)	true	true	true
(2)	true	false	false
(3)	false	true	false
(4)	false	false	false

Even though the use of 'true' and 'false' makes it much easier to write out explanations of non-basic sentences, you should not forget the relationship between the use of these words and the use of pictures. The pictures portray the way things are, or might be; their use makes it evident that sentences in Primitive are intended to connect up with reality in appropriate ways. Using 'true' and 'false' of the sentences of Primitive is no less a way of saying something about the relation between these sentences and reality.

4.4   Truth Tables and Truth Functionality

You may think that it has taken me a great deal of space to say very little. Many lines of print have been used to introduce a language that has so far been shown to contain only a very few sentences. Nonetheless, as I go on to describe further sentences in Primitive, the ways of talking about the language that have been used above will make explanations clearer and shorter. A further aid to clear and concise discussions in the pages which follow are certain terms that can be applied to what you now know about Primitive.

The table used in section 4.3 to explain 'P & Q' (the one without the pictures) is called a *truth table*. It can be abbreviated still further and written in a clearer format as follows:

'P'	'Q'	'P & Q'
T	T	T
T	F	F
F	T	F
F	F	F

Read the *rows* of the table. The first row consists of a *truth value* for 'P', a truth value for 'Q', and a truth value for 'P & Q'. This last truth value is just what you would expect given the values for 'P' and 'Q' and the meaning of the '&'. Each row gives different possible truth values for the combination of 'P' and 'Q'. The four rows display all the possible ways in which these basic sentences could be true or false. As we have discussed, the truth value of the sentence 'P & Q' is fixed by the truth values of its constituent sentences. I have marked the fact that the truth values under 'P' and 'Q' list the four possibilities by dividing them off from those under 'P & Q' with a double vertical line. Each row to the left of the double line describes a way the weather could be at some time.

In section 4.2, I claimed that, in the Primitive language, the meaning of '&' was fully determined by the effect it has on the applicability (truth values) of the sentences in which it occurs. The truth value of any non-basic sentence made with '&' is completely determined by the truth values of its constituent basic sentences. The term for this is *truth-functional*. In saying that '&' is truth-functional, we are saying that the pattern of truth values illustrated in the table for 'P & Q' (above) shows all there is to know about the role of '&' in determining the truth values of non-basic sentences in which it occurs. Moreover, in Primitive, the truth-functional role of '&' is all there is to its meaning. This last comment requires further discussion.

If '&' had meant something like 'and, curse the gods', then the truth table would not *fully* specify its meaning. The truth table can only tell you what contribution '&' makes to the truth values of sentences containing it. To appreciate this, suppose there was a language which differed from Primitive in one and only one respect: in this language (NotPrimitive), '&' really means 'and, curse the gods'. The truth table for '&' in NotPrimitive would be exactly the same as the one for '&' in Primitive. This is because their '&' is used, among other things, for conjoining two basic sentences in the way given in the truth table. But it also has a further blasphemous use which does not affect truth value, and so does not show up in a truth table. The point about the Primitive use of '&' is that it does not have any such further use. Its meaning is fully specified by the pattern of truth values it determines for non-basic sentences in which it occurs.

Exercise 1

Write out truth tables for each of the sentences below:

(a) R & S.
(b) Q & P.

This EXERCISE should contribute to your understanding of both truth tables and Primitive conjoining. First, even though I have never said what 'R' and 'S' mean to speakers of Primitive, you can still write out a truth table for their conjunction. All you need to know is that these sentences are determinately true or false, and, because they are sentences of Primitive, you can be assured of that. Second, the order in which basic sentences occur does not affect the truth values of a non-basic sentence constructed with '&'. The truth table for 'Q & P' has the same value in each of the relevant rows as the one for 'P & Q'.

4.5 Referring to Sentences

I have referred to sentences in Primitive by naming them, and I have used a device with which you are familiar to do so. That device is quotation. To form the name of an English sentence, you merely write the sentence inside quotation marks. (They could be single or double quotes. I have used single, but this is merely a matter of which style you prefer.) Failure to be careful about whether you are using a sentence, or referring to it with its quotation name, can lead to confusion. For example, what would you make of the following?

(i) John wrote said Mary.

I wouldn't expect you to make much of it at all. This is because, as written, the above is gibberish. It makes no more sense than:

(ii) John ate wandered sky.

Of course, there is a temptation to think that (i) is more intelligible than (ii), and this is easily explained. (i) can be 'heard' either as:

(i$_a$) 'John wrote' said Mary.

or as:

(i$_b$) John wrote 'said Mary'.

When quotation marks are put around the appropriate parts of (i), we get perfectly intelligible sentences. This is because the quotation marks prevent us reading the words within them as having their ordinary uses; instead, we read them as part of a name of some bit of language. The effect of this, in connection with (i_b), was to convert the last two words into the name of a two-word phrase of English. This named thing then served as the grammatical direct object of the verb 'wrote'. With such a direct object, the original sentence could be understood in a way that makes sense.

> **Exercise 2**
>
> Use quotation marks to make sense of each of the following:
>
> *(a) Tiny was called Tiny because of his size.
> (b) I think thought Mary.
> *(c) The name Theodore means the same as Dorothy.

So, quotation marks are useful – indeed, in many uses of English, they are necessary. The trouble is that, in discussing Primitive, they are a nuisance. Every time I needed to tell you something about the Primitive sentence 'P', I had to enclose it in quotation marks. Yet you wouldn't be confused if I left them out because Primitive is a recognizably foreign language, and there is little chance that you would confuse the sentence and the name. Taking advantage of this fact about Primitive, I am going to drop the use of quotation marks from here on. Primitive sentences can serve as their own names even without quotation marks. Logicians call items with this feature *autonyms*.

4.6 Disjoining

The next sort of non-basic sentence of Primitive looks like this:

P ∨ Q,

and has the following truth table:

P	Q	P ∨ Q
T	T	T
T	F	T
F	T	T
F	F	F

The 'V' symbol with which it is constructed is called *disjunction*. Can you get some idea of what P V Q conveys to a user of Primitive?

Just as for conjunction, the truth table tells you all you need to know about the meaning of 'V'. To understand disjunction you should read each of the rows of the truth table, seeing what truth value is assigned to the non basic sentence given the values of the basic sentences. Doing this reveals that P V Q is true in each of the first three rows and is only false when both constituent sentences are false.

Strictly speaking, this should suffice to give you an understanding of P V Q: armed with this information, you would be able to go among speakers of Primitive and use sentences constructed with 'V' correctly. You would know that you could use such a sentence truly in every case except when both of its constituent basic sentences were false. In the specific case of P V Q, you would know that it was false only when it was false that it is raining *and* false that it is windy.

It is often helpful in understanding a foreign language sentence to be able to translate it, perhaps only approximately, into your own. So, granting that there might be no *exact* equivalent in English, how best could you convey the meaning of 'V' as it occurs in P V Q using the resources of English?

Remembering how we rendered the basic sentences, consider the following as a translation of P V Q:

(i)   It is raining *or* it is windy.

How closely does this match the truth table account of P V Q? Put it another way, does the English word 'or' have the same meaning as the Primitive 'V'?

These questions can be answered by examining each row of the truth table above. Rows 2, 3 and 4 seem uncontroversial: the truth values assigned to P V Q in each case are just what you would expect to be assigned to (i). Check this for yourself by asking whether you would be prepared to count (i) as true in each of these cases. I think you will agree that they do match. Thus,

Row 2   Given that it is true that it is raining, and false that it is windy, it is true that: it is raining or it is windy.

Row 3   Given that it is false that it is raining, and true that it is windy, it is true that: it is raining or it is windy.

Row 4   Given that it is false that it is raining, and false that it is windy, it is false that: it is raining or it is windy.

The problems arise in connection with row 1, and might be put as follows. P V Q is true in row 1 (when it is true that it is raining and true that it is windy). This might be taken to show that 'or' is not a good translation of 'V'. Someone might argue: the use of 'or' in a sentence conveys the idea that one *or* the other constituent sentence is true; when *both* are true, 'or' is not the appropriate word. So, if it is raining and it is windy, it is false that: it is raining or it is windy.

Is this consideration compelling? Think about the following dialogue:

> Teacher   *(disgruntled)*: Every time we have the school picnic it is raining or windy.
>
> Pupil: No, last year we had the picnic and it was raining *and* windy.

The pupil's remark is (mildly) amusing. Why? Clearly, the teacher did not intend to rule out the possibility of rain *and* wind by his remark. He wanted to make an assertion that included that worst eventuality, but also made provision for the fact that rain alone (or wind alone) had adverse effects on the school picnic. Had the teacher said:

> (ii)   every time we have the school picnic it is raining and windy,

he would not have conveyed the thought he considered true. Using 'or' as in (i) seemed the proper way of expressing the thought.

The pupil's remark draws attention to a somewhat different use of 'or' as illustrated in this dialogue.

> A: What are your holiday plans?
> B: I am going for one week to Paris or Vienna.

It is implicit in this exchange that B has not spoken accurately if he ends up going to Paris *and* to Vienna. In essence, then, the pupil's remark is a play on the word 'or': the teacher intended it one way, while the pupil interpreted it in another.

Does this mean that 'or' is ambiguous – that it has more than one meaning in English? We cannot fully answer this question now, but we can venture this much: 'or' can be used in different ways, and the use that matches 'V' most closely is that in the teacher's lament about the weather. The teacher used 'or' in an *inclusive* way, whereas it was used in an *exclusive* way in B's remark about his holiday. Speakers of Primitive do not have these different uses – the student's joke could not be made in it. This is because 'V' is given an exhaustive and precise meaning by its truth table. Primitive disjunction is always inclusive.

Would you say that 'or' is a good translation of 'V'? At this point I would hope that you were cautious enough to hesitate before answering. There are uses of 'or' that seem at variance with the use of 'V', but a definite answer to the question requires that we be clearer about the notion of translation. This must wait until the Strategy is more fully developed.

NOTE You may wonder why I did not just come out and say that 'or' is ambiguous, and can mean inclusive or exclusive disjunction. My hesitation here is because of the very intricate theoretical issues in linguistics and philosophy which surround the ideas of ambiguity and meaning. We will return to this issue.

Exercise 3

Construct truth tables for the sentences below:

*(i)   Q ∨ P.
(ii)   R ∨ S.

4.7   Negating

Here is another non-basic sentence of Primitive:

¬P.

The '¬' in it is called *negation*, and the explanation of its use is simple. (In fact, its very simplicity will call for more explanation than the symbol itself.)

The truth table for the above sentence is.

P	¬P
T	F
F	T

This truth table has only two rows, and thus differs from the truth tables we have used up to this point. Why?

A negated sentence is a non-basic sentence that is constructed from just one basic sentence. As you can see from the truth table, it has the effect of reversing the truth value of the basic sentence it contains. Since this non-basic sentence is formed from just one basic sentence, its truth table is constructed using only the appropriate sentence. Because P only has two possible truth values, the truth table for ¬P need only have two rows.

The most natural translation of ¬P in English is:

it is not raining,

and I think you can satisfy yourself that there is nothing in the truth table for ¬P which casts doubt on this translation.

The symbols '&', 'V' and '¬' are called *connectives* of Primitive. There are two more to come. You may not think that this is the most appropriate word, since '¬' doesn't appear to do much connecting. However, logicians have been used to calling symbols such as '&' *two-place* connectives (for obvious reasons), and they do not therefore find it odd to think of '¬' as a *one-place* connective.

4.8   Conditionalizing

The next sort of non-basic sentence of Primitive looks like this:

P ⊃ Q,

and has this truth table:

P	Q	P ⊃ Q
T	T	T
T	F	F
F	T	T
F	F	T

The '⊃' symbol used in its construction is called the *conditional*. As before, it is quite easy to use the truth table to master the use of '⊃' in Primitive. A sentence P ⊃ Q constructed with it, can be truly asserted in all cases except where P is true and Q is false. In discussing the conditional, it is helpful to use the following terminology: the first element of the conditional sentence (P in the above) is called the *antecedent*; the second element (Q) is called the *consequent*.

Speakers of Primitive think it correct to use the above example of a conditional sentence in all cases except when, as we would put it, it is raining and it is not windy. Can you think of any close approximation to P ⊃ Q in English? That is, can you think of some form of words in English that translates '⊃' in the way that 'or' was used in connection with 'V'? You will come to appreciate that these questions lead to the unfolding of a complex and fascinating story. Here we can only begin the story.

The most plausible translation in English of P ⊃ Q is:

(i)   *If* it is raining *then* it is windy.

Understanding Primitive speakers as using P ⊃ Q with the sense of (i) goes some way to showing why they assign the truth values they do to the conditional sentences. There are problems, however, so it is best to discuss this in a little detail.

> *Row 1*   It is true that it is raining, and true that it is windy. What verdict would this lead to for (i)?

Many would give the answer 'true', and we would hardly call (i) 'false' in these circumstances. Nonetheless, there may be some hesitancy here. Some people would be reluctant to assert (i) in these circumstances. They think that, in order to feel comfortable about asserting (i), you need to be assured that there is some *connection* between its being rainy and its being windy. Knowing simply that it is both raining and windy does not seem much of a ground for the existence of a connection. But we do not have to examine the merits of this view here. Our question is not 'would you assert (i) in these circumstances?' Rather, it is 'if (i) were asserted would it be true or false?' When we distinguish the question of assertion from the question of a true/false verdict, there seems very little reason to disallow the assignment of 'true' to (i) in row 1.

> *Row 2*   It is raining, and it is *not* windy. What verdict does this demand for (i)?

Here matters are less complicated. The verdict must surely be 'false'. You would neither assert (i) in these circumstances, nor would you think anyone correct who did make such an assertion.

> *Row 3*   It is *not* raining, and it is windy. What verdict does this demand for (i)?

This question seems most peculiar: even more so than in connection with row 1. One is very tempted to protest: what possible sense does it make to use (i) when the antecedent is false? By now you should be able to anticipate the answer. The question before us is whether (i) is true in the circumstances given in row 3. We are *not* interested in whether you would actually use (i) if you knew it was not raining and it was windy.

As in the case of row 1, it is fairly clear that (i) is *not* falsified by having a false antecedent. After all, there could be many other weather conditions that happen to go with its being windy. Sentence (i) does no more than claim that rain is one such condition. It would be unreasonable to think that the truth of:

> it is snowing and it is windy,

makes it false that:

if it is raining then it is windy.

Moreover, there is evidence that English speakers would regard (i) as, in fact, true in the circumstances given in row 3. Consider the following dialogue which makes the point using a different example of an English sentence with 'if . . . then'.

(On Wednesday)
Smith: If England win the toss then they will win the Test Match.

(A week later)
Jones: You were wrong. They lost the toss and won the Test.
Smith: No. I was perfectly right. I never said that winning the toss was the only way they would win the Test. I said that *if* they won the toss, they would win the Match. In saying this, I spoke the truth even as things turned out.

Row 4   It is not raining and it is not windy.
What is the verdict on (i)?

This case shares with row 3 the somewhat puzzling fact that the antecedent is false, but it differs in that the consequent is also false. Does this change things? Not really, though I suspect that the false consequent makes it easier to see (i) as true in this case. Imagine that someone has offered you (i) as a bit of lore about the weather. While out for a walk on a sunny and still day, he says: I told you, if it is raining then it is windy. Isn't what he says true in those circumstances? I expect that many would agree that it is, and certainly would not think it false.

A Concluding Remark about the Conditional

Our discussion of the use of 'if . . . then' as a translation of '⊃' may not have left you completely satisfied. Do not let that cause you to lose sight of this basic point: in Primitive, the meaning of the conditional ('⊃') is clearly set out in the truth table. The issue of translation is, for now, secondary. After all, the aim is to master Primitive.

As a first approximation, we can agree that (i) will do. That is, we can understand '⊃' as something like the English language 'if ... then'. I say this even while recognizing that there seem to be differences between these. In struggling with these differences, we were forced to make some very fine distinctions such as that between a sentence being true and our having grounds to assert it. Understanding the use of 'if ... then' in English, and its equivalents in other natural languages, requires all the resources of philosophical and linguistic theory. As you will see, the conditional in

Primitive plays a crucial role in this issue. So, whilst you should begin to think about 'if ... then', the main business of this section has been about '⊃'. Speakers of Primitive are blissfully unaware of the complexities of English language conditionals: for the present, you can follow them in this.

*Exercise 4

What truth values does the sentence:

Q ⊃ P

have in each of the rows of the truth table we used above to work out the truth values of P ⊃ Q?

Unlike non-basic sentences constructed with '&' and 'V', the result of this EXERCISE should show you that the order in which basic sentences occur makes a difference to the truth value of a non-basic sentence constructed with '⊃'.

4.9   Equalizing

The last sort of non-basic sentence of Primitive is constructed with '≡'. An example of such a sentence is:

P ≡ Q.

The new symbol is called *equivalence*, and has the following truth table.

P	Q	P ≡ Q
T	T	T
T	F	F
F	T	F
F	F	T

P ≡ Q is true when both basic sentences are true, and when both basic sentences are false. In the other two cases it is false. A first attempt to express P ≡ Q in English might come out as:

(i)   it is raining *matches in truth value* it is windy.

The idea would be that (i) will be true in row 1 and row 4, and false in row 2 and row 3. The trouble is that (i) is simply not a sentence of English. This may seem surprising at first, but a moment's thought should convince you. What is the grammatical subject of the verb 'matches in truth value'? You would be correct if you said: the sentence 'it is raining'. The trouble is that these words in (i) do not *name* a sentence; they are used in the ordinary way to say that it is raining. It certainly makes little sense to say: it is raining matches something in truth value. The weather doesn't have a truth value. We could have written:

> (ii)   the sentence 'it is raining' matches in truth value the sentence 'it is windy',

but, though grammatically acceptable, (ii) doesn't do what is required of a translation of P ≡ Q. P ≡ Q is about the weather; it is not about sentences and truth values. Because of the explicit mention of sentences and truth values, (ii) does not convey the same, weather-oriented, message as P ≡ Q.

We can get closer to the required translation of P ≡ Q into English using:

> (iii)   it is raining *if and only if* it is windy.

The phrase 'if and only if' is called the *biconditional*. All the problems that arose in connection with the conditional '⊃', and its translation into English, come up again in regard to (iii). These will be taken up in chapter 10.

Exercise 5

(a) Draw a *single* picture which would make all of the following sentences true:

Q.
P ∨ Q.
Q ⊃ P.

(b) Below is a picture. What sentences would a native speaker of Primitive regard as true of the situation depicted?

(c) Below is another picture. Answer as instructed in (b).

The Main Points of Chapter 4

1 Primitive has four *basic* sentences:

P, Q, R, S.

They are all used to describe the weather, though we have only bothered with translations into English for P and Q. They are:

P   it is raining.
Q   it is windy.

The basic sentences of Primitive are, in every situation, determinately true or false.

2 *Non-basic* sentences of Primitive can be constructed with *connectives*. Below is a list of the connectives, each of which is given with a sample sentence showing how the connective is used in Primitive, and with a suggested English translation for the sample sentence.

CONJUNCTION
      &   P & Q   It is raining and it is windy.

NEGATION
      ¬   ¬ P   It is not raining.

DISJUNCTION
      V   P V Q   It is raining or it is windy.

CONDITIONAL
      ⊃   P ⊃ Q   If it is raining then it is windy.

EQUIVALENCE (or BICONDITIONAL)
      ≡   P ≡ Q   It is raining if and only if it is windy.

3 Each of the connectives is *truth-functional*. That is, the truth values of non-basic sentences constructed with these connectives are wholly determined by the truth values of the constituent basic sentences. The particular way in which a connective contributes to these truth values is given by constructing the appropriate *truth table* for each connective. Moreover, the meaning of each connective is completely determined by its characteristic truth table.

4 The idea of a *truth table* is one of the most important in this chapter. A truth table contains a listing of all possible truth values of the basic sentences relevant to determining whether some non-basic sentence is true. You should be able to write out truth tables for sentences constructed with the connectives of Primitive.

Chapter five

Sentential

5.0 Enlarging Primitive

There isn't much that you can do with a language as limited as Primitive. Given its four basic sentences and five forms of non-basic sentence, it is not possible to say anything profound in it. Even the most devoted followers of the weather would soon tire of speaking it. (Do keep in mind, however, that Primitive is a spoken language only in our imagination.) In this chapter, we are going to enlarge Primitive in two ways. I will call the new language *Sentential*.

Sentential will prove to be a considerably more powerful language, but the enlargements to Primitive that it requires are not difficult to understand. Let us review the main features of Primitive.

(a)   There are four basic sentences: P, Q, R, S.
(b)   These sentences are, in any given circumstance, definitely either true or false.
(c)   There are five ways in which non-basic sentences can be constructed from basic sentences. Each of these uses a different *connective*. They are listed below.

   (i)   Conjunction &
   (ii)   Disjunction ∨
   (iii) Negation ¬
   (iv)   Conditionalization ⊃
   (v)   Equivalence ≡

Each of these is *truth-functional*. That is, in each case, the truth value of a non-basic sentence constructed with the connective is fully determined by the truth values of its basic constituents. The truth table which shows how this determination is made for each connective can be considered a complete explanation of the meaning of the connective.

The move from Primitive to Sentential requires us to look at features (a) and (c).

5.1 The Stock of Basic Sentences

Sentential has many more basic sentences than Primitive. In fact, it has indefinitely many more. This is brought about by our simply stipulating that Sentential has the following basic sentences:

$P_1, P_2, \ldots P_n, \qquad Q_1, Q_2, \ldots Q_n$
where n is not fixed. It is indefinitely large, but finite.

The stipulation is easily made, but it has consequences that might seem odd. The matter needs further discussion.

When you learned Primitive, it was possible for me to give you some idea of what the basic sentences of the language are used to say. I was able both to use pictures, and to use English language sentences, to give you an idea of the content of two of them. Sentential has an indefinitely large number of basic sentences, so neither of these methods is at all practical. This may lead you to wonder how it would be possible to use Sentential as a language. How could speakers ever cope with the fact that there is a very large, open-ended number of basic sentences in their language? They could never learn them one at a time.

One thing that I could say about Sentential would be this: it is not intended as a language spoken by a group of people. It is a language of logic or a *structural* language. It has its place, ultimately, in the study of arguments and validity, and it is part of the Strategy for that study outlined in chapter 3.

This would certainly be true. We are eventually going to use Sentential as a means for testing the validity of arguments in natural language. However, it is helpful to be able to see Sentential as a language, even if it is a highly unusual one. That end is best served by understanding how it *could* be used by some hypothetical population. Moreover, I think that if you do see Sentential as a language, you will be better placed to understand the connection between it and natural languages. Here, then, is a story about speakers of Sentential.

Unlike speakers of Primitive, speakers of Sentential are very casual about their use of basic sentences; they do not think of these sentences as having fixed meanings. When they feel that they want to communicate some thought, they merely choose from the set of basic sentences listed above. If one of them wants to say that it's a lovely day, he might come out with the sentence P_8. On another occasion, he may use P_8 to mean that it is very cold.

This casual use of basic sentences has the consequence that hearers cannot usually pick up the meaning of a basic sentence used on some occasion. After all, it would be surprising if the hearers could tell just from the context what P_8 means, since, in different contexts, it conveys different thoughts. None of this much matters to speakers of Sentential. One could think of them as sometimes feeling great social pressure to have something to say, but not worrying overmuch whether anyone understands exactly what it is that they are saying.

When it comes to non-basic sentences, however, they are quite careful to observe certain rules. For instance, if one of them says:

P_8 & Q_3,

he or she is very insistent that this is true when and only when both constituent sentences are true. That is, they observe precisely the same rules for understanding non-basic sentences as speakers of Primitive did; they use the connectives with their fixed, truth-table meanings. For this reason, speakers expect their hearers to understand at least the connectives used in any non-basic sentence, though they do not much care whether their hearers understand each of the basic sentences. A typical hearer might have no idea what the above sentence was about (its content) because he doesn't understand what P_8 and Q_3 mean. But he would recognize it as having a conjunctive structure.

In view of their singular lack of interest in communicating the specific content of their utterances, and their genuine concern for the structure of these utterances, it seems reasonable to think that the speakers of Sentential are a tribe of logicians.

5.2   More Non-basic Sentences

Primitive offered five ways in which its basic sentences could be used to form non-basic sentences. Sentential uses precisely the same five devices, but it allows non-basic sentences to contain other non-basic sentences as parts. Thus, the most complex sentence of Primitive had three elements – for example:

P & Q,

whereas, in Sentential, each of the following are acceptable, non-basic sentences:

(1) $(P_1$ & $P_2)$ V P_3
(2) $(\neg P_1$ V $P_2) \supset P_3$.

Such complexity brings with it the possibility of certain sorts of misunderstanding, and the parentheses used in (1) and (2) are there to prevent it. Let me spell this out. The above examples of Sentential use parentheses to indicate the grouping of basic sentences and connectives. Consider the first of the sentences, and compare it to the one below:

(3) P_1 & $(P_2 \vee P_3)$.

The basic sentence in (1) and (3) are the same, and so are the type and order of the connectives. Do they say the same thing? The answer is 'No', though I can only expect you to *guess* this for the present. You know that the meaning of these sentences will be given by the meaning of their basic constituents *and* by a table that assigns them truth values on the basis of the truth values of these constituents. If you guessed correctly about the difference between these two sentences, then this was because you suspected that the differences in grouping would make a difference to the assignment of such truth values. (If you did not guess correctly, don't worry. You will see precisely why these differ in the next section. Continue reading this section on the understanding that they *do* differ.)

In view of the difference between the above two sentences, what would you make of the following string of symbols?

(4) P_1 & $P_2 \vee P_3$.

Written without any parentheses, this is an *ambiguous* string. To say that it is ambiguous is to say that it could be interpreted in more than one way: (4) could be interpreted either as (1) or as (3). Given that Sentential contains only truth-functional connectives, this has the following consequence: if an ambiguous string were allowed to count as a sentence, then it would have different truth value assignments depending upon which interpretation was employed. This is unacceptable to speakers of Sentential. For this reason, they do not regard (4) as a sentence of their language; they see it as *merely* a string of symbols. This raises the question of how to tell whether a given string is a sentence.

5.3 Grammar

What is needed is a method of sorting strings of symbols into two groups: those that speakers of the language recognize as well-formed, and those that count as ill-formed. If this is done properly, then we would expect strings like (4) to be placed in the second category. They would not qualify as genuine sentences of Sentential.

The sorting method could be thought of as a *grammar* for the language; it would classify any given string as either grammatical or ungrammatical. (These terms can be thought of as roughly equivalent to 'well-formed' and 'ill-formed'.) For simple languages such as Sentential, this goal can be achieved with *rules* that are called 'rules of *syntax*'. Let me explain.

Here are the rules of syntax for Sentential:

Rule One   Basic sentences are sentences.

Rule Two   If '¬' is used to the left of a sentence, then the result is a sentence.

Rule Three   If either '&', 'V', '⊃' or '≡' is used between sentences, and the connective, together with the pair of sentences, is enclosed in parentheses, then the result is a sentence.

Rule Four   Any string of symbols is a sentence if and only if it is constructed according to Rules One to Three.

I will discuss the details of these rules shortly, but, first, consider this question:

What features of a string of symbols do you have to look at to apply these rules?

It should be clear that you can apply these rules without looking beyond the most superficial feature of any string – its form. You do not have to know what each symbol means or what any basic sentence says. It is for this reason that they are called *rules of syntax*.

You can use the rules either to construct sentences, or to see whether some given string is a sentence. Here is an example of a string which may or may not be a grammatical sentence:

$(P_1 \ V \ \neg(Q_1 \ \& \ Q_2))$.

Begin with the occurrence of 'V'. (You could begin anywhere in the string.) By Rule Three, the correct use of this symbol requires that it be flanked by sentences, and the whole lot must be enclosed in parentheses. On the left of 'V' is P_1. It is a sentence by Rule One. Also, the left-most and right-most parentheses form a pair. So far, so good. On the right of 'V' is the following:

$\neg(Q_1 \ \& \ Q_2)$.

To see whether it is a sentence we have to consult Rule Two – the rule that deals with '¬'. This requires that the '¬' be to the left of a sentence, so we have now to test this:

$(Q_1 \ \& \ Q_2)$.

By Rule Three (again), it is a sentence if what is to the left and right of '&' are both sentences, and if the whole is enclosed in parentheses. The parentheses are clearly there, and Q_1 and Q_2 are sentences by Rule One. This means that the original question of whether the string to the right of 'V' is a sentence, is now settled positively, so the string we began with is, itself, a sentence.

NOTE   Is the following a well-formed sentence?

P_1 & P_2.

Strictly speaking it is *not*. This is because Rule Three requires parentheses, even when the string is unambiguous without them. It is easy enough to see that parentheses aren't really needed in the above. For convenience, we will amend Rule Three to allow us to drop the parentheses that are outermost in any sentence. This makes the above well-formed, and saves us adding unnecessary parentheses.

Applying the rules to determine whether some string is a sentence is straightforward, even if it is repetitious. Even easier is making sure that any sentence *you* construct is well-formed. Just make sure that nothing you write violates Rules One, Two or Three. Sentential is a sophisticated enough language to require a grammar, even if the grammar works in a repetitive and merely syntactical way.

Do you think that it would be possible to devise purely syntactical rules that separated strings of English words into the categories 'grammatical' and 'ungrammatical'? This is a difficult question. Would you classify the strings of words below as grammatical sentences?

(i)   Angry blue concepts slept.

(ii)   Angry blue the slept concepts.

In so far as they are regarded as *both* ungrammatical (and many people would find them so), it is difficult to see how we could have purely syntactical rules for English grammaticality. This is because (i) seems to be syntactically the same as:

(iii)   Tired little boys rested.

So the difference in grammaticality of (i) and (iii) must be explained in ways other than syntactical, perhaps by the meanings of the words. By contrast, no string of words which is syntactically the same as (ii) seems to be grammatical. So, a lot turns on whether we regard (i) and (ii) as ill-formed sentences of English. You can pursue this further through the relevant items on the Reading List.

*Exercise 1

Use the Rules (with the amendment to Rule Three) to test whether
each of the following are well-formed (wf):

(a) $(P_1 \lor \neg(Q_1) \,\&\, Q_2)$
(b) $\neg(P_1 \supset Q_1$
(c) $(P_1 \equiv \neg(Q_1 \lor Q_2)$
(d) $P_2 \lor \neg P_3$
(e) $Q_1 \supset (Q_2 \equiv \,\&\, Q_3)$.

5.4   Scope and Schemata

The grammar or rules of syntax for Sentential can be thought of as a
tool that we need to describe the behaviour of Sentential speakers. The
grammar is part of *our* theory of Sentential, and we can think of
Sentential users as conforming to the grammar, though we cannot think
of them as explicitly in possession of the grammar. This is because the
grammar for Sentential is in English. In this section, I will introduce two
more notions which, like the grammar, should be thought of as part of
the theory of Sentential. These new notions will make it easier to
describe Sentential economically and accurately.

A.   Scope

The negation in the sentence:

$\neg P_1 \lor P_2,$

affects only the basic sentence P_1, whereas the negation in:

$\neg(P_1 \lor P_2),$

affects the non-basic sentence $P_1 \lor P_2$. I take this to be obvious enough,
but we cannot leave matters there. The idea of a connective 'affecting'
certain sentences is too vague. In place of this vague notion, we can
use the rules of grammar to help us define a sharp one: the *scope* of a
connective. The scope of a connective is *the shortest sentence in which
it occurs*. To see what counts as a sentence we appeal to the rules of
syntax.

  Using this definition, you can see that the scope of the '$\neg$' in the first
sentence above is P_1, while its scope in the second is $P_1 \lor P_2$.

*Exercise 2

(a) What is the scope of the 'V' in the following sentence?

$(P_1 \equiv P_2) \vee \neg Q_1.$

(b) What is the scope of '&' in the following sentence?

$P_1 \supset (P_2 \vee (P_3 \,\&\, P_4)).$

The definition of the scope of a connective has this consequence: connectives can occur within the scope of other connectives. This allows us to speak of one connective in a sentence having *wider* or *narrower* scope than another. One connective has wider scope than another if the first includes the second within its scope. Also, given some long non-basic sentence, we can speak about its *main connective* as the one with the widest scope, the scope that takes in the whole sentence. For example, the main connective in:

(1) $(Q_1 \vee Q_2) \supset (P_1 \,\&\, \neg P_2),$

is '$\supset$' since it has the whole of the sentence as its scope. The idea of the main connective of a sentence is useful for allowing us to talk about the structure of sentences of Sentential. The sentence (1) can be described as having the structure of a conditional sentence in virtue of having '$\supset$' as its main connective. This brings me to the second notion we will need.

B.   Schemata

In describing (1) as having the structure of a conditional sentence, we used the notion of scope to work out that the main connective in this sentence is '$\supset$'. In our discussions of Sentential, it will be useful to have a notation for indicating the structure of sentences, a notation which will *show* the structure of a sentence without our having to *say* in so many words what it is. Of course, a sentence such as (1) shows its structure just as it is, so you may wonder why we need to have further notation. The answer is *generality*. I will explain.

Suppose you are asked what the following sentences have in common, what would you say?

$P_1 \supset P_2$
$(Q_1 \vee Q_2) \supset (P_1 \,\&\, P_2)$
$\neg P_1 \supset \neg(P_2 \equiv P_3).$

It is clear that, in each case, the main connective is a conditional, so the correct answer is that they all have the structure of conditional sentences. However, as things now stand, we have no way to show that structure. We have no way to display what these sentences have in common, but which leaves out the differences between them. What we need is a means of displaying the structure of sentences which is general enough to allow us to say what the above sentences have in common, but without including their differences. The natural first choice for such a notation would be to use blanks as in this:

(2)   ... ⊃ – – – .

This expression can be used to display the conditional structure of the above sentences, because it allows us to imagine all sorts of fillings for the blanks on either side of the '⊃', and this is how generality is achieved. Is (2) a sentence of Sentential? Certainly not. It has blanks in it which hold places for sentences, but it is not a sentence. Technically, (2) is called a *schema* (plural: *schemata*); it is a way of allowing *us* to say something general about the actual sentences of Sentential. Speakers of Sentential can happily use their language in complete ignorance of the notation of schema (2). Indeed, you may wonder why I even asked whether (2) is a sentence.

The answer arises from the fact that we will not use blanks to write schemata. Though natural, blanks are less convenient when we need lots of different structural displays, so we will use instead letters from the beginning of the alphabet, which will be called *schematic letters*. (2) will be written as (3) below:

(3)   A ⊃ B.

As you can see, there is a great temptation to see (3) as a sentence of Sentential, a temptation which must be resisted. To resist it just recognize that (3) is merely our way of doing what could have been done with (2).

C.   Truth Tables and Schemata

Schemata allow us to say things of a general nature about Sentential when the need arises, and here I must admit that the need has already arisen, though I allowed it to go unnoticed. Even in the description of Primitive there was a need for schemata, but Primitive was such a simple language that you would not have been led into error by the omission, and the introduction of schemata there would have been tedious.

When the connectives were discussed, I said such things as: '&' can be used to connect two basic sentences of Primitive to give a sentence such as P & Q whose truth table is ... Speaking this way encouraged the idea that there was such a thing as a general truth table for '&', whereas, in fact, all we had were truth tables for specific non-basic sentences. Strictly, the truth tables for the connectives even in Primitive should have been stated in terms of As and Bs. Thus, the truth table for '&' should be written this way.

A	B	A & B
T	T	T
T	F	F
F	T	F
F	F	F

This schematic truth table allows you to see the role of '&' when it occurs between *any two sentences of the language*. Remember that 'A' and 'B' hold places for any sentence. In Primitive, it didn't matter all that much that truth tables were not given in this general way. After all, there are only ever four possible basic sentence fillings for any schematic letter. However, in Sentential, sentences can be quite long and complex. Schematic letters hold places for any basic or non-basic sentence.

Exercise 3

Write out general truth tables for:

∨, ¬, ⊃, ≡.

5.5 Long Sentences

Sentential allows the construction of long sentences. But however long they are, the fact that they are constructed with truth-functional connectives guarantees that the truth value of any non-basic sentence is determined by the truth values of its basic constituents.

Suppose you eavesdrop on a conversation in Sentential that uses the sentences P_1, P_2, Q_1 and Q_2. Imagine that you have some way of knowing that, *in the context*, these sentences are used with the following meanings and truth values:

P_1 The flag is flying.
P_2 The mountain is visible in the distance.
Q_1 The sun is in the sky.
Q_2 There's smoke coming from the chimney.

P_1 is true.
P_2 is false.
Q_1 is true.
Q_2 is false.

Given this information, it is not difficult to work out whether each of the following is true:

(1) $Q_1 \supset P_2$
(2) $\neg Q_2$
(3) $P_1 \equiv Q_1$
(4) $P_1 \vee Q_2$.

You can work this out and, perhaps, even picture what each of them says, because you know the contribution that the connectives make to each of them, and you know the meaning and truth values of the basic sentences.

Exercise 4

(a)   Construct *four true* non-basic sentences other than (1)–(4) using the above basic sentences and the information given in the text about their truth value. Do not use more than two basic sentences in each.

(b)   Taking the meaning of the basic sentences as that given in the text, which of the sentences you have constructed is true of the following (roughly drawn) picture of the way things are?

Above, and in EXERCISE 4, you knew the meanings and truth values of the basic sentences. This was because I told you what they were. In the more usual case, speakers of Sentential do not have such information. They know the meaning of the connectives, and they know that every basic sentence is either true or false. But they do not know the specific meanings and truth values of the basic sentences. Lacking such information, it is impossible to work out whether a given non-basic sentence is *actually* true or false. However, even in the absence of this information, you can work out whether a non-basic sentence is true or false for each *possible* assignment of truth values to its basic constituents. That is, you can work out the truth table for any non-basic sentence of Sentential. All you have to do is to work out what the possibilities are, and what truth value the non-basic sentence has in each of them. The idea is simple enough, it is merely an extension of the truth tables we used for simple non-basic sentences such as P_1 & P_2. But faced with this sentence:

(5) $(Q_2 \lor \neg P_1) \supset (P_2 \& \neg(P_1 \equiv Q_2))$,

putting the idea into practice seems a daunting task. For example, could you tell straight off whether (5) is true when P_1 is true, P_2 is false and Q_2 is true? You know there is an answer, since this list of truth values is one of the possibilities, but I doubt that it is at all obvious. What is needed is some method for working it out. This is the business of the next sections.

5.6 Truth Tables for Sentential: More Possibilities

A truth table tells you when a given non-basic sentence is true (or false) on the basis of information about when each basic sentence is true (or false). The complete list of all possible combinations of truth values of the basic sentences is written in tabular form on the left side of the double line, and the truth values of the non-basic sentence for each possible combination (each row) are written on the right. This procedure applies both to 'simple' non-basic sentences such as P_1 & P_2, and to more complicated examples such as this:

(i) P_1 & $(Q_1 \lor Q_2)$.

The main difference between this non-basic sentence and those of Primitive is that (i) contains 'parts' which are themselves non-basic sentences, and it also contains *three* basic sentences: P_1, Q_1 and Q_2. This difference means that there will be more work involved in writing out the truth table for (i), but no new ideas are needed.

What you have to do first is to figure out a way of writing all the possible combinations of truth values of the three basic sentences. Given *two* basic sentences, there are four possible combinations (rows) to the truth table. This is because each basic sentence can be either true or false and there are two basic sentences. If you cannot see right off why these considerations determine the four possible combinations, you should look at the truth table for P & Q. A row for this truth table is made up of a truth value of P and a truth value for Q. There are as many rows as there are *different* combinations of truth values for these two sentences. Since each sentence could be T or F, you can tell by trial and error that there are four distinct possible combinations, and that these are correctly given in the table.

Precisely the same idea should lead you to work out how many rows there are in a truth table that is constructed around *three* basic sentences. The only trouble is that trial and error is both a trial and can all too easily lead to error. What is wanted is a way of telling straight off how many rows there are in the truth table *and* how to write them. This is where the arithmetical considerations mentioned above come in handy. *Two* basic sentences generate *four* rows: the number of rows is determined by this arithmetical formula:

Number of rows = 2^n,

where n is the number of *different basic sentences* occurring in the sentence for which the truth table is being constructed, and 2^n is 2 multiplied by itself n times. Thus, (i), which has three basic sentences, requires a truth table with 2^3 or 8 rows. There are eight possible combinations of truth values for the basic sentences of (i). All that remains is to work out how to write them down.

It is easy enough to see that one row must look like this:

P_1	Q_1	Q_2
T	T	T

and another like this:

P_1	Q_1	Q_2
F	F	F

but it is not as easy to list the other distinct possibilities.

Exercise 5

Write out all eight possible combinations of truth values for the three basic sentences in (i).

If you managed to do the EXERCISE, you now appreciate how convenient it would be to have a *method* which allows you to list all eight possible rows of the truth table for (i). Even more important, we want a method which will do this for truth tables that contain *any number of basic sentences*. Think how time consuming it would be to guess at the construction of a truth table which was constructed from, say, five basic sentences. It would have 2^5 or $2 \times 2 \times 2 \times 2 \times 2$ or 32 rows!

The method I will use is summarized in the following steps:

(a) Determine the number of rows in the truth table using the formula: number of rows = 2^n, where n is the number of different basic sentences in the non-basic sentence for which the truth table is being constructed.

(b) Under the first basic sentence write a column, half the rows of which are T and half – the second half – are F.

(c) Under the second basic sentence (if there is one) write a column, the first quarter of whose rows are T, the second quarter F, the third quarter T and the last quarter F.

(d) Under the third basic sentence (if there is one) write a column, the first eighth of whose rows are T, the second eighth F, the third eighth T, the fourth eighth F, the fifth eighth T, the sixth eighth F, the seventh eighth T and, finally, the last eighth F.

(e) Steps (c) and (d) are repetitive. What they require is that you alternate the Ts and Fs in each new column twice as often as in the previous one. Thus, if you have a column which alternates Ts and Fs four at a time, the new column requires you to alternate them two at a time. By proceeding in this way, then, no matter how long the initial column is, you are bound to get to a column which alternates T and F in this way:

T
F
T
F
T
F
.
.
.

It will be a strict alternation of T and F. You are now finished with the construction. (Notice that if there were only one basic sentence, you would reach the strict alternation at step (b).) The result of this construction is that each row of the table will be distinct from the others, and the table will contain all the possibilities.

As is so often the case with things in logic, the explanation can seem more difficult than what it seeks to explain. The reason for this is not hard to appreciate: what is wanted is a completely *general* account of the method, one which works for any number of basic sentences. This is given by steps (a)–(e) above. However, when the method is applied to a specific example, it is much easier to cope with. Here is the method applied to our original example (i) with the steps labelled as in the general description given above:

(a)   The sentence:

   (i) P_1 & $(Q_1 \vee Q_2)$

   has three different basic sentences in it. This means that a truth table for it will have 2^3 or 8 rows. The 'shell' of the table will look like this:

	P_1	Q_1	Q_2	P_1 & $(Q_1 \vee Q_2)$
row 1				
row 2				
row 3				
row 4				
row 5				
row 6				
row 7				
row 8				

(b)   The column under the first basic sentence is filled in with half Ts and half Fs as follows:

	P_1	Q_1	Q_2	P_1 & $(Q_1 \vee Q_2)$
row 1	T			
row 2	T			
row 3	T			
row 4	T			
row 5	F			
row 6	F			
row 7	F			
row 8	F			

(c)   The column under the second basic sentence is filled in with one-quarter Ts, one-quarter Fs, one-quarter Ts and one-quarter Fs as follows:

	P_1	Q_1	Q_2		$P_1 \& (Q_1 \lor Q_2)$
row 1	T	T			
row 2	T	T			
row 3	T	F			
row 4	T	F			
row 5	F	T			
row 6	F	T			
row 7	F	F			
row 8	F	F			

(d) The process of increasing the rate of alternation of Ts and Fs each time is continued until a strict alternation of T and F is reached. In this case, such a strict alternation occurs under Q_2 – the third and final basic sentence. The final table of possibilities looks like this:

	P_1	Q_1	Q_2		$P_1 \& (Q_1 \lor Q_2)$
row 1	T	T	T		
row 2	T	T	F		
row 3	T	F	T		
row 4	T	F	F		
row 5	F	T	T		
row 6	F	T	F		
row 7	F	F	T		
row 8	F	F	F		

(e) The table contains all eight different possible combinations of truth values for the basic sentences. These possibilities are just those you were asked to work out for yourself earlier, though they probably occur in a different order. Compare your list with the one above.

5.7 Algorithms

In essence, the method given in steps (a)–(e) above is merely a technique (or trick) for writing out all the possible combinations of truth values for any number of basic sentences. As you have seen, it is cumbersome to explain but, once you have seen it done once or twice, it is easily mastered. Indeed, you may well be wondering why I have spent so much time carefully describing the method in full generality and showing its operation in a step-by-step way.

Part of the answer is that this method illustrates a notion of great importance in logic, and precisely because the method itself is so simple, it offers an ideal opportunity to explain the new notion. The notion is that of an *algorithm*. Here is an explanation of it.

Think back to my asking you the question: what combinations of possible truth values are involved in working out the truth table for *any* sentence of Sentential? In order to answer this question you had to use your knowledge of the general principles of truth table construction, and you had to work out for yourself each of the possible combinations.

By contrast, when you have learned the method of steps (a)–(e), you can set out confidently knowing that, by carrying out each step, you will arrive at the correct answer with no struggle at all. Knowing the method is like knowing a procedure for computing the result of $m \times n$ where m and n are any numbers: even before you are given the values of m and n you know that the arithmetical methods you learned in school will enable you to work out the result.

A procedure for answering a question such as that given in (a)–(e), or that for multiplication, is called an *algorithm*. Such procedures have the important properties of being *effective* and *mechanical*. They are effective because you can be sure that, when they are correctly applied, they will give a definite answer to the original question. They are mechanical because you do not have to use any creative intelligence to apply them: just begin with the first step, and carry out each further step as directed until you reach the step which tells you that you are finished. (Even a computer or other form of machine could apply them, hence the term 'mechanical'.)

Many questions which we face in life cannot be answered by methods which could be described as algorithms. Whether a certain film is good, who will win the 3 o'clock at Goodwood, what am I best suited to do in life, are all questions which take time, intelligence and method to answer, and there seems no way in which effective and mechanical procedures could be formulated for answering them. Other questions such as what is the product of any two numbers, or what is the shortest route from London to Brighton, can be answered by procedures that are effective and mechanical, i.e. algorithmic methods.

The division of questions into those which do, and those which do not, allow of algorithmic methods for answering them invites an intriguing question: can there be an algorithm for validity? That is, will the procedures we devise with the Strategy constitute effective and mechanical means of deciding the validity of arguments? This can only be answered when we have fully implemented the Strategy, but you

should keep it in mind as we develop methods for testing the validity of
Sentential arguments in the next chapter.

Just to make sure you fully understand the method given by (a)–(e),
apply it to the following sentence:

$$(P_1 \mathbin{\&} Q_1) \lor (\neg P_1 \mathbin{\&} Q_1).$$

Step (a) requires you to work out the number of *different* basic sentences. The correct answer here is *two*. The basic sentences P_1 and Q_1
occur twice each but this does not count as four for the purposes of
constructing the list of possibilities. The truth values of the whole sentence depend on the truth values of the component basic sentences. This
sentence has only two component basic sentences even though they each
occur in two places in the whole. Using the rule that the number of possibilities $= 2^n$ where $n = 2$, we know that the number of rows is 4.

Writing these out gives us the familiar set of possibilities given below
on the left of the double vertical line:

P_1	Q_1	$(P_1 \mathbin{\&} Q_1) \lor (\neg P_1 \mathbin{\&} Q_1)$
T	T	
T	F	
F	T	
F	F	

Exercise 6

Construct the table of possible combinations of truth values for each
of the following sentences:

*(a) $(P_1 \mathbin{\&} P_2) \supset P_3$
 (b) $Q_1 \equiv P_1$
*(c) P_1
 (d) $((P_1 \lor Q_1) \lor P_2) \supset Q_2.$

5.8 Truth Tables for Sentential: Finishing the Job

You now know how to work out the relevant possibilities for any non-
basic sentence of Sentential. Each of these combinations of possibility
(rows of truth values for the appropriate basic sentences) will determine
a truth value for the non-basic sentence you are working on. This leaves
us with just one more job: to work out a way to calculate the truth
value of the non-basic sentence given each combination of truth values

for its basic sentence components. This is not at all obvious when the non-basic sentence is complicated.

When a non-basic sentence has a structure with which you are familiar, there is no real difficulty in working out what the truth values should be. Do this for:

P_1 & P_2.

There are two basic sentences so there are four possibilities and they are arranged as follows:

P_1	P_2	P_1 & P_2
T	T	
T	F	
F	T	
F	F	

Filling in the values for the non-basic sentence on the right of the double vertical line requires only that you remember the truth table for '&'. This gives us:

P_1	P_2	P_1 & P_2
T	T	T
T	F	F
F	T	F
F	F	F

Life is more difficult when the non-basic sentence is longer. For example, how would you go about filling in the values on the right for one of our earlier examples (see below)?

P_1	Q_1	Q_2	P_1 & $(Q_1 \lor Q_2)$
T	T	T	
T	T	F	
T	F	T	
T	F	F	
F	T	T	
F	T	F	
F	F	T	
F	F	F	

Is it true in the first row when all its component sentences are true? What about in the sixth row? It is not so easy to see how to answer these questions because, while you know how to construct truth tables for '&' and 'V' (and the other connectives), it isn't easy to do this all at once for two connectives.

Think about multiplication again. If you are asked how much 2934×1768 is, you would find it exceedingly difficult to get the answer by just thinking about these numbers. Instead, you would proceed by making repeated use of the multiplication tables which you learned in school. In essence, you would arrive at your answer by breaking down the question into simpler ones – into questions you can answer straight off such as how much is 8×4. Precisely the same idea is used in constructing truth tables for Sentential.

What we have to recognize is that any non-basic sentence of Sentential can be thought of as *built up* from components which may themselves be either basic or non-basic sentences. The table of possibilities on the left of the double vertical line gives you the truth values of the basic sentence components. What we have to do is to compute the truth values of the component non-basic sentences, and to do so in an order which helps us to work out the truth values of the whole sentence. It is here that the notion of *scope* can be very helpful.

The main connective is the connective with the widest scope. The truth values under this are what we are looking for, they are the truth values of the original sentence. To compute these, all we have to do is order our computations in terms of scope. First, we compute the truth values of the connectives with narrowest scope, then those with wider scope, and we proceed in this way until we get to the main connective. Ordering our computations in this way, means that we will never have to work out the truth values for non-basic sentences with more than one connective, so we only have to remember the truth tables for the five connectives. These function like the multiplication tables in arithmetic. You can perform any multiplication by using the elementary ones of the table. Similarly, you can write the truth table for any non-basic sentence by remembering the truth tables for the five connectives. Here is how it works as applied to our earlier example:

Stage One

P$_1$	Q$_1$	Q$_2$	P$_1$ & (Q$_1$ V Q$_2$)
T	T	T	T
T	T	F	T
T	F	T	T
T	F	F	F
F	T	T	T
F	T	F	T
F	F	T	T
F	F	F	F

The column for Q$_1$ V Q$_2$, is constructed through our understanding of the truth table for 'V'.

Next, we use the result of Stage One (the column under 'V') and the column under P$_1$ to work out the truth value of P$_1$ & (Q$_1$ V Q$_2$), the original sentence. Our decisions about what to write in each row are governed by our understanding of '&'. The result is shown under the '&' in Stage Two below.

Stage Two

P$_1$	Q$_1$	Q$_2$	P$_1$ & (Q$_1$ V Q$_2$)	
T	T	T	T	T
T	T	F	T	T
T	F	T	T	T
T	F	F	F	F
F	T	T	F	T
F	T	F	F	T
F	F	T	F	T
F	F	F	F	F

This finishes the truth table for the original sentence; the column we wrote in Stage Two gives the truth values of the original sentence for each set of possible truth values of the basic sentences. The procedure can be summarized in the following steps.

To write the truth table for any sentence A of Sentential:

1   Write out the table of possibilities for the basic sentences in A.
2   Compute the truth values of the non-basic components of A, and write these under the connectives in the relevant component. Do this in order of increasingly wide scope.

3   The list of truth values under the connective with the widest scope gives the truth values of A in all possible circumstances.

Exercise 7

Construct truth tables for each of the following:

*(i) $P_1 \supset \neg(Q_1 \& Q_2)$
(ii) $Q_3 \& (P_1 \supset P_2)$
*(iii) $P_1 \equiv (Q_1 \lor Q_2)$
(iv) $(Q_1 \& P_1) \supset \neg P_2$.

5.9   A Final Word on Truth Tables (for now)

The construction of truth tables for longish sentences is more a book-keeping job than anything else. Book-keeping is not to everyone's taste so it is worth finishing this part of our work with a few words of encouragement.

A truth table tells a speaker of Sentential what truth value some complicated sentence has, given any set of truth values for its component basic sentences. This is moderately interesting in itself, but it is not the reason why so much space has been devoted to the construction of truth tables. In the next chapter – and this might surprise you – we will see how the construction of truth tables enables us to decide whether any argument in Sentential is valid. This will require a bit of discussion, but it will not require any further skills. The ability to construct a truth table for any sentence in Sentential will suffice to allow you to decide validity. This is especially interesting in that the construction of truth tables is effective and mechanical – the detailed discussions of this chapter, in essence, provided an algorithm for such construction.

5.10   Fewer Connectives

Sentential is a very spartan language. It has any number of basic sentences, but only five connectives. Even so, there can be dialects of Sentential in which the number of connectives is fewer than five. And, perhaps surprisingly, speakers of some of these dialects are able to express the same sentences and arguments as can be expressed in Sentential with its five connectives.

For example, suppose you came across speakers who only used the '¬' and '&'. could they express everything that ordinary speakers of Sentential can? To find out, we must begin with a specific case. Could speakers of Sentential$_{¬\&}$ express this thought?

$P_1 \supset P_2$.

That is, could they express a thought which has the following truth table?

P_1	P_2	$P_1 \supset P_2$
T	T	T
T	F	F
F	T	T
F	F	T

You can convince yourself that they can if you construct the truth table for the sentence below:

$¬(P_1 \& ¬P_2)$.

Assuming, as is reasonable, that the basic sentences mean the same in both cases, you can begin to see that speakers of Sentential$_{¬\&}$ would not be stuck for a way to express the conditional sentence that comes so naturally to speakers of Sentential.

As a matter of fact, it turns out that any truth-functional sentence that is expressible in Sentential can also be expressed in Sentential$_{¬\&}$. Both languages are said to be *functionally complete*. The full-dress demonstration of this is beyond our present resources, but the above sort of consideration should go some way to convincing you.

---

*Exercise 8

(a) Finish the comparison between Sentential$_{¬\&}$ and Sentential by showing how to express the equivalents of the following in Sentential$_{¬\&}$:

   $P_1 \lor P_2$
   $P_1 \equiv P_2$.

(b) Which of the following pairs of connectives do you think are functionally complete?

   (i) ¬, $\lor$
   (ii) $\lor$, $\supset$.

The Main Points of Chapter 5

1　Sentential is an enlargement of Primitive. Both languages contain the same *connectives*, but there are these two differences.

> (i)　Sentential has an indefinitely large number of basic sentences.
> (ii)　Sentential allows the construction of non-basic sentences which have non-basic sentences as components.

2　These differences make Sentential sufficiently complicated for it to require a carefully set out *grammar*. This grammar takes the form of four rules of *syntax*.

3　Because the non-basic sentences of Sentential can be so much more complex than those of Primitive, we had carefully to work out a procedure for constructing the truth table for any non-basic sentence of Sentential. The careful statement of this procedure requires the notion of *scope*. It also required us to introduce *schematic letters* so that truth tables for the connectives could be given in their most general form.

4　In describing the construction of truth tables for Sentential, I introduced the notion of an *algorithm*. An algorithm is an *effective and mechanical* method of answering a given question. Some questions can be answered by algorithms, others seem not to be so answerable. The procedure for the construction of a truth table for any sentence of Sentential is an algorithm.

NOTE　See Appendix 1, Lesson 1, for further help.

Chapter six

Decision

6.0   Sentential and Primitive

We have completed the construction stage: Sentential is the language of logic we will use in the Strategy. In this chapter, we will develop methods for testing the validity of arguments formulated in Sentential, and in the next chapter we will see how to translate natural language arguments into it.

One note must be made before we move on to matters of decision. In the last chapter, I avoided using plain P and Q as basic sentences of Sentential; in every case I used letters with subscripts. This was to prevent any confusion between the basic sentences of Primitive which have fixed meanings, and those of Sentential whose meaning varies from context to context. In this chapter, I will allow myself to use, where reasonable, P and Q as ordinary basic sentences of *Sentential*. This is wholly for convenience, since it is easier to write (and read) sentences without subscripts. When they are used, they should be thought of as in Sentential and *not* as having the fixed meaning given them in our discussion of Primitive.

6.1   Truth Tables and Validity

Consider this simple argument in Sentential:

(a) $(P \lor Q) \supset Q$
     P
     _____
     Q.

My suggestion is that you now know enough to be able to work out a mechanical and effective method of deciding whether it is valid. Moreover, the method will be applicable to *any* argument formulated in Sentential. All you have to do is to focus for a moment on the notion of validity which was discussed at some length in chapter 2.

Recall our original definition:

> A valid argument is an argument in which it is not possible for the premises to be true and the conclusion false.

In the previous chapter, we worked out a procedure for writing the truth table for any sentence of Sentential. Such a table gives the truth values of any sentence in all possible circumstances. This invites the idea that we should extend the construction of truth tables from sentences to arguments.

Argument (a) above contains two different basic sentences. A truth table with four rows will list all the possible ways for these sentences to be true or false. In turn, we can use these truth values to work out the truth values of $(P \vee Q) \supset Q$ in all possible circumstances, and include them in the table. In this way, the final table will list the truth values of both the premises and the conclusion in all possible circumstances. By inspecting the rows of this table, it will be an easy matter to determine if there are any circumstances in which the premises are true and the conclusion false. If there are such circumstances, the argument is *invalid*; and if not, then the argument is *valid*. Here is the truth table:

P	Q	$(P \vee Q) \supset Q$	
T	T	T	T
T	F	T	F
F	T	T	T
F	F	F	T

The first premise is represented in the final column, the second premise in the first column, and the conclusion in the second column. To see whether the argument is valid you have to do two things:

1   Find each row in which *all* the premises are true.
2   Check whether the conclusion is true in *each* of these rows.

If the checking in (2) shows that in *every* case in which the premises are jointly true so is the conclusion, then the argument is valid. Otherwise, it is invalid. In this example, the premises are jointly true only in the first row. In this row, the conclusion is also true. Therefore, the argument is valid. There is no possible circumstance in which the premises are true and the conclusion is false. It is as simple as that.

Extending truth tables from sentences to arguments requires only that you write out a truth table in which every premise and the conclusion are represented. The procedure for testing is then just a matter of inspecting the completed truth table. Here is another example:

Argument

$P_1 \lor P_2$
$\neg(P_1 \,\&\, P_3)$
P_2
_____

$P_3.$

There are three different basic sentences used in the argument, so the truth table needed to represent the premises and conclusion will have eight rows. In the table below, the truth values of the premises are marked with 'p', and the conclusion with 'c'.

	P_1	p P_2	c P_3	p $P_1 \lor P_2$	p $\neg(P_1 \,\&\, P_3)$
	T	T	T	T	F T
*	T	T	F	T	T F
	T	F	T	T	F T
	T	F	F	T	T F
*	F	T	T	T	T F
*	F	T	F	T	T F
	F	F	T	F	T F
	F	F	F	F	T F

I have marked with '*' the rows in which all the premises are true. This makes it easy to do the checking required. As you can see, the conclusion is false in the second and sixth rows – rows in which all the premises are true. Hence, the argument is invalid.

The truth table method for testing arguments is an algorithm. It gives you an effective and mechanical way of telling whether any argument in Sentential is valid. The care with which we discussed the construction of truth tables in the previous chapter has paid off. It requires nothing but patience to construct a truth table for any sentence of Sentential; the same procedure is employed each time, and by going through the finite number of steps carefully, you know that you will finish the job. Truth tables (as above) for use in connection with arguments are no different. Moreover, when you have completed a truth table for an argument, the checking procedure is just as mechanical.

Exercise 1

Use the truth table method to determine whether the following are valid arguments:

*(a) P ⊃ Q
      P ∨ Q
      _____

      Q

(b) (P & Q) ⊃ ¬P
     P
     _____

     ¬P ∨ ¬Q

*(c) P ∨ (Q₁ & Q₂)
      ¬P
      _____

      Q₁ ∨ P

(d) ¬(P & ¬Q)
     Q ⊃ P
     _____

     P ≡ Q

*(e) ¬(P ∨ Q)
      _____

      ¬Q

6.2 Types of Sentence

A. Tautologies

Construct a truth table for this sentence:

(i)   P ⊃ (Q ⊃ P).

It should look like this:

P	Q	P ⊃ (Q ⊃ P)	
T	T	T	T
T	F	T	T
F	T	T	F
F	F	T	T

Under what circumstances is (i) false? According to the truth table, there are *no* circumstances under which it is false: it is true no matter what truth values are assigned to its basic sentences. Such a sentence is interesting enough to be given a name: it is called a *tautology*.

You might think that this is a wonderful type of sentence; it might seem useful to be able to say something true without having to check whether the components of what you say are true. But, while this type of sentence will prove valuable to us shortly, its value does not lie in conversational circumstances. You can appreciate this by considering a simpler example of a tautology, viz.:

P ∨ ¬P,

whose truth table is below.

P	P ∨ ¬P
T	T F
F	T T

Suppose that P is used to say that London has 4,532 pubs. I have absolutely no idea whether this is true but, if it is, it would be (mildly) interesting. However, it is hardly interesting to be told that either London does have 4,532 pubs or it does not. This is true, but it is too obviously true and, therefore, tells us nothing about London's pubs. Regardless of how P is used, the sentence P ∨ ¬P comes out true, and this makes it of little use in conveying genuine information. Even so, speakers of Sentential have an interest in tautologies which we will discuss in section 6.3.

B.   Contradictions

Consider this sentence:

P & ¬(Q ⊃ P).

Its truth table is shown below.

P	Q	P & ¬(Q ⊃ P)
T	T	F F T
T	F	F F T
F	T	F T F
F	F	F F T

This sentence is false no matter what truth values are assigned to its component basic sentences: it is a *contradiction*. We are taught that such sentences are to be avoided in ordinary conversation. A simpler example – one you should think of as the standard case of a contradiction – is this (shown with its truth table):

P	P & ¬P
T	F F
F	F T

Anyone who used P & ¬P would make a strange conversational partner – perhaps even stranger than someone who used P ∨ ¬P. After all, what would you make of someone who confidently said that there both were, and were not, 4,532 pubs in London? Still, like tautologies, contradictions are important in Sentential for reasons not connected with ordinary conversational exchanges.

C. The Contingent

Not all sentences are either tautologies or contradictions. You have had many examples of sentences which were true in some circumstances, and false in others. Such sentences are called *contingent*. They are so-called precisely because their truth (or falsity) is contingent upon the assignment of truth values to their component basic sentences. A sentence is contingent if it has at least one T *and* at least one F in its truth table.

It is not usually obvious whether a sentence is of one of the three types described: the only sure way to tell is to construct a truth table.

---

*Exercise 2

Classify each of the following as a tautology, a contradiction, or as contingent:

(a) P ⊃ ¬P
(b) P ≡ (Q & ¬P)
(c) P ∨ (¬P & ¬P)
(d) P ⊃ (Q ⊃ P)
(e) (P ⊃ Q) & ¬(¬P ∨ Q).

6.3   Tautologies, Validity and Equivalence

Consider the following sentence:

(S)   [((P ∨ Q) ⊃ Q) & P] ⊃ Q.

(The square brackets replace one of the required sets of parentheses as an aid to the eye. It makes it easier to see the correct grouping.) This sentence can be seen as made up from the argument:

(P ∨ Q) ⊃ Q
P
_____

Q.

by conjoining the two premises, and making this conjunction the antecedent of a conditional which has the conclusion as consequent. We call such a conditional the *corresponding conditional* of an argument. The argument in this case was the first example that I used to explain the truth table method for testing validity, and it was most definitely valid. You know how to write a truth table for the sentence (S), but, without doing it, think about what such a table will reveal.

The sentence has the overall structure

$$A \supset B,$$

where A is $((P \lor Q) \supset Q) \& P$, and B is simply Q. Given this, you know that it will only be false in these circumstances: A is true and B is false. Or, in other words, it will only be false when the antecedent is true, and the consequent false. But the antecedent of the conditional is the conjunction of the premises of a valid argument, and the consequent is the conclusion. So, you know that it will never be the case that A is true and B is false. Hence, you can predict that (S) is a tautology.

What this reasoning shows is that, in view of the truth table meaning of '$\supset$', there is the following relationship between an argument and its corresponding conditional: *when the argument is valid, the corresponding conditional sentence is a tautology.*

Tautologies can figure in another way in our understanding of validity. Is the following argument valid?

$$\frac{Q}{P \lor \neg P.}$$

Even without writing the truth table for this, you can see that the conclusion is a tautology, it always has the value true. But this means that it can never happen that the premises of this argument are true and the conclusion false. This is simply because this particular conclusion is never false. So, by our definition, the original argument is valid.

Some logicians find this odd. They cannot see why, as in this case, we should count an argument as valid when its premises are wholly unrelated to its conclusion. Others do not find this at all odd. For the present, it is sufficient that this consequence of our definition of validity is brought to your attention.

Turning our attention to equivalence, work out the truth table for the following sentence:

(E) $(P \supset Q) \equiv (\neg P \lor Q).$

It is a tautology. Sentences of the form $A \equiv B$ which are tautologies are called *logical equivalences*. Unlike ordinary equivalences which are true or false contingently on the truth values of A and B, tautologies of the form $A \equiv B$ are true in virtue of the structure of A and B. As you will have noticed when you constructed the truth table for (E), the truth tables for each side of the equivalence are identical.

As you know from our discussion of functional completeness in chapter 5, various connectives can be defined in terms of one another. Logical equivalence is just the explicit statement of this interdefinability. The Exercise below deals with a number of logical equivalences which should help you in finding your way around Sentential.

---

*Exercise 3

Below are ten sentences. Use truth tables to help you to say which of them are logically equivalent to which others.

(a) P ∨ Q   (b) ¬(P ∨ Q)   (c) ¬(P & ¬Q)   (d) P & Q

(e) P ⊃ Q   (f) ¬P ∨ ¬Q   (g) ¬P & ¬Q   (h) ¬(P & Q)

(i) ¬(¬P & ¬Q)   (j) ¬(¬P ∨ ¬Q)

6.4 Consistency and Validity

Consistency is generally held to be a virtue: we praise those whose deeds and words are consistent. Here we are more interested in the consistency of words than of deeds. What does it mean to say that someone is consistent (or inconsistent) in speaking?

Suppose that, in the course of a conversation, someone makes the following claims:

(1) You can get to the airport either by train or by bus.
(2) The train ceased operating a long time ago.
(3) There never was a bus service.

This person's claims are inconsistent and, quite obviously, unhelpful. No matter how you look at it, one of the things he says must be false, and, since you do not know which of them is false, they cannot be depended on. (Except, of course, as indicating something about the seriousness and state of mind of the speaker.)

Inconsistency is closely related to the notion of contradiction that came up earlier in the chapter. A contradiction is a non-basic sentence whose truth table reveals it to be false regardless of the truth values of its basic components. No one of the sentences (1)–(3) is a contradiction, since any one of them (or any pair of them) could be true. As a group or set, however, they are like a contradiction: if you formed the sentence:

(1) and (2) and (3),

this would be like a truth-table contradiction in that it could never be true. Moreover, it is reasonable to think of (1)–(3) conjoined in this way since they are all assertions from the mouth of one speaker; when someone makes a number of assertions, it's as if the speaker was saying one thing *and* another *and* ... Inconsistency is, therefore, a more general notion than contradiction; it applies to *sets* of sentences. If a set has only one sentence in it, and is nonetheless inconsistent, then that sentence must be a contradiction.

A set of sentences is consistent if it is possible for them all to be true. Do not lose sight of 'possible' here. For example, is the following set consistent?

(4) Whales are mammals.
(5) All mammals are furry.
(6) Whales are furry.

They are consistent even though (5) and (6) are obviously false. The world could have been created in such a way that (4)–(6) were all true, and that is enough to make them consistent.

In Sentential, it is an easy matter to test any list of sentences for consistency. Just write a single truth table for the whole list, and see if there is a row in which every sentence on the list is true. *If you can find at least one row in which all of the sentences in the list are true, then the set is consistent.*

Consistency is an interesting notion because of its connection with validity. This connection can be made explicit by applying the following procedure to an argument:

> Put a negation in front of the conclusion and test whether the list of sentences which consists of the premises of the argument and the *negated* conclusion is consistent.

Thus, given this argument:

$P \supset Q$
P
___
Q

see if the following is a *consistent* set

(i) $P \supset Q$
(ii) P
(iii) $\neg Q.$

If (i)–(iii) is consistent, then you know that it is possible for the premises of the original argument to be true and the conclusion false; or, in other words, the argument is *invalid*. As it happens, in this case, the list (i)–(iii) is inconsistent, so the argument is valid. It is important to remember that the relationship between consistency and validity is:

> if the list that includes the premises and *negation* of the conclusion is *inconsistent*, then the *original* argument is *valid*.

It is all too easy to form the list correctly by negating the conclusion, find out that it is consistent, and then think this shows the original argument is valid. *This would be a mistake.*

---

*Exercise 4

Which, if any, of the following lists of sentences are consistent?

(a) P & ¬Q   (b) Q ∨ (P ⊃ ¬Q)   (c) $P_1 ⊃ Q$
     Q   P $P_2 ⊃ Q$
     P ≡ Q $P_1 ∨ ¬P_2$

Finally, while we are on the topic of consistency, what would you make of the following argument?

$$\frac{P \,\&\, ¬P}{Q.}$$

You probably do not need to apply any of the procedures we have used to this argument to get the answer. The premise of this argument is a contradiction, so it can never happen that the premises are true and the conclusion false. This is simply because the only premise never is true. The same thing could be shown in an example where there are more premises, and they are inconsistent. In essence, the above argument, and others like it, show that inconsistent premises validly imply any sentence you care to choose. Some would see this as just what you would expect. After all, we are taught to avoid inconsistency in conversation, and this case shows why. Anyone who used inconsistent premises would be able to validly imply the truth of any conclusion, and this would be a good reason for our not trusting him.

6.5   Argument Notation

Up to now, we have written arguments in this general form:

Premise.
Premise.

.

.

.
_____

Conclusion.

This 'vertical' display of arguments is clear, but it takes up a lot of space. For this reason, and also because it is traditional, I would like to introduce the following 'horizontal' way of displaying arguments which will be used from time to time:

Premise, Premise, . . . / Conclusion.

Additionally, I would like to use the following to describe a relationship between certain sentences of Sentential:

$P \supset Q, P \vDash Q.$

This is called a *sequent,* and it is constructed with a symbol called the *turnstile*. It says that the truth of the sentences on the left guarantees the truth of the sentence on the right, and it should be obvious that this particular example of a sequent is true. Clearly, any valid argument can be written as a true sequent by putting its premises on the left and its conclusion on the right. When we want to deny that certain sentences guarantee the truth of others, we write it this way:

$P_1, P_2 \nvDash Q.$

This sequent can be used to claim that the argument which corresponds to it is invalid.

   It is important for you to recognize that sequents are not sentences of Sentential in that the turnstile is not an element of Sentential. A sequent is something we use in this book to talk *about* Sentential, to describe a certain relationship between sentences of Sentential.

6.6   Working Backwards

There is an even shorter way to use the idea behind truth tables to test for validity. Aside from saving work, it is worth discussing because it should give you that bit more insight into validity and the truth-table decision procedure. Our sample argument is this one:

$P \lor Q_1, Q_1 \,\&\, Q_2 \,/\, P \supset Q_1.$

The full truth table would have eight rows. However, what we are most interested in is a row that assigns T to each of the premises and F to the conclusion. Such rows are crucial to deciding validity: if there are any rows like this, then the argument is invalid. Instead of writing out the full table, try to see if you can tell if there is such a row.

The place to begin is with the conclusion. This is why the method, so to speak, works backwards. What you should do is to *assign values to the conclusion which make it false, and then see whether, consistently with that assignment, you can make each premise true.* This is illustrated below, in stages, with the truth value assignment written above the appropriate letter, and with the value of the complete sentence written to the right of it.

Stage One $P \lor Q_1$

                  $Q_1 \mathbin{\&} Q_2$

                  T   F
                  $\overline{}$
                  $P \supset Q_1$ F

These assignments of truth values should now be carried over to the premises.

Stage Two   T   F

                  $P \lor Q_1$

                  F

                  $Q_1 \mathbin{\&} Q_2$

                  T   F
                  $\overline{}$
                  $P \supset Q_1$ F

Now see what effect this assignment has on the premises. Remember your object is to try as hard as you can to make the premises *true* by filling in values to basic sentences which have not already been given values at Stage Two.

Stage Three T   F

                  $P \lor Q_1$ T

                  F

                  $Q_1 \mathbin{\&} Q_2$ F

                  T   F
                  $\overline{}$
                  $P \supset Q_1$ F

Notice that without our doing anything further, the first premise gets the value T and the second premise the value F. We can say this of the second premise even though we have yet to assign a truth value to Q_2

because the sentence is a conjunction: it is false so long as one of its conjuncts is false.

This shows that we have failed to find a way of making the premises true and the conclusion false. Are there any other ways of making the conclusion false? If there are, then we must carry through the steps above using these other ways. Remember, an argument is invalid if there is *any* assignment which makes the premises true and the conclusion false.

In this particular case, however, there is only one way in which the conclusion can be false: it is a conditional and this means that it is false only when its antecedent is true and its consequent is false. So, for this example, we need only look at the stages given above to see that it is valid. That is,

$$P \lor Q_1, Q_1 \& Q_2 \vDash P \supset Q_1.$$

Contrast this with this argument:

$$P \supset Q$$
$$\underline{Q \supset P}$$
$$P \equiv Q.$$

There are two ways in which $P \equiv Q$ could be false: either P is true and Q is false, or P is false and Q is true. In using the backwards method, *both* of these possible assignments would have to be investigated. It could turn out that one of them failed to provide a case in which the premises are true and the conclusion false, whereas the other one did. But one such case is enough to establish invalidity. (**Note:** the above is, in fact, valid.)

There are several things to keep in mind when using the backwards method. First, the method consists in trying to do something and seeing if you succeed or fail. You must remember that *failure* shows validity. Since validity is a good thing, it is all too easy to make the mistake of thinking that failure goes with invalidity. Second, the method is most simple and direct when there are very few different ways in which the conclusion can be false. The more different ways in which the conclusion can be false, the more avenues of investigation you have to open up. In some cases, the amount of work involved hardly justifies the use of the method. For example, suppose the conclusion of an argument is as shown below.

$$P \& (Q_1 \& Q_2).$$

There are seven ways in which this could be false! You would have to follow up each of these, and this might well use up more time and space than writing out a truth table. However, in very many cases the backwards method gives you a quicker way of checking for validity than writing out the full table.

The Main Points of Chapter 6

1 A method for deciding the validity of any argument of Sentential was presented. The method is outlined below.

    (a) Construct a truth table for the argument. This means counting the number of different basic sentences in the whole argument, using that number to write the table of possible circumstances, and computing the truth values of all the premises and the conclusion in the same table.

    (b) Mark the rows which assign T to each of the premises.

    (c) Check whether there is *any* row marked in (b) in which the conclusion is false. If there is, then the argument is invalid, otherwise it is valid.

2 Sentences were divided into three types: *tautologies, contradictions,* and *contingent* sentences. A tautology is a sentence which takes the value T in every row of its truth table, a contradiction is a sentence which takes the value F in every row, and a contingent sentence is one which has at least one T and at least one F in its truth table.

3 Given the truth definition of '⊃', there is a close connection between validity and tautologies. If you conjoin all the premises of a valid argument, and make them the antecedent of a conditional which has the conclusion as the consequent, then the conditional is a tautology. Such a conditional is said to be the *corresponding conditional* of the argument.

4 Our definition of validity has the consequence that an argument with a tautologous conclusion is valid regardless of its premises.

5 A list of sentences is *consistent* when it is possible for them all to be true. Consistency is related to validity in this way: if a list containing the premises of an argument and the negation of the conclusion is consistent, then the argument is *invalid.*

6 Our definition of validity has the consequence that an argument with inconsistent premises is valid regardless of its conclusion.

7 A shorter *(backwards)* method for checking validity was introduced.

Note See Appendix 1, Lesson 2, for further help.

Chapter seven

Translating into Sentential

We have now carried out the first two stages of the Strategy: the Sentential language has been constructed and a decision procedure for testing validity has been developed. To complete the Strategy we have to learn how to translate from English into Sentential. Once this is done we will be in a position to evaluate the success of the Strategy.

7.0 A Note on Translation

Translation between languages is a tricky business: the phrase 'lost in translation' is a commonplace used to convey the idea that much of the point of a text in one language can be lost or corrupted when that text is rendered into a second language. It is, in short, very hard to achieve a good translation.

Suppose you are asked to translate a poem that you know and enjoy from English into French. Your knowledge of French may be quite extensive, but we all know how hard it is to convey the sense of a poem in any language other than that in which it was written. Achieving a good translation here is very difficult indeed. At the end of the day you may even decide that, with respect to this particular poem, no good translation can be fabricated. You could very well think this even though you were virtually bilingual in English and French.

On the other hand, suppose you were asked to translate an instruction manual from English into French. For specificity, we can suppose that the manual clearly and accurately describes the setting up and functioning of a washing machine. In contrast to the case of poetry, you would probably consider this a much easier task. The languages between which translation is to be effected are the same, but the task is easier because it is less difficult to see what is wanted in the second case. Successful translation of the washing machine manual requires this: a monolingual reader of French should be able to tell from his reading of the manual how to set up and operate the washing machine. No such simple criterion of success can be stated in the case of poetry translation. There is no one thing that a poem is used for, hence, there is no easy way to say whether a translation works.

What these examples illustrate is that the quality of a translation is relative to the specific purpose for which the translation is required. When people say that translation is very difficult they usually have literary examples in mind, and literature has no simple agreed purpose. Things are different in the case of instruction manuals. Since we know what they are for, it is relatively easy to say whether a translation is adequate.

The moral of this is that we must be careful in judging the quality of a translation: we must keep firmly in mind the purpose of the exercise. No doubt a washing machine manual can be translated from good English into poor French. But, if the French translation suffices to give French readers a grasp of the workings of the machine, it is an adequate translation.

We are about to discuss the details of translation from English into Sentential. Sentential is a very different language from, say, French. It is a language of structure. Nonetheless, the move from English to Sentential does involve many of the problems of translation. Given this, we must keep firmly in mind the purpose of the translation as set out in the Strategy.

What we are interested in is validity. We know how to test arguments in Sentential using truth tables. If we can adequately translate arguments from English into Sentential then we can use the truth-table method to evaluate them. Our view of whether the translation is adequate should, in part, be based on how well the translation serves this need of the Strategy. (The reason that I say 'in part' is that we must be prepared for the eventuality that Sentential is not up to the task the Strategy sets it, however the translation is carried out. Indeed, you will come to see that the fuller implementation of the Strategy will require the development of a further language of logic. But we will leave that for later chapters.)

7.1   Previous Attempts

In chapter 4, where Primitive was introduced, there was some discussion of the translation between Primitive and English. This was intended to make it easier for you to understand the non-basic sentences of Primitive. Strictly speaking, so long as you understand how a truth table is constructed, and know the meanings of the basic sentences, you can understand each non-basic sentence of Primitive by reading its truth table. An important feature of simple languages such as Primitive and Sentential is that truth tables give us everything we need to understand the non-basic sentences. Nonetheless, it seemed reasonable to give you a feel for the connectives by trying to find close equivalents for them in English. Here is a summary of those previous attempts at translation:

Connective	English translation
&	and
∨	or
¬	not
⊃	if . . . then
≡	if and only if

As you no doubt recall, there are genuine questions about the adequacy of these translations. But, given what I have just said about how we should judge the translation of English into Sentential, a full evaluation of any proposed translation must wait until we can translate whole arguments. *Only when we can translate whole arguments, can we tell whether the translation scheme preserves validity.* If it does, then piecemeal questions about the translation of this or that connective will assume very little importance.

In setting out the translation scheme – the business of this chapter – we have no choice but to begin with sentences. The full scheme for translating arguments can only come at the end, since arguments are made up of sentences and these, in turn, are made up of various elements such as basic sentences and connectives.

7.2   The Elements: Basic Sentences

Translating the basic sentences of English into Sentential should be very easy. For example, here is a sentence of English:

The cat is on the mat.

It can be translated into Sentential simply by choosing from this huge list:

$$P, P_1, \ldots, P_n, Q, Q_1, \ldots, Q_n,$$

and stipulating that the Sentential sentence you have chosen is the translation of the English one. Remember that speakers of Sentential do not care much about the content of basic sentences, so long as the same sentence expresses the same thought throughout a given context of argument. This means that if you choose P as the translation of 'The cat is on the mat', you must continue to use P as the translation of this sentence in the context of an argument. On some future occasion, though, you could use P to translate:

The cow jumped over the Moon.

The basic sentences of Sentential are, unlike the sentences of natural languages, *variable*: a given sentence, say, P can have different meanings from one time to another. The only important thing is that, in a given context of argument, the meaning of P is thought of as fixed. This is just what you would expect of Sentential inasmuch as it is a language of structure: it is imagined as the language spoken by a tribe of logicians who are not interested in what you have to say so much as in the *structure* of what you have to say. By contrast, speakers of Primitive (and English) use their sentences as *constants*.

This feature of Sentential makes the translation of English basic sentences child's play – or almost. The fly in the ointment is the idea of 'basic' sentences of English. Is this such a sentence?

(i)   The man who came to dinner never left.

Or this?

(ii)   Fire will not spread unless there is oxygen present.

Each of these could be treated as a basic sentence, and translated by a basic sentence of Sentential. However, in so doing, it is quite possible that something would be lost. In Sentential, a non-basic sentence is one which contains one or more expressions from the list: & V, ¬, ⊃, ≡. This is the list of *connectives*. So, in order to be able to recognize a non-basic, or basic, sentence when you come across it, you have to know what the connectives are. The problem is we do not have a complete list of English connectives. We do have the list of approximate English translations of Sentential connectives, but that is hardly a complete list for English. For example, as you will see shortly, 'unless' functions as a connective in (ii), whereas there seems to be no such connective expression in (i). This means that, if we translated (ii) as, say P_1, we would be hiding the fact that (ii) contains two 'simpler' sentences and a connective.

Some appreciation of traditional 'school' grammar can help here. The sentence:

The man who came to dinner never left,

is what is called a *complex* sentence. Very roughly, this means that it contains at least one *clause* in addition to subject/predicate structure. In this case, the clause is:

who came to dinner.

A clause is a sentence-like expression which is distinguished from a sentence by the fact that it cannot be used on its own. What we get when we subtract the clause is this:

The man never left.

This is no longer complex, but it is a sentence. If it were the only utterance you used on a given occasion, your audience would think you strange, but would not doubt your understanding of English grammar. In contrast to this, if you used the clause on its own, then your audience would think your grasp of the English relative pronoun 'who' was shaky. Used on its own, the clause encourages an audience to think that the speaker is using 'who' as someone's name – perhaps as short for Dr Who. (Obviously, the very words in the clause could be used to ask a question, but then we would no longer be dealing with the clause as it is understood in (i).)

Things are quite different in regard to:

Fire will not spread unless there is oxygen present.

This sort of sentence is traditionally known as a *compound* sentence. Roughly, this means that it contains two or more sentences, and not merely clauses, as parts. Either:

fire will not spread,

or:

there is oxygen present,

is a perfectly good sentence which could be used on its own.

The distinction between complex and compound sentences can help to sort English sentences into basic and non-basic for purposes of translation into Sentential. Sentential has no way of representing clauses. This means that any complex sentence will be, from the perspective of Sentential, a basic sentence. Even a long sentence such as:

The door which is to the left of the room used as a store was repaired by the man who came to dinner,

counts as a basic sentence and can be translated as, for example, Q. This is because it contains no parts which themselves are complete sentences, even though it does contain three clauses and a number of prepositional phrases such as 'to the left' and 'by the man'.

By contrast, (ii) contains two complete sentences each of which can be translated as follows:

The fire will spread	P_1.
There is oxygen present	P_2.

The complete translation of (ii) then requires some way of dealing with the connective 'unless'. We will come to this shortly, but, for now, you can see that the translation of (ii) into Sentential could be of this general form:

$$P_1 * P_2,$$

where '*' is one, or some combination of, the connectives of Sentential.

Why did I say that the translation 'could' be of this general form, rather that that it is required to be? The answer to this is very important. The aim of translation, as I have now said several times, is to allow us to test natural language arguments for validity. It can happen that, in some argument, we do not need to translate sentences such as (ii) as non-basic sentences of Sentential in order to show validity. For example, suppose you came across this argument:

> If the fire will not spread unless there is oxygen present, there is nothing to worry about.
> The fire will not spread unless there is oxygen present.
> _____
> There is nothing to worry about.

Even before we have finished discussing translation, it is clear that this is a valid argument. More to the present point, it is an argument whose validity does not depend on our translating the second premise (and the antecedent of the first) into anything more complicated than a basic sentence, P. And notice that this second premise is (ii) above. Of course, we *can* translate it as non-basic, it wouldn't be incorrect. It is just more effort to do so, and, in this case, we need not expend it.

In this chapter, we will consider ways in which translation can be effected by uncovering the maximum structure: every non-basic sentence of English will be translated into a non-basic sentence of Sentential. When you deal with arguments, you will not go wrong if you continue to do this, but many logicians urge one to adopt this maxim: uncover as much logical structure as you need to show validity, and don't waste your effort doing more.

7.3   The Elements: The Connectives

How many connectives are there in English, or any other natural language? This is, perhaps unsurprisingly, a very difficult question to answer. Fortunately, we will not try to answer it in its full generality. I propose to consider a number of important examples of expressions in English that function as connectives. My discussion of these should serve our purposes well enough, and it should give you a sufficient grounding to see how to go about translating any that I overlook.

Since our object is the translation of English into Sentential, we can organize our investigation around the connectives of Sentential. That is, we will determine how to translate a number of expressions of English into the much more restricted set of logical expressions of Sentential.

A.   Conjunction

The word 'and' in, for example:

(1)   Napoleon was born in Corsica and he died in St Helena,

seems straightforwardly translated by '&'. Using the basic sentences of Sentential shown below, the translation of (1) comes out as:

P & Q,

where P is 'Napoleon was born in Corsica', and Q is 'Napoleon died in St Helena'. Notice that, in making this translation, we assumed that 'he' in the original sentence refers back to Napoleon. You will find that, in translating into Sentential, you will often have to use your knowledge of such matters to clarify the precise content of the basic sentences. Also, (1) could have been:

Napoleon was born in Corsica and died in St Helena,

and the translation proposed would have been unaffected.

The above use of 'and' is uncontroversial, but look at this case:

(2)   Napoleon liked water and wine.

Can we assume that this goes into Sentential as the following?

P & Q
where   'Napoleon liked water' is P
'Napoleon liked wine' is Q.

The matter is not so clear because (2) may be claiming that he liked both drinks, or it may be claiming that he liked the mixture. If he liked neither drink on its own, then our translation into Sentential would seem to be distorting the truth. In this case, 'and' seems to function like 'with'.

Consider now:

(3)   Bradman hit the ball and he ran down the wicket.

Suppose we translate this as follows.

> P & Q
>
> where   'Bradman hit the ball' is P
> 'Bradman ran down the wicket' is Q.

You can tell from the truth table that, in Sentential, P & Q has precisely the same truth table as Q & P. The '&' is insensitive to the *order* of basic sentences. (Remember that this is *not* true for '⊃'.) However, you do not need to know too much about cricket to recognize that (3) would not be considered equivalent to:

(4)   Bradman ran down the wicket and he hit the ball.

In so far as (3) and (4) are not equivalent, this is because the 'and' is understood as functioning like 'and then'. When this element of time sequence is read into 'and' it ceases to be so obviously well-translated by '&'.

What are we to say of examples (2), (3) and (4)? Is it simply wrong to translate these uses of 'and' into the Sentential '&'?

The answers to these questions illustrate something both interesting and important. What I suggest is that it is a mistake to translate the 'and' in (2) by '&', whereas it is not a mistake to do so in (3) and (4). The reason for saying that translation in (2) is a mistake is that (2) does not contain any genuine sentential connective, i.e. any word or expression which connects two or more sentences. Since no such connective occurs in the English sentence, you would hardly expect the translation into Sentential to have one. It just so happens that 'and' can be used in English both as a sentence connective and as another sort of connective device, one which connects nouns like 'water' and 'wine'. I will say more about this use later in the book.

The sentences (3) and (4), however, do contain connective uses of 'and'; the only question is whether they are fully translated by '&'. Here I urge caution. A translation is adequate if it meets the particular purposes set for it. Clearly, '&' does not convey the sense of time sequence that comes across in the use of 'and' in (3) and (4). However, if you read P & Q as you should – as containing no hint of time sequence – then this translation at least preserves part of the *truth* common to (3) and (4). That is, it is true when (3) is true *and* it is also true when (4) – the reversal of (3) – is true. It may matter to cricket historians whether Bradman hit the ball and *then* ran or ran and *then* hit the ball. But our translation P & Q at least applies to both cases. So, something is 'lost' in translation and something is preserved. In advance of using the translation as part of the Strategy, we cannot say whether what is lost matters; we will, therefore, work on the assumption that all uses of 'and' as a sentence connective in English are translated by '&'.

Related problems show up with this sentence:

(5)   Computers are unintelligent, but they save time.

The word 'but' functions as a sentence connective something like 'and': think about it and you'll see that (5) is true only in the case where it is true both that computers are unintelligent and that they save time. Yet, it seems that something is missing from the following translation of (5) into Sentential:

P & Q
where   'computers are unintelligent' is P
'computers save time' is Q.

This is because 'but' conveys something further about the nature of the connection between the sentences, somewhat in the way that 'and' in (3) does. This something is lost in translation even though truth is preserved. As above, we will not worry about this extra message: we will use '&' to translate all sentence connective uses of 'and' and 'but'.

B.   Disjunction

We will translate the sentence connective (italicized) in each of the following as 'V':

(6)   The fuse is blown *or* the switch is damaged.
(7)   Dessert is *either* cheese *or* fruit.

(Note that from now on, I will not always include the full translation of each sentence into Sentential. Unless there is a special problem, I will assume that you know how to translate the component sentences of examples such as (6) and (7).)

The proposed translation of 'or' and 'either ... or' by 'V' might be controversial. As we saw in chapter 4, the problem is that the truth table for a sentence containing 'V' makes that sentence true when both of its component sentences are true. Thus, if we translate (6) as P V Q we are committed to saying that (6) is true when:

it is true that the fuse is blown
AND
it is true that the switch is damaged.

In some cases, perhaps in this one, this seems all right. In others, it is felt that this is odd, that the use of the word 'or' excludes the possibility that both of its components are true. For example, many would be prepared to say that the summary of the menu in (7) is just mistaken (false) if, in fact, both cheese and fruit are on offer.

In view of this controversy, there are two things that we could do here, and the choice between them can teach us something about language. First, we could say that English has two *senses* or *meanings* for the word 'or': one the *inclusive* sense captured by 'V', the other the *exclusive* sense as in (7). We could even go on to design a new symbol for Sentential which has this truth table:

P	Q	P ψ Q
T	T	F
T	F	T
F	T	T
F	F	F

where 'ψ' is now the exclusive 'or'.

On the other hand, we could insist that there is only one sense or meaning of 'or'. In cases where this use seems to require an exclusive interpretation of the word, this is because of the *background knowledge we have of the context*. We all know about menus and choices, so it seems inappropriate to think of (7) as true when we are told that customers can have cheese and fruit, but this is not due to the meaning of 'or'. The claim is that this meaning is inclusive, but that the context gives us this further information: you cannot have both. On this view, if such further information is important to an argument, it can always be included by adding a 'not-both' rider to the translation of (7). This would give us:

(P V Q) & ¬(P & Q).

This non-basic sentence has precisely the same truth table as that of the 'ψ' symbol above.

How do we decide between these two proposals? Both give us what we want: a way to translate sentences using 'or'. One suggests that 'or' is ambiguous, and that context tells us which meaning is being used; the other that it has one meaning, but that the context sometimes adds something. The notions of ambiguity and context-dependence are very important tools in the description of language. If we had some general theory about when an expression was ambiguous, we might be able to decide this issue. Without such a theory the choice here can seem like that between six and a half dozen.

Even so, there is a piece of evidence that might be of some help in deciding this issue. Consider this sentence:

(8)   Money can neither buy friendship nor happiness.

Clearly, there is a relationship between 'neither ... nor' and 'either ... or': plausibly, 'neither ... nor' is the negation of 'either ... or'. Thus, in clumsy English, we could rephrase (8) as:

It is not the case that: either money can buy friendship or money can buy happiness.

This, in turn, would be most naturally translated into Sentential as:

¬(P ∨ Q)
where   'money can buy friendship' is P
'money can buy happiness' is Q.

Notice two things: first, the negation is of the whole disjunction, and not merely a negation of each of its parts; and second, I have used the inclusive disjunction '∨' here. The first of these is justified by the observation that (8) is certainly *not* adequately translated by:

¬P ∨ ¬Q,

which says that either money does not buy friendship or money does not buy happiness. This is true, for example, if it turns out that money *does* buy friendship, even though it does not buy happiness. The author of (8) could hardly agree to that.

The second point is the one directly relevant to our discussion above. If 'either ... or' is ambiguous, then you would expect 'neither ... nor' to be ambiguous too. Thus, faced with (8), we should wonder whether to use '∨' or 'ѱ'. I used '∨' and I think that no plausible translation of (8) could do otherwise. If (8) were translated as ¬(P ѱ Q), it would come out true when both of these are true:

Money can buy friendship.
Money can buy happiness.

This certainly runs counter to the thought expressed by (8). So, if you agree that 'neither ... nor' is the negation of 'either ... or', you should agree that '∨' is best used in both translations, and that the so-called 'exclusive meaning' of 'either ... or' is best handled by conjoining the not-both rider when the context demands it.

Defenders of the ambiguity thesis could argue that 'neither ... nor' does not offer the scope for ambiguity that 'either ... or' does. Hence, the matter isn't finally settled by my discussion of 'neither ... nor'. Still, we will use 'V' as the translation of 'or' and 'either ... or', and in the translation of 'neither ... nor'.

C.   Negation

Negation occurs in many ways in English. Here are some.

(9)   (a)   It is not the case that sugar is healthy.
       (b)   It isn't true that sugar is healthy.
       (c)   Sugar is not healthy.
       (d)   Sugar is unhealthy.

All of these are translated as ¬P. For obvious reasons, the first pair are *external* negations; the second pair are *internal* negations. In most cases, this difference is not important, but it can cause trouble. Watch out for sentences like:

(10) All fats are unhealthy.

This quite clearly does not mean:

Not all fats are healthy.

The problem is that, in some cases, you cannot move between internal and external negation. Later in the book we will come back to examine this sort of case, but I do not think that it will cause you much trouble in connection with Sentential.

D.   Conditionals

Using '⊃' to translate 'if ... then' is generally the cause of the greatest dissension among newcomers to logic. As you have seen, the truth table for '⊃' makes it seem as if there is a very great difference between the way speakers of Sentential use this connective, and the way speakers of English use their conditional.

In chapter 4, I tried to cross this gulf by invoking a distinction between the conditions under which a conditional is true, and the conditions in which it would normally be asserted. When the sun is shining and the wind is strong, speakers of Sentential are quite happy to say:

(11) The sun is shining ⊃ the wind is strong.

(Here I use a mixture of English and Sentential for clarity.)

Yet it seems bizarre to think that, in these circumstances, we would say:

(12) If the sun is shining then the wind is strong,

merely because both happened to be true. If we were to make such an assertion, it would be more likely because we had a particular theory about the cause of strong winds.

Nonetheless, there is still reason to think that we would regard (12) as true when both conditions obtain: in the absence of a special theory of winds, we may be reluctant to assert (12) but, if someone does assert it, many would regard it as true, and the presence of sun and wind hardly falsifies it.

Whether this is an adequate way to deal with the differences between '⊃' and 'if ... then', will not be pursued here. Remember that the only way to test our translation scheme is as part of the whole Strategy. For the present, you can simply assume that the correct translation of the English conditional is '⊃'. that is, any English sentence of the form:

　　　if ... then _ _ _,

is to be translated into Sentential as:

　　　P ⊃ Q.

What other sorts of conditional connectives are there in English? Below are a number of conditional sentences that are not in the straightforward 'if ... then' form. See if you can restate them so that they are:

　　　(13)　Britain will leave the EEC if Labour wins.
　　　(14)　Britain will leave the EEC only if Labour wins.
　　　(15)　Britain will not leave the EEC unless Labour wins.
　　　(16)　Britain will leave the EEC provided that Labour wins.

The first of these is the easiest. English allows us to change around the order in which the antecedent and consequents of conditionals are presented. This gives us scope for emphasizing one or the other. (13) can be recast as:

　　　(13′) If Labour wins then Britain will leave the EEC,

and this is then translated by P ⊃ Q.

(14) is more tricky. I expect that you can 'hear' that it means something quite different from (13). Someone who asserted (14) would not give up the assertion just because Labour won and did *not* leave the EEC. However, even though we use 'only if' naturally and easily, many find it difficult to recast it into the 'if ... then' form. The correct way to do this for (14) and all similar sentences is:

　　　(14′) If Britain will leave the EEC then Labour wins.

This slightly awkward sounding sentence has the same truth conditions as (14): it is false if:

It is true that Britain will leave and false that Labour wins.

(15) is probably the most difficult. The problem is that 'unless' interacts with the negation, and it is not always obvious how to move between this construction and the straightforward conditional. Most would agree that (15) is either:

If Labour wins then Britain will leave the EEC,

or,

If Britain leaves the EEC then Labour wins.

But which is it? The answer is the second. (15) is equivalent to:

(15′)   If Britain leaves the EEC then Labour wins.

It is also equivalent to:

(15″)   If Labour does not win then Britain does not leave the EEC.

The last sentence in the list is very much like the first. Instead of '. . . if _ _ _', it is '. . . provided that _ _ _' which is merely another way of invoking the conditional. Thus, (16) has precisely the same translation as (13), i.e. (13′). Incidentally, it is quite common to find either 'on condition that' or simply 'when' in place of 'if'; all of them come out as (13′).

E.   Biconditionals

Our discussion of conditionals should make it much clearer why '≡' is the translation of 'if and only if'. To see what I mean, write out the truth tables for both P ≡ Q and (P ⊃ Q) & (Q ⊃ P). *They are exactly the same.* Given our discussion of conditionals, the second sentence is the translation of an English sentence of this form:

(17)   . . . if _ _ _ and . . . only if _ _ _.

You can now see why the Sentential '≡' is the translation for 'if and only if': this English phrase is merely a compressed version of (17).

The problems that beset '⊃' as a translation of 'if . . . then' carry over to the biconditional. Remember, regardless of what P and Q mean, a Sentential speaker will be prepared to assert P ≡ Q in any circumstance in which they have the same truth value. Thus, using the 'mixed' idiom again, such a speaker will be quite happy to assert:

(18) snow is white ≡ grass is green,

whereas it sounds very odd indeed to say:

(19) snow is white if and only if grass is green.

Still, if someone were to assert (19), it is reasonable to think that he would be prepared to claim (18) as true. The final word on this matter must rest with our evaluation of the Strategy in chapter 10 where the problems with conditionals and biconditionals will be further aired.

7.4   Complicated Sentences

We have now discussed the translation scheme for basic sentences and for the connectives. All that remains is the translation of English sentences which contain multiple occurrences of basic sentences and connectives.

You might think that longer English sentences introduce no new difficulties – that having covered all the parts, the wholes should look after themselves. This thought isn't completely wrong, but there are aspects to the construction of longer English sentences which deserve special mention.

A.   Grouping

When translating from English into Sentential, you must be careful about grouping. In Sentential, all grouping of sentences occurs by means of parentheses or, if it is visually clearer, by square brackets. Grouping devices exist in natural languages such as English, but they are not the same as in Sentential. Instead, grouping in natural language is accomplished by a mixture of indicators: commas, word order, special words, stress, general context. The following pair of examples will help to make the point:

1   George will go to Oxford and Jane will go to Cambridge, or *their* mother will be disappointed.
2   George will go to Oxford and Jane will go to Cambridge, or *her* mother will be disappointed.

I would suggest that both of these should be translated as

$$(P_1 \,\&\, P_2) \lor Q$$

with the '&' within the scope of the '∨'. In both cases, this is because of the ',' but in (1), the use of 'their' is a contextual factor that reinforces this pattern of grouping. After all, since the mother in question belongs to both of them, it seems only reasonable that she would be disappointed if things didn't go well for both her children. To judge just how effective 'their' is, try to write (1) in such a way that it requires this translation.

$$P_1 \ \& \ (P_2 \lor Q).$$

It might be enough to write:

(3)   George will go to Oxford, and Jane will go to Cambridge or their mother will be disappointed.

But without special stress (which I cannot easily reproduce in writing), (3) is liable to misinterpretation. To make absolutely sure, you would have to insert some extra word as in:

(3′)   George will go to Oxford, and additionally Jane will go to Cambridge or their mother will be disappointed.

It would be tedious to describe every little trick that we use in English to make grouping clear, but with these examples to make you conscious of the possibilities, I do not think that you will have trouble in translation.

B.   Ellipsis

Long sentences make for difficult listening and reading. For this reason, we tend to shorten our messages, and use various devices to make sure that they are understood. One of the most obvious ways to accomplish this is to leave out certain words or phrases while marking their absence. The word for this, derived from the Greek, is *ellipsis*. As an example, consider:

(4)   If Henry and Ann go to Crete for a holiday, then so will I.

We have no difficulty in understanding this sentence, and no one sensible would use the unelliptical:

(4′)   If Henry and Ann go to Crete for a holiday, then I will go to Crete for a holiday,

except for special emphasis. Sentential, however, is a language spoken by those more interested in clarity than in style. (Not that these are always in competition.) For this reason, you must be prepared to expand (4), at least for yourself, as part of translating it into Sentential.

7.5   Skill

This chapter offers guidance rather than detailed instructions about translating from English into Sentential, and I have tried to include guidance on the most common and important words, phrases and constructions. Nonetheless, there is some skill to translating even into a language as simple as Sentential. This skill consists in your taking care about the English sentences you are trying to render into Sentential.

We constructed Sentential in order to help with our search for a way to decide whether arguments are valid. The need to translate English idiom into Sentential is part of that enterprise. However, in carrying out the translation, you will deepen your understanding of English and, indeed, natural language generally. This, as promised earlier, is almost as important a part of learning logic as the testing of arguments.

---

*Exercise

Translate each of the following sentences into Sentential. In each case, say precisely what basic sentence of English your Sentential sentence translates. (Also, translate so as to reveal the maximum Sentential structure you can find in each English sentence.)

(a)   I will take my holiday abroad this year unless the weather improves.
(b)   Neither love nor money would persuade him to help with the project.
(c)   Greek is a difficult but worthwhile language to learn.
(d)   You can't win if you do not play.
(e)   If Smith comes to the dinner, and if Jones does not, then we can all travel in the same car.
(f)   Robert cannot be both travelling to London and dining in Paris.
(g)   Only by working hard can you succeed.
(h)   If the fuel holds out and we get either a following wind or a calm sea, then we'll be in harbour today.
(i)   I'll be there provided the trains are running.
(j)   Smoking is unhealthy.

The Main Points of Chapter 7

1   Translation from one language to another can be a very difficult undertaking. Just how difficult it is depends on the purpose for which the translation is to be used. In translating from English (or another natural language) into Sentential, our interest is in validity. Part of what counts in favour of a translation scheme is whether it preserves validity. Ideally, an argument which is valid in a natural language should have as a translation an argument valid in Sentential, and vice versa. This means that the translation scheme cannot really be judged in a piecemeal way. We need to see how it works in connection with arguments. (Also, we must see how close to the goal of the Strategy Sentential can take us.)

2 In order to identify sentences in English that correspond to basic sentences of Sentential we have to have some idea of the connectives used in English. No complete list was given, but a number of the most central cases were discussed.

3 The list included:

(a) NEGATION: 'not', 'it is not the case', 'it is not true that' and a number of prefixes such as 'un-' and 'im-'.
(b) CONJUNCTION: 'and', 'but' (be careful about uses of 'and' and 'but' which are not genuine sentence connectives).
(c) DISJUNCTION: 'or', 'either . . . or', 'neither . . . nor'.
(d) CONDITIONAL: 'if . . . then', 'if', 'only if', 'unless', 'provided that'.
(e) BICONDITIONAL: 'if and only if', 'when and only when'.

4 There are various devices used in English to indicate grouping. These play the role of parentheses and brackets in Sentential.

NOTE   See Appendix 1, Lesson 6, for further help.

Chapter eight

The Strategy Applied and Extended

We have reached the point envisaged in chapter 3: each stage of the Strategy has been worked out, and the first task will be putting it to work to evaluate natural language arguments. The second thing we will do is to extend Sentential methods for dealing with arguments. This will spill over into chapter 9.

8.0 The Elements of the Strategy Reviewed

The three stages of the Strategy are as follows:

(I)   The *construction* of a language of logic, more particularly, Sentential.

(II) The development of a *method of logic* for determining the validity of arguments couched in the Sentential language.

(III) The *translation* of arguments from English into Sentential.

When these are combined they should give us a way of telling whether arguments in English are valid: you simply translate into Sentential and test for validity. The complete success of the Strategy depends on the truth of this claim:

an argument in English is valid *if and only if* it is valid in Sentential.

In chapter 10, we will take up the question of whether this claim is true, i.e. whether Sentential is adequate to the demands of the Strategy. As has already been indicated, there are grounds for thinking that Sentential must eventually give way to a richer language of logic; Sentential is not itself adequate to the demands of the Strategy. But you will come to appreciate that Sentential is a reasonable foundation for further work, so our effort on it is well spent.

8.1 Two Examples

(A) The food was marvellous, but the wine was poor. If Max selected the wine, it was not poor. Thus, Max did not select the wine.

Is this valid? First, translate each premise and the conclusion into Sentential.

Premise (1)   The food was marvellous, but the wine was poor.
P_1 & Q

Premise (2)   If Max selected the wine, it was not poor.
$P_2 \supset \neg Q$

Conclusion   Max did not select the wine.
$\neg P_2$

Next, evaluate the Sentential translation of the argument using the truth table method

	P_1	P_2	Q	p P_1 & Q	p $P_2 \supset \neg Q$	c $\neg P_2$
	T	T	T	T	F F	F
	T	T	F	F	T T	F
*	T	F	T	T	T F	T
	T	F	F	F	T T	T
	F	T	T	F	F F	F
	F	T	F	F	T T	F
	F	F	T	F	T F	T
	F	F	F	F	T T	T

The only row in which *both* premises are true is the third. In this row, the conclusion is also true, so the argument is valid. I expect that this result agrees with your initial judgement of the argument: it seemed valid when you were confronted with it in English, and it has now been shown to be valid by the Strategy.

(B) We will have a gale unless the wind changes direction. The wind will change direction only if the anticyclone moves further south. The anticyclone will move further south. Therefore, we will have a gale.

I cannot be sure, but I would expect that this argument is less easy to evaluate at a glance, so to speak, than (A). Also, it is a little more difficult to translate into Sentential. Try to translate the argument your-self before reading on, and then compare your answer with that below.

Premise (1)   We will have a gale unless the wind changes direction.

$\neg P_1 \supset P_2$ or $P_1 \lor P_2$

where P_1 is 'we will have a gale' and P_2 is 'the wind changes direction'.

Premise (2)   The wind will change direction only if the anti-cyclone moves further south.

$P_2 \supset P_3$

Premise (3)   The anticyclone will move further south.

P_3

Conclusion   We will have a gale.

P_1

The truth table for this argument is below.

c P_1	P_2	p P_3	p $\neg P_1 \supset P_2$	p $P_2 \supset P_3$
* T	T	T	F T	T
T	T	F	F T	F
* T	F	T	F T	T
T	F	F	F T	T
* F	T	T	T T	T
F	T	F	T T	F
F	F	T	T F	T
F	F	F	T F	T

Examination of the table should convince you that the argument is invalid. The premises are true in the first and third rows, and so is the conclusion. But the premises are also jointly true in the fifth row, and here the conclusion is false. So, the fifth row is a circumstance which shows the argument to be invalid.

8.2   Algorithms and the Strategy

(A) and (B) illustrate something important which we have discussed pre-viously. (A) was obviously valid, while (B) was much less obviously invalid. However, the truth table method works in exactly the same way for each of them, and is no more difficult to apply to (B) than to (A). Because the method of logic we developed (truth tables) for Sentential is an algorithm for validity, no particular argument is more difficult to test than any other. (Except in a book-keeping sense, when the number of basic sentences is very large.)

This does *not* mean that the Strategy itself constitutes an algorithm for testing arguments in natural language. The translation step in the Strategy is not reducible to an algorithm. That is, there is no mechanical and effective set of procedures which will take an English sentence and generate its translation into Sentential. Translation, even at this simple level, requires some intellectual effort.

Nonetheless, even though the Strategy is not itself an algorithm for testing the validity of natural language arguments, it is a distinct improvement over everyday methods. After all, translation may require some skill and practice, but it is not all that difficult. And once you have translated an argument into Sentential, the answer is given you by the truth table algorithm for testing validity in Sentential.

Exercise

Use Sentential to tell whether each of the following are valid arguments.

*1 Mark went to the restaurant around the corner. Therefore, he either went to the restaurant around the corner or to Mexico.

2 The universe is either finite or infinite. The universe is unbounded. Therefore, the universe is either finite and unbounded or infinite and unbounded.

*3 If I don't finish this book by Christmas, it won't be published until 1987. If it is not published until 1987, I'll forfeit my advance on royalties. I will not forfeit my advance. Therefore, the book will be finished before Christmas.

4 The serum must arrive in 24 hours or Sherlock will die. If the expert on jungle diseases is available and the serum arrives, then Sherlock will live. The expert will be available. However, if the expert is available, the serum will arrive in time. So, Sherlock will live.

*5 Neither the Americans nor the Soviets have been able to solve the problem of the arms race. If the Americans don't solve these problems, then we face certain annihilation. So, if the Soviets do not solve the problems, we face certain annihilation.

6 If the temperature does not rise tonight, we can go skating tomorrow. If either the temperature rises or the ice is rough, then we cannot skate. The ice will not be rough. Therefore, we can go skating tomorrow.

*7 Unless Emily gets a bicycle for her birthday she will be unhappy. So, if she gets a dress, she will be unhappy.

8.3   Extending the Methods of Logic

In what remains of this chapter, we will discuss a further method of logic for dealing with Sentential arguments. The rest of the Strategy will remain as before.

This might strike some of you as excessive. After all, you now know how to apply the truth table method, and this provides us with just what we wanted: an effective and mechanical method for deciding whether an argument is valid. So, why introduce yet another method? The full answer to this will become apparent as you proceed further into the book.

8.4   Sentential Conversations

In developing Primitive and then Sentential, I have from time to time asked you to imagine these as spoken languages. I find it useful to look at them that way. Admittedly, the tribe of logicians who speak Sentential have very strange conversational habits. Sentential is a structural language – one which can be used very effectively to display the logical structure of sentences and arguments. This feature is what we exploited in implementing the Strategy. Since its main purpose is to display structure, the behaviour of its imagined speakers can appear bizarre to us: they use sentences even when their hearers are unlikely fully to understand them. Imagine that a Sentential speaker has the thought we might express as:

> the road on the right leads home, and the one on the left to the sea.

This thought could come out in Sentential as, for example, any of the following:

P & Q
P_1 & Q_1
Q_4 & Q_8.

A Sentential speaker doesn't care which is chosen, and what is more likely to matter to a speaker is the fact that the thought is expressed in conjunctive form. I said that it is 'more likely' to matter because there are circumstances in which the above sentence would be treated as itself simply a basic sentence. *Our* interest in Sentential is in its potential for dealing with arguments. As I mentioned in chapter 7, there are times when you have a choice as to whether to translate an English sentence as basic or non-basic,

a choice which is governed by the needs of testing the validity of the argument in which the sentence occurs. Similarly, users of Sentential are really
only interested in arguments; they are, after all, logicians. So, in framing
some argument, it is possible that a thought of theirs can be treated as a
basic sentence, even though, in the context of another argument, the same
thought needs to be displayed with its more detailed structure.

The idea that speakers of Sentential express their thoughts only in
presenting arguments allows us to sharpen our understanding of
Sentential. Earlier in the book, I said that while the basic sentences of
Sentential have variable meanings, they are to be thought of as fixed in
a given context, a given 'stretch' of conversation. We can now say that
a stretch of conversation in Sentential consists in whatever exchanges
are needed to present and evaluate an argument. Thus, the basic sentences of Sentential should be thought of as having a fixed meaning in
any argument in which they figure. Indeed, this is precisely the way we
used them in implementing the Strategy.

Below is a record of two typical Sentential conversations. The speakers are S_1 and S_2.

> (1) S_1:   P & Q, pause, Q
> S_2:   Q.
>
> (2) S_1:   P ⊃ Q, ¬P, pause, ¬Q
> S_2:   silence, conversation ends.

It is not difficult to work out what is going on in these conversations. In
conversation (1), speaker S_1 puts forward a sentence and, by pausing,
indicates his interest in the question of whether this sentence validly
implies the one that follows the pause. S_2 shows that he thinks it does
by asserting the conclusion. In conversation (2), speaker S_1 puts forward
two sentences and pauses to mark off a sentence which may or may not
follow from these. By remaining silent, S_2 shows either that he thinks it
does not follow, or cannot tell.

The arguments in these conversations are very simple so there is no
difficulty in imagining S_2 responding as he does. What if they were very
much more complex? *We* have the truth table method at our disposal;
with a bit of time (and paper and pencil) we can work out our
responses. How is this done by speakers of Sentential?

There are two things we *could* say here:

> (a)   members of this tribe of logicians have the uncanny ability to
>   tell whether any argument is valid merely by having it pre-
>   sented to them;
> (b)   they also use the truth table method.

However, I do not want to say either of them (and it is *my* fantasy, after all). Here are my reasons.

It seems implausible to imagine that Sentential speakers have a built-in capacity to recognize valid arguments. There are an infinite number of possible valid arguments, and it seems a cheat to simply credit speakers with this recognitional capacity. On the other hand, it is no less a cheat to imagine them using truth tables. The Sentential language does not contain words for the concepts of truth and falsity. To be sure, the speakers presumably can recognize when sentences are true or false, since these sentences are used to express their thoughts about how things are. However, in order to construct truth tables, and to use them to test for validity, you have to have words (or, at least, letters) that stand for the concepts of *true* and *false*. There are no such words in the Sentential language itself. Truth tables are *our* invention which we apply to Sentential. The truth-table method is really part of natural language reasoning *about* Sentential and does not take place *in* Sentential.

This last point is important enough to merit some special terminology. The premises and conclusion of the argument:

P & Q / Q,

can be expressed in Sentential. Further, we can count Sentential users as recognizing this as an argument simply by treating their pauses as having the significance described earlier. A pause for them is what '/' is to us.

We will call Sentential the *object language*. Reasoning *about* this language takes place in the *metalanguage* (the prefix 'meta' is from a Greek word which has come to be used roughly for what we mean by 'about'). The metalanguage of chapters 5 through 7 is English supplemented by the various schemes we concocted for writing out truth tables, including our use of schematic letters. In other words, our metalanguage contains the object language plus a lot more. This is unsurprising as you have been fluent in both English and Sentential since you read chapter 5. In the conversations described earlier, speakers of Sentential too are imagined as reasoning about their own language. Typical conversational exchanges can be seen as inquiries into (broadly) the logical relationships between various sentences. But the sort of metalinguistic reasoning they employ does not involve any mention of truth. They seem able to conduct their investigations into arguments without the need of truth tables.

This brings us back to our original question: how do the logicians who speak Sentential work out whether arguments are valid? If we can answer this question, if we can develop a theory of what their reasoning is like, then we will have uncovered a method of logic which does not employ truth tables, but which does show when a conclusion validly follows from premises. Moreover, as you will come to see, this method of logic is one that comes more naturally to *us* than truth tables.

8.5   Sentential Games

The examples of Sentential conversations given above were very simple. This might encourage you to think it easy to work out a theory of the reasoning which takes place in Sentential conversations. You may be tempted to say: when the second speaker recognizes that an argument is valid, he simply repeats the conclusion of the argument. Otherwise he stays silent. The trouble is that, since there are an infinite number of arguments formulable in Sentential, such a theory of Sentential reasoning would require us to see its practitioners as having mastery of an infinite number of distinct arguments. This is hardly a method of logic which we could use, nor is it an accurate account of what goes on in Sentential. The earlier examples of Sentential conversations were misleadingly simple. Below is a more typical example. (In it I have used '/' to indicate Sentential pauses.)

S_1: $P \mathbin{\&} Q_1, P \supset Q_2 / Q_2$
S_2: P, Q_2.

S_1 offers two premises and then, in effect, asks whether a conclusion follows from them. S_2 responds by first asserting P and then the conclusion. What we have here is a conversational *game*.

The idea of such a game is this: the first player (speaker) presents an argument for consideration, and the second player has to show how to *derive* the conclusion of the argument from the premises according to certain *rules* which every Sentential speaker knows. The example above illustrates the operation of two of these rules. As applied to the specific case, the effects of the rules are as follows:

(1)   Given $P \mathbin{\&} Q_1$, you are allowed to assert P.
(2)   Given $P \supset Q_2$ and P you are allowed to assert Q_2.

S_2 knew that, in order to derive the conclusion from the premises, he had first to use (1) to get P, and then to use (2) to get Q_2. He showed this by asserting first P and then the conclusion Q_2.

How do these conversational games help with the question of

validity? (1) and (2) each embody *elementary* valid arguments. That is, in each case, it can never happen that the move from what you are given to what you are allowed to assert will lead you from truth to falsity. Saying that they are 'elementary' means that we can see them as truth-preserving with little or no effort. A successful Sentential game can be seen as a stringing together of these sorts of move. The premises offered by the first speaker are strung together with the assertions of the second speaker that are allowed by the rules, and the game ends with assertion of the conclusion. So long as every move is truth-preserving, the whole can be seen as guaranteeing the truth of the conclusion given the truth of the premises. We will call such a completed game a *deduction* or *derivation* of the conclusion from the premises. The idea is that if a deduction can be constructed, then one can be sure that the conclusion of the argument validly follows from the premises. Further, so long as there are only a finite number of rules used by speakers of Sentential, it will not be implausible to credit them with knowing all the rules. The rules are essentially permissions to assert certain sentences given others. By seeing Sentential speakers as working with these rules, we can understand how it is they can investigate the validity of arguments without having the explicit means for claiming the truth of their sentences. A deduction is after all only a list of sentences of Sentential, albeit a special sort of list.

What we have to do is to work out the rules that are used in deduction games. There are only a finite number of them – in fact there are ten – so the job is not too difficult. However, the very fact that there are so few rules raises an important question. How do we know that these rules will suffice for any valid argument of Sentential? That is, how do we know that the particular set of rules used by Sentential speakers will allow them to construct a deduction for every valid argument in Sentential? This question will be addressed in the next chapter where the rules will be presented.

The Main Points of Chapter 8

1   The stages of the Strategy were put together to work out the validity of natural language arguments.

2   Although the truth table method is an algorithm for validity in Sentential, the Strategy itself does not offer an algorithm for validity in natural language. This is because the process of translation is by no means mechanical and effective.

3   A new method of logic was outlined. As applied to an argument, the idea is that we use certain rules which allow us to *deduce* (*derive*) the conclusion from the premises. This *deduction* shows the argument valid in so far as we have been careful to make each of the rules truth-preserving.

NOTE   See Appendix 1, Lesson 7, for further help.

Chapter nine

Deduction

The sort of reasoning that takes place in Sentential deduction games is the basis for a new method of logic. In the previous chapter, I urged you to see that method as our theory of how, and with which rules, speakers of Sentential play deduction games. However, instead of carrying on with the pretence that we are theorizing about Sentential speakers, the aim of this chapter will be to teach *you* how to play deduction games. As promised, you will find the deduction method natural to use, but it has a more fundamental importance that will be apparent in the later chapters of the book.

9.0 Deductions

The aim of a deduction is to derive a conclusion from whatever premises you are given by proceeding in a step-by-step fashion. Each of these steps contains a sentence of Sentential. You choose which steps to take, and in what order, but you have to make sure that your steps are sanctioned by the rules we are about to discuss. The construction of a deduction is a lot like playing a game of chess. The rules tell you how you may, or may not, move each piece, but they don't tell you which pieces to move at which point in the game. Partly for this reason, my story about Sentential deduction 'games' was not all that fanciful.

Two important things follow from even this preliminary description of a deduction, and they must be aired before I can go on to present the rules. First, since each step in a deduction can contain any sentence of Sentential, the rules must be stated in the most general way. This will be done by using the schematic letters I introduced in chapter 5.

Second, in order to make deductions clear, we will have to introduce some notation for keeping track of what is going on in each step. Sentential deduction games were seen as a sequence of sentences culminating in a conclusion. Each sentence was allowed to take its place in the sequence by the rules, and with reference to the sentences that preceded it. Unless you are very good at playing such games, it can be

very difficult to tell whether some sentence is really allowed in the
sequence. To make it easier, and given the analogy between deductions
and games, we will introduce with each rule a notation for *score-
keeping*.

As a last preliminary point, the steps of a deduction are arranged ver-
tically in sequentially numbered *lines*. This is certainly different from
the way I wrote Sentential deduction games, but, as you will see, it
makes it much easier to keep score.

9.1 The Rules of the Game

There are ten rules that you must master in order to enter into deduction games. Each of them is a way of reasoning from certain premises to
a conclusion. In presenting them, I will offer grounds for thinking that
each of them is truth-preserving. This is vital. A deduction is a sequence
or chain of linked steps. If the whole is to carry a guarantee of truth
from its premises to its final step, then we must be sure that each link
does so as well.

The rules fall naturally into two types: *Elimination* and *Introduction*.
For each connective (&, ¬, ⊃, V, ≡), there is one rule that tells you how
to break down a premise containing that connective (how to *eliminate*
it) and one rule that tells you when you may *introduce* the connective
into the deduction.

I. *CONJUNCTION ELIMINATION* (&E)
   Given any sentence of this form:
      A & B
   you are allowed to write a sentence of this form:
      A
   or a sentence of this form:
      B.

Here is an example which both illustrates the rule and introduces you to
the conventions of score-keeping.

   1   (1) $(P_1 \equiv P_2)$ & Q   Premise
   1   (2) $P_1 \equiv P_2$ 1 &E

Look at the first line. The number in parentheses is the number of the
line in the deduction. The number on the left indicates which line this
particular line *depends* on. This notion of dependency needs some
explaining.

Steps in a deduction do not, by and large, come from thin air.

In keeping track of the lines, we want some way to indicate which other lines, if any, serve as the premises for each line. That is, we want some way to indicate which lines any given line depends on for its truth. In line (1) above, $(P_1 \equiv P_2)$ & Q depends for its truth on itself. You could as well have said: it is true if it is true, and this is just what you would expect for a premise. If someone were to challenge this deduction, and ask by what right have you written line (1), you would justifiably answer: it is a premise for the steps which follow. These answers explain why I have written the '1' on the left-hand side, and 'Premise' on the right-hand side. The answers to these questions in connection with line (2) will make things clearer.

On the *right-hand* side of a line, you indicate your justification for writing the line, the rule you used. Line (2) is sanctioned by our newly introduced rule of &E. In addition to naming the rule, you must write the line numbers to which this rule was applied – in this case, line (1). If asked what guarantees the truth of the sentence in line (2), you would point to line (1). That is why the '1' appears on the *left-hand* side of line (2). It indicates that this line depends on line (1) for its truth.

By keeping score in this way, you make it possible for someone to tell *at every stage in a deduction* what rule sanctions a given line, and which other lines serve as truth guarantors (premises) for that line.

The rule of &E certainly passes the test we set for rules: if a conjunction is true, then so will be both of its conjuncts.

Finally, we can clean up the presentation of the rules by using a dashed line to indicate what the rules sanction. Thus, the final version of the two parts of &E can be written as follows:

A & B   A & B
– – – –   – – – –
  A   B

II.   *CONJUNCTION INTRODUCTION* (&I)

A   B   A   B
– – – –   – – – –
A & B   B & A

SCORE-KEEPING   A simple deduction using this rule is given below to show you how you keep score.

1	(1)	P ⊃ Q	Premise
2	(2)	Q	Premise
1,2	(3)	(P ⊃ Q) & Q	1,2 &I

Notice that &I licenses you to write a line *given two other lines*. That is, the rule requires two premises. This is shown on the right-hand side where two lines are cited, and on the left-hand side where there is a dependency on both premises. (By the way, in the example deductions for both rules, the citations on the right and the dependencies on the left were the same line numbers. Do not think this is always the way things will turn out. The left-hand and right-hand numbers serve different purposes. You will see cases where they diverge shortly.)

The reasoning supporting &I is simple and obviously valid: the truth of both A and B certainly guarantees the truth of either of the conjunctions A & B or B & A.

III. *NEGATION ELIMINATION* (¬E)

¬¬A

- - -

A

SCORE-KEEPING   On the left you cite the truth guarantor of the line number of ¬¬A, and on the right the line number of ¬¬A and the abbreviated name of the rule.

The effect of negating a sentence is to give that sentence the opposite truth value. If you negate the negated sentence (double negation) you get back the original truth value. Hence, since ¬¬A plausibly has the same truth value as A, it is not possible for ¬¬A to be true and A false. In short, the above pattern always has valid instances.

NOTE   We are always told to avoid 'double negatives' in our writing. Why? It might not be obvious why we should not use double negatives. This last sentence with its double negative is hard to construe. That is why we should avoid them: they are often difficult to construe in English. The above rule shows that this is not a problem in Sentential.

Preamble to the Next Rule

We often make assumptions in our everyday reasoning. For example, in the course of an argument, you may be told that something is being assumed 'for the sake of the argument'. The rule about to be discussed involves such an assumption, and it would help to get a bit clearer about assumptions before the rule is stated.

What is an assumption, and what do we mean by the phrase 'for the sake of the argument'? A first answer might be: an assumption is some thought which is introduced into the argument in an effort to reach the conclusion. This isn't entirely wrong, but great care must be exercised in understanding it. The trouble is that it does not distinguish between an assumption made in the course of an argument, and a premise used in the argument. Premises are, after all, thoughts we begin from in an effort to reach a conclusion. If an assumption is seen as a further thought introduced into the argument, then it sounds as though it is merely another premise. This hardly explains why we qualify assumptions with such phrases as 'for the sake of the argument', phrases which seem inappropriate when applied to premises.

In order to distinguish an assumption from a premise, we have to recognize that an assumption is *used* in an argument, but is itself 'dropped' from the argument before the final conclusion is reached. Because it serves temporarily as a premise this explains why the first answer above isn't completely wrong. The fact that it is dropped from the argument after it has served its purpose is what distinguishes an assumption from a premise.

But what does it mean to say that an assumption is 'dropped'? It means that, even though an assumption is used on the way to reaching a conclusion, we do not, in the end, need to see the conclusion as dependent for its truth on the assumption. Or, in other words, the assumption does not serve as one of the premises for the conclusion. When an assumption is made and then later dropped, we will say that it has been *discharged*. This, and the general functioning of assumptions, can be illustrated by the first rule (below) which makes use of them.

IV.   *NEGATION INTRODUCTION* (¬I)
IF, by making an assumption A, we can use the rules to deduce a sentence of the form B & ¬B, i.e. if we can show:

A

- - - - -

B & ¬B

THEN we are allowed to deduce:

¬A

from whatever premises were used in the deduction of B & ¬B from A, but *not* including A itself. That is, A is discharged at the point we write ¬A.

SCORE-KEEPING   This is best illustrated with a deduction using the new rule.

1	(1)	P	Premise
2	(2)	¬P & ¬Q	Assumption
2	(3)	¬P	2 &E
1,2	(4)	P & ¬P	1,3 &I
1	(5)	¬(¬P & ¬Q)	2,4 ¬I

At line (2) we introduced an assumption. That it is an assumption is written on the right, and its self-dependence (as with premises) is shown by writing its own line number on the left. From this assumption and the premise we deduced the contradiction in line (4) using the two rules for '&'. Having deduced this contradiction, we are then entitled to deduce the negation of the assumption which we do at line (5). On the right, you must cite the line number of the assumption, and the line number where the contradiction was reached, together with the name of the rule. On the left, you can see the result of discharging the assumption: its line number no longer figures as one of the things that (5) depends on. However, line (5) does still depend on the original premise given in line (1), since this was used in the deduction at line (4), and is not discharged. This deduction illustrates clearly the fact that the left-hand numbers can diverge from those on the right. Line (5) is shown as dependent on line (1), but the steps we cite to justify our writing of line (5) are those required by the rule, namely lines (2) and (4).

The process of reasoning described in the rule is sometimes called *'reductio ad absurdum'* and sometimes simply 'indirect proof'. The Latin phrase means 'reduction to absurdity' and it is an apt name because, in using the rule, you first make an assumption and then reduce it to absurdity (i.e. deduce a contradiction from it). Having carried out the reduction, you are then allowed to draw the negation of your assumption as a consequence.

The reason that this rule preserves truth is best appreciated by asking what would happen if the original premises did *not* guarantee the truth of the conclusion ¬A? In such a case, we would be justified in thinking it possible for those premises to be true and ¬A false. If ¬A is false, then A is true. This would mean that it is possible for the original premises *and* A to be true together. But this is just what we showed to be *impossible* when we derived B & ¬B from the original premises and A. In deriving this contradiction *using rules which we have already shown to be truth-preserving*, we know that the premises and A cannot be true together. (Remember, if the conclusion of a valid argument is false – and B & ¬B certainly is – then at least one of the premises must be false.) Thus, *we must have been wrong* in our original assumption that the premises did not validly lead to the conclusion ¬A. So, those premises *do* validly lead to the conclusion ¬A.

Think hard about the previous paragraph. It is quite densely argued and it does two things: it argues in favour of the validity of applying the rule, and it does so by using a pattern of reasoning exactly like that given in the rule. It is thus both an explanation and an illustration of the acceptability of Negation Introduction.

NOTE   Assumptions may be made at any stage of a deduction and you may assume anything you like. This sounds too good to be true, but that is only an appearance. Remember, the point of making an assumption is to help in the deduction. You do not want such assumptions to end up as further premises in the argument, and this means that you have to discharge them. Since, there are quite strict guidelines about how and when to discharge assumptions, you will find them useful only in cases where rules such as ¬I show you how to deal with them.

V.   *CONDITIONAL ELIMINATION* (⊃E)

A ⊃ B

A

- - - - -

B

SCORE-KEEPING   On the left you cite whatever A ⊃ B and A depend on, and on the right you cite the line numbers of A ⊃ B and A together with the name of the rule.

This rule requires very little comment. The pattern of reasoning it depicts is one we have had examples of before, and it is certainly truth-preserving. Notice that the elimination of '⊃' is brought about by having as premises the conditional sentence *and* its antecedent. This should come as no surprise since you wouldn't expect to be able to eliminate '⊃' in the way we did '&'. (This rule is sometimes known by its Latin name *modus ponendo ponens*, or *modus ponens* (method of bridging) for short. Logic has offered a home to various Latin phrases because of its long history, but that is another story. I will bring in traditional names in cases where they are still current enough to be encountered in the literature.)

An example of the use of this rule is given below.

1	(1)	$P_1 \supset P_2$	Premise
2	(2)	$P_2 \supset P_3$	Premise
3	(3)	P_1	Premise
1,3	(4)	P_2	1,3 ⊃E
1,2,3	(5)	P_3	2,4 ⊃E

Here it will be useful to introduce the idea of a *deduction sequent*. This last deduction shows that the rules allow the deduction of P_3 from $P_1 \supset P_2$, $P_2 \supset P_3$ and P_1. We can express this fact in the following sentence.

$$P_1 \supset P_2, P_2 \supset P_3, P_1 \vdash P_3$$

The turnstile in this sequent has a single horizontal bar which distinguishes it from '⊨'. The double turnstile is used to claim that the truth of the sentences on the left imposes truth on the sentence on the right. The single turnstile is used to say that you can deduce the sentence on the right from those on the left by using the rules. The above sequent is clearly true in view of the deduction given earlier.

VI. *CONDITIONAL INTRODUCTION* ($\supset$I)

IF we are able to show that B can be deduced from A, i.e. that:

A
- - -
B

THEN we are allowed to deduce:

A $\supset$ B

from whatever premises were used in the deduction of B from A except A itself. Thus, in deducing A $\supset$ B, A is discharged.

SCORE-KEEPING   On the left of the line with A $\supset$ B, you write the numbers of the truth-guaranteeing lines used in deducing B from A. But you do not include A here, since A is treated as an assumption which is discharged in this line. On the right, you write the line numbers of A and B, and the name of the rule. Here is a deduction which shows the following sequent to be true using the new rule.

Sequent $P_1 \supset P_2, P_2 \supset P_3 \vdash P_1 \supset P_3$

Deduction	1	(1)	$P_1 \supset P_2$	Premise
	2	(2)	$P_2 \supset P_3$	Premise
	3	(3)	P_1	Assumption
	1,3	(4)	P_2	1,3 $\supset$E
	1,2,3	(5)	P_3	2,4 $\supset$E
	1,2	(6)	$P_1 \supset P_3$	3,5 $\supset$I

To convince yourself that this pattern of reasoning preserves validity follow this argument: since the rules so far introduced are truth-preserving, the first stage of the rule establishes that it is not possible for A to be true, and B false. Since this is so, and given the meaning of '⊃', there is no way in which A ⊃ B could be false. The only way a sentence of the form A ⊃ B could be false is when A is true and B is false. But we showed that to be impossible in this case by deducing B from A using truth-preserving rules.

VII. *DISJUNCTION INTRODUCTION* (VI)

$$
\begin{array}{cc}
A & A \\
\text{----} & \text{----} \\
A \lor B & B \lor A
\end{array}
$$

SCORE-KEEPING   On the left, you write the numbers of the lines that A depends on, and on the right, the line number of A together with the name of the rule.

This often strikes people as the something-for-nothing rule. From a premise A, you are allowed to deduce A ∨ B where B can be any sentence whatsoever. It can seem odd at first, but a little reflection should remove any doubt. For, it could never happen that A is true and A ∨ B or B ∨ A are false, given the truth-table meaning of 'V'.

VIII. *DISJUNCTION ELIMINATION* (VE)

IF we are able to show that C can be deduced from A and that C can be deduced from B, i.e. that:

$$
\text{Stage One} \quad \begin{array}{ccc}
A & & B \\
\text{---} & \text{and} & \text{---} \\
C & & C
\end{array}
$$

THEN we are allowed to take ourselves as having deduced C from A ∨ B, i.e.:

$$
\text{Stage Two} \quad \begin{array}{c}
A \lor B \\
\text{-----} \\
C
\end{array}
$$

SCORE-KEEPING   On the left of C you write the line numbers on which the truth of A ∨ B depends and the numbers of the truth-guaranteeing lines used in the two deductions in stage one, *not* including the line numbers of A and B. These are discharged at the point of writing the line with C. On the right, you write: the line number of A ∨ B; the numbers of the lines where you assumed A and B; the numbers of the lines where, having assumed A you deduced C, and having assumed B you deduced C again. There are, therefore, five line numbers needed on the right.

This is the most complicated rule of the ten, and you should go through the following informal justification of the rule slowly. What we want to show is that VE is truth-preserving.

For the sake of argument, assume that A V B is true because A is true. Since you have shown that C can be deduced from A, you know that C must be true. So, if it is A that makes A V B true, A V B must also make C true. Assume now that A V B is true because B is true. Since you have also shown that C can be deduced from B, you know that C must be true. So, if what makes A V B true is that B is true, A V B must also make C true. But A V B is a disjunction and, hence, is true only if one or both of its disjuncts are true. So, the two sides of our reasoning above show that in any of the circumstances in which A V B is true, C must be true too.

The rule is called an 'elimination' rule and this might give you pause because the final part of the rule seems to introduce the 'V' for the first time. However, notice that the 'V' occurs as one of the premises in the final line. If you look carefully at the other rules, you will see that a rule is called an elimination rule if the logical particle occurs in a premise but not in the conclusion. For this reason, the above rule is indeed an elimination rule.

Here is an example of the rule at work showing that the following sequent holds:

P V Q, ¬P ⊢ Q

1	(1)	P V Q	Premise
2	(2)	¬P	Premise
3	(3)	P	Assumption
4	(4)	¬Q	Assumption
2,3	(5)	P & ¬P	2,3 &I
2,3	(6)	¬¬Q	4,5 ¬I
2,3	(7)	Q	6 ¬E
8	(8)	Q	Assumption
1,2	(9)	Q	1,3,7,8,8 VE

This is the most tricky deduction we have had so far. It repays careful consideration. In line (3), we made the first assumption needed for VE. Our aim was to get to Q. There seems to be no way forward except by also assuming ¬Q, and trying to get Q by ¬I. You should see why this will work. We already have a contradiction contained in lines (2) and (3). We only have to assume ¬Q, introduce the '&' to get the formal contradiction in line (5), and then 'blame' ¬Q. This means that we can write ¬¬Q at line (6), and discharge the assumption of ¬Q made at line (4). But ¬¬Q is Q. So, line (7) completes the *first* of the Stage One deductions. The second of these is very easy indeed. In line (8), we assume Q. However, having assumed it, we have deduced it. After all, Q is certainly true if Q is. This completes Stage One. We have deduced Q from both sides of the disjunction in line (1). We are, therefore, entitled to re-assert Q in line (9) discharging the assumptions made at lines (3) and (8), and adding a dependency on line (1).

IX.   *BICONDITIONAL ELIMINATION* (≡E)

A ≡ B

- - - - - - - - -

(A ⊃ B) & (B ⊃ A)

X.   *BICONDITIONAL INTRODUCTION* (≡I)

(A ⊃ B) & (B ⊃ A)

- - - - - - - - - -

A ≡ B

SCORE-KEEPING   In both rules for the biconditional, the bottom line depends on the one above, so you write the truth-guaranteeing line number of the upper sentence on the left. On the right, you write the line number of the upper sentence, and the name of the relevant rule.

The truth-table explanation of '≡' should provide you with all the justification of these rules that you need. If you recall, A ≡ B has the same truth table as (A ⊃ B) & (B ⊃ A). They are logically equivalent. Given this, it is hardly surprising that if either of them is true, then so must be the other one.

This completes the presentation of the rules.

9.2   Putting the Rules to Work

Having worked your way through the ten rules, you are well-placed to see why I said earlier that constructing deductions is like playing chess. Learning the rules of chess is a necessary first step in playing, but someone can be an 'expert' on the rules without having much of an idea how to go about playing a decent game. However, if you read through the last section carefully, you are not in such a bad position as a beginner at chess. In the course of explaining the rules, a number of deductions were used as examples, and these should have given you some idea of how to construct further deductions.

A further source of encouragement is that, in a deduction, you know exactly what you have to do, whereas in a game like chess, you only know this in a general way. There are countless (almost) ways in which chess victory can be achieved, but, in any given case of deduction, you know what the conclusion you are aiming for looks like. It may seem an obvious piece of advice, though it is worth saying anyway: look first at the conclusion. This will give you an idea of whether you are likely to need elimination or introduction rules, and which ones. Having done this, turn your attention to the premises. With some idea of what your goal is, your examination of the premises should reveal their potential for achieving it. In the end, though, the only sure way to learn how to construct deductions is to construct a number of them. With that in mind, here are a few examples. In each case, the deduction is preceded by the sequent it shows to be true, and followed by an informal exposition of the tactics used.

Example 1

$P \equiv Q, P \vdash Q$

1	(1)	$P \equiv Q$	Premise
2	(2)	P	Premise
1	(3)	$(P \supset Q) \& (Q \supset P)$	$1 \equiv E$
1	(4)	$P \supset Q$	$3 \& E$
1,2	(5)	Q	$2,4 \supset E$

Here the conclusion is a single letter, so some elimination rule is in the offing. The premises do not provide any immediate route to the conclusion, but you should always think of eliminating '$\equiv$' as this gives you lots of further possibilities. Indeed, when you do this, you can begin to see how to get Q using $\supset$E from the first conjunct of the sentence in line (3).

Example 2

$P \supset Q \vdash \neg Q \supset \neg P$

1	(1)	$P \supset Q$	Premise
2	(2)	$\neg Q$	Assumption
3	(3)	P	Assumption
1,3	(4)	Q	$1,3 \supset E$
1,2,3	(5)	$Q \& \neg Q$	$2,4 \& I$
1,2	(6)	$\neg P$	$3,5 \neg I$
1	(7)	$\neg Q \supset \neg P$	$2,6 \supset I$

Here the aim is to get a conclusion with a conditional in it. This points to the need for ⊃I, and this requires us to assume the antecedent of the conditional with the aim of deriving its consequent ¬P. Now look at the premise. The rule for breaking down a conditional is ⊃E, which requires the antecedent as a further premise. And you haven't such a further premise. However, all is not lost. If you assume the antecedent P, then you have the materials for a contradiction (Q & ¬Q) close at hand. By blaming P for this contradiction, you can derive ¬P, and this is just what you need, given your previous assumption of ¬Q, for the final step.

Example 3

$\neg P_1 \lor Q_1$, $Q_1 \supset P_2$, $\neg P_2 \vdash \neg P_1$

1	(1)	$\neg P_1 \lor Q_1$	Premise
2	(2)	$Q_1 \supset P_2$	Premise
3	(3)	$\neg P_2$	Premise
4	(4)	$\neg P_1$	Assumption
5	(5)	Q_1	Assumption
6	(6)	P_1	Assumption
2,5	(7)	P_2	2,5 ⊃E
2,3,5	(8)	$P_2 \,\&\, \neg P_2$	3,7 &I
2,3,5	(9)	$\neg P_1$	6,8 ¬I
1,2,3	(10)	$\neg P_1$	1,4,4,5,9 VE

Here the conclusion is a basic sentence, so this points to elimination rules. The premises contain one basic sentence, but it is not immediately helpful in reaching a conclusion. Also, the first premise is a disjunction, so you should ask yourself what is required for a disjunction elimination culminating in $\neg P_1$. The first part is easy. Assuming $\neg P_1$ gives you $\neg P_1$. But how does one get $\neg P_1$ from Q_1? The answer is to assume P_1 as in line (6), and aim to get a contradiction. This will allow you to assert $\neg P_1$ by ¬I. Finally, you are entitled to re-assert $\neg P_1$ as the direct consequence of the disjunctive premise and the others by the rule of VE.

Playing deduction games requires skill, and skill requires practice. The EXERCISES below are designed to give you the necessary practice with the minimum of suffering.

Exercise 1

Construct a *quick reference card* of the rules for yourself on *one side of a sheet of paper*. This card should contain each of the rules and some indication of how you would keep score when you use each rule. You will use this card in doing the remaining **Exercises**.

*Exercise 2 (*for the left hand*)

Below are deductions which leave out the score-keeping items on the left, *those items which indicate truth dependencies*. Write out the sequent which each deduction shows true, and fill in the missing numbers on the left-hand side. (In doing this, give a thought to the tactics that each deduction uses.)

(a) (1) $P \supset Q$ Premise
     (2) $\neg Q$ Premise
     (3) P Assumption
     (4) Q 1,3 $\supset$E
     (5) $Q \& \neg Q$ 2,4 &I
     (6) $\neg P$ 3,5 $\neg$I

(b) (1) $P \lor Q$ Premise
     (2) P Assumption
     (3) $Q \lor P$ 2 VI
     (4) Q Assumption
     (5) $Q \lor P$ 4 VI
     (6) $Q \lor P$ 1,2,3,4,5 VE

(c) (1) $P \supset Q_1$ Premise
     (2) $Q_1 \supset Q_2$ Premise
     (3) P Assumption
     (4) Q_1 1,3 $\supset$E
     (5) Q_2 2,4 $\supset$E
     (6) $P \supset Q_2$ 3,5 $\supset$I

(d) (1) $P_1 \supset P_2$ Premise
     (2) $(P_1 \& P_2) \supset Q$ Premise
     (3) $\neg Q$ Premise
     (4) P_1 Assumption
     (5) P_2 1,4 $\supset$E
     (6) $P_1 \& P_2$ 4,5 &I
     (7) Q 2,6 $\supset$E
     (8) $Q \& \neg Q$ 3,7 &I
     (9) $\neg P_1$ 4,8 $\neg$I

*Exercise 3 (*for the right hand*)

Below are deductions which leave out the score-keeping items on the right, *those items which indicate which rule is used and which earlier steps this rule invokes.* Write out the sequent which each deduction shows true, and fill in the right-hand items. (Give a thought as to the tactics used in each deduction.)

(a) | 1 | (1) | $\neg(P \& \neg Q)$
|---|---|---
     | 2 | (2) | P
     | 3 | (3) | $\neg Q$
     | 2,3 | (4) | $P \& \neg Q$
     | 1,2,3 | (5) | $(P \& \neg Q) \& \neg(P \& \neg Q)$
     | 1,2 | (6) | $\neg\neg Q$
     | 1,2 | (7) | Q
     | 1 | (8) | $P \supset Q$

(b) | 1 | (1) | $P \supset Q$
|---|---|---
     | 2 | (2) | $P \& \neg Q$
     | 2 | (3) | P
     | 1,2 | (4) | Q
     | 2 | (5) | $\neg Q$
     | 1,2 | (6) | $Q \& \neg Q$
     | 1 | (7) | $\neg(P \& \neg Q)$

(c) | 1 | (1) | $P \supset (Q_1 \lor Q_2)$
|---|---|---
     | 2 | (2) | $Q_1 \supset \neg Q_3$
     | 3 | (3) | $Q_2 \supset \neg Q_3$
     | 4 | (4) | P
     | 1,4 | (5) | $Q_1 \lor Q_2$
     | 6 | (6) | Q_1
     | 2,6 | (7) | $\neg Q_3$
     | 8 | (8) | Q_2
     | 3,8 | (9) | $\neg Q_3$
     | 1,2,3,4 | (10) | $\neg Q_3$
     | 1,2,3 | (11) | $P \supset \neg Q_3$

(d) | 1 | (1) | $P \supset Q$
|---|---|---
     | 2 | (2) | $\neg(\neg P \lor Q)$
     | 3 | (3) | P
     | 1,3 | (4) | Q
     | 1,3 | (5) | $\neg P \lor Q$
     | 1,2,3 | (6) | $(\neg P \lor Q) \& \neg(\neg P \lor Q)$

1,2	(7)	¬P
1,2	(8)	¬P ∨ Q
1,2	(9)	(¬P ∨ Q) & ¬(¬P ∨ Q)
1	(10)	¬¬(¬P ∨ Q)
1	(11)	¬P ∨ Q

*Exercise 4 (*for both hands*)

Below are deductions which leave out both the left- and right-hand score-keeping items except for an indication of the premises. Write out the sequent shown in each case, and fill in the left- and right-hand sides. (Before you begin each example, it would be useful for you to try to construct the deduction yourself and then compare yours with those given.)

(a) (1) P & Q   Premise
     (2) P
     (3) Q
     (4) Q & P

(b) (1) P ⊃ Q   Premise
     (2) Q ⊃ Q₁   Premise
     (3) ¬Q₁   Premise
     (4) P
     (5) Q
     (6) Q₁
     (7) Q₁ & ¬Q₁
     (8) ¬P

(c) (1) P ⊃ Q   Premise
     (2) ¬Q   Premise
     (3) P
     (4) Q
     (5) Q & ¬Q
     (6) ¬P

Exercise 5

Construct deductions for those arguments that you decided were valid by the truth table method in the EXERCISES of chapters 6 and 8.

Exercise 6

Construct deductions for each of the following.

*(a)   Lewis will win neither the 100 m nor the 200 m. Therefore, he will not win the 100 m and he will not win the 200 m.

*(b)   If dinner is not ready, we will be late for the theatre. Therefore, either dinner is ready or we will be late for the theatre.

*(c)   If the horse I bet on comes in first, I will win £50 and if he comes in second I will win £25. I didn't win £50 and I didn't win £25. Therefore, the horse didn't come in first and didn't come in second.

*(d)   I am not hungry and I am not thirsty. So, I'm neither hungry nor thirsty.

*(e)   Sylvia will either be a poet or an accountant. If she is an accountant, she will be unhappy but solvent. Thus, if Sylvia is not a poet, she will be unhappy.

 (f)   Charles will eat in tonight, or he will have Chinese food and a rich dessert. If he eats in tonight, he will have Chinese food. If he doesn't have a rich dessert, he will have a glass of port. Therefore, he'll have a rich dessert, or he'll have Chinese food and a glass of port.

*(g)   The murder of Sir Alfred was motivated by the hatred he inspired or by a calculated desire to gain his fortune. If it was a calculated crime, then it must have been perpetrated by his mistress S. But if it was done out of hatred, then either the butler James or Lord Alfred's brother Jonathan did it. Now S could not have done it and Jonathan has the unassailable alibi of being in Brighton on the evening of the murder. Therefore, the butler did it.

9.3   Validity and Deductions

We have shown how to deduce the conclusions of Sentential arguments from their premises using the ten rules. There are two fundamental sorts of question that can be asked about the deduction method.

1   Are the deductions we construct truth-preserving? Is it the case that, in any correct deduction, if the premises are true, then so must be the conclusion?

2   Do the rules suffice to allow the construction of a deduction for every valid argument in Sentential?

The questions listed under (1) are ways of asking whether the rules are *sound,* and (2) asks whether the rules are *complete.* Ideally, the answer to both these questions should be 'Yes', and this is, in fact, the correct answer. However, showing this in detail requires more sophisticated techniques than we have at our disposal. (You can acquire them from a number of the more advanced texts given in the Reading List at the end of the book.)

Of course, we haven't been working on the deduction method unaware that such questions needed to be faced. In presenting the rules, something was said to convince ourselves that each particular rule was truth-preserving. Nonetheless, we cannot simply assume that because informal considerations support the idea that each rule is truth-preserving, we have thereby shown that the whole deduction method is too.

Completeness is clearly a very important requirement for any system of rules, but it is not at all easy to demonstrate. There are an infinite number of valid arguments and only ten rules. We have constructed deductions for many valid arguments, and, while this might raise our confidence, it scarcely constitutes a demonstration of completeness.

These general questions about the relationship between validity and deduction lead to a specific one: what does the deduction method have to say about tautologies? Remember, a tautology is a sentence which is true in every row of its truth table, and we can express the fact that some sentence is a tautology this way:

$\models P \supset P.$

Sequents claim that the truth of the sentences on left of the turnstile impose truth on the sentence on the right. When there are no sentences on the left, the sequent can only hold if the sentence on the right is a tautology.

In this chapter, we have used the single bar turnstile in writing sequents like this:

$P \vee Q, \neg Q \vdash P,$

which claim that the sentence on the right can be deduced from those on the left by using the ten rules. The soundness and completeness of Sentential invite the thought that the two turnstiles should overlap in all their uses. (This is *not* to say that the two styles of sequent make the same assertion. I have been careful to say that they do not: one is about truth and the other about rules.) For example, you would expect that a sequent of this form:

$\vdash P \supset P,$

would be demonstrable when the sentence on the right of the turnstile is a tautology. However, what this sequent actually says is that the sentence can be deduced by the rules from no premises at all. How can that happen? Here is the deduction needed for the above sequent:

1   (1) P   Assumption
    (2) P ⊃ P   1,1 ⊃I

The deduction has a single assumption, and it is discharged in the second step by ⊃I. Notice that the concluding line of the deduction depends on no premises or assumptions. It is this fact that warrants the assertion of the above sequent.

Deductions such as that above, and the sequents they establish, provide us with a way to use the rules as a means of investigating which sentences are tautologies. (Remember, this is so because of the soundness and completeness of Sentential.) Below is a longer example in which the 'standard' tautology is deduced.

⊢ P ∨ ¬P

1	(1)	¬(P ∨ ¬P)	Assumption
2	(2)	P	Assumption
2	(3)	P ∨ ¬P	2∨I
1,2	(4)	(P ∨ ¬P) & ¬(P ∨ ¬P)	1,3 &I
1	(5)	¬P	2,4 ¬I
1	(6)	P ∨ ¬P	5 ∨I
1	(7)	(P ∨ ¬P) & ¬(P ∨ ¬P)	1,6 &I
	(8)	¬¬(P ∨ ¬P)	1,7 ¬I
	(9)	P ∨ ¬P	8 ¬E

Exercise 7

Deduce the following sequents. Give an explanation of why the sentences in them are shown to be tautologies by your deductions.

*(a)   ⊢ ¬(P & ¬P)
 (b)   ⊢ P ⊃ (Q ⊃ P)
*(c)   ⊢ P ≡ (P ∨ P)
 (d)   ⊢ P ≡ ¬¬P.

9.4   Truth Tables and Deductions

Accepting that the deduction method is sound and complete, it delivers the same results as the truth-table method discussed in chapter 6. In this section, I will discuss general differences between the methods.

The truth-table procedures of chapter 6 constituted an algorithm for validity: no matter which argument you set out to test, following the same finite number of steps was guaranteed to give you the answer. If you have worked your way through the EXERCISES of this chapter, you will probably think of the construction of a deduction as anything but an algorithm for validity. Indeed, a great deal of skill and ingenuity seems required to construct deductions in certain cases. Moreover, if you failed in some attempt to deduce a conclusion from given premises, you would not have taken this as showing that the argument was invalid. Humility would have required you to think that you just hadn't seen the way to do it. Yet, in spite of these appearances, the method of deduction can be set out so as to constitute an algorithm. Why didn't I offer you this way of setting it out to save you all the puzzling over particular deductions? The answer is apparent enough from the merest sketch of the algorithm:

> Take the premises and list every different sequence of steps which the rules allow you to generate from these premises. Examine each of these deductions (for that is what the sequences are). If one of them ends with the appropriate conclusion, the original argument is valid. If none of them does, then it is invalid.

Putting this procedure into practice for any given example could take hours. However difficult it seemed to master the more intelligent use of the rules, it is certainly more efficient and interesting. Even so, it is important for you to recognize that the method of deduction could be set out as an algorithm. (Note that this fact about deduction is, like soundness and completeness, true, though not *demonstrated* in this book. In particular, to demonstrate it I would have to convince you that every listing generates only a finite number of such sequences. Only if the number of possible deductions is finite can you be sure that you can check them in a finite number of steps.)

The second difference between the truth-table method and that of deduction is a real one. It can be put in the following way. The method of deduction is a *syntactical* method, whereas truth tables are *semantic*. This should be spelled out.

In the last chapter, I noted that deduction games were the most appropriate way for us to understand how Sentential speakers were able to tell whether an argument was valid. By crediting them with a grasp of the ten rules, we now know we were crediting them with a way to demonstrate the validity of any argument. The reason that deduction is most appropriate to them is that, in order to construct a deduction and check whether it is correct, you need only look at the *form* of the sentences in each step. Deciding whether some sequence is a deduction that obeys the rules is no less a syntactical matter than deciding whether a string is a sentence of Sentential.

By contrast, the truth-table method brings in the notion of truth explicitly. After all, that was the point of writing all the Ts and Fs in the table. In doing this, you are acknowledging that the sentences have meanings, and are true or false depending on the way things are in the world. Admittedly, you do not need actually to know what the meanings and truth values of specific sentences are in order to construct truth tables. They are tables of all possible truth values. Nonetheless, the truth-table method depends on the notions of truth and meaning, and it is therefore thought of as a semantical method.

The Main Points of Chapter 9

1   The method of logic known as *deduction* was introduced, and the rules which operate in the construction of deductions were discussed and justified.

2   The deduction method for Sentential is *sound* and *complete*. Soundness consists in the fact that every deduction is truth-preserving, and completeness consists in the fact that a deduction can be constructed for every valid argument.

3   In spite of appearances, the method of deduction can be set out as an algorithm for validity, though a demonstration of this is beyond the scope of this book.

4   The method of deduction is *syntactical*; you can recognize whether something is a deduction by examining the structure or form of the sentences in each step. This contrasts with the need to think of sentences of Sentential as being true or false and having meaning in order to see the point of the truth-table method. This makes the truth-table method *semantical*.

NOTE   See Appendix 1, Lessons 3–5, for further help.

Chapter ten

Sentential and the Strategy

We have now constructed a language of logic – Sentential – and used it, as the Strategy dictates, to evaluate arguments in natural language. As has more than once been said, Sentential is not a rich enough language to give us a means of evaluating *any* natural language argument. But it is an important first stage in the construction of the richer languages of logic. In this chapter, we will look in some detail at the shortcomings of Sentential.

10.0   The Aim of the Strategy

The practical justification of the Strategy was to provide us with a replacement for the trial and error methods we ordinarily use to evaluate arguments. (Its deeper justification was the insight it gives us into language, but we will leave this on one side for now.) We can count the Strategy as successfully completed when the following is true:

(G)   Any argument formulated in natural language is valid if and only if its translation into a language of logic is demonstrably valid by the methods of logic.

In determining whether this is true, we seem to be called on *first* to evaluate arguments in natural language, and *then* to compare our findings with the result given us by using the Strategy. But if we can do this, there doesn't seem to be much point in using the Strategy in the first place. Nor is this the only problem.

Suppose we come across an argument which seems, for example, invalid, at least by our everyday procedure for checking such matters. Suppose further that translation into a language of logic, and evaluation by the methods of logic, shows the original argument to be valid. Such a conflict would certainly make (G) false, but it also would raise this further question: how can any conflicts between the results of the Strategy and our ordinary judgements be resolved? To what tribunal can we appeal? There would seem to be no higher authorities than either our everyday methods, or those of logic.

There are no easy answers to these questions. On the one hand, we cannot survey all actual and possible natural language arguments by everyday methods. We developed the Strategy precisely because everyday methods are not adequate, and nothing has turned up to change our judgement about this. On the other hand, the particular uses of the Strategy do need to be evaluated and, since we cannot survey every possible argument, we must proceed case by case. However, in proceeding case by case we run up against the problem just mentioned: when there is a conflict do we accept our intuition, or the result of the Strategy?

The only sensible thing to do in this predicament is to carry on, but *with caution*. In deciding the adequacy of a particular language of logic in the Strategy, we will have to look at specific cases. Caution comes into the picture this way: we will not rest content with isolated cases that make trouble. If there are difficult cases, we will insist that we understand the basis of their construction, so that we can see the *reason* for any difficulty they cause. This will also allow us to construct further similar cases. You could look at it this way: if there is to be trouble, we *insist* that it comes (at least) in threes.

In the remainder of this chapter, our aim is to evaluate the use of Sentential in the Strategy. We will examine specific cases for which (G) seems to be false when Sentential is the language used. Our maxim of caution dictates that we must be able to put our finger on what has gone wrong in each case.

10.1 Inside Basic Sentences

Suppose we set about evaluating the following argument using the Strategy:

(a)   All dogs are mammals.
       All mammals have backbones.
       _____

       All dogs have backbones.

Translation into Sentential would yield:

(b) P_1
       P_2
       ___
       P_3.

Each of the premises and the conclusion of (a) are treated as basic sentences in (b). This seems reasonable enough since they do not contain the sort of connective we have been led to expect in non-basic sentences: items like 'and', 'or', 'not', 'if', etc.

It doesn't take much thought to see that (b) is invalid. (If you have any doubt about this, construct the truth table.) Indeed, it would be surprising if two distinct basic sentences validly led to a third basic sentence. So where does this leave us?

The argument in (a) seems clearly *valid*; that in (b) seems as clearly *invalid*. Moreover, it is easy to see how to construct an indefinitely large number of cases just like this one. One look at (a), and you realize what a large range of valid arguments in natural language do not come out as valid in Sentential. Just as obviously, the problem in these cases is not with translation. The recommendations on translation given in chapter 7 were followed, and there simply isn't any way in which we can translate (a) so that the result comes out valid in Sentential.

The problem is that (a) contains elements of structure which are responsible for validity, but which are not capturable in Sentential. In particular, the interaction between words like 'all' and those for classes of thing ('mammals', 'dogs') are what makes us think that the premises of (a) guarantee the truth of its conclusion. The validity of (a) comes from structure *within* what are merely basic sentences from the point of view of Sentential. The remedy is clear, and in chapter 11, we will begin the construction of a language of logic which can cope with this *subsentential* structure.

10.2   Operators

The following argument seems to be valid. (Imagine it as part of a conversation about whether it is necessary that one work hard to pass exams.)

(c)   John did not work hard in passing his exams.
Therefore, it was not necessarily the case that John worked hard in passing his exams.

If you translate it into Sentential, the best you can do is:

$$\frac{\neg P}{Q,}$$

which is clearly invalid. The problem comes in the conclusion, so we should look more closely at it.

Given our translation of the premise as ¬P, you should be able to discern the basic sentence P in the conclusion. However, the conclusion also contains the phrase 'it was not necessarily the case that', and this cannot be heard as a basic sentence of English. Indeed, on its own, it is not a sentence at all, and that is why we had to treat it together with 'John worked hard in passing his exams' as a single basic sentence distinct from P. Remember, you are supposed to translate, as basic sentences of Sentential, those sentences of English which can stand on their own to make assertions. Sentential does not provide a way to divide up the conclusion of (c) so as to show that it contains P. The temptation is to write something that looks like this:

> it is not necessarily the case that P,

and, while this is in the right direction, it is not as yet something we can handle in Sentential. The untranslated phrase in this can be seen as an *operator* on the basic sentence P, and it is crucial to the validity of (c) that we have some means for dealing with such operators. There will be further discussion of this in chapter 16.

10.3   Non-structural Validity?

The next example raises a hornet's nest of problems, and not just for Sentential. First the example.

> (d)   My car is red. Therefore, my car is coloured.

Remember, in saying whether you think this is valid, you have to ask yourself whether you think it possible for the conclusion to be false and the premise true. It certainly seems impossible for a car to have no colour at all, and yet be red, so the argument passes the everyday test for validity. Its translation into Sentential would be:

$$\frac{P}{Q,}$$

and this is certainly an invalid argument. However, unlike the cases examined in sections 10.1 and 10.2, this case raises a fundamental question about the Strategy itself, and not just about the use of Sentential in it. This is because (d) seems to be valid, but its validity does not appear to depend on any *structural* element within the sentence. Let me spell this out.

The basic assumption of the Strategy is that arguments are valid in virtue of their structure. This is what set us on the search for structural languages, languages of logic, which could be used to capture the structure of natural language arguments. The trouble with (d) is that its validity does not seem to be based on anything that we can recognize as structural. The argument is valid because of the relationship between the concepts of redness and having a colour. One could say that it is valid because of the meanings of the specific words 'red' and 'coloured'. Another argument with what seems precisely the same structure, but using different words, may well be invalid. Here is an example:

(e)   My car is damaged. Therefore, my car is old.

The Strategy was designed to cope with structural validity, and, as we have seen, there is a lot of it about. Indeed, examples (a) and (c) show that we have not yet exhausted the field. You should think of (d) as raising questions about the eventual scope of the Strategy, but not as a reason to give it up.

10.4   Problems More Specific to Sentential

Examples (a) and (c) involved structural features of natural language arguments which Sentential offered no real hope of expressing. The next examples are arguments which we have some reason to believe Sentential should get right. You will be better placed to understand what I mean if you first do the **Exercise** below.

Exercise

Below are four arguments. Do not pause to ask yourself whether they are valid. Just translate them into Sentential, and see whether the resultant arguments are valid using one of the methods of logic you have learned.

(a)   If Smith gets the job, Jones will resign next week. If Jones dies, Smith gets the job. Therefore, if Jones dies, he will resign next week.

(b)   If you pressed the Return button on the computer, it printed your letter. Therefore, if you pressed the Return button on the computer and it was not plugged in, it printed your letter.

(c)   If you were to get a good night's sleep, you would not be tired. Therefore, if you were tired, you would not get a good night's sleep.

(d)   The sun is shining. Therefore, if it is cloudy then the sun is shining.

(e)   It is not the case that if the butler is innocent then the gardener is guilty. Therefore, the butler is innocent.

The point of asking you to do the EXERCISE first was to make a point in the most vivid terms possible. If you followed my directions, you will have reached the conclusion that each of these arguments is *valid*: translating them into Sentential and constructing truth tables gives this result unequivocally. Now look back at the arguments. Would you judge them valid? My own judgement, and that of numerous writers on this subject, is that they are *invalid*. Indeed, you probably couldn't help noticing this when you read them through. This result is most unwelcome. The culprit in these examples is not difficult to identify. Each of them involved the English conditional construction 'if . . . then'. Given our earlier suspicions about the translation of 'if . . . then' by '⊃', the discrepancies between the natural language and Sentential arguments seem to fall squarely on this translation. The '⊃' connective, defined as it is by its truth table, is called the *material conditional*. The problem which the EXERCISE highlights is that the material conditional is a poor translation of the natural language conditional (which I will call simply the conditional from now on).

In earlier chapters, I defended the translation by saying that resistance to seeing the conditional as a material conditional comes, in part, from a failure to distinguish conditions for truth from conditions for assertion. This is a defence one often comes across in logic texts. In more detail, here is how to spell it out.

Suppose that you have just come back from the library and, while you were there, you saw Jones deep in study at one of the tables. When Smith asks you where Jones is, you say: he is either in the library or having a drink in a pub. Since you have no reason at all for believing that Jones has raced out of the library and into the pub, this is an uncooperative answer. By giving it, you certainly seem to be misleading Smith. But, and this is crucial, have you said anything false? Upon reflection it would seem that you haven't. Since you believe that Jones is in the library (and this is true), your remark to Smith is certainly true; Jones *is* either in the library or in the pub. However, in using the disjunction, you are giving Smith less than all the information you have at your disposal. The disjunctive claim is weaker than the straightforward assertion that Jones is in the library; and this is an assertion you were in a position to make. In usual conversational situations, we rely on cooperation, we expect people to make claims consistent with what they know or think probably true. Smith relies on this cooperation so, when he hears your reply, he assumes there is not much better reason for thinking Jones is in the library than that he is in the pub. In thinking this, in thinking this to be what you believe, Smith is misled. But he is not misled by your telling him a falsehood. Instead, he is misled by the conversational background and by your weakened claim.

In somewhat the same way, it has been argued that the natural language conditional is true or false under precisely the conditions laid down for the material conditional. The difference between them is a result, not of divergence of truth value, but of things conveyed indirectly by the conversational background. Strictly speaking, even such an apparently odd claim as

If grass is green then snow is white,

is true because both antecedent and consequent are true. But, in *asserting* the above, you lead your hearers to think that you believe the greenness of grass to be a factor responsible in some way for the whiteness of snow. In so saying, you mislead without actually saying anything false.

We will not stop here to investigate this proposal in further detail, though much more needs to be said about how it works in the conditional case. The example of disjunction seems much easier to spell out. What is much more pressing is that, even if we were attracted to this defence, it does not appear to help with the examples in the Exercise. Those examples come out as valid when the conditional is translated by the material conditional. The only way in which the above defence could help is if you could get yourself to believe that the natural language arguments were also valid. But this seems very hard to swallow.

In view of all this, why do logicians carry on with the translation of the conditional by the material conditional? There are a number of things to be said here. First, the material conditional does appear to give the right results in a number of central cases. Given an argument like this:

If Harry ate the last doughnut, Martin will be angry.
Harry did eat the last doughnut.

Martin will be angry.

the Sentential translation comes out as valid; it comes out as a simple instance of ⊃E.

Second, it is possible to find evidence in favour of the material conditional translation by examining certain other interrelationships between the connectives of Sentential and those of natural language. For example, in Sentential, the sentence ¬P ∨ Q is equivalent to the sentence P ⊃ Q. This equivalence seems to be matched by the apparent equivalence of the following two sentences in English:

Either the butler or the gardener did it.
If the butler didn't do it, then the gardener did.

If we give up the translation of the conditional by the material conditional, then we will have to give up these sorts of equivalence between conditionals and disjunctions.

Third, as you will see, the material conditional plays a very useful role in the new language of logic which we will begin to construct in the next chapter. It will help us in dealing with those elements of logical structure which examples like (a) brought to light, examples of sub-sentential structure.

10.5   What is to be done?

The examples in the EXERCISE have shown that the translation of the conditional by the material conditional allows counter-examples to (G). That is, the translation puts us in the position of translating invalid natural language arguments by valid arguments of Sentential.

Of course, this is in no way an indictment of the material conditional. As a truth-functional connective of Sentential, it is unexceptionable. Only as a translation of the natural language conditional does it lead to trouble. Since this is so, why not translate into Sentential in some other way? Unfortunately, the material conditional cannot be improved upon *within Sentential* as a prospect for translating the conditional. Here is a sketch of the reason for this.

If ever there was a sentence whose translation should come out as a tautology, it would be:

If Smith wins and Jones loses, then Smith wins.

And this is just what you get when you translate this sentence using the material conditional. The translation and the truth table are as follows. (I included the truth table for P ⊃ Q for reference.)

(P & Q) ⊃ P

P	Q	P ⊃ Q	(P & Q) ⊃ P	
T	T	T	T	T
T	F	F	F	T
F	T	T	F	T
F	F	T	F	T

However, if you change any row of the truth table for the material conditional except the one which makes it false – the second row – then (P & Q) ⊃ P will cease to be a tautology. And if you change the one which makes it false, you will end up making all conditionals into tautologies.

The conditional outruns the resources of Sentential. In a way, one of the useful functions of Sentential has been to show us just that. After all, who would have expected that connectives such as 'and' and 'or' can be handled with very little trouble in Sentential, but that 'if ... then' would be so recalcitrant. In this book, we will not consider further proposals for dealing with the conditional. However, you can track down the literature on this fascinating and important topic by consulting the Reading List.

The Main Points of Chapter 10

1 The aim of the chapter was to investigate whether it is true that a natural language argument is valid if and only if its translation into Sentential is valid.

2 The first sort of counter-example showed that we need to supplement Sentential with a language of logic capable of dealing with *sub-sentential* structure. This is the main business of the next few chapters.

3 A second sort of counter-example showed that there are expressions which function as *operators* on sentences. These cannot be adequately handled by Sentential, and you are referred to chapter 16 for further guidance.

4 Briefly, we discussed the possibility of arguments which are valid, but not in virtue of their structure.

5 The translation of the conditional in natural language by the *material conditional* ('⊃') of Sentential leads to many counter-examples to the claim mentioned in **(1)** above. The upshot was that no connective of Sentential can fully capture the conditional, and you were referred to the Reading List for further enlightenment.

Chapter eleven

Predicate: Part I

In this chapter, we begin the construction of a new language of logic, a language which enables us to capture the logical structure found *inside* basic sentences. In introducing Sentential, I indulged myself in the fantasy that it was a language spoken by a tribe of logicians, and I will not drop that idea here. In fact, the new language, Predicate, should be thought of as spoken by a tribe of more sophisticated logicians.

11.0 Foreign Languages

You will shortly be learning Predicate and, since it is a fairly complicated language, it is sensible to begin with a few remarks about learning second languages. There are all sorts of ways in which people acquire second languages, but current theories favour what has been called the *direct method*.

If you were to go to a French class, or consult a book on learning French at home, you would find that you are encouraged to acquire the language by applying French expressions and sentences to situations familiar to you from your everyday experience. We all know about shops, airports, hotels and the like. The idea is that you learn to use French in dealing with, and describing, these environments and the events that take place within them. This is in contrast to the old-fashioned method of first isolating the ways in which you describe these situations in English, and then learning to translate from English into French. The up-to-date French class is conducted, as far as is possible, in French: the situations are brought into the classroom by imagined scenes in which you act out roles, pictures and, if you are lucky, by video portrayals. You learn to apply French to the world as a French speaker does; only later, if at all, do you consider how English ways of describing situations relate to these. It should be obvious why this is called the direct method.

There are two reasons why this way of learning a second language is superior to any other. First, it allows you to use the vast amount of knowledge you have of the world, knowledge which is not itself linguistic. The teacher can presume, as a background, that you know about shops, airports, other people, etc., and that your knowledge of these situations is not essentially tied to English ways of describing them. This knowledge acts as a kind of non-linguistic medium of communication. Second, by learning to describe these situations in French, you avoid the well-known traps that one falls into when a language is learned by translation into your native tongue. Each language has its own ways of describing situations, ways which are loosely called 'idioms'. Given this, the indirect, translational method often leads to misunderstanding and unnecessary difficulty. For example, when it is warm and the sun is shining, *we* might describe matters this way:

the weather is fine.

A French speaker confronted with the same circumstances would be likely to describe it this way:

il fait beau.

If we were to render this last expression into English, it would come out approximately as:

it makes beautiful,

and this little piece of nonsense would be more of a hindrance than a help in learning French. Much more sensible is the approach that gets us to use 'il fait beau' in the appropriate circumstances; English/French translation can come later.

In a sense, the direct method is something like the method we use to teach children their native tongue. Since we cannot presume knowledge of any language, we have no choice but to teach by using features of the world with which the child is acquainted.

In chapters 4 and 5, I used something like the direct method in teaching you Primitive and Sentential. My drawings portrayed the very simple situations these languages could be used to describe; these drawings fulfilled the same role as the imagined encounters in shops and airports play in learning French. I didn't there emphasize the directness of the teaching method, but this was solely because Primitive and Sentential are simple languages: they do not present the sort of language-acquisition problems which the direct method is designed to handle. Sentential is a fairly rich language, but not so rich that you require drawings and other non-linguistic aids to master it.

As you will soon appreciate, Predicate is more complex than Sentential. In fact, it is complex enough to justify the use of something like the direct method. That is, you will find it easier to learn, and will be less likely to misunderstand, if you learn how to apply Predicate as if you were being trained as a native speaker. For the purposes of this chapter, and the next one, you can consider yourself a rather sophisticated child who has fallen among speakers of Predicate; the idea is to acquire the language without relying on your undoubted mastery of English. The relations between Predicate and English will be considered in chapter 13.

11.1   Situations

Books on teaching yourself French tend to be filled with all sorts of pictures. These are aids to your imagination, they help you conjure up the real life situations with respect to which you can try out your incipient French. I too need some such aid but, you might be glad to hear, Predicate is considerably simpler than French, so the situations you have to conjure up need not be very complicated. Since it is to hand, I will use my desk, and the things on it, as the medium through which to explain Predicate. You are to understand that each frame (see below) contains a depiction of how things are at a given time in respect of my desk: for our purposes, the arrangement of things on my desk will constitute the whole of our world. Admittedly, my desk may seem a poor substitute for the whole world but it contains sufficient material for your training in Predicate. Below is a depiction of how things are arranged on my desk first thing on Monday morning. What is depicted is called a *Situation* – a way things are. What we have to do now is to see how Situations can be described using Predicate. Once you are fluent enough in Predicate to say how things are with respect to my desk, you will be able to use the language to describe much more complex Situations.

There is one last thing to note before doing this. Ever since I said that we should avoid using English in the process of acquiring Predicate, I have done nothing but use English. In fact, given the circumstances of my communication with you, this is unavoidable. However, when I introduce elements of Predicate, focus on these elements and their relationship to the Situation they describe. English will come into my explanations, but do not let it distract you from the connections between the Predicate language and Situations.

11.2 Simple Descriptions: Designators and Predicates

A. Designators

In order to describe matters in the Monday morning Situation (Situation (1)) pictured below, we need:

(i) some way to pick out the items that figure in the situation;
(ii) some way to characterize those items.

Predicate has a large stock of expressions called *designators* which are used for the first of these jobs. They are lower case letters with and without subscripts as shown below:

$a, a_1, a_2, \ldots, a_n$
$b, b_1, b_2, \ldots, b_n$
$c, c_1, c_2, \ldots, c_n.$

They function rather *like* labels for the items in the Situation. Actual labels might be provided as in:

Situation (1)

but designators have the advantage of being, so to speak, detachable: they enable us to pick out an item for discussion, even though they are not glued to it. They also can be re-used: you can designate some item as a_1 and, in a different Situation, use a_1 for some other item. However, having designated some item as a_1 in a given Situation, you must continue to use that designator as a label of that item for so long as the Situation figures in discussion.

B.   Predicates

The task of characterizing items in a Situation, saying what features they have, is carried out by *predicates*. Predicates do their characterizing in a variety of ways, so we should discuss two examples before giving a complete list of predicate expressions.

First example   Speakers of Predicate might use:

> Fa, Gb, Hc

to describe the items in Situation (1). The designators a, b and c are written after upper case letters, and these latter are the predicate expressions. Each combination of upper and lower case letters is a *sentence*. In this example, the predicate expressions are used in each sentence to say what *property* an item has. A rough translation of each sentence would yield:

> Fa – a is rectangular,
> Gb – b is a telephone,
> Hc – c is a book.

Second example   You might also come across sentences that looked like this:

> Rba, Sabc.

These have more than one designator after each predicate expression, and they are used to say what *relations* items in the Situation have to one another. Their rough translations are:

> Rba – b is to the right of a,
> Sabc – a is in between b and c.

In these sorts of sentence the order of the designators is very important. Given the meaning that has been assigned to 'R', had the sentence Rab been used, it would have made the false claim that a is to the right of b. The predicate expression 'R', as used in this example, not only conveys the idea that one item is to the right of another, it is also understood as saying that the item designated in the *first* place is to the right of that designated in the *second* place.

Additionally, each of these predicate expressions is understood as having a fixed number of places. 'R' is *two-place* or *binary*: no speaker of Predicate would allow that:

Ra or Rabc,

are proper sentences since, as used in connection with Situation (1), 'R' conveys the idea that one item is to the right of another. Similarly, it is part of the meaning of 'S' as used above that it is *three-place* or *ternary*. The only way in which 'S' could be part of a proper sentence is for it to be followed by three designators. In general, a predicate expression is said to be n-*place* when it requires *n* designators to form a complete sentence. Given this, the predicates in the first example are *one-place*.

Finally, all of the sentences so far discussed are examples of *basic* sentences of Predicate. They differ from the basic sentences of Sentential in having the extra structural elements of designators and predicates, but they are basic because they do not contain other sentences as parts.

So far I have indicated how many places a predicate has either by writing it out with its places filled in with designators as in:

Gb, Rba, Sabc,

or by saying explicitly how many places it has, i.e. 'G' is one-place. In order to be able to list the predicate expressions of Predicate, I need to have some way to *show* how many places a predicate has without using specific designators. This is because when we do use designators, we end up with a list of basic sentences rather than a list of predicate expressions.

What we need are expressions which mimic the role of designators, but which do not function as designators of specific items in Situations. Such expressions are called *variables*. Predicate uses lower case letters with and without subscripts as variables:

$x, x_1, x_2, \ldots, x_n$
$y, y_1, y_2, \ldots, y_n$
$z, z_1, z_2, \ldots, z_n$

They mimic the grammatical role of designators, but you can think of them as *place-holders* for designators, rather than as themselves having any designating function. They indicate the number of places that a predicate has in this way:

$Gx, Hy_1, Rxy, Sx_1x_2x_3.$

You will come to see that variables have a more important job in Predicate than merely to indicate how many places a predicate has, but that can wait. Below is the list of predicate expressions in Predicate.

One-place
$Fx, F_1x, F_2x, \ldots, F_nx$
$Gx, G_1x, G_2x, \ldots, G_nx$
$Hx, H_1x, H_2x, \ldots, H_nx$

Two-place
$Rxy, R_1xy, R_2xy, \ldots, R_nxy$

Three-place
$Sxyz, S_1xyz, S_2xyz, \ldots, S_nxyz$

.

.

.

n-place
$Tx \ldots x_n, T_1x \ldots x_n, T_2x \ldots x_n, \ldots, T_nx \ldots x_n$

This is a vast number of different predicate expressions, but you will be relieved to hear that you need use only a small fraction of them in learning Predicate. Notice that I left you to imagine the predicates that are more than three-place. It would have been very tedious to list them when what is really important is the fact that Predicate allows the formation of predicates of *any finite number of places*. This is adequately shown by the last row above and the three dots that lead to it.

NOTE   Predicate is very like Sentential in one important respect. Certain elements of Sentential, the basic sentences, are thought of as having variable meaning, though this meaning remains settled in a given context of argument. The same variability figures in the understanding of the designators and predicates of Predicate. We can assign them whatever meaning is consistent with their structural role, and this meaning can vary from context to context. Only in the context of a given argument must we think of the meaning as settled. This should be obvious enough from the text, but I emphasize it here to forestall any misunderstanding.

C. Choice of Variables

Predicates can be written with all manner of different variables. We could write:

Rxy,

or:

Rx_1x_2.

But nothing hinges on this difference. What matters is only that 'R' is shown to be a two-place predicate, and this requires that there be two different variables, the choice of which is up to you.

When a two-place predicate is used in a basic sentence, you will find designators in place of the variables. Thus, you may find that the predicate:

R_2xy,

is applied to Situation (1) in this sentence:

R_2ac.

This sentence says that a and c are the same shape, and since they are both rectangular, this is true. However, do *not* let the occurrence of different variables in the predicate mislead you into thinking that each of them must hold a place for a different designator. The sentence:

R_2aa,

contains the predicate R_2xy, and is true of Situation (1), since 'a' certainly has the same shape as 'a'.

Using two *different* variables shows that a predicate requires two designators in order to make a basic sentence. Basic sentences so formed *may* have two different designators, but they may not. However, suppose you came across the predicate below:

R_3xx.

This has two variable occurrences, but they are the *same* letter. Here we are *obliged* to form a sentence by replacing 'x' in both its occurrences with the same designator. We thus count R_3xx as a one-place predicate.

In sum, the choice of specific variables in the display of the predicate is up to you, but:

(i) if two different variables are used, you *may* find them replaced with different designators in a sentence;

(ii) if the same variable is used it *must* be replaced with the same designator.

Exercise 1

Above is Situation (2). Make up as many Predicate sentences as you can which truly describe this Situation. (List the designators and predicates that you use, indicating which items the designators stand for, and what the predicates mean.)

Exercise 2

Below is a list of basic sentences of Predicate together with their translations. Draw a single Situation of which they are all true.

Fa – a is a pen.
Gb – b is a notepad.
Hc – c is an ink bottle.
G_1b – b is square.
F_2c – c is half full.
Rab – a is on b.
R_1cb – c is to the left of b.

Exercise 3

Use your own desk (or imagine one if you are not sitting at a desk) as a Situation. Make up *five* predicate sentences that truly describe the items on it.

11.3   Further Descriptions: Generality and Quantifiers

When you did EXERCISE 2 just now, you probably realized that there are any number of ways in which you could draw a Situation that makes all seven sentences true. Those sentences mention three items, and give you some information about them, but if your drawing ability is up to it, you could include any number of *further* items in your sketch. Also, there are any number of *different* ways in which you could draw the items that would nonetheless make the predicates true of them. Quite clearly, any set of sentences is not going to determine a Situation precisely.

While the above sorts of indeterminacy cannot be fully eliminated, there is a way which Predicate speakers have of cutting down on a different sort of indeterminacy. Sentences using predicates and designators are useful for giving *specific* information about the items in a Situation. What they fail to provide is *general* information about Situations. And general information is exceedingly important for precise description. For example, consider this Situation.

Situation (3)

This can be described using:

> Fa,
> Fb,
> Fc,

where 'F' means 'is a book'. But these three sentences leave out of account the fact that *all* the items are books. Moreover, no further sentence made up from designators and predicates can make this omission good. What we need is some additional resource in the language. This is where *quantifiers* come into the picture.

11.4   The Universal Quantifier

The first new element of Predicate to be mastered is this:

$$\forall.$$

This symbol is pronounced 'every', and it just so happens that there are close parallels between '$\forall$' and the word in English with which it shares pronunciation. In fact, we might as well say that '$\forall$' *means* 'every'. You can assume that Predicate happens to overlap with English here.

This symbol will enable us to frame general descriptions of Situations. For example, in addition to saying of each item in Situation (3) that it is a book, we might want to say that the Situation contains books and only books. This is a general claim as opposed to each of the specific claims: Fa, Fb and Fc. To do this, we must have some way of combining '$\forall$' with a way of picking out the items in the Situation, so that we can go on to say that they are books. As a newcomer to Predicate, you might think that we could do this by using our new symbol in combination with a designator in this way:

$$\forall a.$$

This expression would be read as 'every a', and if it is prefaced to 'Fa' we would get something which, in the mouths of Predicate speakers, comes out as: *every a is such that a is a book*. Now, while this sounds true, it should be obvious that this does not do what we want. In Situation (3), the designator 'a' picks out *one* of the books: it is certainly true that every 'a' is a book but this says nothing *general* about the Situation. It is at this point that variables come into their own.

Variables have the same grammatical role as designators; this is what was meant by my saying earlier that they mimicked the role of designators. However, they do not pick out *specific* items in Situations. If you hear:

$$Fx,$$

and are asked which item in Situation (3) is under discussion, the correct answer is that you do not know. The variable holds a place for a designator of some specific item, but it doesn't itself designate. Using this fact, we can combine the new symbol '$\forall$' with variables to get expressions such as:

$$\forall x, \forall y, \forall x_1, \text{etc.}$$

By the conventions of Predicate, these are then enclosed in parentheses so that we get the following series of symbols:

$(\forall x), (\forall y), (\forall x_1)$.

These are called *universal quantifiers*. They are pronounced (using the first of them as an example): 'every x is such that'. Combined with the predicate expression 'Fx' meaning 'x is a book', the universal quantifier allows us to comment generally on Situation (3) with this sentence:

$(\forall x)Fx$.

It is read:

every x is such that x is a book.

This *universally quantified sentence* tells us just what we could not express by using Fa, Fb and Fc. Even when these three basic sentences are conjoined into the one sentence:

Fa & Fb & Fc,

we do not quite capture what is expressed by $(\forall x)Fx$. Given the truth of the universal sentence, you should certainly expect the conjunction to be true. But the truth of the conjunction can never guarantee the truth of the universal sentence, since the conjunction only gives us information about specific items in Situation (3). It leaves out of account the fact that a, b and c are the only items there are, a fact which no designator + predicate sentence could express.

11.5   Three Important Notes on Quantifiers

Note (i)   You can use any variable in the universal quantifier without changing what is said. Thus, the following are all equivalent ways of saying that everything in Situation (3) is a book:

$(\forall x)Fx, (\forall y_1)Fy_1, (\forall x_2)Fx_2$.

Note (ii)   The choice of variable in a quantifier is up to you, and does not affect the content of the sentence. However, in any particular sentence, you must use the same variable in the quantifier as in the relevant predicate: the variables in the quantifier and predicate must *link up*. For example, the sentence:

$(\forall x)Fx$,

says, as you know, that every x is such that x is a book. Contrast this with the following expression:

(∀x)Fy.

This expression is read: 'every x is such that y is a book', which, since the variables do not link up, does not make an intelligible claim.

Note (iii)   In the above examples, quantifiers were attached to one-place predicates. What about the predicates that are more than one-place? Here I must ask you to be patient. Predicate has a very special place for multiple-place predicates with multiple quantifiers. Indeed, the use of such sentences is the crowning achievement of this language. But I have reserved the explanation of this achievement for the next chapter, since we have a little more preliminary work left for this one.

11.6   The Existential Quantifier

There is one other quantifier in Predicate. It is called the *existential* quantifier, looks like this:

(∃x),

and is pronounced (and means): 'there is at least one x such that'.

I have said that quantifiers are used in the making of general claims about Situations – claims that cannot be made using only designators and predicates. This *might* get someone to thinking that the existential quantifier is out of place. After all, what could be more *specific* than the claim that there is at least *one* of some item? While I can see the motivation for this thought, it is misguided. Here is why.

Situation (4)

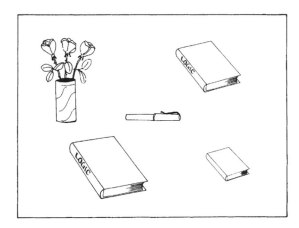

Focus on the flowers (which I was given). Obviously, a Predicate speaker could designate each of them, and supply a one-place predicate, say 'Gx', to indicate their flowerhood. However, consider this sentence:

$(\exists x)Gx.$

It says that there is at least one x such that x is a flower (or, more briefly, there is at least one flower). Which flower is it? I hope you see that this is an unanswerable question. It is unanswerable because even though the above sentence says that there is at least *one* flower, it doesn't, so to speak, mention any names. What it does is to make a general claim about Situation (4). It is not a universal claim, but this is not surprising since the quantifier is existential.

11.7   Generality within Limits

Take another look at Situation (4). I was lucky enough to be given roses to put on my desk. Is there any way I can use Predicate to indicate that the flowers are roses? Since every flower (in the Situation) is a rose, you might think that:

$(\forall y)Hy,$

would serve the purpose. This says that every y is such that y is a rose. However, there are a number of books on my desk, as well as a pen and a vase, so the above sentence fails to say specifically of the *flowers* that they are roses. Indeed, the above sentence is simply false with respect to Situation (4). It is not true that every y is such that y is a rose.

Here I expect you to protest. Up to now I have not indicated which items the quantifiers quantify. Does '$(\forall y)$' take into account everything in Situation (4)? Or, only the flowers?

We need some terminology to help with these questions. The sorts of things which the quantifier takes into account are said to be in the *domain* of the quantifier, and the quantifier is said to *range* over this domain. The domain of the quantifier '$(\forall y)$' above has been understood to take into account *all* the items in Situation (4). That is, it is said to range over all items and not simply the flowers. For this reason, the sentence above is false: it is not true that every *item* in Situation (4) is a rose. Note that the range of the quantifier *could* have been understood as being just the flowers in Situation (4), and this would have made '$(\forall y)Hy$' true. Used in this way the domain of the quantifier is said to be *restricted* to flowers. Speakers of Predicate do not like to use quantifiers in this way. This is because of the role that quantifiers play in representing arguments. I do not expect you to understand this fully, since evaluating arguments is a subject that is still some way off. However, I can say this much. In an argument, there may be many quantified premises, and if each quantifier is restricted in its own way, there will be great difficulty when it comes to putting them together to judge the possibility of their joint truth. For this reason, Predicate speakers use their quantifiers unrestrictedly to range over all the items in a Situation, and we will follow them in this. This brings us back sharply to the original question: how do Predicate speakers say of Situation (4) that the flowers are roses?

Would the sentence '$(\exists x)Hx$' do? This sentence is read:

> there is at least one x such that x is a rose.

You should be able to see that this is true of Situation (4), but it doesn't help us in our present search for a way to say that *all* the *flowers* are roses. To solve our problem we must have a way to specify that it is the flowers we are talking about, and we must be able to do this in the sentence itself, since the quantifier is understood as unrestricted.

Here is how Predicate speakers manage the task:

> $(\forall y)(Fy \supset Hy)$,

where 'F' means 'is a flower' and '$\supset$' is the material conditional familiar from Sentential. This sentence is read:

> every y is such that *if* y is a flower *then* y is a rose.

It is very important that you understood both *why* this sentence is true of Situation (4), and *that* it says precisely what we have been trying to say.

The universal quantifier invites us to look at all the items in Situation (4) *and* it claims that every such item fulfils the condition that follows it. That is, it claims that every item meets this condition:

> $Fy \supset Hy$.

Is this true? Well, to see whether it is begin by thinking of the items as divided into flowers and non-flowers. Imagine each non-flower – each book, the pen and the vase – as labelled with designators. When such designators are put in place of 'y' in the above condition, every resulting sentence:

> $Fa \supset Ha, Fb \supset Hb, Fc \supset Hc \ldots$,

is *true*. They are true because in each case the item is *not* a flower, so the antecedent of each conditional is false. And when the antecedent of a material conditional is false, the conditional is true. The non-flowers in Situation (4) make 'Fy ⊃ Hy' true trivially in that they falsify the antecedent. What about the flowers? Each flower is, of course, an F. This means that the conditionals:

$$\text{Fd} \supset \text{Hd, Fe} \supset \text{He, Ff} \supset \text{Hf,} \quad \text{(where d, e and f designate the flowers)}$$

will have true antecedents, and each whole conditional will be true only in so far as the consequent is true too. Now because d, e and f happen to be roses, they are indeed H, so each of the above conditionals is true. In sum, all the items in Situation (4), the flowers and the non-flowers, make 'Fy ⊃ Hy' true and this means that

$$(\forall y)(\text{Fy} \supset \text{Hy})$$

is true. The only circumstance in which it would be false is that in which you found a flower (an F) which was *not* a rose (an H). Since there are no such cases in Situation (4), we can be confident in asserting the universally quantified conditional. Also, given the sort of case which would make it false, we can be confident that this sentence asserts just what we need: it says that all the flowers are roses.

One small (but important) terminological matter. In the above discussion we made use of the expression 'Fy ⊃ Hy'. The role of this expression should be clear enough to you, but what should we call it? It contains the connective '⊃', but it isn't itself a sentence. You can appreciate this by asking yourself whether you think it could ever be true or false. Well, is 'Fy ⊃ Hy' true of Situation (4)? This question should leave you puzzled. You cannot answer it, since the expression contains no hint about which item or items you are supposed to look at in Situation (4); remember 'y' is not a designator. In fact, this expression bears more than a little resemblance to a predicate. It contains variables and predicate letters, and only the presence of '⊃' complicates matters. In view of all this, we will call expressions like 'Fy ⊃ Hy' *non-basic predicates*. Retrospectively, this means that 'Fy', 'Hy', 'Rxy', etc., are *basic predicates*. This should appeal to those of you who like things tidy. After all, the basic/non-basic distinction here is simply a Predicate language counterpart of that in Sentential.

Now consider this sentence:

$$(\forall y)(\text{Fy} \,\&\, \text{Hy}).$$

Can you see why this does not say that all the flowers are roses? The trouble with it is that it says something too strong and is, therefore, false. It says that every y is such that y is a flower *and* y is a rose. This is clearly made false by the presence of the books and the pen (not to mention the vase). They are items which are neither flowers nor roses. What this shows is just what an important part the material conditional plays in Predicate: it has just the right meaning to allow speakers of Predicate to make universally general claims about specific sorts of item.

One last note before we move on. The universally quantified conditional has *two* sets of parentheses: one around '∀y' and one around the conditional, 'Fy ⊃ Hy'. The first pair we have discussed already: Predicate users include them as part of the quantifier expression itself. The second pair, however, are more interesting. They serve to show us how far into the sentence the quantifier has 'influence'. This is a somewhat vague way of putting it, and I will improve on it in the next chapter. For now, though, it should be clear enough what I have in mind: a quantifier with its variable has influence or, more correctly, *scope* within a sentence. In order that the quantifier be understood as connected to the right predicates, its scope must extend as far as those predicates. Since quantifiers are understood as having within their scope the smallest complete expression to their right, we need the above parentheses to make 'Fy ⊃ Hy' into one complete expression. Only in this way can we guarantee that the scope of '(∀y)' includes 'Hy'. This might sound complicated but think back to the way we used '¬' and parentheses in Sentential. If we write:

¬P ∨ Q,

the '¬' has scope only so far as 'P'. In order to extend its scope to the whole sentence, we have to write:

¬(P ∨ Q).

Think of quantifiers as having the same sort of influence or scope as negation, and you will appreciate why we need the second set of parentheses in '(∀y)(Fy ⊃ Hy)'.

11.8   More Generality within Limits

In the last section, we saw how Predicate can be used to make general and universal claims about restricted domains. Take a look at Situation (4) again (below).

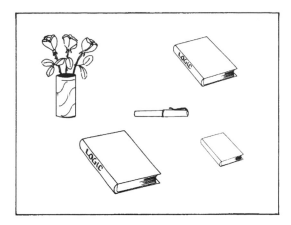

Can you think of a way in which we can use Predicate to say that at least one of the books is about logic? This is certainly true of Situation (4). Moreover, it is a claim restricted to the *books* in Situation (4), and it is existentially general rather than universally general. That is, it claims only that there is at least one book on logic, and not that all books are on logic. Here is the Predicate sentence that does the job:

$(\exists y)(F_1 y \ \& \ G_1 y)$
where '$F_1 y$' means 'y is a book' and
'$G_1 y$' means 'y is on logic'.

This sentence is made true by our finding any one item which is both a book and on logic. In fact, there are two such items in Situation (4). Notice again, however, that this sentence does not refer to, or use, designators of any particular book in the Situation. It is, after all, general.

You may wonder here why we didn't use:

$(\exists y)(F_1 y \supset G_1 y)$.

The trouble is that this sentence is far too 'weak'. It is made true by our finding any one item which is *not* a book. Remember that a material conditional is true whenever its antecedent is false. Thus, the above is true merely in virtue of there being a vase in Situation (4).

There is a very important moral in the work of the last two Sections.

The Moral

In English we make restricted universal and existential claims merely by varying the quantifier expressions. We say: 'every book is on logic' when we want to make a universal claim restricted to books, and we say: 'at least one book is on logic' when we want to make an existential claim restricted to books. This is sometimes put in the following terms: a natural language quantifier is made up of a *determiner* (such as 'every') and a common noun or noun phrase. The restriction is therefore built into the quantifier.

In Predicate, the quantifiers alone do not make the restriction. Instead, the content and structure of the predicate plays this role. Therefore, *we need to be careful about the connective used within the predicate.* We must use '⊃' for restricted universal sentences, and '&' for the existential.

11.9   Something about Nothing

What do you make of this?

Situation (5)

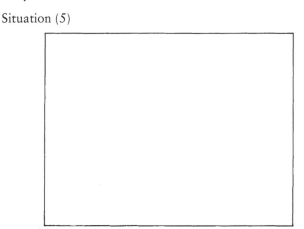

In particular, what truth value would you assign to the sentences below as applied to Situation (5)?

(i)   (∀x)Fx,
(ii)   (∃x)Fx,
where 'Fx' means 'x is a book'.

The first sentence says that every x is such that x is a book. We know from our earlier discussions that the domain of 'every x' is unrestricted – it takes into account whatever there is. Given this, and given the fact that there is nothing, it is pretty clear that (i) is trivially true of Situation (5). If you doubt this then ask yourself whether you can find anything in Situation (5) which is not a book. Surely, if (i) is false then you should be able to produce such an example. Unsurprisingly, you cannot find a counter-example to (i), since there isn't anything, there isn't anything which is not a book. (Nor, of course, is there anything which is a book. Hence, the sentence '(∀x)¬Fx' is also true of Situation (5).)

What now about (ii)? This says that at least one x is such that x is a book, and as before 'at least one x' has an unrestricted domain.

However, in order for '(∃x)Fx' to be true, we are required to find at least one item in that domain which is a book. But there is no such item because there is nothing at all. So, (ii) is false.

In consequence of these truth values for (i) and (ii), the sequent:

$$(\forall x)Fx \vDash (\exists x)Fx,$$

does not hold for Situation (5). That is, '(∀x)Fx' is true and '(∃x)Fx' is false. This bothers Predicate logicians because they think of the above sequent as true. (And we follow them in this.) Since, the possibility of empty domains threatens this sequent, the simplest thing to do is to rule them out as acceptable Situations. That is, from now on we will not think of Predicate as applying to Situations which are empty. (This is not a very burdensome restriction, since we are not likely to do much talking about nothing at all.) The restriction does the trick because, if a domain is *non-empty*, then:

$$(\forall x)Fx,$$

is true or false depending on whether the one or more objects in the domain are books. If it is true, then all the objects are books and:

$$(\exists x)Fx,$$

will certainly be true. If it is false, then the existential sentence can be true or false without affecting the truth of the above sequent.

Remember, in requiring the domain (or *universe of discourse* as it is sometimes called) to be non-empty, we do not require that there are *books*, only that there is at least *something*.

11.10   The Relationship between the Quantifiers

The two quantifiers of Predicate are used to say rather different things, but it would be sensible to have some idea of how they are related. In English, the universal and existential quantifiers are related in an interesting way. The sentence:

there is at least one book,

says no more nor less than can be said with:

not everything is not a book.

Similarly, the sentence:

everything is round,

can be heard as equivalent to:

it is not the case that there is at least one thing which is not round.

In Predicate these same relationships hold. That is, the following pairs of sentences are equivalent, and they give you the idea of how the quantifiers are related:

Pair a: $(\exists x)Fx$, $\neg(\forall x)\neg Fx$
Pair b: $(\forall x)Fx$, $\neg(\exists x)\neg Fx$.

As you can see, these pairs give us the possibility of defining one quantifier in terms of the other. Thus, there could be dialects of Predicate which had only universal, or only existential quantifiers, but which would be no less expressive than the full version. This should remind you of an earlier discussion of a similar fact about Sentential. In chapter 5, it was pointed out that Sentential can have dialects with fewer than all five connectives, but with no less expressive power. Of course, with regard to Sentential, we can understand the notion of *expressive power* as the clear notion: *expressibility of all possible truth functions*. My remark about the interdefinability of the quantifiers is not grounded on such a clear notion. Or, at least, it is not *yet* so grounded. The matter will be taken up again briefly in chapter 14.

Since we are on the subject of Sentential, it is worth ending this chapter with a note about the connectives. I have said nothing very rigorous about their removal from Sentential to Predicate. It is clear that they play a crucial role in Predicate, but it is a different one. In Sentential, they occur between and within sentences, whereas in Predicate they can occur in predicates. In the further exposition of Predicate, we will continue to operate on the assumption that this dual role is one to which the connectives are suited. More rigour comes in chapter 17.

Exercise 4

Below are two groups of Predicate sentences. Each group describes a different Situation. Using the key to the predicate expressions given, draw the two Situations that make each different group of sentences true.

(a)   Fa, Fb, Hc, Gd, H_1e, $(\exists y)F_2y$, $(\forall x)(Fx \supset F_2x)$, Rab.
(b) $(\exists y)(H_1y \ \& \ F_2y)$, F_2a, Rbc, $(\forall x)(F_2x \supset H_1x)$.

Key

Fx – x is a book
Hx – x is a pen
Gx – x is an ink bottle
H_1x – x is a vase
F_2x – x is red
Rxy – x is to the right of y

Exercise 5

Below are two Situations. Write four true sentences about each of them, including at least one general sentence in each group.

(a)

(b)

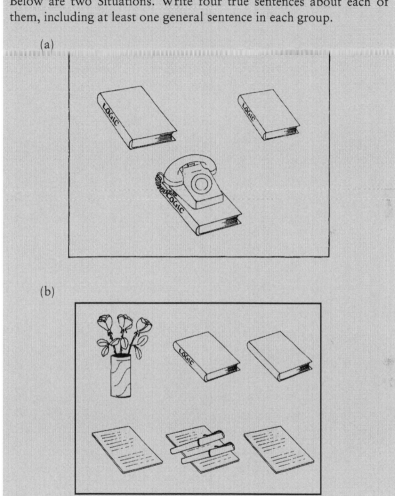

The Main Points of Chapter 11

1 Predicate contains the following sorts of expression:

    (a) *Designators* Lower-case letters from the beginning of the alphabet with or without subscripts. These are used to pick out or label items on Situations.

(b)   *Variables*   Lower-case letters from the end of the alphabet with or without subscripts. These occupy the same grammatical place as designators but they are not used to label specific items in Situations. For their real uses read on.

(c)   *Predicates*   Upper-case letters with or without subscripts. These are used to say what properties an item has or what relations it bears to other items. The number of places in any given predicate is shown by the use of variables.

   Predicates as just described are *basic* predicates. When these are combined with the logical connectives from Sentential, e.g.:

   Fy $\supset$ Hy, Gx & Hx,

we get *non-basic* predicates. For more on these read on.

(d)   *Quantifiers*   There are two such quantifiers each formed by using a special symbol ('$\forall$' or '$\exists$') followed by a variable with the whole lot enclosed in parentheses. Here is how you are to understand each quantifier.

   ($\forall$x) – every x is such that . . .
   ($\exists$x) – at least one x is such that . . .

(e)   *Sentences*   There are two sorts of sentence in Predicate.

   (i)   Those formed from predicates and designators, e.g.:

      Fb, Hc, Rab.

      These are *specific*: they are used to say things about specific items in Situations.

   (ii)   Those formed by prefixing quantifiers to basic or non-basic predicates, e.g.:

      ($\forall$y)Fy, ($\exists$x)Hx, ($\forall$x)(Fx $\supset$ Gx), ($\exists$y)(Fy & Gy).

      These are *general*. They are used to make general claims about Situations. Of special importance are the sentences which combine quantifiers and non-basic predicates. These can be used to make general, but limited, claims about Situations, claims such as these:

      ($\forall$y)(Fy $\supset$ Gy)   –   Every y is such that if y is F then y is G,or, more succinctly, every F is a G.

      ($\exists$y)(Fy & Gy)   –   At least one y is such that y is an F and G, or, at least one F is G.

2 In using the quantifiers of Predicate, there are a number of things to watch out for.

(a) The *scope* of a quantifier is the expression over which the quantifier exerts an influence. The scope of quantifiers is something like that of '¬', so you need to use parentheses. Without parentheses, the scope only extends to the basic predicate immediately to the right of the quantifier. More will be said about this in the next chapter.

(b) The *domain* over which quantifiers *range* is unrestricted. That is, you are to understand each quantifier as surveying all the items in a Situation or *universe of discourse*. It is for this reason that I attached such importance to the use of non-basic predicates to limit the generality of sentences using quantifiers. Without this, Predicate would forever be making implausibly general claims about Situations. (See the end of **1** above.)

(c) The universe of discourse is assumed to contain something. That is, users of Predicate do not apply the language to the empty domain.

Chapter twelve

Predicate: Part II

You should now be able to use Predicate to describe Situations in specific and in general ways. A specific sentence is one which uses only designators and predicates. It is true when the things designated in a Situation are indeed as they are said to be by the relevant predicates. The general sentences so far discussed come in two flavours: those beginning with a universal and those beginning with an existential quantifier. A universally general sentence is true of a Situation when the predicate in it applies to every item in the Situation; an existentially general sentence is true when the predicate applies to at least one item in the Situation. In this chapter, we are going to focus more sharply on general sentences.

12.0   Mixing Generalities

Consider carefully the Situation below.

Situation (6)

Focus particularly on the relative location of the books and the glasses. Well, the books are to the left of the glasses. That is, *every* book is to the left of *every* glass. Can you use Predicate to make this claim about Situation (6)? Let us review the resources we have.

You know how to say that every book has some property or other. Suppose that 'Fx' means 'x is a book', then the pattern:

$(\forall x)(Fx \supset .. x ..),$

can be used to say that every book has a certain property. All you have to do is to fill in the gap on the right with a predicate that specifies the desired property. Similarly, in order to say that every glass has a certain property, you need a pattern of this form (where 'Hx' means 'x is a glass'):

$(\forall x)(Hx \supset \underline{\quad} x \underline{\quad}).$

Finally, you know how to express the idea that one object is to the left of another. You choose a two-place predicate:

$R_2xy,$

which you understand as 'x is to the left of y'.

Putting all of this together should be easy enough. What you are aiming at is a way of saying of Situation (6) that every book is to the left of every glass. This is true and obviously so. But, while it is not difficult to combine the above resources of Predicate, you must be careful. Here is how a speaker of Predicate would frame the required description:

(1) $(\forall x)(Fx \supset (\forall y)(Hy \supset R_2xy)).$

This is read:

> every x is such that:
>> if x is a book then every y is such that:
>>> if y is a glass, x is to the left of y.

I have presented the reading of (1) in a more perspicuous way. This is because (1) can seem quite a mouthful to a speaker of English, and the above display makes it easier to take it in at a glance. Concentrating on (1) and the way it is read, you should be able to see why it conveys, quite precisely, the idea that every book is to the left of every glass. However, it is the most complicated sentence we have met with so far, and you no doubt have a number of questions about it. The next section should help.

12.1   Scope and Free/Bound Variables

In the last chapter, we learned how to make complex general claims using non-basic predicates such as:

$Fx \supset Gx,$
$H_1x \& H_2x,$
$F_1x \supset \neg F_2x.$

In each case, we turned these predicates into sentences by prefixing a single quantifier. We also made sure that this quantifier linked up with all the variables in the predicate. This last task was accomplished by choosing the same variable for the quantifier and predicate, and by enclosing the whole predicate in parentheses.

In contrast, sentence (1) has *two* quantifiers in it, and this makes the whole question of linkage more intricate. This is a good place to return to the notion of *scope* introduced in chapter 11. It will allow us to introduce other notions we need to describe the linkages in sentences of Predicate.

The *scope* of a quantifier was said to be the extent of influence of the quantifier within the sentence. Thus, using underlining to indicate scope, the scope of the quantifier in:

$$(\forall x)Fx \supset Gx,$$

is:

$$\underline{(\forall x)Fx} \supset Gx.$$

Whereas, the scope of the quantifier in:

$$(\forall x)(Fx \supset Gx),$$

is

$$\underline{(\forall x)(Fx \supset Gx)}.$$

In essence, the quantifiers have a weakness for the *nearest complete expression to the right*, so you need to use parentheses if you want to extend the scope. As I mentioned in the last chapter, the scope of quantifiers is very much like that of negation in Sentential.

In order to give a precise definition of the scope of a quantifier, we have to define the idea of a *complete expression*. In the above examples, 'Fx' and '(Fx ⊃ Gx)' were treated as complete expressions, whereas 'F' and '(Fx' were not. A general definition of *scope* and *complete expression* is given below.

> The scope of a quantifier is the complete expression which immediately follows it. A complete expression is defined by the following conditions (where 'C' and 'D' are schematic letters which hold a place for Predicate expressions).
>
> (i)　A basic predicate is a complete expression.
> (ii)　If C is a complete expression then so is ¬C.
> (iii)　If C and D are complete expressions then so are:

(C & D),
(C ∨ D),
(C ⊃ D),
(C ≡ D).

(iv)   If C is a complete expression then so are:

(∀x)C,
(∃x)C.

Notice that the conditions defining a complete expression bear a resemblance to the grammar we used for Sentential. One important difference, however, is that the grammar defined the notion of a well-formed *sentence* of Sentential, whereas the above defines well-formed *complete expressions*. A complete expression need not be a sentence. For example, by clause (i) any basic predicate is a complete expression. You could consider these conditions to be *part* of the grammar for Predicate, but their main use is to make the notion of scope precise.

---

*Exercise 1

Use underlining to indicate the scope of every quantifier in the following:

(a)   (∀y)(Fy) ∨ Gy
(b)   (∃x)((Fx & Gx) ∨ Fy)
(c)   (∀x_1)(Gx_1 ⊃ Gx_2) ⊃ Fx_1
(d)   (∃y)Fy & Gy
(e)   (∀x)(((Fx ∨ Gy) ∨ Hy) ⊃ F$_2$x).

The scope of a quantifier is *part* of what we need to make precise the notion of a linkage between quantifiers and variables. In addition, we must say something about the choice of letters. We will say that a variable is *bound* by a quantifier (linked to it) when it is in the scope of a quantifier *and* it alphabetically matches the variable in the quantifier. (We can assume that variables in quantifier expressions themselves are automatically bound.) Thus, in the expression:

(∀y)(Fx ⊃ Hy),

the variable 'y' in the quantifier and the one in 'Hy' are both bound, but the variable in 'Fx' is not, *even though it occurs within the scope of a quantifier*. This is because it does not alphabetically match the variable in the quantifier within whose scope it lies. When a variable is *not* bound we will say that it is *free*.

*Exercise 2

Go back to the previous EXERCISE and indicate which variables are bound and which are free.

Armed with the notions of free and bound variables, we can return to consider sentences of Predicate that have more than one quantifier.

12.2   Multiple Universal Quantifiers

The sentence:

(1) $(\forall x)(Fx \supset (\forall y)(Hy \supset R_2xy))$,

says of Situation (6) that every book is to the left of every glass. One of the questions that this sentence may have raised in your mind was why we used two different variables. The answer should now be clearer.

The first quantifier is needed to say of *every book* that *it* is to the left of every glass. This means that this quantifier must be linked to the first variable place in 'R_2xy'. This is accomplished by making its scope the whole sentence, and by choosing the letter 'x' for it. However, the result of this is that the second quantifier – the one that ranges over the glasses – occurs within the scope of the first. The only way to keep the link between those things which are books and those things which are to the left, while also *separately* linking those things which are glasses with those things that have books on the left, is to use different letters for each of the quantifiers. If we used the same letters throughout, we would get:

$(\forall x)(Fx \supset (\forall x)(Hx \supset R_2xx))$,

which (at best) could be understood as saying that everything which is both a book and a glass is to the left of itself!

In order fully to describe Situations, we need to resort to multiple-place predicates like 'R_2xy'. When such predicates are combined with generality the result can seem quite complicated: we are forced to write long sentences with one quantifier occurring within the scope of another. However, if you take a further look at:

(1) $(\forall x)(Fx \supset (\forall y)(Hy \supset R_2xy))$,

you should by now be able to discern a certain simplicity. The real heart of the sentence consists of the two quantifiers and the two-place relation to which they both link. The rest serves to tell us that one of these universally quantified domains consists of books and the other of glasses.

We are now going to investigate the effects of quantifiers occurring within the scope of other quantifiers, so it will be helpful if we can confine our discussion to the essential elements of sentences such as (1). To achieve this we will have to take liberties. Remember that speakers of Predicate insist on treating the domain of quantification as extending to everything in a Situation. That is why we need one-place predicates in (1) to restrict attention to books in respect of the first quantifier, and glasses in respect of the second. However, if we 'cheat' a little, we can leave out these one-place predicates and, instead, *assume* that the domain of quantification for '$(\forall x)$' is books and for '$(\forall y)$' is glasses. This use of restricted domains of quantification is harmless, since we know how to re-introduce unrestricted domains by means of the appropriate predicates. The simplified version of sentence (1) is:

(2) $(\forall x)(\forall y)R_2xy.$

This can be understood as saying that every book is to the left of every glass by virtue of our assumed restrictions on the domains of quantification. It is certainly easier to take in at a glance. For the purposes of further discussion, we will let this consideration override the fact that speakers of Predicate would regard (2) as highly colloquial. (For them, (2) *literally* says that everything is to the left of everything. This is certainly not true of Situation (6), or indeed of any Situation, since nothing is to the left of itself.)

Given that we understand (2) as saying that every book is to the left of every glass, what do you think this sentence claims?

(3) $(\forall y)(\forall x)R_2xy.$

The only difference between (2) and (3) is the order in which the quantifiers are written. But quantifier order affects scope. You can see that in (2) the quantifier '$(\forall y)$' occurs within the scope of '$(\forall x)$', whereas this is reversed in (3). But what effect do you think this has? Is (3) simply another way of saying that every book is to the left of every glass? In order to answer these questions we must think again about universal quantification.

12.3   Recasting

When I say truly of some Situation that:

(4) $(\forall x)Fx,$

I thereby claim that everything has the property indicated by 'F'.

Suppose that there are only three things and that these are designated a, b and c. Then, since the above universal claim is true, we could as well have said:

(5)   Fa & Fb & Fc.

We know that the conjunction (5) does not say precisely what the universal (4) does; (5) does not convey any generality. However, without thinking of (5) as equivalent to (4), we can use the relationship between them to gain insight into the workings of the universal quantifier. A universal claim is something like an indefinitely long conjunction. Where there is only a small number of designated objects in the domain, we can think of the universal as *recast* into a conjunctive form. It is as if someone were to say: there are only three items in the domain, now say that they are all F. The generality would, in this case, be implicit in this description of the Situation, so we can write (5), comfortable in the knowledge that it covers every item. Recasting in this way can show us something about the effect of quantifier order.

   In Situation (6), there are four objects: two books and two glasses. Assume that the books are designated a and b, and the glasses c and d. How would you recast (2)? The procedure for recasting is this: drop the universal quantifier and write out as many conjuncts as there are designators of objects in the domain of that quantifier. The designators are written in place of the variable of the discarded quantifier in each conjunct. In the case of (2) this gives us:

(2′) $(\forall y)R_2ay$ & $(\forall y)R_2by$.

This says:

   a is to the left of every glass and b is to the left of every glass.

As you can see, the 'inner' quantifier still figures in each conjunct. This is not surprising since our recasting involved only the outer quantifier in (2). However, there is nothing to stop us recasting *each* of the conjuncts in (2′). Remember that the domain of '$(\forall y)$' is the glasses c and d, this gives us:

(2″) $(R_2ac$ & $R_2ad)$ & $(R_2bc$ & $R_2bd)$,

which says:

   a is to the left of c *and,*
   a is to the left of d *and,*
   b is to the left of c *and,*
   b is to the left of d.

The point of all this recasting, and the tedious (though true) conjunctive description of Situation (6), will be apparent if you carry out the recasting on (3) – the sentence with the quantifiers in reverse order to those in (2). Without further detailed explanation, the steps in this recasting are below.

(3) $(\forall y)(\forall x)R_2xy$.

Recasting '$(\forall y)$' gives:

(3') $(\forall x)R_2xc$ & $(\forall x)R_2xd$.

Recasting '$(\forall x)$' in both occurrences gives:

(3") $(R_2ac$ & $R_2bc)$ & $(R_2ad$ & $R_2bd)$,

which says:

> a is to the left of c *and*,
> b is to the left of c *and*,
> a is to the left of d *and*,
> b is to the left of d.

The difference between the recast forms of (2) and (3) is merely the order in which the conjuncts are written. I say 'merely' because the order in which conjuncts are written does not change either the truth of the whole conjunction, or its meaning. This should be familiar from Sentential.

This result indicates that the difference in the order of quantifiers in (2) and (3) makes no difference to our understanding of these sentences. In short, they are equivalent. Of course, we reached this conclusion on the basis of recasting, and we know that recast sentences are not themselves equivalent to the originals. However, the point of recasting is not that of getting conjunctive equivalents of universal quantifications. Rather, we have used very small domains as a way of seeing what happens when quantifier order is reversed. You can see that quantifier order in (2) and (3) makes no difference in such a domain, and there is no reason to think that it will make a difference as the domains get larger. It is as if recasting allows us to take a microscopic look at the workings of the quantifier.

It has taken us quite a long time to get clear about this first example of multiple quantification. However, you will find that the effort is repaid in our further investigations of other examples.

12.4   Multiple Existential Quantifiers

Consider the state of my desk pictured below (writing a book isn't easy, and it is Christmas).

Situation (7)

Here is a sentence that Predicate speakers could use to describe the Situation:

(6)   (∃x)(Fx & (∃y)(Gy & R₃xy)).

This is read:

> there is at least one x such that:
>> x is a book and there is at least one y such that:
>>> y is a bottle and x is leaning on y.
>>>> (Or, at least one book is leaning on at least one bottle.)

In this case we have two existential quantifiers, one occurring within the scope of the other. As before, we can simplify this by restricting '(∃x)' to books and '(∃y)' to bottles. With such restricted quantification, the essentials of sentence (6) can be captured by:

(7)   (∃x)(∃y)R₃xy.

Sentences like (7) allow us to describe Situations in a way not available to us before now. By using multiple existential quantifiers, we can express *relationships* between things which are general, but not universally so.

How do you think (7) stands with respect to (8) below?

(8)   (∃y)(∃x)R₃xy.

The only difference between these sentences is the quantifier order, so we have now to look into existential quantifier order by means of recasting.

If it is true of some Situation that:

($\exists$x)Fx,

then this is like saying that

Fa $\lor$ Fb $\lor$ Fc . . . ,

where a,b,c . . . designate the items in the Situation. That is, the claim that at least one x is F, could be understood as an indefinitely long *disjunction*: if at least one thing is F, then it is either a, or it is b, or it is c, . . .

Returning to the above Situation, we can use this information to recast:

(7)   ($\exists$x)($\exists$y)R_3xy,

as:

(7')   ($\exists$y)R_3ay $\lor$ ($\exists$y)$R_3$by.

Given that books are designated a and b, this says either that a is leaning on at least one bottle or that b is leaning on at least one bottle. Finally, we can recast each of the quantifiers in (7') to get

(7")   (R_3ac $\lor$ R_3ad) $\lor$ (R_3bc $\lor$ R_3bd).

This says:

a is leaning on c *or,*
a is leaning on d *or,*
b is leaning on c *or,*
b is leaning on d.

The stages in the recasting of:

(8)   ($\exists$y)($\exists$x)R_3xy,

are:

(8')   ($\exists$x)R_3xc $\lor$ ($\exists$x)R_3xd,
(8")   (R_3ac $\lor$ R_3bc) $\lor$ (R_3ad $\lor$ R_3bd).

This final form is read:

a is leaning on c *or,*
b is leaning on c *or,*
a is leaning on d *or,*
b is leaning on d.

As you can see, the only difference between the recast versions of (7) and (8) is the order of the disjuncts. But the *order* of disjuncts makes no difference to our understanding of a disjunction, so (7) and (8) are equivalent. That is, it does not matter which of the existential quantifiers comes first.

At this point, you may feel that our checking of quantifier order by lengthy recasting is unnecessarily fussy. After all, the pairs of existential and universal sentences *sound* the same when you read them out. However, my fussiness will be vindicated shortly.

12.5   Multiple Universal and Existential Quantifiers

The next Situation to consider is this one.

Situation 8

At least one vase contains every flower. That is obvious. How would you express this thought in Predicate? Try:

(9) $(\exists x)(F_1x \, \& \, (\forall y)(F_2y \supset R_4xy))$,

which is read:

    at least one x is such that:
      x is a vase and every y is such that:
        if y is a flower then x contains y.

Before we make the usual simplifying assumptions about the domains of quantification, notice that (9) contains both '&' and '⊃'. Because the overall structure of (9) is existential, the connective needed in the non-basic predicate is conjunction (see chapter 11, section 11.8). However, an ingredient in the complex predicate of (9), viz.:

$(F_1x \,\&\, (\forall y)(F_2y \supset R_4xy)),$

contains a universal quantifier. As you would expect, the non-basic predicate governed by this quantifier is constructed with a conditional. (If you do not remember why this is to be expected, see chapter 11, section 11.7.)

By assuming that the domain of '$(\exists x)$' is vases, and of '$(\forall y)$' is flowers, we can capture the essentials of the thought expressed by (9) in this simpler sentence:

(10) $(\exists x)(\forall y)R_4xy.$

Does the order of the quantifiers make a difference in (10)? When we have multiple *existential* quantifiers, the order doesn't affect the truth conditions of the sentence. Similarly for multiple *universal* quantifiers. So, does the mixing of quantifiers make any difference? Reversing the order of quantifiers in (10) gives us:

(11) $(\forall y)(\exists x)R_4xy.$

We have to work out the relationship between (10) and (11).

You can begin to understand these sentences better by thinking carefully about how they are read.

(10) At least one x (vase) is such that every y (flower) is such that x contains y.
    Or, more colloquially:
    at least one vase contains every flower.

(11) Every y (flower) is such that at least one x (vase) is such that x contains y.
    Or:
    every flower is contained in at least one vase.

Do they sound equivalent? I would expect you to judge them *not* equivalent, but don't worry if your judgement does not follow my expectations. The how-do-they-sound test is not definitive enough by itself and, as before, we must now recast (10) and (11) into a quantifier-free form. We have done this often enough so, without a lot of explanation, here are the steps using a, b to designate the vases and c, d to designate the flowers in Situation (8).

(i) To recast (10):

    recast the existential quantifier to get:
        (10′) $(\forall y)R_4ay \lor (\forall y)R_4by,$
    then recast the universal quantifiers to get:
        (10″) $(R_4ac \,\&\, R_4ad) \lor (R_4bc \,\&\, R_4bd).$

(ii)   To recast (11):

recast the universal quantifier to get:
(11′)   ($\exists$x)R₄xc & ($\exists$x)R₄xd,
then recast the existential quantifiers to get:
(11″)   (R₄ac V R₄bc) & (R₄ad V R₄bd).

Are (10″) and (11″) equivalent? You do not have to rely on intuition here. These two non-basic sentences are *not* equivalent, even though they contain the same basic sentences. This is because (10″) is a *disjunction* of conjunctive sentences, while (11″) is a *conjunction* of disjunctive sentences. This difference in connectives prevents the re-arrangement of elements that we appealed to when we had only universal or only existential quantifiers. A sentence of this form:

$(P_1 \text{ & } P_2) \text{ V } (P_3 \text{ & } P_4)$,

is not equivalent to one of this form:

$(P_1 \text{ V } P_3) \text{ & } (P_2 \text{ V } P_4)$.

(You can prove this for yourself with truth tables.)

So, when you mix universal and existential quantifiers, the order makes a great deal of difference. But this is not the end of the story. We now know that (10) and (10″) have different truth conditions from (11) and (11″). However, we have yet to see how this difference carries over to Situations.

12.6   Two Situations

We can see more clearly what is going on with (10) and (11) by focusing on the following two Situations.

Situation (8)

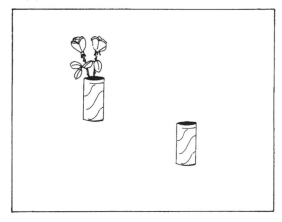

Situation (9)

(The first of them we discussed earlier, but I reproduced it here so that you could compare it directly with the new one.) We know that:

(10) $(\exists x)(\forall y)R_4xy$
       (at least one vase contains every flower),

is true of Situation (8), and we know that this sentence is *not* equivalent to:

(11) $(\forall y)(\exists x)R_4xy$
       (every flower is contained in at least one vase).

What consequences does all this have for the truth of (11) with respect to Situation (8)? This is not an easy question so think carefully about it.

Sentence (11) happens to be true of Situation (8). You can see that every flower is contained in at least one vase: none are lying around on the desk. This shouldn't be all that surprising. After all, (10) and (11) are not equivalent, but this doesn't prevent them both being true of Situation (8). What is much more interesting, however, is that *whenever* a sentence like (10) is true of a Situation, then so will be a sentence like (11). That is, (10) validly implies (11). Of course, I cannot prove this now, since we have not yet discussed validity and arguments in Predicate. The best I can do is to appeal to your intuitions about these sentences, so take another close look at the readings of (10) and (11). Can you imagine any circumstance in which the first is true and the second false? I expect not and, for the present that will have to do.

So, (10) is not equivalent to, but does imply, (11). At this point, I have asked you to look at these sentences so often that you probably cannot distinguish the one from the other. Here is where Situation (9) comes in. Once you grasp the difference between it and Situation (8), you should have no trouble keeping sentences (10) and (11) apart and understanding them.

In Situation (9), there are no flowers lying around on the desk: every flower has a place in a vase. However, unlike Situation (8), there isn't one particular vase which holds them all. So, it is true that:

(11) $(\forall y)(\exists x)R_4xy,$

but it is *not* true that:

(10) $(\exists x)(\forall y)R_4xy.$

Situations (8) and (9) illustrate precisely what happens when a universal quantifier occurs within the scope of an existential, and vice versa. The clear difference between how things are in Situation (8), and how they are in (9), is neatly captured by taking care over the order in which quantifiers are written. As you will see in chapter 13, Predicate has some advantage here over natural languages. In English, for example, it is not always easy to describe Situations like (8) and (9) in such a precise way.

Exercise 3

Below are four sentences of Predicate. In each case:

   *(i)   indicate how to read the sentence;
   (ii)   draw a Situation which makes it true. To save you work in drawing, the predicates are those of simple geometric figures. Here is a key:

   F_1x – x is a square
   F_2x – x is a circle
   F_3x – x is a triangle
   R_1xy – x is to the left of y
   R_2xy – x is in y.

(a) $(\forall x)(F_1x \supset (\exists y)(F_3y \;\&\; R_2xy))$

(b) $(\exists x)(F_2x \;\&\; (\exists y)(F_3y \;\&\; R_1xy))$

(c) $(\exists x)(F_3x \;\&\; (\forall y)(F_1y \supset R_2xy))$

(d) $(\forall x)(F_2x \supset (\forall y)(F_1y \supset R_2xy)).$

Exercise 4

Below are two Situations. In each case, make up a sentence of Predicate which uses two quantifiers and is true of the Situation. Use the expressions whose key is given in EXERCISE 3.

(a)

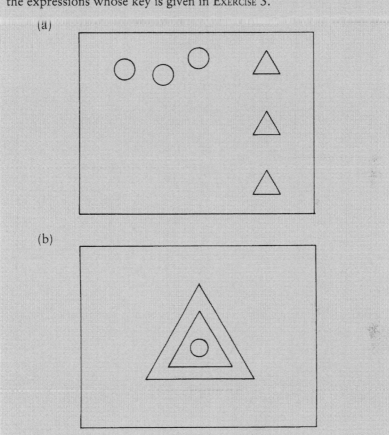

(b)

*Exercise 5

(a) Recast each of the following sentences for a domain of two objects:

($\exists$x)Fx

($\forall$y)(Fy $\lor$ Gy).

(b) Explain why the recasting method shows that quantifier order makes a difference to the truth conditions of a sentence that has both a universal and an existential quantifier.

Exercise 6

The Situations that we have used so far are not very exciting. My desk and geometric objects are hardly the stuff of novels. However, there is in principle no restriction on Situations; any way the world is counts. This Exercise should broaden your horizons a bit.

(a) Think of some portion of your family tree and use designators and Predicates to indicate who everyone is and what relation they have to one another.
(b) Make *six* true general claims about the members of your family. At least three of these claims should use multiple quantifiers.

12.7   A Special Relationship

In the following Situation:

the items depicted are both copies of a little known work on logic. Given this, it would not be unreasonable for someone to say that both items were the *same*; they are, after all, copies of a single work. On the other hand, it is no less reasonable for someone to say that these items are *not* the same. They are distinguishable in all sorts of ways from one another, not least by their being located in different places.

What all this shows is that the words 'the same' can be used in some what different ways. We will call the first way the *similarity* notion of sameness, and the second the *numerical* notion. ('Numerical' is appropriate here because, for this notion, it matters what number of items there are. If you can count two items, then those items cannot be the *same* in this rather stricter use of the word.)

Keeping this in mind, look at this Situation:

Suppose that *you* had described this Situation using the sentence:

Fa,

where you chose 'F' to mean 'is a book' and 'a' as the designator. Further, suppose that *I* had described this Situation with the sentence:

Fb,

using 'F' as you had, but using 'b' as the designator. What do you think should be said about the relationship between a and b? I suggest that the most appropriate reply would be: a and b are *the same*. Moreover, in this reply, the phrase 'the same' is used in the numerical way. There is only one item in the Situation, so it can hardly be otherwise.

Notice that my question was about the relationship between a and b, and *not* about the relationship between 'a' and 'b'. That is, I was asking you about the items a and b, and not the names. This can seem puzzling. After all, you know that there is only one item, so it seems a bit odd to talk about the relationship between the items a and b. This puzzlement should disappear, however, when you think of cases where you do not *begin* with knowledge of numerical sameness. Here is one: the police find a television in Jones's house, and it is very much like a television that was recently stolen. (It is the same television in the similarity way of speaking about sameness; it is the same size, brand, age, etc.) Jones's guilt turns on this question: is the television in Jones's house numerically the same as the one recently stolen? This is not a question about the designators of televisions, but about the televisions themselves. Of course, it may well turn out that there is only one such television: Jones may indeed be guilty. In this case, my talk of televisions will have been inaccurate. But it would be no less misleading to speak of *the* television before I find out that the one in Jones's house is the one missing.

Returning to the Situation in which there is a single book, here is a way in which Predicate speakers could make the connection between a and b:

$$R_5ab.$$

In this sentence, the two-place predicate is read: a is numerically the same as b, or: a is *identical* to b. This sentence could be used to clear up any confusion that might arise as the result of your using a different designator from me in your description of the above Situation. (A suitably adjusted sentence using this predicate would, if true, incriminate Jones. That is, if 'a' and 'b' were exchanged for designators of the relevant television sets, then the resulting sentence's truth would form part of any case against Jones.)

The relationship of identity is held in high regard by speakers of Predicate. So high, in fact, that they write it in a special way. Instead of using one of the ordinary two-place predicates such as 'R_5xy' as we did above, they write:

$$a = b.$$

This sentence introduces a new symbol in Predicate, but is read in the same way as 'R_5ab': a is identical to b. The negation of this sentence can be written either as:

$$\neg(a = b),$$

or as:

$$a \neq b.$$

I have used the example of a Situation with one item and two designators to motivate interest in this predicate, but I could as well have introduced identity more directly. Leaving out the question of multiple designators of an item, it is certainly true that:

a = a.

It must be admitted that this doesn't seem to be a very informative truth. Indeed, because it is obvious that claims of this form are always going to be true, we could generalize to get:

(∀x)(x = x).

This universal claim says that everything is identical to itself and this, like its specific instances, isn't news. In this respect, there is a close resemblance between this claim and the tautologies discussed in chapter 6: neither sticks its neck out by claiming something which *could* be false.

Given all this, why is the relation of identity so important to Predicate speakers? Why have they chosen to represent, with a special symbol, a relation only useful so far for clearing up confusion in multiple designator cases, and for making a blindingly obvious universal claim? The answer follows.

12.8 The Uses of Identity: The Other

Consider the Situation below.

Situation (10)

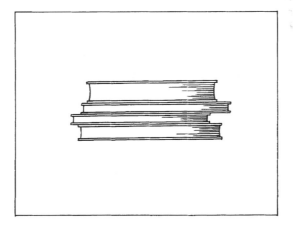

How could we express the thought that one of the books is on top of the pile, i.e. that one of the books is on top of every other book? You might try:

$(\forall x)(Fx \supset Rax),$

where 'Fx' means 'x is a book', 'Rxy' means 'x is on top of y' and *a* designates the topmost book. This sentence is read:

> every x is such that if x is a book then *a* is on top of x.

The trouble is that this sentence isn't even true. It says that *a* is on top of *every book*. But what about *a* itself? The topmost book is after all a book. So, the above sentence must be seen as claiming that *a* is on top of itself, and this is quite clearly false. The thought we want to express is that *a* is on top of every *other* book. Here is where identity can help. Look at this sentence:

$(\forall x)((Fx \ \& \ x \neq a) \supset Rax).$

It is read:

> every x is such that if x is a book and x is not *a*, then *a* is on top of x.

This sentence conveys precisely what we tried for earlier. By conjoining the 'not identical to a' condition with 'Fx' we restrict attention to *books other than a*.

---

*Exercise 7

Express in Predicate the thought that:

> every child other than Mary has an ice-cream.

Choose your own symbols. Does your answer include the claim that Mary does *not* have an ice-cream? Should it?

12.9   Uses of Identity: How Many?

Predicate has two quantifiers, two symbols to indicate how many of the items in a Situation meet the conditions set by predicates. The universal quantifier is used to make claims about every item. (See the Situation depicted below.)

Situation (11)

With it, and a suitable choice of predicates, we can say things about every book, every pen, every telephone, etc. However, this quantifier tells us nothing about the number of things which meet certain conditions. Indeed, using 'Fx' for 'x is an ashtray' and 'Gx' for 'x is round', the following is true of Situation (11):

$$(\forall x)(Fx \supset Gx),$$

even though there are no ashtrays at all on my desk. (I've given up smoking.)

In contrast, the existential quantifier does tell us something more about the number of items in a Situation that fulfil a given predicate. The claim that:

$$(\exists x)(Fx \ \& \ Gx),$$

says that there is at least *one* round ashtray, and it is quite clearly false of Situation (11).

While the existential quantifier tells us something about the number of items, it is very limited. For instance, the following are true thoughts we could have about Situation (11), and yet they do not seem to be expressible using the quantifiers of Predicate:

(i)   *There are at least two* books.
(ii) *There are at most two* pens.
(iii) *There is exactly one* telephone.

Speakers of Predicate have developed ways of using the identity relation to express these, and related sorts of numerical thoughts. That is, instead of having to invent new quantifier symbols for use in each of the above quantified thoughts, they manage with the two quantifiers already introduced. The key to this is their clever employment of the identity predicate. Here's how it works.

A.   At least . . .

We will begin with (i) (see above). A first try at expressing this thought in Predicate would be:

(i′) $(\exists x)(\exists y)(F_1x \ \& \ F_1y)$.

This is read: at least one x is such that at least one y is such that x is a book and y is a book; or: at least one x and at least one y is a book.

You might be tempted to think that this already says that there are at least two books, but you would be wrong. Situation (12) shown below should show you why.

Even though there is only one book, the sentence (i′) would be true of this Situation. There is nothing to stop our thinking of the one and only book making *both* quantified predicates true. In effect (i′) rather redundantly says:

at least one thing is a book, at least one thing is a book,

and this falls short of our hoped for way of saying that there are at least *two* books in Situation (11).

However, if we insert a non-identity claim as in:

(i″) $(\exists x)(\exists y)((F_1x \ \& \ F_1y) \ \& \ x \neq y)$, then we can achieve our aim. This last sentence says that there is at least one x which is a book and at least one y which is a book, where x and y are distinct. In order for it to apply to a Situation, there must be at least two different books. But this is just what we set out to capture.

B.   At most . . .

To express the thought in (ii), that there are at most two pens, requires a completely different strategy from the one just used. In Situation (11) it is true that there are at most two pens, even though there is only one. Indeed, it would be true even if there were no pens at all, so we cannot use existential quantifiers to make the claim expressed in (ii).

What we have to do is to sneak up on our prey. Suppose someone said that he believed in at most one God. (This is said to be the belief of a certain unzealous sect.) Such a belief could be expressed in this round-about way:

> every God is identical to every God.

This form of words does not actually say that there is a God; it only claims that every God is identical to every item which is a God. This has the effect of ruling out the possibility of *two distinct* Gods. For, if there were two distinct Gods, then they would not be identical, and the above would be false.

Using this hint, we can express the thought that there are at most two pens in Situation (11) in this way:

(ii′) $(\forall x)(\forall y)(\forall z)[(F_2x \ \& \ F_2y \ \& \ F_2z) \supset (x=y \lor x=z \lor y=z)]$.
(I have left out some parentheses for ease of reading.)

This may seem a very difficult sentence, but the difficulty is merely one of length. Essentially, it says that every x, every y and every z are such that if they are pens, then there must be at least one true identity between any two of them. That is, there cannot be *three distinct* things which are pens. But this is precisely what we need to express the thought that there are *at most two* pens. Notice that this sentence does *not* say anything about what there is. Its truth is consistent with a Situation in which there are no pens, one pen or two pens. Try the **Exercise** which follows as it will give you insight into the way (ii′) works.

C.   Exactly . . .

The final thought about Situation (11) that we must consider is:

(iii)   There is exactly one telephone.

Given the work we have done so far, this will prove quite easy. For it is clear that the thought in (iii) comes to:

there is at least one telephone,
AND
there is at most one telephone,

and we know how to express each of these thoughts. Using 'H_1x' for 'x is a telephone', we can combine these into a single sentence

(iii′) $(\exists x)(H_1x \ \& \ (\forall y)(H_1y \supset x = y))$

which is read roughly as follows:

There is at least one telephone and every item which is a telephone is identical to it.

This guarantees that there is a telephone, but it rules out the possibility of there being two or more distinct telephones. In short, there is exactly one telephone.

The Main Points of Chapter 12

1 In the first sections of the chapter, we discussed how to express thoughts that involved more than one general element. This is done by using sentences of Predicate which contain more than one quantifier.

2 Such *multiple generality* results in sentences that have quantifiers occurring within the *scope* of other quantifiers. Here we introduced a more precise definition of scope, and the notions of *free* and *bound* variable.

3 Using the method of *recasting*, we showed that scope differences did not have much effect in simple sentences when all of the quantifiers were universal, or all were existential. However, scope differences have considerable effect in sentences which mix universal and existential quantifiers.

4 In the remainder of the chapter, we discussed the notion of *identity* (or *sameness*) and its uses within Predicate.

5 The notion of sameness is as in:

this is the very same coat I wore yesterday,

rather than as in:

this coat of mine is the same as you bought for yourself.

6 The relationship of identity is a two-place predicate, but it is written in this special way in Predicate:

$a = b$.

7 Combining this two-place predicate with universal and existential quantifiers, we were able to express any of:

(a)   there are at least n . . .
(b)   there are at most n . . .
(c)   there are exactly n . . .

8 We were able to use this predicate to express 'otherness' as in:

(a)   every other student . . .
(b)   at least one person other than Mary . . .

Note   See Appendix 1, Lessons 8–12, for further help.

Chapter thirteen

Translating into Predicate

You should now be a Predicate speaker. Since you are also a speaker of a natural language, you are well prepared for translating *into* Predicate. I have left discussion of validity to the next chapter, since I want to consider the relationship of your natural language (I will assume English) to your newly acquired language of logic while the latter is still fresh in your mind.

13.0 A Note Before We Begin

It comes as a surprise to many people that Predicate is as rich a language as it is. Though some of my explanations have been quite involved, Predicate isn't all that complicated. In particular, there aren't that many different types of symbol in the language. It has designators, predicates, variables, two quantifiers and the identity relation. Compared to any natural language this is a very sparse list indeed.

Nonetheless, Predicate can be used to make claims of great subtlety and precision. This has led to all sorts of speculation about the role of Predicate in human intellectual life. Here are some examples.

(i) Some would go so far as to say that Predicate can be used to give the structure of any true thought that scientists and mathematicians (not to mention logicians) could have. If, as these writers would also say, there are no other true thoughts than those of science, mathematics and logic, then Predicate gives the structure of whatever language you need to express true thoughts about the world.

(ii) From another perspective, there are those who think that Predicate captures, if not all, then at least the core structure of natural language. Roughly, they would tell this story: the structure of our *thoughts* is given by something like Predicate. When the occasion arises, these thoughts are processed in various ways before they are communicated. The effect of such processing is to convert Predicate structures into sentences of English, German, French, etc. Natural language is what thoughts wear when they leave home.

(iii) Still further, many regard the details of the relationship between Predicate and natural language as having profound consequences for questions about the nature of things (metaphysical questions), and questions about human knowledge. For example, there is a lively debate in philosophy about which elements of natural language, if any, function like designators in Predicate. This debate is central to the metaphysical subject of ontology, the study of what sorts of thing *really* exist.

(iv) And last, but not least, many who work with computers in the area known as 'artificial intelligence' believe that Predicate provides the backbone for computational languages that will enable machines to perform feats we would consider intelligent. The idea is that a computer which can read and reason with Predicate sentences will be able to perform many of the intellectual tasks that we do. Included here will be the ability to understand natural languages.

These are bold claims and big issues. To assess them would take us deep into their home territories – philosophy, linguistics, computer science, and psychology – and we haven't got time for such forays. For instance, before you can even understand the boldest of these claims, you must track down the notion of science, and this lives in an extensive forest of philosophical writing. In any case, you don't need to be able to evaluate or fully understand these sorts of claim to see this: *the relationship between Predicate and natural language is itself an important area of study in philosophy, linguistics, psychology and computer science.* Proposals for translation between natural language and Predicate can have consequences which extend far beyond the modest use to which we will put translation in this chapter.

We want a validity-preserving way of translating from natural language into Predicate. That is what is required by the Strategy, and that is what I have promised you ever since chapter 3. The bigger issues that such translation raises will have to be put on one side. However, I am on record as saying that the reason for being interested in logical languages is not merely to develop more efficient ways of testing the validity of arguments. This preface to translation invites you to recognize that Predicate *both* is the most efficient means for displaying the validity of arguments *and* provides a rich source of insight into language and, perhaps, thought.

One last caveat: our survey of translation will be systematic, but I cannot cover every area of interest. The point of this chapter is to help you to acquire a *skill* in translation which you can then go on to develop further on your own. As in chapter 7, our work will be organized around the elements of the logical language, and we will discuss the ways of translating that reveal the maximum of structure in any given case. It may happen that, in the context of a particular argument, you will not have to translate so as to reveal all the structure for which Predicate provides. But, in this chapter, translation will be discussed outside the context of particular arguments.

13.1   Designators

Situation (13)

In this Situation, Predicate speakers would pick out the items using designators such as 'a', 'b' and 'c'. How would you pick them out using the resources of English? Here are four ways.

(1)   You could think of the items as having *proper names*. For example, suppose the much used pen was a gift, and I call it 'Fred' in honour of its donor. Those who know this will ask for Fred when they need to borrow my pen. In more usual circumstances, however, proper names are used to label persons, places, and things which are of some generally recognized importance to our lives. Still, there is nothing to stop us labelling any item with a name, and then using it like a Predicate language designator.

(2)   In some ways simpler than using a proper name is the use of words like 'this' and 'that'. These are *demonstratives*, and they usually work in conjunction with gestures such as pointing. Unless you direct my attention to a particular place on the desk, I would be at a loss to understand the remark:

that is a book.

There are all sorts of things within sight of us, so I have to be shown which thing is the subject of your remark in order fully to understand it. Of course, we don't point every time we use demonstratives. Once the subject of conversation is fixed, the repetition of 'that' will usually work without further gesture.

(3)   You could pick out items in discussion by using what are called *definite descriptions*. For example, you would all know which thing I was talking about if, with respect to Situation (13), I said:

the book on top of the pile.

The phrase 'book on top of the pile' is a description (predicate) which, when combined with the definite article 'the', results in the above definite description. My claim is that definite descriptions can be used to designate items in Situations.

NOTE   The descriptive element in a definite description is suspiciously like a one-place predicate. This may make you wonder whether definite descriptions in natural language really are like the designators of Predicate. Designators point to items, but they do not describe them, whereas definite descriptions pick out items *by* describing them. We will return to this later.

---

(4)   *Pronouns* can be used to pick out items for discussion, though these, like demonstratives, usually require some background to make the reference clear. In speaking of Situation (13), I might say:

they are on logic,
it has no ink in it,

and I suspect you would understand me perfectly well as talking about the books in the first instance, and the pen in the second. Your understanding of these sentences, and your background knowledge (logic is a subject matter for books, and pens use ink), make it clear which items are *they* and which is *it*. Pronouns have number and gender built into them, and this could be seen as a descriptive element. Thus, it is (usually) inappropriate to pick out Fred using 'she', or to speak of the pen as 'they'.

Possessive pronouns like 'my' and 'his' combined with a predicate result in phrases which designate in the way that definite descriptions do. Thus, the phrase:

my pen,

functions as a definite description referring to the same item as is referred to by 'the pen on the left of the pad'.

NOTE   Pronouns are very slippery customers. Accepting, as you ought, what I have said above, look at this sentence:

> He who hesitates is lost.

Suppose a novice in English asked you to which male person this sentence referred. I suspect such a question would make you smile. The pronoun 'he' in this sentence does not designate anyone in particular, nor is that what it is used to do. Instead, it plays a role something like that of a variable in Predicate. Pronouns lead a double life: they function sometimes as designators and sometimes as variables. In the present context, it is only their role as designators that interests us; we will return to the other role later.

Summary

In English and in other natural languages, there are a number of devices that mimic the role of designators in Predicate. Of these, proper names come closest to being like designators, but demonstratives, definite descriptions and pronouns also serve in this capacity.

These devices can be translated by designators of Predicate. For example, when discussing Situation (13), the following:

> 'Fred' (given the story of how the pen came to have a name),
> 'this' (said pointing to the pen),
> 'the pen on the left of the pad',
> 'it' (where the pen is what is being discussed),

can be rendered into Predicate as 'a'. There is more to be said about some of these devices, and about this simple scheme of translation, but it can wait. You must learn to walk before you can run.

13.2   Predicates: the Preliminaries

Once you know which devices do the designating, it is a fairly easy matter to isolate the predicates. For example, if I gave you the following sentences:

> Fa,
> Gb ⊃ Hc,
> Rab,

and asked you to tell me which predicates occur in them, you would have very little trouble answering. Indeed, it would seem to be too easy a task. All you have to do is to substitute variables for the designators, taking care to use a different variable for each different designator within a sentence. Here are the predicates:

Fx,
$Gx \supset Hy$,
Rxy.

The move between sentences and predicates in Predicate is child's play because there is never any doubt about which expressions are designators. Now that we have discussed possible designators in natural language, it should be fairly clear how to proceed. First, we must isolate the predicate-like expression in the natural language sentence. I will call this the *predicate frame*. Then, we have to translate this into Predicate.

The first stage requires you to substitute a variable for one or more of the designating expressions in the sentence. Below are three examples.

Sentence – John is hungry.
Predicate frame – x is hungry

Sentence – That pen is to the left of the pad.
Predicate frame – x is to the left of y

Sentence – Robert caught the ball in his hand.
Predicate frame – x_1 caught x_2 in x_3

In order to translate these predicate frames into Predicate, you simply choose a Predicate language predicate that has the appropriate number of places, and stipulate that this is the translation of the predicate frame. Here are translations for the above examples:

(i) F_1x,
(ii) R_3xy,
(iii) $S_1x_1x_2x_3$.

Could you have used different letters? Of course. Remember that Predicate speakers, like those of Sentential, are interested in structure. They do not feel bound to use predicates in the same way on every occasion, though within a given context of argument they do use them consistently. For example, in one context, they may use 'Fx' to mean 'x is a book', and they will continue to use it this way in current discussion. But, in another context, they might use 'Fx' to mean 'x is a pen'. This will make it difficult to hearers to understand precisely what content is being conveyed on any specific occasion, but that is not what Predicate is for. Predicate is a language of logic – a structural language. It is used primarily as a medium to communicate the structure of thoughts, rather than as a medium to communicate the thoughts themselves.

Do you have to replace *all* the occurrences of designating expressions with variables? That is, given a sentence like:

Robert caught the ball in his hand,

do we have to isolate a three-place predicate frame: 'x_1 caught x_2 in x_3'? Or, could we see this sentence as giving rise to a simpler *and different* one-place predicate frame: 'x caught the ball in his hand'? The correct response is that it is up to the translator. Put more clearly: you do have some latitude as to the predicate frame you isolate and, hence, some latitude with respect to translation. For example, the sentence:

John stood between Harriet and Ilke,

yields the following possible predicate frames:

(i) x_1 stood between x_2 and x_3,
(ii) x_1 stood between x_2 and Ilke,
(iii) x_1 stood between Harriet and Ilke,
(iv) x_1 stood between Harriet and x_2,
(v)   John stood between x_1 and x_2,
vi)   John stood between x_1 and Ilke,
(vii) John stood between Harriet and x_1.

Which of these you choose determines whether you will use a one-, two- or three-place predicate as your final translation and which one it is. I say 'which one it is' because the number of places is not the only element of choice. For instance, compare (ii) and (iv). These are both two-place, but they are different predicate frames and this would require you to think of your chosen Predicate translations differently. If you choose 'Rx_1x_2' for (ii), then you cannot at the same time use this to translate (iv). 'Standing between someone or other and Ilke' is not the same predicate as 'standing between Harriet and someone or other'. The choice of predicate frame is up to you, but you must keep track of the choice when you translate into Predicate.

Most choices in life are not a matter of whim, and the choice here is certainly not intended to be whimsical. Our ultimate aim in translating is to check the validity of natural language arguments. Given this, it is sensible to isolate and translate predicates in as much structural detail as is needed to show validity. We have yet to discuss the issue of validity in Predicate, but the following example should give you some idea of what I mean.

Here are two arguments:

(a) John stood between Harriet and Ilke.
     Therefore, at least one person stood between Harriet and Ilke.
(b) John stood between Harriet and Ilke.
     Therefore, at least one person stood between two others.

Since the conclusion of (a) uses the predicate frame 'x stood between Harriet and Ilke', there is no real reason to isolate a more complicated predicate frame in the premise. On the other hand, the conclusion of (b) involves existential quantification in respect of *three* places, so you will have to make sure to translate the premise so that it embodies the three-place predicate 'x_1 stood between x_2 and x_3'.

NOTE   In this section, we have gone from sentences to predicate frames, and then to full translations, by substituting variables for designating expressions. We depended on the fact that sentences in Predicate are often made up according to the formula:

SENTENCE = PREDICATE(S) + DESIGNATOR(S).

The sharp-eyed among you may have noticed that in my remark about argument (a), I isolated the predicate frame in the conclusion, not by deleting a designator, but by deleting a quantifier. That is, I used the fact that sentences in Predicate can also be made up according to this formula:

SENTENCE = QUANTIFIER(S) + PREDICATE(S),

as a second way of isolating predicate frames. The conclusion of (a) is:

at least one person stood between Harriet and Ilke,

and the deletion of the quantifier (with the substitution of the variable) gives the predicate frame.

The reason that I haven't yet exploited this way of isolating predicate frames is simple: we have yet to discuss natural language quantifier expressions. Until we have some idea of how they look, we are in no position to use this second method to any advantage. (The conclusion of (a) used a natural language quantifier expression that a speaker of Predicate couldn't miss. It won't always be that clear.)

13.3   Predicates and Reflexive Pronouns

Consider this sentence:

(A)   Ralph injured himself.

How would you translate this into Predicate? On the one hand, given what has been said so far, we might expect 'Ralph' and 'himself' to mark two places in a predicate. After all, the first is a proper name and the second a pronoun. This would give us the predicate frame:

x injured y.

On the other hand, there is something special about the pronoun in this case. It would be incorrect to think of the 'him' in 'himself' as referring to anyone other than Ralph. What we have here is a pronoun which attaches itself to a proper name, something grammarians call a *reflexive* pronoun.

Precisely because of this reflexivity, (A) is best understood as containing the predicate frame:

x injured x,

and this is translated by the predicate:

Rxx.

As mentioned in an earlier chapter, this predicate, containing two occurrences of the same variable, is nonetheless one-place.

Anticipating somewhat, you may feel that this translation has left something out. If Ralph did truly injure himself then someone injured someone. And you might feel that this consequence is denied us if we translate (A) using 'Rxx'. However, this would be wrong, though you will have to wait until chapter 14 to appreciate it. Even though the predicate is one-place, we can validate the inference from (A) to:

(B)   Someone injured someone.

*Exercise 1

Below are a number of sentences of English. Indicate which phrases or expressions in them could be translated as designators.

(a)   Byron died in Greece.
(b)   This book is not meant to be read in one sitting.
(c)   John ran himself down.
(d)   My favourite stories are those by Balzac.
(e)   This will serve as a table.

13.4 Universal Quantifiers

The Predicate sentence:

> (∀x)(Fx ⊃ Gx)
> where: 'Fx' means 'x is a glass'
>   'Gx' means 'x is empty'.

is true of this Situation.

> Situation (14)

How would you use English to describe this Situation? Here are a number of ways:

Every glass is empty.
All the glasses are empty.
Each glass is empty.
Any glass is empty.
The glasses are empty.

Does this mean the Predicate sentence above can be treated as a good translation of these sentences? That is, can we translate 'every', 'all', 'each' and 'any' using the '∀' of Predicate? As a first approximation, the answer is yes. However, English and, of course, other natural languages, are not so profligate with their resources as to have a large number of ways of doing the same job. There are subtle differences between each of these natural language quantifiers, differences which I can only describe when we consider matters such as *scope* later in this chapter.

What now of the last sentence in the above list? It doesn't seem to have any word whose job is that of quantification and, to make matters worse, it contains a phrase that looks suspiciously like a designator, viz. 'the glasses'. There can be no doubt that you understand this sentence as conveying the right message, but it is not clear how, since the quantifier is merely *implicit*. I will leave discussion of implicit quantifiers until after we have considered existential quantification.

13.5   Universal but Negative Quantifiers

Look again at Situation (14) focusing on whether the books are open or not. A perfectly natural way to describe what you see would be:

no book is open,
OR
none of the books is open.

These sentences contain a universal quantifier expression, but it is negative. Does the fact that Predicate lacks such a quantifier prevent our translating them? Of course not. The translation is given below.

(a) $(\forall x)(F_1 x \supset \neg F_2 x)$
where   '$F_1 x$' means 'x is a book'
'$F_2 x$' means 'x is open'.

This Predicate sentence is read:

every x is such that if x is a book then x is not open,

and it is easy enough to see that this conveys the thought that no book is open. So, universal negative forms of quantifier in natural language can be translated into Predicate using '∀' and an appropriately placed negation.

Another way to capture the force of 'no book is open' is to use this sentence:

(b) $\neg(\exists x)(F_1x \,\&\, F_2x)$.

This is read:

it is not the case that there is a book that is open.

Given the quantifier equivalences (see chapter 11), it is unsurprising that there should be a way to capture a universally negative quantifier with an existential quantifier and a shift in the negation. Your knowledge of quantifier equivalences should convince you that (a) could be written this way:

$\neg(\exists x)\neg(F_1x \supset \neg F_2x)$.

But, when Sentential equivalences are exploited, this converts (a) into (b). More will be said about this in chapter 14.

13.6   Existential Quantifiers

Look again at Situation (14). Here is another sentence of Predicate which truly describes it:

$(\exists x)(Fx \,\&\, Hx)$
where: 'Fx' is 'x is a glass'
        'Hx' is 'x is upside-down'.

Here are four ways in which this Situation might be described in natural language:

  (i)   At least one glass is upside-down.
  (ii)   There are upside-down glasses.
  (iii) Some glasses are upside-down.
  (iv)   Glasses are upside-down.

The question is whether the above Predicate language sentence can be considered an adequate translation of (i)–(iv).

There cannot be much argument about the first of these sentences. The Predicate sentence is read:

there is at least one x such that:
x is a glass and x is upside down.

This is somewhat awkward English, but it is recognizably the same as (i). The trouble comes with (ii) and (iii). A good many students of logic baulk at using the Predicate sentence as a translation of these sentences. They think that '∃' is not a good translation for 'some'. I think that it *is* a good translation, and I think I can convince you that I am right, though I can understand the hesitation. I suppose the most graphic way to illustrate the problem is in terms of this Situation.

Situation (15)

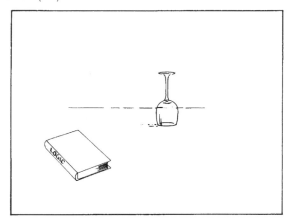

The Predicate sentence remains true of this Situation, but I expect that many of you would hesitate if asked whether:

some glasses are upside-down,

is true. (I will consider only sentence (iii) and 'some'. Sentence (ii) is problematic for precisely the same reasons, so there is no need to consider it separately.)

Since I think that the Predicate sentence is a good translation of the 'some'-sentence, I think that the latter *is* true of Situation (15). Here is my story.

In natural languages such as English, there is a complicated grammatical apparatus of number (singulars and plurals) which you are forced to apply in constructing many sorts of sentence. In particular, most verbs are marked for number, so that it is not usually possible to use a verb which is neutral between singular and plural. Suppose, for example, that a murder has been committed. You believe that the crime was the work of possibly one, but possibly more than one, person in the room. What would your audience think if you said:

(A)   some person in this room is guilty.

Surely, they would think your view was that *one* person committed the crime. Suppose, instead, you said:

(B)   Some persons in this room are guilty.

Plausibly, they would think you had fallen for the multiple murderer theory. Neither (A) nor (B) expresses precisely the thought you have. In either of its grammatical settings, it is bound to create the wrong impression.

You could get around this by using this more complicated sentence:

(C)   some person or persons in this room is guilty,

which could be put this way:

at least one person or persons in this room is guilty.

This seems clear evidence that the word 'some' means 'at least one', and, thus, that it can be translated as '∃'. The impression of singularity or plurality that you get in (A) or (B) does not come from the word 'some', but from the necessity of choosing singular or plural verb forms. Indeed, all that (A) and (B) have is an *impression* of number. If you had the thought expressed by (C), then you would not strictly be wrong if you asserted either (A) or (B), but their use in certain contexts can mislead an audience. For example, if you know (and your audience doesn't) that things are as in Situation (15), then it would be unfair to your audience to say that some glasses are upside-down. It would be unfair, but not untrue. Contrary to some first thoughts, sentences using 'some' are correctly translated by the existential quantifier of Predicate.

What now of the last of our natural language sentences:

(iv)   glasses are upside-down.

This sentence has no obvious quantifier expression. It manages to convey the idea of quantification implicitly, and we must now re-open our discussion of implicit quantifiers.

13.7   Implicit Quantifiers

Here are four sentences. Can you tell which are quantified and, for those that are, whether they are universal or existential?

(i)   The whale is a mammal.
(ii)   The marsupial wrecked the sitting room.
(iii) Gorillas are herbivorous.
(iv)   Logicians are visiting.

The answers are as follows: (i) and (iii) are universal and could be translated, with suitable readings of the predicates, as:

$(\forall x)(Fx \supset Gx)$.

(ii) has a definite description, and does not contain an implicit quantifier in the way that (i) does. (I am being cagey here. You'll see why when we get to section 13.10, though what I have to say there will not undermine present discussion.) Sentence (iv) is existential and can be translated as:

$(\exists x)(Fx \ \& \ Gx)$.

These are my answers, and I suspect that they are yours too. But how do we know such things? After all, these sentences do not contain typical quantifier expressions.

The answer lies partly in features of English to which you are sensitive, and partly in facts about the world which you happen to know. The definite article and plural construction alert us to the *possibility* that what is being spoken of is a whole species. However, these same constructions could very well point to particular items, whether by designation or by existential quantification. What makes the difference is non-linguistic knowledge. For example, we know that being a mammal and being herbivorous are general properties; they tend to be used of every member of a species. In contrast, wrecking the sitting room is hardly likely to be a general property of marsupials.

In the last sentence, the predicate 'visiting' is a clue which alerts us to the fact that this sentence is existential. (After all, one would have to be implausibly unfortunate to be in the position of having all logicians visiting.)

*Exercise 3

Translate the following into Predicate. Write out a dictionary indicating the meaning of each predicate you use.

(a)   There are people unemployed.
(b)   Each violin is handcrafted.
(c)   Apples are seeded.
(d)   Apples were eaten.
(e)   Any train will do.
(f)   Everything I said was to no avail.
(g)   The Dodo is extinct.
(h)   Something in the text was misleading.

13.8   The Accent on Whole Sentences

Our discussion so far has centred around ways of translating from natural language into the elements of Predicate, viz. designators, predicates and quantifiers. In doing this, you learned how to translate some whole sentences of English into Predicate, but the accent has been on the elements. We are now going to shift the emphasis to the translation of whole sentences. In doing so, you will see just how much of natural language can be efficiently expressed in Predicate. The business of this section (and the next) will be conducted largely through examples.

Also, up to now I have explained matters mostly in terms of how things are on my desk. This is a very narrow conception of the world; it hardly needs saying that the resources of natural language are used to describe more complex Situations. Nonetheless, in considering examples from now on, you should not forget that Situations still play a part, even if they are far from drawable. The basic idea of using simple Situations was to apply Predicate directly to the way things are. In translating from natural language into Predicate, you can keep faith with this by using the following procedure.

(I)   Read the natural language sentence carefully and try to visualize the way the world is (the Situation) when this sentence is true.

(II)   Having done this, you can use your knowledge of how Predicate describes Situations to arrive at a translation.

Here we begin with examples.

(i)   If *anyone* was late *he* wasn't seated.

This sentence illustrates how pronouns (italicized) in natural language do the work of variables in Predicate; pronouns, when they're not busy designating, are used to show links between predicates and quantifiers. For example, it would be merely comical if, with respect to (i), you were asked the name of the man who was late and wasn't seated. The function of the word 'he' is not to designate, but to link to the 'one' in 'anyone'. The following hybrid Predicate/English version of (i) makes the point:

(i')   If any x was late x wasn't seated.

In examples like this, the linkage between pronouns is not all that complex, but when sentences involve multiple quantification the complexity increases. We will discuss multiple quantification in the next section. The translation of (i) into Predicate is:

$(\forall x)(Fx \supset \neg Gx)$
where: 'Fx' means 'x was late'
        'Gx' means 'x was seated'.

Strictly, one should read the predicate 'Fx' as 'x was late and a person' since the pronouns imply that the domain of quantification is persons. Or, you could translate the sentence as:

$(\forall x)((Fx \,\&\, Hx) \supset \neg Gx)$

where the extra one-place predicate indicates personhood. In general, such pedantry will not be called for. The object of translation is validity testing, and it is unlikely that you will need to be so fussy to accomplish such translation. You can allow yourself some freedom in choosing domains of quantification, but you should aim to make them unrestricted enough to have a single domain for all the quantifiers in any given sentence you translate. We will return to this topic in chapter 14, since what is at issue will be clearer when we have to test whole arguments.

Suppose you were given the following sentence:

(ii)   All employees are not insured.

How would you translate this into Predicate? There seem to be *two* possibilities. They are as follows:

(a) $\neg(\forall x)(Fx \supset Gx)$,
(b) $(\forall x)(Fx \supset \neg Gx)$.

(From now on I will be more casual about specifying the precise translation of each predicate. It must be insulting to be given a dictionary each time when the meaning of the predicates is so obvious.)

That is, either:

(a)   not all of the employees are insured
or
(b)   all of them, as a group, do not have insurance – none of them are insured.

In short, the English sentence is ambiguous. The two Predicate sentences capture these two readings precisely, but how do you decide which of them is correct?

I suppose most people would think that (a) was the most likely reading, but suppose that you heard the following dialogue.

A: Which persons are not insured?
B: All employees are not insured.

In this case, I think that reading (b) is the most natural. So, the actual context of (ii) would be needed before we could decide the matter completely. This is a lesson we have learned before about natural language, and it is one that cannot be repeated too often. Natural language can be used as precisely as Predicate, or any other artificial language such as a computer language. However, the key to precision in natural language does not lie wholly in the grammatical structure of a sentence; the linguistic and non-linguistic background or context must be taken into account. This may mean that precision is harder to achieve in using natural language, and it certainly means that translation into Predicate can be a subtle task, but it places no limit on the degree of precision obtainable. Since I cannot always supply background to each sentence used as an example or for an exercise, I have had to be careful to choose sentences that do not rely too much on context. This can make the examples somewhat stilted, and for this I apologize.

Notice, by the way, that the difference between (a) and (b) turns on just one thing: the placement of the negation. You could say that the ambiguity of this sentence arises from our being unsure of the *scope* of the negation.

Finally, have a look at:

(iii)   Only pedestrians came this way.

Clearly, it involves universal quantification, such quantification is implicit in the word 'only'. The problem is to say which of the following is the correct translation.

(a) $(\forall x)(Fx \supset Gx)$
(b) $(\forall x)(Gx \supset Fx)$
        where: 'Fx' means 'x is a pedestrian'
                    'Gx' means 'x came this way'.

(You need the dictionary in this case to tell the two possibilities apart.)

That is, does (iii) claim that every pedestrian came this way or that everyone who came this way was a pedestrian? Put this way, the answer is obvious enough: (b) is correct. The word 'only' operates as a universal quantifier, though when you translate this with explicit quantifiers, you have to be careful to get the order of the predicates right.

*Exercise 4

Translate the following into Predicate. Provide a dictionary indicating the meaning of the predicates you use.

(a)   Not only politicians are dishonest.
(b)   The whale is not a fish.
(c)   All that glistens is not gold.
(d)   He is a lucky man that is talented.
(e)   Every apple was not edible.

13.9   Multiple Quantifiers and Other Complexities

There are two sorts of thing to watch out for when translating sentences with multiple quantifiers:

(A)   making sure that you have the right idea of the pronoun linkages,

(B)   taking care over ambiguities of scope.

A.   Pronouns, Variables and Linkages

This is a subject dear to lawyers' hearts. Consider this sentence:

(i)   Anyone who enters into any contract to buy any car is responsible for making sure that it is sound.

Is 'it' connected with the predicate 'contract' or 'car'? When there is more than one quantificational element, there is the possibility of getting the pronoun links wrong, and in this sentence, there are three quantificational elements. In legal documents, a great deal of trouble is taken over just such problems and the result is usually very complex English. In this case, the problem is dealt with fairly easily by replacing 'it' with either 'the contract' or 'the car', but I am sure that you can find numerous examples where matters are not so easy.

In contrast with natural language, linkage ambiguities cannot arise in Predicate. The above sentence would be represented either as:

(i_a) $(\forall x)(\forall y_1)(\forall y_2)(Sxy_1y_2 \supset Rxy_1)$,

or as:

(i_b) $(\forall x)(\forall y_1)(\forall y_2)(Sxy_1y_2 \supset Rxy_2)$,
    where: '$Sx_1y_1y_2$' means 'x_1 enters into y_1 to buy y_2'
             'Rxy' means 'x is responsible for making sure y is sound'.

(Notice that I have assumed the appropriate restricted domains of quantification, so that the sentences are easier to read: x is restricted to persons, y_1 to contracts, and y_2 to cars.)

The occurrence of either y_1 or y_2 in the last variable place of (i_a) or (i_b) is what determines which sort of thing must be sound, cars or contracts.

B. Scope Ambiguities

Suppose you were told:

(ii)   Everyone went home in a car.

This could be understood either as:

(ii_a) Everyone went home in some car or other
Translation $(\forall x)(\exists y)Rxy$,

or as:

(ii_b) Everyone went home in the same car
Translation $(\exists y)(\forall x)Rxy$.

It just isn't possible to construct sentences in Predicate that have ambiguities of scope. You are forced to put the quantifiers in an order, and this order will determine one or other reading of the original English sentence. This is one of the virtues of Predicate.

This precision forces you to determine which reading of the sentence is intended before you translate. You would know right away how to translate (ii_a) and (ii_b), but the original sentence, on its own, gives you no clue. You know that it has two readings, and you know how to represent them in Predicate, but that is all. Why then do speakers use sentences like (ii) to express their thoughts? The answer is that these sentences are usually *not* ambiguous when they are used in a setting; the trouble with (ii) is that you don't know what the setting is. For example, what if it was known that the number of persons was more than 50? It is hardly possible that everyone of these went home in the same car, thus ruling out the second reading. Of course, the same car may have been used many times to ferry them, but, if this had been the case, the original sentence would have been an extremely bad choice to describe it.

Scope in Predicate comes with the ordering of the quantifiers. In natural language, it is signalled in many more ways than this, and quantifier order is not always a sure guide. Indeed, the *order* of the quantifiers in (ii) above was not a sure guide as to their real scope.

Consider these two sentences:

Every mathematician can add two and two.
Any mathematician can add two and two.

They are equivalent, and would both be translated as:

($\forall$x)(Fx $\supset$ Gx).

In this example, the words 'any' and 'every' seem to be merely stylistic variants for universal quantification. However, consider these two sentences:

(iii)   if any pig can fly, John will be surprised,
(iv)   if every pig can fly, John will be surprised.

Most of us would be surprised by a flying pig – we are like John as portrayed in (iii). However, (iv) makes John out to be quite blasé about flying pigs: the existence of one or two flying pigs does not occasion his surprise. Only if they all fly, will he be surprised. In short, these two sentences are *not* equivalent, even though they differ only in that one has 'any' where the other has 'every'. Here are translations of these sentences into Predicate:

(iii')   ($\forall$x)(Fx $\supseteq$ (Gx $\supset$ Ha)).

This sentence is read: every x is such that *if* x is a pig *then* if x can fly, John will be surprised. Or, more idiomatically, it can be read: every x is such that *if* x is a pig and x can fly *then* John will be surprised.

(iv')   ($\forall$x)(Fx $\supset$ Gx) $\supseteq$ Ha.

This is read: *if* every x is such that if x is a pig then x can fly *then* John will be surprised.

I have italicized the main 'if . . . then' connective in each reading, and underlined the main '$\supset$' in each translation. You can see that the only difference between these Predicate sentences is one of scope. The universal quantifier in (iii') has scope over the whole sentence including, of course, the main conditional. In (iv'), the scope of the universal ends before the main conditional; indeed, the conditional has the quantifier within its scope. (This is because the scope of a conditional is the two components it connects. Those components include the quantified sentence in (iv'), but not in (iii').) We can put the point more simply using two terms whose meaning will be obvious: in (iii'), the quantifier has *wide* scope; in (iv'), it has *narrow* scope. (The converse is true of the conditional: it has narrow scope in (iii') and wide scope in (iv').)

The upshot is that 'any' and 'every' do make very different contributions to our understanding of quantified sentences: they lead us to have different expectations of scope. The word 'any' tends to be understood as having wide scope, whereas 'every' has narrow scope. This is clear in (iii) and (iv) where these words both occur *after* 'if', though one does, and the other does not, include the conditional in its scope. You can also see why this difference doesn't show up in sentences like:

> any mathematician can add two and two,
> every mathematician can add two and two.

In such cases, there simply isn't room for a quantifier scope difference, since there is no way to link the variables except by giving the quantifier wide scope.

NOTE   There is another way to express (iii) which is quite revealing. It is:

> if some pig can fly, then John will be surprised.

It would be translated as:

> (iii″) $(\exists x)(Fx \mathbin{\&} Gx) \supset Ha.$

Here the conditional has wide scope just as it does in (iv), but this is achieved by changing the quantifier. As you would expect, (iii″) is equivalent to (iii′). What this shows is that scope difference *can* be important enough to add up to a difference of quantifier.

Exercise 5

Translate into Predicate the sentences below. (Indicate whether the English sentences are ambiguous and allow two translations.)

* *(a)   Everyone likes at least one Vermeer.
* (b)   If John invites someone to the party, he will be unpopular.
* (c)   Any politician can fool all of the people some of the time. (Hint: Take 'some of the time' literally by including times as items to be quantified over.)
* *(d)   If everyone stands up, someone will get wet.
* (e)   Each person is allowed to choose at least one dessert from any menu.
* *(f)   Somebody is always late. (Hint: you can quantify over times to handle 'always'.)

13.10   Definite Descriptions Revisited

Suppose it was claimed (in 1986) that:

The President of the UK is not a woman.

If this remark is addressed to someone ignorant of the politics and constitution of the UK, it might be taken to say that, as a matter of constitutional decree, the office of President is not occupied by a woman. The correct Predicate translation of the sentence would be:

$(\forall x)(Fx \supset \neg Gx).$

It would be like the sentence:

the whale is not a fish,

which has an implicit universal quantifier.

If we changed the example somewhat so that it was:

(i)   the incumbent President of the UK is not a woman

then the universal reading would be ruled out. The addition of the word 'incumbent' seems to force us to see this sentence as more particular than universal. However, there are still two ways in which this sentence might be taken and they point to something very important.

On one reading – a reading available perhaps only to someone ignorant of the constitution of the UK – (i) would be translated as

(a)   ¬Fa

where 'a' is the translation of the definite description 'the incumbent President of the UK'. So understood, the definite description is thought of as playing the role of a designator.

The other reading can be brought out by imagining the following dialogue:

American (*thinking of Mrs Thatcher*):   The incumbent President of the UK is a woman.
Briton: That is not true.

Here, the Briton, who we will presume conversant with the UK constitution, is not denying that a certain person is a woman. Instead, what is denied is that there is an incumbent President of the UK.

These two readings differ in their understanding of the scope of the negation. In the first, the negation goes with the predicate 'is a woman', in the second, something else is negated. But it is here that things get interesting. For, if we translate the sentence as in (a), there isn't any other place to put the negation. 'Fa' is a basic sentence and the scope of any negation will be the whole of it. Also, and no less important, we can hardly treat the definite description as a designator when the point of the sentence in the dialogue is to deny that there is any object answering to the description.

Both of these problems can be dealt with at once if we take up a famous proposal made by Bertrand Russell. He suggested that sentences containing definite descriptions be understood so as to rule out a designating role for definite descriptions. The American's claim:

(ii)   the incumbent President of the UK is a woman,

which, on our previous understanding, was translated as 'Fa' should instead be understood as:

there is exactly one person who is an incumbent President of the UK and that person is a woman.

This sentence involves the numerical quantifier 'there is exactly one' which we discussed in chapter 12. Translation into Predicate is effected by treating this sentence as made up of two interwoven claims:

there is at least one person who . . . AND
there is at most one person who . . . .

The translation is:

(ii′) $(\exists x)[(Fx \,\&\, (\forall y)(Fy \supset x = y)) \,\&\, Gx]$.

This is read: at least one x is such that x is an incumbent President of the UK, and every y which is an incumbent President of the UK is identical to x, and x is a woman.

There is certainly a more complicated translation than 'Fa', but its advantages are numerous. In fact, its very complication offers us something we were looking for: different places in which to insert negation. Thus,

(i)   the incumbent President of the UK is not a woman,

gives us at least *two* relevant Predicate translations, viz.

1   $\neg(\exists x)[(Fx \,\&\, (\forall y)(Fy \supset x = y)) \,\&\, Gx]$,
2   $(\exists x)[(Fx \,\&\, (\forall y)(Fy \supset x = y)) \,\&\, \neg Gx]$.

On the first of them, we have captured precisely what the Briton said to the American: there simply is no such person as the President of the UK. The second is that in which what is denied is not the existence of a unique incumbent President, but merely the fact that the President is a woman. This case is the counterpart of the earlier translation, i.e. '¬Fa'. (There could also be a third negation, if the '¬' was put just before the universal quantifier. The sentence would then claim that there was no *unique* incumbent President. However, this is a less natural denial of (i) than the other two.)

The availability of these translations confirms what we thought originally: that (i) is ambiguous because of uncertainty about the scope of negation. Moreover, this proposal of Russell's, known as the *theory of definite descriptions*, has further useful features.

In our original discussion of definite descriptions, I noted a certain unease about the fact that these expressions contained predicate-like elements that were 'buried' in the designator translation. The element 'a' is hardly a fair summary of the information contained in the phrase 'the incumbent President of the UK'. Russell's proposal offers us a way to display this complexity.

The Main Points of Chapter 13

1   There are two sorts of sentence in Predicate:

(i)   sentences made from PREDICATE(S) and DESIGNATOR(S),
(ii) those made from QUANTIFIER(S) and PREDICATE(S).

Discussion of translation from natural language into Predicate was based on this division.

2   The first task was to isolate natural language candidates for the role of DESIGNATOR. The list included:

(a)   proper names,
(b)   definite descriptions,
(c)   pronouns,
(d)   demonstratives.

Definite descriptions and pronouns play roles other than that of designators, so one must be careful.

3   Having identified natural language expressions which can be translated as designators, it is possible to identify the *predicate frames* which are translated as predicates. A predicate frame results from deleting one or more designating expressions from a natural language sentence and replacing it (them) with variables from Predicate. The final step consists in choosing predicates with the appropriate number of places to serve as translations of the predicate frames.

4   Quantifier expressions in natural language are many and varied. Below are some examples. (Note dual role of 'any'.)

Universal	*Universal and Negative*	*Existential*
Every	No	At least one
Each	None	Some
All	Nothing	There are
Any		Any

In addition, it is often the case that quantification in natural language is conveyed implicitly, i.e. without any of the above sorts of words.

5   In natural language, unlike Predicate, ambiguity of structure is possible. For this reason, you must take care over the intended scope of various expressions, and over the variable-like linkages made by pronouns.

6   Finally, Russell's account of definite descriptions was set out. On this view, definite descriptions are not treated as designators. Instead, the sentences in which they occur are construed as general sentences which combine an existence claim and a uniqueness claim. This can be very useful in cases where there is no item to be designated, even though the sentence with the description is meaningful and true.

NOTE   See Appendix 1, Lesson 13, for further help.

Chapter fourteen

Validity

Our second run through the Strategy is nearly complete. You can speak Predicate or, more accurately, you can write it; you can translate English into it. All you need now is a way to test Predicate arguments for validity. That is the main business of this chapter. Also, since we have already discussed translation into Predicate, we might as well complete the application of the Strategy in this chapter. That is, we will combine the tasks of validating Predicate and natural language arguments.

14.0   What about Truth Tables?

A first thought might be: why not just use the truth tables familiar from Sentential to test validity. Alas, while it would be very nice if we could use them, a little thought will show that Predicate has outgrown them. And I mean this quite literally.

Start with this very simple argument:

> All men are mortal.
> Socrates is a man.
> _____
> Socrates is mortal.

(So well known is this example that its absence from the book would shock logicians and I wasn't willing to do this.)

Translating this into Predicate would give us this:

> $(\forall x)(Fx \supset Gx)$
> Fa
> ___
> Ga.

How would you use truth tables here? The first thing to do is to work out how many different basic sentences there are in this argument. The conclusion counts as one, and so does the second premise. That is, from the perspective of Sentential, these can be treated as, say, P_1 and P_2. But what about the first premise? There do not seem to be *any* basic sentences in it; there is a quantifier and a non-basic *predicate* which is itself made up of two basic predicates. But no basic *sentences* at all. Of course, the whole of this first premise could be treated as, say, P_3, but, in doing this, we would destroy any possibility of showing the argument valid. Its validity quite clearly comes from the structure of elements *within* the quantified sentence. The argument:

$$P_3$$
$$P_1$$
$$\overline{}$$
$$P_2$$

would not be validated by truth tables.

Still, you may think, all is not lost. From our discussion of universal quantification, you know that this premise is like a long conjunction; it is of the form:

$$(Fa \supset Ga) \And (Fb \supset Gb) \And (Fc \supset Gc) \ldots$$

Each of these conjuncts contains basic sentences: you can count six different ones in the display. Unfortunately, that is just the trouble. If there are an infinite number of items in the universe of discourse, there are going to be an *infinite* number of basic sentences hidden (so to speak) in the universally quantified premise. And it would be rash to insist, in our logic, that there are only a finite number of things in the universe. Remember, since we want the logic to apply to mathematical reasoning, numbers must be counted as items, and there is certainly an infinite number of them.

In consequence, when you come to compute the number of rows of the truth table for this argument, you will get:

$$2^\infty, \text{ i.e. } (2 \times 2 \times 2 \ldots \text{ infinitely}),$$

and this is a very large number indeed. Any truth table with that many rows would be unwritable. So, even for the very simple Predicate argument above, the truth table method is no use.

NOTE   It is even worse. You can only think of a universally quantified sentence as equivalent to an infinite conjunction if you also think that everything in the universe could have a designator. However, there are good reasons to think that this is not so. The number of what mathematicians call 'real' numbers is said to be uncountably infinite, and this would preclude their all having designations. (Because the number of possible designators in the universe is 'smaller' than the number of reals, i.e. there is plausibly only a countable infinity of designators.)

14.1 Deductions

We have drawn a blank with truth tables, so you will not be surprised to hear that the next option is to look at the use of deductions. Sentential arguments could be shown to be valid by either method; we have now to see whether deductions can help us with Predicate.

Something that came out of the failure of the truth-table method does give us a reason to be hopeful. To see what I am getting at, reconsider the discussion of the argument about Socrates, and, in particular, the conjunctive expansion of the first premise. The first conjunct in the infinite expansion is:

Fa ⊃ Ga.

This is simply a conditional construction from two basic sentences. If we had this conditional as a premise, then we could use the other premise to reach the conclusion in three quick steps, viz.

1	(1)	Fa ⊃ Ga	Premise
2	(2)	Fa	Premise
1,2	(3)	Ga	1,2 ⊃E

(You may well be a bit rusty on the rules and score-keeping used in deductions. It might be a good idea to have a quick review by skimming through chapter 9.)

So, if we had a rule which allowed us to go from:

(∀x)(Fx ⊃ Gx),

to:

Fa ⊃ Ga,

it would be an easy matter to derive the conclusion. Moreover, there doesn't seem to be any reason why we shouldn't have the rule. Given that it is true that every man is mortal, it is surely true that each designated man is mortal – including Socrates.

With such overwhelming reason in its favour, we are certainly entitled to have a rule of inference that sanctions the move from a universally quantified sentence to one without quantifiers. Such a rule would be a Universal Quantifier Elimination Rule (∀E, for short) and could be used to construct the following deduction.

1	(1)	(∀x)(Fx ⊃ Gx)	Premise
2	(2)	Fa	Premise
1	(3)	Fa ⊃ Ga	1 ∀E
1,2	(4)	Ga	1,2 ⊃E

The only thing that stands in our way is that we haven't yet got the means to formulate the rule in an appropriately *general* way. You remember how careful one has to be about the presentation of the rules. It must not turn out that ∀E is appropriate to the above argument, but not to other more complex arguments. The statement of ∀E and other Predicate rules is the business of the next sections. The point of the present section is to show how rules like ∀E can be combined with the ten from Sentential to give us a way to construct deductions for Predicate language arguments. (Can you guess how many quantifier rules there are? Four. There are two quantifiers, and we will need an Elimination and an Introduction rule for each of them.)

One last point: we will assume that the rules of Sentential do carry over to Predicate. For example, the argument:

Fa ⊃ Ga
Fa
―――――
Ga,

counts as an instance of ⊃ E. We could be more precise about this; we could re-introduce the rules, one by one, having re-defined the notions of basic and non-basic sentence for Predicate. However, having pointed out this assumption, I think we can let matters rest.

14.2 A Notation for Predicate Rules

What we need to display Universal Elimination in the most general way is to represent Predicate arguments in schematic form. Remember that in giving the Sentential rules we used the letters 'A', 'B' and 'C'. These were not themselves sentences, they are rather like the blanks on a questionnaire which have to be filled in with sentences. However, unlike Sentential, Predicate sentences have components which are not sentences. (In saying this I am ignoring logical components such as '⊃'. They are, of course, parts of Sentential sentences, even though they are not themselves sentences. In the schematic presentation of Sentential rules, they were not replaced by schematic letters – they portrayed themselves, and will continue to do so in Predicate rules.)

The required schematic presentation of designators, predicates, and variables is achieved as follows:

(i)   't' will be used as a blank for designators. This letter is chosen because designators are often called *terms* by logicians.

(ii)   'Φ' (Greek phi) will be used as a blank for predicate expressions, however complicated. That is, 'Φ' holds a place for any expression that has at least one free variable in it. Here are some possible substitutions for 'Φ':

Fx, Fx & Hx, Hy ⊃ Rxy, (∀y)(Fy ⊃ Rxy).

Notice that the last of these has a quantifier, but the whole of the expression still counts as a complete predicate expression because of the free 'x' in it. (There can, of course, be multiple occurrences of 'x' as in the second example above.)

(iii) 'v' will be used as the blank for variables. (Subscripts are allowed if needed.) In particular, we can understand:

Φv,

as a place-holder for a predicate with *one* free variable. If you see:

Φv₁v₂,

this means that the predicate has *two* free variables in it.

These conventions will allow us to write out the rules of inference so that they are completely general. For example, the claim that all men are mortal, in Predicate:

(∀x)(Fx ⊃ Gx),

could be a filling for:

(∀v)Φv.

But this same schematic form would serve for:

(∀y)(∃x)((Fy & Hx) ⊃ Rxy).

The variable 'y' takes the place of 'v', and:

(∃x)((Fy & Hx) ⊃ Rxy),

takes the place of 'Φv'.

Notice that the quantifier symbols are treated as place-holders for themselves. They behave in schemata exactly like '⊃' and the other Sentential connectives.

14.3   Universal Quantifier Rules

A.   Universal Quantifier Elimination (∀E)

We can now state the Universal Quantifier Elimination rule that allows the move from every person's mortality to that of Socrates.

(∀v)Φv

Φt

SCORE-KEEPING   The conclusion depends on whatever premises

'(∀v)Φv' depends on, so you have to indicate this on the left-hand side of the line number of 'Φt'. Also, you have to cite the line number of '(∀v)Φv' on the right-hand side of the deduction.

NOTE   We will assume that 't' replaces *all* occurrences of 'v'. *This convention in the formulation of the rule will apply to the other rules unless it is expressly overridden.* The reason for it should be fairly obvious; without it, the following would be an instance of ∀E:

(∀y)(Fy ⊃ Hy)

Fa ⊃ Hy

and we would have a free variable in the conclusion. In essence, this would be a case where a predicate was inferred from a sentence. We cannot make sense of such an inference as valid, since validity requires the preservation of the truth, and a predicate isn't assessable as true or false. The convention that 't' and 'v' replace each other in each and every occurrence will be called the *replacement convention.*

The deduction we constructed for the mortality example, unsurprisingly, turns out to be in line with this rule. However, it would be as well to consider a more complicated example:

All logicians are pedantic.
Everyone who is pedantic is hard to live with.
Fred is not hard to live with.
Therefore, Fred is not a logician.

Translation

(∀x)(Fx ⊃ Gx)
(∀y)(Gy ⊃ Hy)
¬Ha

¬Fa

Deduction

1	(1)	(∀x)(Fx ⊃ Gx)	Premise
2	(2)	(∀y)(Gy ⊃ Hy)	Premise
3	(3)	¬Ha	Premise
1	(4)	Fa ⊃ Ga	1 ∀E
2	(5)	Ga ⊃ Ha	2 ∀E
6	(6)	Fa	Assumption
1,6	(7)	Ga	4,6 ⊃E
1,2,6	(8)	Ha	5,7 ⊃E
1,2,3,6	(9)	Ha & ¬Ha	3,8 &I
1,2,3	(10)	¬Fa	6,9 ¬I

Here we used two applications of the new rule and then introduced 'Fa' as an assumption. This was done because it was obvious that we could use this assumption to derive 'Ha' and this stands in direct contradiction to the third premise. The final line uses this contradiction to derive the wanted conclusion, the negation of the assumption. As you can see from the left of the last line, the conclusion depends only on the original premises since the assumption is discharged by the use of ¬I.

B.   Universal Quantifier Introduction (∀I)

Not all of our reasoning proceeds from the general to the specific; often we use general premises as the basis for general conclusions. Below is an example.

> All jobs worth doing are worth doing well.
> Anything worth doing well is time consuming.
> _____
> All jobs worth doing are time consuming.

Translating this into Predicate, we get

$$(\forall x)(Fx \supset Gx)$$
$$(\forall x)(Gx \supset Hx)$$
$$(\forall x)(Fx \supset Hx).$$

If we proceed using the means at our disposal, we get the beginning of a deduction which looks like this.

1	(1)	$(\forall x)(Fx \supset Gx)$	Premise
2	(2)	$(\forall x)(Gx \supset Hx)$	Premise
1	(3)	$Fa \supset Ga$	1 ∀E
2	(4)	$Ga \supset Ha$	2 ∀E
5	(5)	Fa	Assumption
1,5	(6)	Ga	3,5 ⊃E
1,2,5	(7)	Ha	4,6 ⊃E
1,2	(8)	$Fa \supset Ha$	5,7 ⊃I
	(9)	??	

Here we are stuck. We have established a connection between 'Fa' and 'Ha', just as the conclusion seems to require. But we can hardly jump from this specific connection to the universally general conclusion of the original argument. Then again, perhaps we can.

It is well-known that people are always jumping to general conclusions, and it is no less well-criticized. After all the care we have taken, we cannot allow ourselves a rule which would allow as valid such inferences as this one:

> The butcher on the corner is dishonest.
> Therefore, all butchers are dishonest.

Yet, the earlier argument seems quite different from this blatantly invalid one. If we could capture that difference, we could formulate a rule that would prevent the 'butcher' inference while allowing the earlier one. This requires some further thought.

It is often easier to reason with particular things in mind, even when the reasoning is general in spirit. An instructor of veterinary medicine may well find it easier to get his message across by saying:

> Fido has sweat glands in the pads of his paws.
> Fido has 13 thoracic, 7 cervical and 7 lumbar vertebrae.

In these remarks, 'Fido' is a proper name. Yet, it has a role unlike that of any ordinary proper name: it would be only funny if one of the students in the class asked whose dog Fido was. (I suppose the lecturer would be justified in saying that Fido was everybody's dog.) Names used in this way are called *arbitrary names* because they purport to designate arbitrarily chosen representatives of some collection of things. The idea is that if you want to make a point about, for example, dogs, you can do so by imagining a representative of the species. This representative, however, must be chosen carefully; it must have only characteristics true of any dog chosen at random.

Of course, when proper names are used in this way, we don't actually choose a representative; we just speak as though we have one in mind. That is why it is a gross misunderstanding to wonder to whom Fido belongs. First, there is no specific dog answering to the name, and, second, the point of this use of a name is precisely to exclude non-general features.

Arbitrary names are very closely related to universal quantification. The lecturer could as well have said: 'all dogs . . .' He didn't, presumably because he wanted to make his point in a graphic way; arbitrary names are commonly used for this purpose. (Think of how some instructions for filling up forms use names like 'John Doe'.) However, our present interest is solely in the relationship between arbitrary names and universal quantification. If we could formulate a rule of inference that allowed a universal conclusion only from a premise that had an arbitrary name, this would give us what we need while avoiding 'butcher' inferences.

The first step is to introduce a new category of designator: arbitrary designators. In honour of Fido, we will use 'f' (with subscripts, if needed). This means that terms, items that fill the 't' position, can either be designators like 'a', 'b', 'c' or arbitrary designators like 'f'. In the rule of Universal Elimination, the slot for the conclusion, viz.:

    Φt,

could be filled by something like:

    $Fa \supset Ga$,

or by:

    $Ff \supset Gf$.

We can now state the Universal Quantifier Introduction Rule ($\forall$I).

$$\Phi t$$
$$- - - - - - - -$$
$$(\forall v)\Phi v$$

Where: (i)   't' is an arbitrary designator.
            (ii) 'Φt' does *not* depend on any line in which 't' occurs.

SCORE-KEEPING   In using this rule, '$(\forall v)\Phi v$' depends on whatever 'Φt' depends on, so you put the relevant line number(s) to the left of '$(\forall v)\Phi v$'. To the right, you cite the line number of 'Φt'.

The statement of this rule seems complicated, but a closer look should show that it is really quite straightforward. Condition (i) demands that the designator we are generalizing about is arbitrary. This condition helps to keep out 'butcher' inferences.

Condition (ii) makes sure that we do not smuggle in 'butcher' inferences while using arbitrary designators. If 'Φt' does depend on a line in which 't' occurs, then it may well be the case that the arbitrary name is not so arbitrary after all. Here is a blatant example:

    Rover is a dog with three legs.
    Therefore, all dogs have three legs.

Translation

$$\frac{Ff_1 \ \& \ Gf_1}{(\forall x)(Fx \supset Gx)}$$

'Deduction' (the error is marked in line 5)

1	(1) $Ff_1 \ \& \ Gf_1$	Premise
2	(2) Ff_1	Assumption
1	(3) Gf_1	1 &E
1	(4) $Ff_1 \supset Gf_1$	2,3 $\supset$I
1	(5) $(\forall x)(Fx \supset Gx)$	4 $\forall$I

Of course, I'm sure that you would not have used an arbitrary name in the premise of this argument, since you would have recognized that Rover is hardly an arbitrarily chosen dog. However, not everyone is as clear-thinking as that, so we have to state the rules without loopholes. Condition (ii) rules out this attempted deduction because (4) depends on (1) which has f_1 in it.

The argument we considered earlier, the one about jobs worth doing well, can be shown to be valid by this deduction.

1	(1)	$(\forall x)(Fx \supset Gx)$	Premise
2	(2)	$(\forall x)(Gx \supset Hx)$	Premise
1	(3)	$Ff \supset Gf$	1 $\forall$E
2	(4)	$Gf \supset Hf$	2 $\forall$E
5	(5)	Ff	Assumption
1,5	(6)	Gf	3,5 $\supset$E
1,2,5	(7)	Hf	4,6 $\supset$E
1,2	(8)	$Ff \supset Hf$	5,7 $\supset$I
1,2	(9)	$(\forall x)(Fx \supset Hx)$	8 $\forall$I

Here we introduced an assumption with 'f' in it at line (5). This caused no harm, since it was discharged before we got to the line to which $\forall$I was applied. That is, line (8) is the 'Φt' line with the arbitrary designator, and it depends on lines (1) and (2). Neither of these, however, has 'f' in it, so all the conditions for $\forall$I are met. This is unsurprising. The original premises of the argument were universally general, so we would expect to be able to derive a universal conclusion from them.

Also, notice that I used $\forall$E in lines (3) and (4) to derive sentences with arbitrary designators. This is because I anticipated the need for such designators at the end of the deduction. Had I used 'a' instead of 'f', I would not have been able to finish the deduction. However, if you ever get yourself in that position, you need only go back and change the ordinary designators to arbitrary ones. Just make sure, though, that you do not thereby violate condition (ii). The possibility of such replacement is more significant than it might seem. It is precisely because the deduction up to step (8) could have had any designator in it that it is all right to make the universal claim in step (9). That is, because there were no special assumptions made about the item designated in line (8), there is no reason to doubt the universally general claim in (9).

Just like $\forall$E, $\forall$I requires the replacement convention. That is, 'v' in 'Φv' must replace each and every occurrence of 't' in 'Φt'. However, the need for the convention has a different basis in the case of $\forall$I. For $\forall$E, we required it because we wanted to block the deduction of non-sentences from sentences, since this would not have accorded with our

242   *Validity*

conception of validity as truth preserving. This would not be a problem for ∀I, though, because one always begins with a sentence (with arbitrary names), and adds quantification. So, the question is why do we need the convention to block moves like that from 'Rff' to '(∀y)Rfy'. The following unquestionably *invalid* argument and its supposed deduction provide the answer.

> Everyone resembles themselves.
> Therefore, everyone resembles everyone.

Translation

> (∀x)Rxx
> ―――――――
> (∀x)(∀y)Rxy

'Deduction' (violation of convention is marked)

1	(1)	(∀x)Rxx	Premise
1	(2)	Rff	1 ∀E
1	(3)	(∀y)Rfy	2 ∀I
1	(4)	(∀x)(∀y)Rxy	3 ∀I

Only the replacement convention blocks the construction of a deduction for this invalid argument.

14.4   Existential Quantifier Rules

A.   Existential Quantifier Introduction (∃I)

After the lengthy discussion of ∀I, it will be a relief to get back to a simpler case. The following inference seems obviously valid, and does not need to be hedged about with all sorts of special conditions.

> Tony is late,
> Therefore, there is at least one person late.

The move from the specific to the existentially general is bound to be valid. Or is it?

There is one fly in the ointment. What would you say about this argument?

> Santa Claus does not exist.
> Therefore, there is at least one thing that does not exist.

On the face of it, the conclusion is self-contradictory. Yet I suspect that the premise would be judged true, and the argument seems to follow the same pattern as the one about Tony. To be honest, this example raises a problem that I have so far kept from you: what to do about 'designators' that fail to designate. We can't simply disallow them in Predicate, since the sentence about Santa Claus is a perfectly intelligible natural language claim which we ought to be able to translate into Predicate. For the present, however, I will continue to ignore the mess they make, neither dealing with it, nor sweeping it under the rug. Everything I say now about the existential rules of inference will be applied only to designators which *do* in fact pick out an appropriate item.

The rule of inference for Existential Quantifier Introduction (∃I) follows:

$$\Phi t$$
$$\rule{3cm}{0.4pt}$$
$$(\exists v)\Phi v$$

> Where: it is *not* required that 'v' in 'Φv' replace *every* occurrence of 't'.

SCORE-KEEPING   When using this rule, '(∃v)Φv' depends on whatever 'Φt' depends on, so you put the relevant line number(s) to the left of '(∃v)Φv'. To its right you cite the line number of 'Φt'.

Notice that we have here relaxed the convention about 'v' in 'Φv' replacing all and only occurrences of 't' in 'Φt'. It is worth explaining this.

We can relax the replacement convention for ∃I because, unlike ∀I, the existential rule doesn't generate conclusions 'strong' enough to lead us astray. Here is the premise that we used in discussing the issue with respect to ∀I:

> Everyone resembles themselves
> Translation (∀x)Rxx.

We can use ∀E on this premise to get:

> Rff.

Now, without the replacement convention, ∃I allows the move to any of the following:

> (∃x)Rxx,
> (∃x)Rfx,
> (∃x)Rxf.

Taking the second one as an example, we could use ∃I as a final Introduction step to get:

> (∃y)(∃x)Ryx.

It was this sort of multiple quantification that got us into trouble when ∀I was used without the replacement convention. Here there is no trouble at all. The multiple existential says simply that someone resembles someone, and this certainly is true given that everyone resembles themselves.

Could you have used ∀I instead of ∃I in the final step? Of course, and I chose 'f' in the application of ∀E to allow this possibility. What you would end up with is

$(\forall y)(\exists x)Ryx.$

This says that everybody resembles somebody or other, and this seems a perfectly reasonable consequence of the claim that everybody resembles themselves. What you could never get is the existential on the *outside*, i.e. having wide scope. Try it and you will see that the ∀I replacement convention stops you.

B.   Existential Quantifier Elimination (∃E)

Smith and Jones are sitting at a table in a pub when they are told:

someone at this table is a raffle winner,
Translation: $(\exists x)(Fx \;\&\; Gx).$

Quite clearly, it would be a mistake to conclude from this that Smith is a raffle winner. Equally, it would be a mistake to conclude that Jones is. The original claim is general, and makes no reference to a specific individual. So, if 'a' designates Smith, we would not be justified in inferring:

Fa & Ga.

If *Smith* 'eliminated' the existential quantifier in this way, the inference would be a case more of wishful than of logical thinking.

However, suppose that Smith and Jones know that all raffle winners will be toasted. They can surely conclude from this, and the previous claim, that someone at this table will be toasted. That is, the following is a valid inference.

(a)   Someone at this table is a raffle winner.
       All raffle winners will be toasted.
       Therefore, someone at this table will be toasted.

Translation

$(\exists x)(Fx \;\&\; Gx)$
$(\forall x)(Gx \supset Hx)$
———————————
$(\exists x)(Fx \;\&\; Hx)$

Our task will be to work out a rule for eliminating existential quantifiers so that we can construct a deduction for this argument. But it must be a rule that doesn't involve the sort of wishful thinking that Smith engaged in when he heard that someone at the table was the raffle winner. That is, the rule must not allow inferences from existential claims to claims about known individuals.

Even though the elimination of existential quantifiers cannot be accomplished in the way that Smith thought, there is a useful clue in his reasoning. Suppose that Smith and Jones are both given to wishful thinking. That is, Smith thinks:

Fa & Ga,

and, allowing 'b' to designate Jones, Jones thinks:

Fb & Gb.

Each of them might then reason as follows.

	Smith				*Jones*		
1	(1)	Fa & Ga	Premise	1	(1)	Fb & Gb	Premise
2	(2)	$(\forall x)(Gx \supset Hx)$	Premise	2	(2)	$(\forall x)(Gx \supset Hx)$	Premise
1	(3)	Fa	1 &E	1	(3)	Fb	1 &E
2	(4)	Ga $\supset$ Ha	2 $\forall$E	2	(4)	Gb $\supset$ Hb	2 $\forall$E
1	(5)	Ga	1 &E	1	(5)	Gb	1 &E
1,2	(6)	Ha	4,5 $\supset$E	1,2	(6)	Hb	4,5 &E
1,2	(7)	Fa & Ha	3,6 &I	1,2	(7)	Fb & Hb	3,6 &I
1,2	(8)	$(\exists x)(Fx$ & $Hx)$	7 $\exists$I	1,2	(8)	$(\exists x)(Fx$ & $Hx)$	7 $\exists$I

These two deductions are precisely the same *except* in one respect: where the one on the left has claims about Smith, the one on the right has claims about Jones.

As I said earlier, we cannot condone the move from someone at the table won to Smith won, nor can we condone the inference from someone won to Jones won. All we know is that at least one person won; we don't know who. However, if we did know who it was, then a deduction like those above could be constructed, and it would validate an argument very close to argument (a). It would be just like (a) except for having a non-general premise in place of '$(\exists x)(Fx$ & $Gx)$'.

In this example, it was either Smith or Jones who won. This made it easier to see what is going on, but it isn't essential. Suppose that the number of possible winners was indefinitely large. Still, as long as someone won, a deduction of the above form can be constructed by using a designator of the relevant individual. After all, an existentially quantified claim such as:

$(\exists x)(Fx \ \& \ Gx),$

can be understood as an open-ended disjunction:

$(Fa \ \& \ Ga) \lor (Fb \ \& \ Gb) \lor (Fc \ \& \ Gc) \ldots$

If the existential is true, then somewhere in the disjunction there must be at least one true sentence of the form:

F___ & G___.

Since there is some such sentence, you will be able to use the deduction pattern which is exemplified above in Smith's and Jones's reasoning. All you have to do is to find out what name fills in the '___'.

In view of this, does it really matter for the argument in question whether you know who *actually* won? It would seem not. As long as you know someone won *and* you can construct a deduction that goes from a designator of that individual, *whoever it is*, to the conclusion, you can count yourself as having reached that conclusion simply from the fact that someone won. That is, given:

someone at the table is a raffle winner,

and given that you can construct a deduction FROM:

___ is at the table and is a raffle winner,
AND
all raffle winners will be toasted,

TO:

someone at the table will be toasted,

you can take yourself to have shown how to construct a deduction for the original argument (a), viz.:

Someone at the table is a raffle winner.
All raffle winners will be toasted.
_____

Someone at the table will be toasted.

This is justified because the first premise tells us that there is a person who won, and the deduction shows us how to get from the claim that a *particular* person won to the desired conclusion.

But what are we to make of '___'? We cannot construct deductions with blanks in them. It is meant to be filled in by a designator of the raffle winner. We know that someone won the raffle. We just don't know the name of the winner, and that is why we needed the blank. Does this sound familiar? Why not use an arbitrary designator in place of '___'?

As long as we are careful, we can formulate a rule for Existential Elimination using arbitrary designators and following the reasoning described with '___'. Here is the formulation of the rule for Existential Quantifier Elimination (∃E).

IF you can show that:

(1)   Φt

      – – –

      C

THEN you have shown this:

(2)   (∃v)Φv

      – – – – –

      C

WHERE: (i)   'Φt' is obtained by replacing all and only occurrences of 'v' in 'Φv' by an arbitrary designator 't'. That is, the replacement convention is in force.

  (ii)   C is any sentence of Predicate which does not contain 't'.

  (iii)   C is deduced from 'Φt' without depending on any line containing 't' except, of course, the line where 'Φt' itself is introduced.

SCORE-KEEPING   C in (1) may well have depended on lines besides that of 'Φt'. You must write these dependencies to the left of C in (2). In doing this you do *not* include dependency on the line where 'Φt' was assumed, but you do include the line with '(∃v)Φv'. On the right you cite the line with '(∃v)Φv', the line where 'Φt' is assumed, and the line in (1) where C is deduced.

This is the most complicated of our rules. Since it is easier to see in operation, here is the correct deduction of argument (a) using it.

1	(1)	(∃x)(Fx & Gx)	Premise
2	(2)	(∀x)(Gx ⊃ Hx)	Premise
3	(3)	Ff & Gf	Assumption
2	(4)	Gf ⊃ Hf	2 ∀E
3	(5)	Gf	3 &E
2,3	(6)	Hf	4,5 ⊃E
3	(7)	Ff	3 &E
2,3	(8)	Ff & Hf	6,7 &I
2,3	(9)	(∃x)(Fx & Hx)	8 ∃I
1,2	(10)	(∃x)(Fx & Hx)	1,3,9 ∃E

This deduction contains both stage (1) and stage (2) as described in the rule, but they are squashed together. Stage (1) goes from line (3) to line (9). These constitute a deduction of C which, in this case, is '$(\exists x)(Fx \And Hx)$' from 'Φt' which is 'Ff & Gf'. As the rule says, once you have such a deduction, you are entitled to draw the conclusion C from the original *existential* premise, wiping out any dependency on the assumption made at line (3). Line (10) embodies this move. It re-asserts C, but it no longer depends on the assumption; instead it depends on the existential premise and any other premises used in the deduction of C.

In using arbitrary designators as part of Existential Elimination we have to be very careful. Arbitrary designators were introduced to allow for Universal Introduction, and we must ensure that there is no illicit move from existential to universal quantification. This is where conditions (i)–(iii) come in. I won't stop to justify each of them separately, but, to give you some idea of their importance, consider this argument:

> Something is green.
> Therefore, everything is green.

Translation

$(\exists x)Fx$
$\overline{(\forall x)Fx}$

If it weren't for condition (ii), it would be easy to construct a deduction for this unquestionably invalid argument. Here is how.

1	(1)	$(\exists x)Fx$	Premise
2	(2)	Ff	Assumption
1	(3)	Ff	1,2,2 $\exists$E
1	(4)	$(\forall x)Fx$	3 $\forall$I

The third step is marked to show that it falls short of being a proper application of $\exists$E. The trouble is condition (ii). In this 'deduction', 'Ff' is treated as C, and this violates the requirement that 't' (in this case 'f') must not occur in C.

14.5   Operating with the Rules

The quantifier rules are much more difficult to formulate precisely than the Sentential rules. However, they are not difficult to work with. You will find deductions are often easier in Predicate than in Sentential, and, while you must understand the conditions that effect each quantifier rule, you are not likely inadvertently to violate these conditions. The most appropriate use of a rule in a specific case will probably satisfy the conditions.

In this section, there are three worked out examples followed by Exercises which should help you extend your skill in constructing deductions. Before presenting these examples, however, I have to ask an important question, a question which may have already occurred to you: *what about identity?* In all this talk about quantifier rules, I have so far left out of account any rules for inferences involving this relation. It is easy to see that some such rules are needed. The rules we now have would not help us with even this simple example of a valid argument:

> Mark Twain wrote *Huckleberry Finn*
> Mark Twain is Samuel Clemens.
> Therefore, Samuel Clemens wrote *Huckleberry Finn*.

Translation

> Rab
> $a = c$
> ———
> Rcb

The premises of this argument are non-quantified sentences of Predicate, and they are each different basic sentences when viewed from the perspective of Sentential. So, the fourteen rules we now have would not suffice to validate this argument. In spite of this, I will not stop here to formulate the rules for identity. For reasons you will appreciate, they are more naturally part of the subject matter of the next chapter. Now for some examples.

Example 1

> Some deductions are not easy.
> Anything not easy is a challenge.
> Therefore, some deductions are a challenge.

Translation

> $(\exists x)(Fx \ \& \ \neg Gx)$
> $(\forall y)(\neg Gy \supset Hy)$
> ———
> $(\exists y)(Fy \ \& \ Hy)$

Deduction

1	(1)	(∃x)(Fx & ¬Gx)	Premise
2	(2)	(∀y)(¬Gy ⊃ Hy)	Premise
3	(3)	Ff & ¬Gf	Assumption
2	(4)	¬Gf ⊃ Hf	2 ∀E
3	(5)	¬Gf	3 &E
2,3	(6)	Hf	4,5 ⊃E
3	(7)	Ff	3 &E
2,3	(8)	Ff & Hf	6,7 &I
2,3	(9)	(∃y)(Fy & Hy)	8 ∃I
1,2	(10)	(∃y)(Fy & Hy)	1,3,9 ∃E

At line (3) we made the assumption necessary for the first stage of Existential Elimination. Using the other rules, we finally got line (9) which depends on the assumption and the universal premise. Since line (9) does not contain 'f', it can count as C in the Existential Elimination rule. All that is needed is to make that explicit in line (10). Here we are entitled to re-assert the sentence in line (9) as depending on lines (1) and (2).

Example 2

> John likes something made of chocolate.
> Everything made of chocolate is fattening.
> Anything fattening is not good for you.
> Therefore, John likes something that is not good for him.

Translation

$$(∃x)(Fx \& R_1ax)$$
$$(∀x)(Fx ⊃ Gx)$$
$$(∀x)(∀y)(Gx ⊃ ¬R_2xy)$$
$$\overline{(∃x)(R_1ax \& ¬R_2xa)}$$

Where   'Fx' is 'x is made of chocolate'
               'R_1xy' is 'x likes y'
               'Gx' is 'x is fattening'
               'R_2xy' is 'x is good for y'.

NOTE   In the third premise, we have an interesting case. What is the function of 'you'? As a pronoun it could be used to designate the addressee of the remark, but it is unlikely that this is its function here. After all, it isn't clear who the addressee is. A more reasonable interpretation is that it is used as a mark of generality, rather as one uses 'one'. As such it is understood as implicitly universal and that explains the second universal quantifier in the translation. Note, additionally, that the domains of quantification have been restricted to 'things' for x and 'persons' for y.

Deduction

1	(1)	$(\exists x)(Fx \,\&\, R_1ax)$	Premise
2	(2)	$(\forall x)(Fx \supset Gx)$	Premise
3	(3)	$(\forall x)(\forall y)(Gx \supset \neg R_2xy)$	Premise
4	(4)	$Ff \,\&\, R_1af$	Assumption
2	(5)	$Ff \supset Gf$	2 $\forall$E
3	(6)	$(\forall y)(Gf \supset \neg R_2fy)$	3 $\forall$E
3	(7)	$Gf \supset \neg R_2fa$	6 $\forall$E
4	(8)	Ff	4 $\&$E
2,4	(9)	Gf	5,8 $\supset$E
2,3,4	(10)	$\neg R_2fa$	7,9 $\supset$E
4	(11)	R_1af	4 $\&$E
2,3,4	(12)	$R_1af \,\&\, \neg R_2fa$	10,11 $\&$I
2,3,4	(13)	$(\exists x)(R_1ax \,\&\, \neg R_2xa)$	12 $\exists$I
1,2,3	(14)	$(\exists x)(R_1ax \,\&\, \neg R_2xa)$	1,4,13 $\exists$ E

Here line (4) is the assumption needed for Existential Elimination. The steps from (4) to (13) are those necessary to show that the conclusion follows from the premises and the assumption. Having established this, and given that the conclusion does not itself contain 'f', we are entitled to re-assert the conclusion in line (14). However, as per the rule for Existential Elimination, this line depends on (1) and the other premises and no longer on (4). Thus, it is only in line (14) that the conclusion of the argument is shown to follow from the originally given three premises.

Example 3

> Somebody kissed everybody at the party.
> Therefore, everybody at the party was kissed by somebody or other.

Translation

$$(\exists x)(\forall y)Rxy$$
$$\overline{(\forall y)(\exists x)Rxy}$$

(Notice that, in translating this argument, simplifying assumptions were made about the domain of quantification. There is no need to include predicates such as 'x is a person' and 'x was at the party' when simpler translation with restricted domains of quantification suffices for showing validity.)

Deduction

1	(1)	$(\exists x)(\forall y)Rxy$	Premise
2	(2)	$(\forall y)Rf_1y$	Assumption
2	(3)	Rf_1f_2	2 $\forall$E
2	(4)	$(\exists x)Rxf_2$	3 $\exists$I
1	(5)	$(\exists x)Rxf_2$	1,2,4 $\exists$E
1	(6)	$(\forall y)(\exists x)Rxy$	5 $\forall$I

In this deduction, we make the assumption at line (2) as the first stage in Existential Elimination. This assumption is then stripped of its universal quantifier (line (3)) and the existential quantifier is re-introduced at line (4). This is a most important line. It contains no occurrence of 'f_1', so it can legally count as C in the $\exists$E rule. But it also has the existential quantifier in the inside position and this is what the conclusion requires. Line (5) is the final stage in Existential Elimination. It confirms our right to assert the sentence in line (5) as the consequence of the original existential premise, and that is why we are allowed to say that line (5) depends on (1) and no longer on (2). The final line applies Universal Introduction to line (5). This is perfectly legal; line (5) depends only on line (1) and there is no occurrence of 'f_2' in line (1). In effect, the last line merely re-introduces the universal quantifier that was dropped in line (3), but the quantifier is now on the outside as required.

What would happen if we tried to deduce the converse of the above? That is, what would happen if we tried to construct a deduction for the following argument?

> Everyone at the party was kissed by someone or other.
> Therefore, someone kissed everyone at the party.

This is a blatantly invalid argument; the premise guarantees that a lot of kissing took place, but it does *not* point to one particular person responsible for all of it. For this reason, you would expect the rules to block any deduction in this case, and that expectation is not disappointed. Here is the beginning of an attempted deduction.

1	(1)	$(\forall y)(\exists x)Rxy$	Premise
1	(2)	$(\exists x)Rxf_1$	1 $\forall$E
3	(3)	Rf_2f_1	Assumption

At this point the deduction cannot proceed further. What is wanted is '(∀y)Rf₂y', but you cannot use ∀I to get it. Because line (3) depends on itself (it is an assumption) and contains 'f₁', you are not allowed to use ∀I.

Exercise 1

Construct deductions for each of the following:

*(a) (∀x)Fx ⊢ (∃x)Fx
 (b) (∃x)(∃y)Rxy ⊢ (∃y)(∃x)Rxy
 (c) (∀x)(Fx ∨ Gx), (∀x) ¬Gx ⊢ (∀x)Fx
*(d) (∀x)(Fx ⊃ Gx), (∃x)Fx ⊢ (∃x)Gx.

Exercise 2

Translate the following arguments into Predicate and show them to be valid by constructing the appropriate deduction.

 (a) All cereals are healthy.
      Anything healthy isn't tasty.
      Therefore, no cereal is tasty.
*(b) Any lie is immoral.
      Some lies are a kindness.
      Therefore, some kindnesses are immoral.
 (c) New York always has hot summers.
      Any place that always has hot summers is not a place I would
      live in.
      Therefore, I would not live in New York.
*(d) Nigel borrowed *War and Peace* from Inga.
      Nigel returned every book he borrowed from anyone.
      Therefore, Nigel returned *War and Peace* to Inga.
 (e) All holidays are disappointing.
      Nothing disappointing depresses Susan.
      Therefore, any holiday does not depress Susan.

14.6 Logical Truth and Vanishing Premises

Some sentences of Sentential were tautologies, their truth tables had T in every row. For example, the following is a very simple tautology:

P ⊃ P.

Using '⊨' we were able to indicate this by writing:

⊨ P ⊃ P.

The double-bar turnstile says that the truth of the sentence(s) on the left *impose(s)* truth on the sentence on the right. It is this property that justifies its use when the set of sentences on the left are the premises of a valid argument and the sentence on the right is the conclusion. When there are no sentences on the left, as in the above example, we are forced to understand it as saying that *no sentences at all* are required to impose truth on the right-hand sentence. That is, the sentence is true in and of itself, its truth is self-imposed or *necessary*. In Sentential, the only sentences that are like this are tautologies and that is why the above use of the double-bar turnstile is a convenient way to indicate that a sentence is a tautology.

Also, you will remember this sort of assertion:

⊢P ⊃ P.

The single-bar turnstile asserts that the sentence(s) on the left allow(s) the construction of a deduction of the sentence on the right. More pedantically, it asserts that there is a deduction in which the right-hand sentence is the last line, and in which this last line depends on the line(s) containing the sentences on the left. In the above case, there are no sentences on the left. Hence, what is claimed is that there is a deduction in which the above sentence is the last line, and in which this last line depends on no previous line. Here is such a deduction.

1	(1)	P	Assumption
	(2)	P ⊃ P	1,1 ⊃I

Though we haven't actually proved it, it is provable that every assertion made about sentences in Sentential with the double-bar turnstile can be matched by an assertion with the single-bar turnstile (and vice versa). In every case in which a set of sentences imposes *truth* on another sentence, we can construct a *deduction* of this latter sentence using those in the former set, and vice versa.

Unsurprisingly, then, when the set of sentences on the left is *empty*, as in the above cases, we would still expect the truth turnstile to be assertible whenever the deduction turnstile is (and vice versa); and this is precisely how it turns out in Sentential. But what about Predicate?

The only way we have of showing an argument valid is by constructing a deduction. Thus, if you did EXERCISE 1(a) above you are now sure that:

(∀x)Fx ⊢ (∃x)Fx.

Does this entitle you to assert the following?

(∀x)Fx ⊨ (∃x)Fx.

That is, does the existence of a deduction in Predicate entitle you to assert that the premises of the deduction impose truth on its conclusion? Of course. What would have been the point of my long explanations of the quantifier rules if this wasn't so? Strictly speaking all of this is informal, we haven't the advanced logical machinery needed to prove it, but you can take my word for it.

Suppose now we were to construct a Predicate deduction which had no premises at all? This is easily done.

1	(1)	(∀x)Fx	Assumption
1	(2)	Fa	1 ∀E
1	(3)	(∃x)Fx	2 ∃I
	(4)	(∀x)Fx ⊃ (∃x)Fx	1,3 ⊃I

This deduction entitles us to assert:

⊢(∀x)Fx ⊃ (∃x)Fx,

and, following our discussion above, we are also entitled to assert:

⊨(∀x)Fx ⊃ (∃x)Fx.

But what are we to make of this assertion? Strictly, it says that this conditional imposes truth on itself, it cannot but be true. However, unlike such sentences in Sentential, it is not a tautology. This is because the method of truth tables is not applicable to the quantified sentences of Predicate, and a tautology is, by definition, a sentence whose truth table has T in every row.

What we need is a notion of a sentence which cannot but be true even though it is not a simple tautology. Such sentences will be called *logical truths*.

Logical truths can be very useful. For instance, in chapter 11, we discussed the relationship between the universal and existential quantifiers and came to the (informal) conclusion that '(∀x)' means the same as '¬(∃x)¬'. If we can construct a deduction to show that:

⊢(∀x)Fx ≡ ¬(∃x)¬Fx,

then by our earlier reasoning this equivalence will be counted as a logical truth. We will have proven something that we took on trust. Here is how to do it.

First, think of the task as broken down into two smaller ones, viz. showing that:

(i)   ⊢ (∀x)Fx ⊃ ¬(∃x)¬Fx
       AND
(ii)   ⊢ ¬(∃x)¬Fx ⊃ (∀x)Fx.

It is easier to see what you are doing in each of these and they can be put back together at the end by ≡I. The deductions presented consecutively, and with the stages indicated, are as follows.

	1	(1)	(∀x)Fx	Assumption
	2	(2)	(∃x)¬Fx	Assumption
	3	(3)	¬Ff	Assumption
	1	(4)	Ff	1 ∀E
	1,3	(5)	Ff & ¬Ff	3,4 &I
	3	(6)	¬(∀x)Fx	1,5 ¬I
	2	(7)	¬(∀x)Fx	2,3,6 ∃E
	1,2	(8)	(∀x)Fx & ¬(∀x)Fx	1,7 &I
	1	(9)	¬(∃x)¬Fx	2,8 ¬I
(i)		(10)	(∀x)Fx ⊃ ¬(∃x)¬Fx	1,9 ⊃I
	11	(11)	¬(∃x)¬Fx	Assumption
	12	(12)	¬Ff	Assumption
	12	(13)	(∃x)¬Fx	12 ∃I
	11,12	(14)	(∃x)¬Fx & ¬(∃x)¬Fx	11,13 &I
	11	(15)	¬¬Ff	12,14 ¬I
	11	(16)	Ff	15 ¬E
	11	(17)	(∀x)Fx	16 ∀I
(ii)		(18)	¬(∃x)¬Fx ⊃ (∀x)Fx	11,17 ⊃I
		(19)	[(∀x)Fx ⊃ ¬(∃x)¬Fx] &	
			[¬(∃x)¬Fx ⊃ (∀x)Fx]	10,18 &I
		(20)	(∀x)Fx ≡ ¬(∃x)¬Fx	19 ≡I

This is the longest deduction we have had, and it repays study. As is so often the case, the secret of success lies in the assumptions made. In the first stage, we assume the antecedent of the conditional (i), the conclusion without its initial negation, and '¬Ff' which is needed for Existential Elimination. The strategy is to get a contradiction (line (5)) and blame the assumption in line (1). At this point, Existential Elimination can be applied to discharge the '¬Ff' assumption. By re-using the assumption in line (1), we can get a second contradiction (line (8)) and this is now blamed on the assumption in line (2). The result is '¬(∃x)¬Fx' depending on line (1), so we can discharge all assumptions to get the conditional in line (10). This completes stage (i).

The second stage requires the assumption of the antecedent of (ii) and the assumption of '¬Ff'. By Introducing an existential quantifier, we get '(∃x)¬Fx' and this contradicts the first assumption. Negation Introduction is effected on '¬Ff' giving us '¬¬Ff', i.e. 'Ff'. Since this last sentence depends only on line (11) which does not contain 'f', we can Introduce a universal quantifier to get '(∀x)Fx'. The deduction is then completed by discharging the assumption at line (11) to get (ii), and then putting (i) and (ii) together to get line (20) by Equivalence Introduction.

Exercise 3

Construct deductions to show the following are logical truths.

*(a)   (∀y)Fy ≡ (∀x)Fx
 (b)   (∃x)Fx ≡ (∃y)Fy

Note: these two should convince the most pedantic of you that I was right when I claimed that the choice of letter in a quantified sentence does not affect its content.

*(c)   [(∀x)(Fx ⊃ (∀y)(Gy ⊃ Rxy))] ⊃ [(∀x)(∀y)((Fx & Gy) ⊃ Rxy)]
 (d)   [(∀x)(Fx ⊃ P)] ⊃ [(∃x)Fx ⊃ P]

Note: This shows something about scope. Look back to chapter 13, where John's surprise about pigs' flying abilities was discussed.

 (e)   (∃x)Fx ≡ ¬(∀x)¬Fx

14.7   Predicate, Rules and Algorithms

Truth tables are an effective and mechanical way to decide the validity of Sentential arguments; they provide an algorithm for validity. Constructing a deduction in Sentential seems altogether different. To see how to proceed in a deduction can require considerable thought. Also, if the argument you are working on is invalid, you will never be able to construct a deduction. Yet, you would not know how to distinguish this case from one in which the argument is valid, but the construction of its deduction is beyond your ability. The deduction method seems non-effective and non-mechanical.

However, as I pointed out in chapter 9, this appearance is deceptive. Though it is beyond the scope of this book to prove it, the deduction method for Sentential is, in principle, mechanical and effective. For any given argument, valid or not, you can mechanically go through every possible application of rules to the premises, generating thereby every possible deduction. (This claim does not directly apply to the particular set of rules used in this book. Special provision must be made for repetitive introduction rules like &I and VI. However, the general point about rules of deduction remains true.) There will be a no doubt large but *finite* number of these, so all you have to do is systematically search through them. If one is a deduction of the conclusion, the argument is valid; if there is no such deduction, then the argument is invalid.

Crucial to this procedure working are:

(i)   the systematic application of rules to any given set of premises generates only a finite number of possible deductions;

(ii) the rules suffice to construct a deduction for any valid argument of Sentential, they are *complete*.

Of course, we do not go about constructing deductions in this way. It would take a great deal of time and would be tedious beyond belief. Instead, we exercise our ingenuity in examining the premises and the rules. With sufficient skill, we can see how to construct the deduction for a valid argument without going through too many detours. Nonetheless, it is worth your knowing that, in respect of Sentential, rules can be shown to constitute an algorithm for validity, even if it is only in principle and not in practice. It is worth your knowing this partly because matters are different with respect to Predicate.

It can be shown that the application of rules to Predicate language arguments cannot be arranged so as to constitute an algorithm for validity. The skilful use of rules is a necessity and not merely a convenience. Further, the reason for the difference between Sentential and Predicate has nothing to do with completeness. It has been demonstrated that a deduction can be provided, using the fourteen rules, for every valid argument of Predicate. The problem is not the completeness of the rules, but the fact that there is no guarantee of a *finite* number of possible deductions for any given set of premises. Since we cannot depend on finiteness here, we cannot describe an algorithm which asks us to check over every possible deduction to see if there is one that meets our requirements. Remember, an algorithm must be a procedure with a finite number of steps.

Nor is this all. Logicians have been able to show, not only that the deduction method is not an algorithm, but that *there cannot be any algorithm for validity in Predicate*. This is a very interesting result. It means that in developing a sufficiently rich language – Predicate – to give the Strategy some hope of dealing with natural language arguments, the possibility of an algorithm for validity has disappeared. I suppose some of you might think this an unfortunate result for the Strategy, but I urge you to reconsider. It is only because of the Strategy that we are in a position to appreciate this fact about natural language arguments. Our patient working through the Strategy has helped us to discover that natural language arguments of a certain degree of complexity cannot be tested for validity by any algorithmic procedure.

The Main Points of Chapter 14

1 We first showed why truth tables could not be used to decide the validity of Predicate arguments. The obvious next move is to consider the method of deduction.

2 A notation for expressing the Quantifier Rules was then introduced. This included schematic presentations of variables and predicates.

3 The four Quantifier Rules were presented and justified as truth preserving.

4 Since Predicate does not allow us to use truth tables, there are no Predicate tautologies except in the trivial sense of sentences of Sentential which we count as incorporated into Predicate. However, there are sentences of Predicate which cannot but be true, since they are deducible from *no* premises or assumptions. These are called *logical truths*. In calling sentences which are deducible from no premise or assumptions logical *truths*, we depended on the fact that the Quantifier Rules are wholly truth preserving. In more advanced logical texts, this fact, called *soundness*, can be demonstrated in detail.

5 Though we haven't the tools needed to prove it, Predicate is *complete*, every logical truth is deducible. In this sense, Predicate is just like Sentential. However, Predicate differs from Sentential in an important respect: there can be no algorithm for validity in Predicate, whereas both truth tables and deduction are algorithms for validity in Sentential. This lack of any possible decision procedure for Predicate can be demonstrated, but, as with soundness and completeness, you should consult the Reading List if you want to track down the advanced texts which contain such demonstrations.

NOTE   See Appendix 1, Lesson 14, for further help.

Chapter fifteen

Identity, Problems and Prospects

Using Predicate in the Strategy has allowed us to increase the scope of logical methods. The combined resources of Sentential and Predicate allows us to express and, within interesting limitations, evaluate many of the complex and subtle arguments of natural language. The purpose of this chapter is to give you some idea of the problems that remain. As in chapter 10, we must search out arguments which are intuitively valid, but whose validity does not seem capturable in Predicate. Having done this, I will sermonize (briefly) on the nature of, and prospects for, further developments in languages of logic.

15.0   Identity: The Rules

The first thing to do is to remove the self-imposed limitation I placed on deductions in the last chapter. Until we are provided with deduction rules for the identity relation, the vast range of arguments that use this relation will be beyond our method of validation. Remember, identity allows the expression in Predicate of such sentences as the following:

> At least two sailors jumped ship.
> Samuel Clemens is Mark Twain.
> Everyone other than Jim was early.
> Three boats sank in the Fastnet Race.

In any case in which it figures in the expression of a premise or conclusion, we are going to need some deduction rules to deal with the contribution it makes to the argument. In fact, as you will be completely unsurprised to hear, we are going to need precisely two rules for identity: an Introduction rule and an Elimination rule.

Why did I wait until this chapter to present these rules? The correct rules for identity in Predicate are easy to formulate and no less easy to justify as truth-preserving. However, certain features of these rules impose limitations on the sorts of natural language arguments that can be accommodated. In other words, the first problems for Predicate are revealed by the rules we need to handle identity. For this reason, I thought it better to tell the whole story about identity here in the chapter where problems are surveyed.

A.   Identity Introduction (=I)

When we first discussed identity, there was something tediously uncontroversial that could be said with it: things are identical to themselves. This simple truth is the basis for the Identity Introduction Rule (=I).

At any stage in a deduction you can write:

t = t

WHERE: this line depends on no line at all.

SCORE-KEEPING   To the left you write nothing. On the right you cite only the line number of that line itself and '=I'.

Remember, in our earlier discussion of identity, I pointed out that:

everything is identical to itself,

was very much like a tautology. That is, it seems to be a truth based on our understanding of the logical structure of a sentence, rather than on any fact about the world. In Predicate, this sentence is translated as:

(i) $(\forall x)(x = x)$.

Is it a tautology? In view of our discussions of truth tables and Predicate, you know that it can't strictly speaking be a tautology. A tautology is a sentence whose truth table shows the value true no matter what truth value its component sentences have. But we know that no truth table can be constructed for (i). As with those sentences of Predicate which can be deduced from no premises at all, (i) would seem to be a logical truth. Here is a deduction which makes this surmise official.

1   f = f   1 =I
2   $(\forall x)(x = x)$ 1 $\forall$I

Given the rule for =I, '$(\forall x)(x = x)$' in (2) has been deduced from no premises or assumptions. Hence, it takes its place as a logical truth along with those discussed in chapter 14.

B.   Identity Elimination (=E)

There isn't too much you can do with =I on its own, though we need it for the completeness of the set of rules. Matters are quite different with the Elimination rule. It is no less easy to grasp, but it is exceedingly useful in constructing deductions.

The basis for the Elimination rule is this: suppose something is true of a person called 'Jim', and it happens that Jim is identical to James. Then isn't it reasonable to infer that whatever is true of Jim is true of James? Of course. In formal dress, the Identity Elimination Rule ($=$E) follows.

Φt_1

$t_1 = t_2$

$- - - -$

Φt_2

Where: 'Φt_2' is got from 'Φt_1' by replacing some or all occurrences of 't_1' by 't_2'.

SCORE-KEEPING   'Φt_2' depends on whatever 'Φt_1' and '$t_1 = t_2$' depend on. The line numbers of these dependencies are written to the left. On the right you indicate the line numbers of 'Φt_1' and '$t_1 = t_2$'.

It is easy to see that this rule gives us a deduction for the argument considered in chapter 14, viz.:

> Mark Twain wrote *Huckleberry Finn*
> Mark Twain is Samuel Clemens.
> Therefore, Samuel Clemens wrote *Huckleberry Finn*.

Translation

Rab

a = c

―――――

Rcb

Deduction

1	(1)	Rab	Premise
2	(2)	a = c	Premise
1, 2	(3)	Rcb	1,2 =E

A more challenging example is below.

> J. Mill was the father of J. S. Mill.
> Nobody is their own father.
> Therefore, J. Mill is not J. S. Mill.

Translation

Rab

$(\forall x)(\neg Rxx)$

―――――

$a \neq b$

Deduction

1	(1)	Rab	Premise
2	(2)	$(\forall x)(\neg Rxx)$	Premise
2	(3)	$\neg Raa$	2 $\forall$E
4	(4)	$a = b$	Assumption
1,4	(5)	Raa	1,4 =E
1,2,4	(6)	Raa & $\neg Raa$	3,5 &I
1,2	(7)	$a \neq b$	4,6 $\neg$I

On the *assumption* that J. Mill is J. S. Mill, then J. Mill is the father of J. Mill, that is, that he is the father of himself. This, however, leads to the contradiction in line (6). In turn, this allows us to discharge the assumption by introducing its negation, and this is just the conclusion we are looking for.

15.1 Problems with Designators

Each of these rules works perfectly well within Predicate, and each of them contributes to our understanding of natural language arguments. However, there are cases where we run into trouble.

Children would applaud us, but I take it as obvious that we do not want the rules of logic to make the following a logical truth:

> there is a Santa Claus.

Yet, as things stand, we should show this to be a logical truth by treating 'a' as 'Santa Claus' in the following deduction

1	$a = a$	=I
2	$(\exists x)(x = a)$	1 $\exists$I

The conclusion depends on no premises, so it counts as a logical truth. What has gone wrong, of course, is that we had no business in using a designator for Santa Claus in the first place. When the rule of Identity Introduction was given, this restriction should have been made explicit. If we agree that any designator is assumed genuinely to refer, if this is part of the understanding with which we use Predicate, then you could not get started on the deduction given above.

Does this solve the problem? Unfortunately, it does not. The trouble is that we all understand claims using names like 'Santa Claus', so we would hope that the logic of the Predicate language would allow for this. The whole point of Predicate is to give us a way to represent the structure of natural language sentences, so we can scarcely rest content if we simply rule certain sentences out of court.

NOTE   You might think that the use of =I creates problems even when we know that a name designates. Take 'b' to be a designator of yourself. Unlike Santa Claus, you exist. Therefore there should be no problem with the above deduction using 'b'. However, the result of the deduction is that the claim of your existence comes out as a logical truth. Surely, however self-centred we are, we do not think that our existence is guaranteed by the laws of logic.

This second problem is less difficult to deal with than the one about 'Santa Claus'. It does sound strange to say that logic guarantees our existence – that the sentence asserting our existence is a logical truth. However, if we insist that any proper use of Predicate and its rules begins with the assumption that designators must designate, then it is less puzzling that Predicate can be used to show that a designated item exists as a matter of logical truth. It is not puzzling to be told that:

> on the assumption that 'b' designates something, there is something that it designates,

is a logical truth. Since the existence assumption lies behind the use of every designator of Predicate (while we have rule of =I as stated above), it is unsurprising that the '$(\exists x)(x = b)$' comes out as true in virtue of the workings of Predicate.

You might think that we could take a liberal attitude toward names like 'Santa Claus' by thinking of them as designating fictional entities. This would work well enough to allow us to construct deductions for arguments like this:

> Santa Claus lives at the North Pole.
> The North Pole is a cold place.
> ───────────────────────────
> Santa Claus lives at a cold place.

and that might seem enough. But here you must be careful. The sort of case in which such liberality could lead to trouble is with sentences such as:

> Sherlock Holmes does not exist.

This asserts something perfectly intelligible; indeed, you probably think it true. Yet, in using Predicate with a liberal attitude toward fictional entities, the most straightforward translation would yield:

> $\neg(\exists x)(x = a)$.

That is, it is not the case that there is anything such that it is identical to a. The trouble with this can be graphically illustrated by applying $\exists$I to the designator in it:

$(\exists y)\neg(\exists x)(x = y)$.

This says, in effect, that there is something not identical to anything, and this is of course absurd, given that everything is identical to itself. Naturally we don't want this as a Predicate consequence of the sensible and true sentence 'Sherlock Holmes does not exist.'

What are we to do about the translation of natural language sentences with so-called 'empty' (non-designating) names? There are two courses of action open. The first is to allow them to be translated as designators, but to change the rules of identity and quantification so that we do not get into trouble. This is a course of action which you can follow up using the Reading List. The second course is less drastic.

It has seemed to many that here is a place to think again about definite descriptions. Remember that we were able to use Russell's proposal for definite descriptions to help us with such sentences as:

the President of the UK is not a woman.

The Russellian suggestion is that we translate sentences such as:

the President of the UK is a woman,

as:

$(\exists x)((Fx \ \& \ (\forall y)(Fy \supset x = y)) \ \& \ Gx)$,

so that we can insert the negation in one of two places depending upon the correct construal of the original natural language sentence. And, crucially for the present subject, one of these negated sentences answers to the construal in which it is claimed that there is no such item as 'the President of the UK'.

Applying Russell's suggestion to proper names in natural language, we could treat, say, 'Santa Claus' as an abbreviation of a definite description, perhaps:

the man in the red suit and white beard who comes down the chimney with presents at Christmas.

If 'Santa Claus' is short for some such description, then it is easy enough to see that translation into Predicate need not involve using 'Santa Claus' as a designator at all; treat it like 'the President of the UK'. This blocks the deduction that 'shows' the existence of Santa Claus to be a logical truth, and it allows us a way to deny his existence without descending into contradictions. All you have to do is to put a negation in front of the claim that there is a man in a red suit and white beard ... The literature on the subject of proper names and definite descriptions is vast. In fact, Russell's proposal has come in for considerable criticism even as an account of definite descriptions. See the Reading List at the end of the book for further guidance.

15.2 Problems with Predicates: Thoughts

It was $=$I that brought out the problem with designators, and it is $=$E that we must look at next. Here is a story which will serve as a background to our next example.

> Louise believes that George Eliot wrote *Silas Marner* because she read the book in school and owns a copy of it. However, never having studied the historical background, it never occurs to her that George Eliot is Mary Ann Evans. Indeed, so convinced is she of the gender of the author of *Silas Marner*, that she would think it a silly question if she were asked whether Mary Ann Evans wrote the book.

I take it that this story is perfectly plausible. What then are you to make of the following argument?

> Louise believes that George Eliot wrote *Silas Marner*.
> Louise does not believe that Mary Ann Evans wrote it.
> Therefore, George Eliot is not Mary Ann Evans.

The obvious translation of this into Predicate gives

$Rabc_1$ where: 'a' is 'Louise', 'b' is 'George'
$\neg Racc_1$ 'Eliot', 'c' is 'Mary Ann Evans'
          and 'c_1' is '*Silas Marner*'.
_____

$b \neq c$

And it is easy to show this valid by following deduction.

1	(1)	$Rabc_1$	Premise
2	(2)	$\neg Racc_1$	Premise
3	(3)	$b = c$	Assumption
1,3	(4)	$Racc_1$	1,3 $=$E
1,2,3	(5)	$Racc_1 \ \& \ \neg Racc_1$	4,5 &I
1,2	(6)	$b \neq c$	3,5 $\neg$I

But, given the plausibility of the story, our intuition is clearly that the premises of the original natural language argument are true and the conclusion false. Louise does have those beliefs, so do many others. Yet George Eliot *is* Mary Ann Evans.

What has gone wrong? The source of the trouble is the translation of the premises. In each case, the phrase 'believes that' was treated as a three-place relation between Louise, George Eliot (or Mary Ann Evans) and *Silas Marner*. This came about because, by our usual procedure, a predicate frame is isolated from a sentence by substitution of variables for designators. This procedure yields the predicate frame:

$$x_1 \text{ believes } x_2 \text{ wrote } x_3,$$

for both of the premises. The trouble is that believing seems not to be a simple relationship between persons and things. Louise has a belief relation to George Eliot, but not to Mary Ann Evans even though these are one and the same individual. Surely, if Louise was standing next to George Eliot, then she would have been standing next to Mary Ann Evans, and the same could be said about almost any other relation. Roughly, what makes the difference in the case of belief is that it is a psychological relation. Our psychological relations to things seem to be mediated by our conception of, or way of describing, those things. Louise did not know the author of *Silas Marner* by the name 'Mary Ann Evans'; it wasn't part of her psychological equipment for ordering things in the world. For this reason, we get into trouble when we translate psychological relations as open to =E. This is because =E is insensitive to the fact that our psychological relations to things are mediated by our conceptions of (names for) those things.

There is another way to look at this problem. We can say that, in sentences depicting psychological relations, names do not function in the ordinary way. In most cases, 'George Eliot' picks out an individual who can be named or described in any number of further ways, among which is 'Mary Ann Evans'. In psychological cases, it makes all the difference what name is used in the characterization of the subject's relation to an object. Louise bears the right relation to George Eliot, but not to Mary Ann Evans.

This is a fascinating and important subject in philosophy, and, careful though I have been, even my brief remarks are bound to be seen as controversial in some quarters. What is not controversial, however, is that we are going to have to restrict the way we isolate predicate frames in order to prevent inferences such as that above. For it is easy enough to see that you could use such an inference to prove you were not identical to yourself. All you would have to do is to find someone who believes you (under one description or name) to have a property, and also believes you (under another description or name) to lack that property.

What we have to recognize is that psychological relations such as believing, fearing, wanting and the like cannot be handled as simple predicates in the Predicate language. Proposals for dealing with them in extended versions of Predicate are thick on the ground; see the Reading List for further enlightenment. We can take ourselves to have put them on one side, having labelled them 'Handle With Care'.

15.3   Problems with Predicates: Adjectives

Do you think that the following is a valid argument?

> Everest is the tallest mountain.
> Therefore, Everest is taller than Ben Nevis.

It certainly seems to be, and we can show that it is by careful translation. Restricting the domain of quantification to mountains, we can translate the premise by:

$(\forall x)(x \neq a \supset Rax).$

Here 'a' designates Everest, and 'Rxy' means 'x is taller than y'. The idea is that we define 'x is tallest' by 'x is taller than any other y'. With 'b' as a designator of Ben Nevis, the conclusion can be translated as:

Rab.

In order to construct the deduction we need the non-identity of Everest and Ben Nevis, but this is surely implicit in the argument, so we can add it as a premise. The deduction (below) is now quite easy.

1	(1)	$(\forall x)(x \neq a \supset Rax)$	Premise
2	(2)	$b \neq a$	Premise
1	(3)	$b \neq a \supset Rab$	1 $\forall$E
1,2	(4)	Rab	2,3 $\supset$E

The adjective 'tallest' is called a *superlative* by grammarians, and they call 'taller' a *comparative*. What we have just shown is that you can define the superlative form of an adjective in terms of the comparative plus universal quantification. (And non-identity to restrict attention to *other* mountains. Here we were being fussy because we didn't want to have a premise with the implication that Everest was taller than itself.)

This argument uses both the superlative and the comparative forms of the adjective 'tall'. 'Tall', the non-superlative, non-comparative, is called simply the *positive* form. Most, but not all, adjectives have all three forms, sometimes using 'more' in the comparative and 'most' in the superlative. Here are some examples.

Positive	*Comparative*	*Superlative*
heavy	heavier	heaviest
green	greener	greenest
beautiful	more beautiful	most beautiful

But no comparative or superlative of, e.g. 'six-foot tall'.

So far, so good. But what do you think about the following?

Elephants are heavy.
Some whales are heavier than any elephant.
Therefore, some whales are heavy.

Surely this is a valid argument. Yet, translating this adequately into Predicate is an interesting and unsolved problem. It is easy enough to come up with this:

$(\forall x)(Fx \supset Hx)$	(Every elephant is heavy.)
$(\exists x)(Gx \,\&\, (\forall y)(Fy \supset Rxy))$	(Some whales are heavier than every elephant.)
$(\exists x)(Gx \,\&\, Hx)$	(Some whales are heavy.)

But this translation does not give rise to a deduction of the conclusion from the premises. This is because, while, in English, the comparative 'heavier' somehow seems to involve the positive 'heavy', this involvement is completely lost in translation. 'Heavy' is represented as 'Hx', while 'heavier' is represented as 'Rxy'. No sensible rule of Predicate will allow the deduction of one from the other.

Proposals for dealing with this abound in the literature. For example, it has been suggested that we can use the comparative form to define the positive in the following way:

'heavy' means 'heavier than most'.

I will not be able to comment in detail on this and related proposals (see Reading List), but I can say this much: first, the proposal requires a Predicate language treatment of 'most'. This tricky matter is discussed in the next section. And, second, the above definition will only begin to look plausible when an answer is provided to the question 'most *what*?' I will explain.

There is something incomplete about many adjectives when used on their own, i.e. unattached to nouns. To see what I mean, translate the following arguments into Predicate.

(a)   All bears are furry mammals.
      Ned is a bear.
      _____

      Ned is furry.

(b)   All fleas are big eaters.
      Wilf is a flea.
      _____

      Wilf is big.

The translations of these two arguments would seem to be structurally the same. That is, we could use the following as a translation of both arguments by allowing different interpretations of the Predicate symbols.

$(\forall x)(Fx \supset (Hx \,\&\, Gx))$
Fa
_____

Ha.

But, intuitively, there seems to be an important difference between (a) and (b). In fact, many people would go so far as to say that (a) is valid, and (b) invalid. (The Predicate argument is valid and its deduction is easy.) This difference between the natural language arguments is lost in translation. What causes the trouble is that 'big' gives the wrong impression when used on its own in (b). Only when it is attached to a noun like 'eater' can we be confident that we have taken it in the right way. In contrast, 'furry' can be used either on its own, as in the conclusion of (a), or in connection with a noun, as in the first premise of (a).

Adjectives which require nouns to anchor them are called *attributive* adjectives. Others, like 'furry', 'red', 'six-foot long', are called *predicative*. The reason is that the latter can be adequately translated as *predicates* in Predicate, while the former cannot be so translated. The natural language Predicate frame 'x is a furry mammal' comes out, without distortion, as 'x is furry and x is a mammal', whereas 'x is a big eater' is distorted when understood as 'x is big and x is an eater'.

You might be tempted to think that the problem can be handled by treating 'x is a big eater' as a single predicate.
Thus, (b) would be translated as follows:

$(\forall x)(Fx \supset G_1x)$
Fa
_____

$G_2a.$

Since 'G_1' ('big eater') is a wholly different predicate from 'G_2' ('big'), the argument is no longer valid. But, how would you handle the following variation on (b)?

(c)   All fleas are big eaters.
       Wilf is a flea.
       _____
       Wilf is an eater.

This argument *is* valid, yet we could not show this in Predicate if 'big eater' were translated as a single predicate.

Attributivity is yet another problem for the move from natural language to Predicate. However, were it not for the development of Predicate, this problem would not have come to light in such a clear way.

15.4   Problems with Quantifiers

There is an extensive range of natural language quantifiers that can be translated into Predicate. Aside from forms of universal and existential quantifiers, there is the indefinitely large number of numerical quantifiers such as 'at least . . .', 'at most . . .', and 'exactly . . .'. Unfortunately, this is still not sufficient. There are a few natural language quantifiers which resist any obvious translation into Predicate. In fact, you might have noticed that I just used one, viz. 'a few'. Here are some sentences containing the most difficult cases:

(i)   *Many* logicians drink to excess.
(ii)   *Few* tigers are tame.
(iii) *Most* logicians do not drink to excess.

These are not the only natural language quantifiers that cause problems. However, examples (i)–(iii) do raise all the issues that we need to examine, so we will confine our attention to them.

It hardly needs pointing out that these quantifiers are common in everyday parlance, and this gives us considerable motivation to translate them into Predicate. But motivation and means are two different things. Consider (ii). It is clear that the assertion of (ii) commits a speaker to the truth of:

(a)   at least one tiger is tame.

It also seems to commit him to:

(b)   at least one tiger is not tame.

But the conjunction of (a) and (b) simply does not add up to the assertion of (ii). You will find that people have rather fixed ideas about the minimum number needed to justify 'few', though these vary dramatically from person to person. What you will not find is anyone who thinks that *one* is a sufficient number. If only one tiger was tame, then (ii) would not be true.

Could we capture 'few' by changing (a) to:

(c)   at least n tigers are tame,

for some given number n? I don't think so. First of all, it is part of the very point of words like 'few' that we use them without numerical precision; that is why it is so odd that people argue about how many count as 'few'. Second, words like 'few' are used with reference to the number of things in what is unsurprisingly called the *reference* class. In (ii) the reference class is that of tigers. If tigers were as numerous as alley cats, then the number of things that would satisfy us in connection with 'few' would be different from what it is.

The point about relativity to reference class is much clearer for 'most', though I do think it applies to 'few' as well as to 'many'. In the case of 'most', most people are tempted by the view that it means 'more than half'. If it did mean that then the need for the reference class would be obvious. However, I think that 'most' retains the fuzziness of 'few' and that, for this reason alone, it cannot mean simply 'more than half'.

Both because of fuzziness and relativity to reference class, it is not possible to be precise about 'few', and this is why we cannot accept (c) as a way to understand (ii). It would seem, then, that the available resources of Predicate do not offer us a way to translate (i)–(iii). This raises the natural question: why not add some more quantifiers to Predicate? For example, why not use 'f' to mean 'few' and translate (ii) as follows?

(iv) $(fx)(Gx \ \& \ Hx)$

This is read: few x's are such that x is a tiger and x is tame. Unfortunately, while this proposal seems to capture something of the 'shape', so to speak, of the natural language quantifier, it does not properly respect the standards of Predicate. It is one of the virtues of Predicate that we can tell *definitely* whether or not a sentence in this language applies to a Situation. This is not something that Predicate users expect merely because they are pedantic. Predicate, and Sentential before it, were constructed in order to express the structure of arguments. More particularly, these languages of logic are used to show how certain sentences impose truth on others; they show us the workings of validity. If we allowed Predicate to contain sentences whose conditions of truth are vague, then the whole point of logic would be lost. And '$(fx)(Gx \& Hx)$' certainly qualifies as vague.

As with other topics in this chapter, the story does not end here, and you should consult the Reading List for further leads. Logicians are resourceful, and various intricate extensions to Predicate have been proposed to deal with the problems of these sorts of quantifier, and with problems such as vagueness, which was touched on briefly.

15.5 Prospects

Two things should by now be obvious.

(i)   Predicate has its limitations.
(ii) There are further languages of logic to be explored.

I will say something about each of these.

A.   The Limitations of Predicate

The problems raised in this chapter show that certain forms of natural language argumentation cannot be fully captured in Predicate. This means that Predicate, like Sentential, does not provide everything the Strategy requires. However, unlike Sentential, Predicate offers us a great deal of what is required. In a precise, austere and yet subtle way, Predicate allows us to see deep into the movements of our thoughts. That it does not allow us to see to the bottom of them is itself an important result. For, in reaching the limit of its application, we can see more clearly into the sometimes murky waters that lie beyond. Less metaphorically, it is, for example, in virtue of the failure of Predicate to properly account for our intuitions about this argument:

> Louise believes that George Eliot wrote *Silas Marner*.
> Louise does not believe that Mary Ann Evans wrote it.
> Therefore, George Eliot is not Mary Ann Evans.

that we have been able to see why belief claims have some of the interesting properties that were long recognized but not understood.

B.   Further Languages of Logic

That there are further languages of logic is no less than you would expect given the way the book has developed. The limitations of

Sentential in the Strategy led to the development of Predicate. The limitations of the latter, together with my repeated advice to consult the Reading List, point to the existence of yet more subtle languages of logic. What will not be clear, and is worth saying, is how much these more sophisticated languages owe to Predicate. The concepts you have acquired in learning Predicate are not *replaced* in these further languages so much as *exploited*. For example, you will find that treatments of belief sentences do not drop the predicate/quantifier approach. Rather, they introduce the necessary subtlety by insisting on distinctions in the items over which the quantifiers range. Special kinds of entity are introduced to figure in belief sentences, and this imposes all sorts of complication on the language, but it is still a recognizably quantificational language.

So, while Predicate has its limitations, you will find that, in mastering it, you have mastered the fundamental language of logic.

The Main Points of Chapter 15

1 We first gave the Introduction and Elimination rules for identity. The application of these rules to certain elements of natural language causes some trouble for the smooth translation from natural language into Predicate.

2 Beginning with the problems arising from identity, we surveyed further problems. These were arranged under the categories of Predicate expressions, viz. problems with:

   (a) designators
   (b) predicates
   (c) quantifiers.

3 Finally, I claimed that Predicate has given way to many more sophisticated proposals which, not without some controversy, claim to give a better account of many of the phenomena of natural language. However, the quantifier–predicate structure of Predicate still remains the basic format of even the more sophisticated languages.

Chapter sixteen

Modal

The Predicate language described so far is the fundamental logical language. Like an old family house, it does not have all the modern conveniences and not everything in it works as well as it could, but one can live in it and it offers the scope necessary for further improvement. The efforts of logicians, philosophers and linguists detailed in the Reading List will give you some idea of the improvements which have been suggested. What I have tried to do in this book is to portray the structure of the original house before too many builders moved in.

As is often the case with additions to old houses, there is likely to be disagreement about their value and about how well they fit in. In this chapter, I will sketch an important new wing of the edifice, though it is by no means universally agreed to be an improvement. Less metaphorically, this chapter introduces elements of a logical language which can be grafted onto Sentential and Predicate. Because of its importance, I did not think even a basic account of the languages of logic would be complete without it. But what follows is only meant as an introduction. In particular, most of the discussion will be confined to the blending of the new elements with Sentential rather than Predicate, as this gives you an uncluttered view of the issues.

16.0   A Sample Argument

Below is an argument in natural language. Do you think it is valid?

(M)   It is possibly the case that Jones is a bachelor.
It is necessarily the case that if Jones is a bachelor then Jones is not married.
Therefore, it is possibly the case that Jones is not married.

It certainly seems valid. Can it be translated into a language of logic which preserves this appearance? The first thing to note is that nothing in the argument seems to require the *full* resources of Predicate. There are no quantifiers in the argument and it could be partially translated in either of the following ways:

(M₁) It is possibly the case that Fa.
      It is necessarily the case that (Fa ⊃ ¬Ga).
      _____
      It is possibly the case that ¬Ga.

(M₂) It is possibly the case that P.
      It is necessarily the case that (P ⊃ ¬Q).
      _____
      It is possibly the case that ¬Q.

Since Predicate isn't called for, we will stick with the Sentential version (M₂). However, we are still short of a full translation. Nothing in Sentential (or Predicate) was designed to cope with notions such as 'possibly' or 'necessarily', yet the validity of the argument here seems to depend crucially on them. If these notions were dropped, then the argument would be a simple instance of ⊃E, and this cannot be all there is to it. The conclusion of the argument is not:

Jones is not married,

but:

it is possibly the case that Jones is not married.

Suppose we create two new symbols to go with those already in Sentential, thereby creating a new language. They are:

'◇' meaning 'it is possibly the case that'
'□' meaning 'it is necessarily the case that'.

We could then represent the argument in this way:

(M₃) ◇P
      □(P ⊃ ¬Q)
      _____
      ◇¬Q.

These new symbols are commonly called *modal operators*, and they are treated, for purposes of scope, like the negation in Sentential. However, it is one thing to introduce symbols and another to give an explanation of them. Suppose, for example, you tried to test (M₃) for validity by constructing a truth table. The argument contains two basic sentences, so it would begin like this:

P	Q	◇P
T	T	T
T	F	T
F	T	
F	F	

But here you are stuck. As the table indicates, it is reasonable to think it true that P is possible when you already know that P is true. This is the ground for the Ts in rows one and two. However, the fact that P is false is not a reason to think it false that P is possible. One of the main uses of the idea of possibility is to say something *true* about what may well be false as things stand. In any case, if rows three and four were assigned Fs, then the table for P and ◇P would be exactly the same. This would mean that the new symbol would be adding absolutely nothing to the argument, and that is just wrong. (And if we put Ts in these rows, the truth table for ◇P would make it a tautology! This is no more acceptable.) The original argument (M) turns on the relationship between possibility and necessity. As was noted above, (M) is not merely another way of presenting ⊃E.

Though I did not get as far as including it in the table, the '□' symbol is no less recalcitrant. Consider a row in which P ⊃ ¬Q is false. In such a row, it is reasonable to think that □(P ⊃ ¬Q) is false, since if a sentence is false we would not count it as necessarily true. However, when (P ⊃ ¬Q) is *true*, we are again stuck. If adding the '□' to the sentence produces another truth, then the table for □(P ⊃ ¬Q) will be indistinguishable from the one for plain P ⊃ ¬Q. In which case, the '□' is redundant.

Introducing the symbols is a first step, but all the work lies ahead. What is missing is some account of these new symbols that tells us how they are to be treated in the evaluation of arguments.

16.1   Modalities

Instead of beginning directly with the new symbols, we will take a step back and examine sentences in English such as:

(a)   it is possibly the case that Jones is a bachelor.

This sentence can be paraphrased as:

(b)   Jones might be a bachelor.

In fact, many would think that (b) is a more natural way of expressing the thought that underlies (a). But what is that thought?

The word 'possibly' in (a) and the word 'might' in (b) are the key to understanding these sentences. These words were classified by early logicians (and grammarians) as *modalities* because it was held that they characterize the mode with which a thought is expressed. The idea is, I suppose, that some thoughts get expressed rather forcefully as assertions in the indicative, e.g.:

the cat is on the mat.

But an essentially similar thought can be expressed in a different mode as the more tentative:

> the cat might be on the mat
> (it is possible that the cat is on the mat),

or, further still as the even more forceful:

> the cat must be on the mat
> (it is necessary that the cat is on the mat).

We don't have to swallow this whole story to accept the classification of certain words and phrases as modals. These include: 'possibly', 'necessarily', 'could have', 'might have' and 'must have'. However, we have to be able to say much more about the contribution of modalities to sentences than that they give the mode with which a thought is expressed. In this further discussion we will continue to focus on (a) and (b).

16.2　Kinds of Modality

There are two ways in which sentences (a) and (b) can be taken. To appreciate them try the following thought experiment. Imagine that you had asserted either of them, and then suppose that someone were to show you a certificate clearly showing that Jones is married. I realize that forgeries are possible, but let us suppose that the certificate is genuine, and that you accept it as absolutely certain proof that Jones is married. Would you still be prepared to think (a) and (b) true? If you would *not* be so prepared then you were taking them as *epistemic*. That is, if the marriage certificate convinced you that you were mistaken in saying that Jones might be a bachelor, then this is because the possibility in question has to do with the state of your knowledge. ('Epistemic' comes from the Greek word meaning 'knowledge'.) In the absence of any real information about Jones's marital state, it is only sensible to say that he *might* be a bachelor. When the certificate is presented to you, this increases your stock of knowledge and it is no longer reasonable to think that Jones might be a bachelor. It is no longer reasonable, that is, *when the kind of possibility in question is epistemic.* But there is another way in which (a) and (b) can be taken.

If, even while you accept that Jones is married, you are still prepared to assert that he might be a bachelor, then you have this second kind of possibility in mind. There is no universally accepted label for this kind of possibility, but labels aren't needed to get hold of the notion. When you think that the married Jones might nonetheless be a bachelor, you are probably thinking one or more of the following sorts of thing.

(1) Jones could have led a different life. For example, if he had become a priest, an idea he in fact entertained when he was younger, he would not now be married.
(2) The world might not have contained the institution of marriage when Jones was of marrying age. For example, suppose that the ideas of certain groups of people in the 1960s took hold, and by the time Jones was of age, there was no longer any institution of marriage.

With (1) or (2) in mind, it becomes reasonable to think that the modality in 'Jones might be a bachelor' is independent of the state of our knowledge about Jones's marital state. It is a kind of modality which depends on how the world could be, and not on what we happen to know about it. For this reason, it is tempting to think of non-epistemic modality as *real* modality, but, since this is not a widely accepted label, we will continue to think of this second kind merely as *non-epistemic.*

Given that there are two general ways in which modalities can be understood, epistemically and non-epistemically, which of them is behind argument (M), and which of them gives us insight into the way in which '□' and '◇' work? These are surprisingly difficult questions to answer. Before we can even begin we need to do a bit more groundwork.

16.3   Modal Speakers

In earlier chapters, I asked you to imagine that Sentential was a language spoken by a tribe of logicians. With it, they are able to make claims about Situations. For example, supposing things to be like this:

Situation (16)

and supposing P to express the thought that the apple is on the book and ¬P to express the thought that the apple is not on the book, then the first claim truly describes the Situation and the second does not.

What I would now like you to imagine is that there are certain individuals in this tribe who, when looking at Situation (16), see more than is portrayed in the above picture. In fact, they see Situation (16) this way.

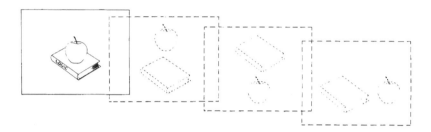

As my portrayal shows, these individuals see that the apple is on the book, but they also cannot help seeing a number of fainter scenes in which the apple and the book occupy different relative locations. (The drawing captures only three of the very many fainter scenes which these individuals would claim to see.)

If you asked any of them whether P was true, they would unhesitatingly say 'Yes'. They would as quickly agree that ¬P is false. In these judgements they agree with other members of the tribe. However, if you asked them whether □P was true, they would say 'No', and if you asked them whether ◇¬P was true, they would say 'Yes'. The other members of the tribe, the ones who cannot see the fainter scenes, are simply mystified by these answers. In view of the idea behind '□' and '◇', we will call those individuals who find the above answers obvious and natural *Modal logicians*, and we can explain their behaviour in the following way.

The fainter scenes which they see, so to speak, *in* Situation (16) are alternative arrangements of the items in the actual Situation. They think of these Alternative Situations as *ways the world might have been*, as possibilities. When they are asked whether □P is true, or whether ◇ ¬P is true, they rely on their appreciation of these Alternative Situations in giving answers. For example, they say that □P is false because they can see Alternative Situations in which P is false. They say that ◇ ¬P is true because they recognise Alternative Situations in which ¬P is true. Underlying these answers are the following interpretations of the modal symbols:

'□A' means 'A is true in *every Alternative Situation*',
'◇A' means 'A is true in *at least one Alternative Situation*',

where A is a schematic letter which can be replaced by any sentence of Sentential.

What would Modal logicians say about ◇P? P is true in the Actual Situation (16) but not in any of the Alternatives pictured. Nonetheless, if you asked whether ◇P was true in the above Situation, they would say 'Yes'. This is because they count the Actual Situation, the one which is not faint, as an Alternative Situation. In their view, if the apple is, in fact, on the book, then it is only reasonable to think it possible that the apple is on the book. Nonetheless, even though the Actual Situation is counted as an Alternative, it is still the case that it is special. The Modal logicians in this example have as robust a sense of reality as their non-modal compatriots, and they recognize that the truth of non-modal sentences depends solely on the way things are in the Actual Situation.

What does this talk of Alternative Situations tell us about modality? Does it commit us to regarding '□' and '◇' as epistemic or non-epistemic? And what does it tell us about the way these symbols work in arguments? These very important questions deserve treatment in separate sections.

16.4   Alternative Situations and Kinds of Modality

It is pretty clear that, in the example above, the modality is non-epistemic. Given that the Modal logicians were portrayed as *knowing* that the apple is on the book, and given that they still regard ◇ ¬P as true, they must understand ◇ ¬P non-epistemically. However, this is just a feature of the way the example was presented, and it does not show that the explanation of modality in terms of Alternative Situations commits one to the view of modality as non-epistemic.

For instance, suppose that one of the Modal logicians is extremely sceptical of the deliverances of his senses. In his view, the appearance of things in Situation (16) does not constitute knowledge of where the apple is, and he marks his doubt by claiming that it is possible that the apple is *not* on the book (◇ ¬P). The sceptic would still accept that the truth of ◇ ¬P comes down to: ¬P is true in at least one Alternative Situation. Where he would differ from the Modal logicians described earlier is that he would have a different conception of the Alternatives. He regards as Alternatives all those Situations which are not ruled out by what he knows. The Alternatives are understood epistemically. In particular, since he does not regard himself as knowing which Alternative is the Actual Situation, he is prepared to count all of the scenes portrayed as on a par.

What this shows is that the explanation of modality in terms of Alternative Situations can serve *both* as the explanation of epistemic *and* non-epistemic modality; though, in any particular case, we can tell which kind of modality is in question by discovering what kinds of Alternative are allowed.

Nor is this all that talk of Alternative Situations buys us. Fix in your mind the responses of the Modal logicians who regard ◇ ¬P as non-epistemic. They are the ones who know perfectly well that the apple *is* on the book, but they still regard it as possible that it is not so placed. That is, they regard the fainter Situations that I drew as genuine Alternatives to the Actual One. However, even within the non-epistemic realm of possibility, there are distinctions to be made. For example, as I've drawn it, there is an Alternative Situation in which the book is floating freely above the apple. We can imagine that some Modal logicians would, and others would not, count this as an Alternative. Those who wouldn't would argue as follows: the world as we know it is governed by certain physical laws or regularities. In so far as the items on the desk are governed by the law of gravity, as they are in the Actual Situation, it is not reasonable to think of an Alternative Situation from which gravity is absent. For these logicians, it is *not* possible that a book can float freely above the desk, whereas, for others, this and even more 'bizarre' Alternatives are possible. Modal logicians who think that the laws of physics constrain the range of Alternatives can be said to have a notion of *physical* possibility.

There are other notions of non-epistemic modality, though, for reasons which will be obvious, I have to go outside simple drawable Situations to give them. Consider these two sentences:

(i)   It is not possible that John got to London from Oxford in ten seconds.
(ii) It is not possible that Smith killed Jones.

Someone who regards these two as true, could very well claim that they were to be understood in the following ways.

(i') There are no Alternative Situations in which John travels from Oxford to London in ten seconds.
(ii') There are no Alternative Situations in which Smith killed Jones.

In each case, however, the constraints on choices of Alternatives are different. It is certainly physically possible to travel from Oxford to London in ten seconds: just imagine that British Rail devote all their resources to StarTrek-like molecular transportation. Even so, the person who made the claim in (i) is not likely to be impressed by this. In its most natural reading, (i) should be understood as about what is *practically* possible; (i) implies that only those Alternatives which are practical are to be countenanced in (i').

In (ii), we can assume that there is no physical or practical reason why Smith could not kill Jones. What is at issue here is what may be called *moral* Alternatives. The underlying thought in (ii') is that the only Alternatives countenanced are those constrained by the various moral principles which it is presumed that Smith holds. The point made in (ii) is that it is not *morally* possible for Smith to have killed Jones.

What all this shows is that there are any number of ways in which we can understand 'possibility' and 'necessity'. There is the basic division into epistemic and non-epistemic and a number of further divisions of which the physical, practical and moral are examples. In all these cases, we can express the modality in terms of Alternative Situations; they provide a way of thinking about modality which is not tied to any one kind. The distinction between kinds of modality can be captured, but only by adding constraints on the choice of Alternatives. Armed with a conception of modality in terms of Alternative Situations, we have now to see what can be said about modality and inference.

16.5 Modality and Validity

Alternative Situations do not trade under this name in the logical literature, so the first thing we must do is bring our discussion into line by expanding our horizons. In your imagination, think of the whole of our world and its history down to such specific things as where you are seated (I will assume you are seated). This is the Actual World. Imagine next a world in which everything is exactly as it is in the Actual World except that, instead of being seated, you are standing. Notice, I did not say that you got up. Rather, in this second world, you were not seated in the first place. This second world is not very different from the Actual World but, in being different at all, it is distinct from the Actual World. We will call this second world a Possible World. (It is a sort of larger-scale Alternative Situation.) Imagine now the whole spectrum of Possible Worlds, each one of which differs in small or large respects from the Actual World. It should be clear that there are going to be a great many Possible Worlds, and we will say:

'◇A' means 'A is true in at least one Possible World',
'□A' means 'A is true in every Possible World'.

As with Alternative Situations, we will count the Actual World as itself a Possible World. In sum, everything we said about modality in terms of Alternative Situations can now be spelled out in terms of Possible Worlds.

What we have to do now is to see whether, using the idea of Possible Worlds, we can find out enough about modality to help us understand its role in inference. The hope is that we can do this *without* having to be all that specific about which sorts of world count as possible. Some grounds for this hope can be found in the fact that we were able to judge this argument:

> (M)   It is possible that Jones is a bachelor.
> It is necessary that if Jones is a bachelor, then he is not married.
> Therefore, it is possible that Jones is not married.

valid without being clear what kind of modality is in question.

The first thing to do is to rewrite (M) in terms of Possible Worlds. This gives the following:

> (M/PW)   There is a Possible World in which Jones is a bachelor.
> Every Possible World is such that if Jones is a bachelor in it then he is not married in it.
> Therefore, there is a Possible World in which Jones is not married.

This Possible World version lends itself naturally to translation into a special sort of Predicate. All we have to do is allow ourselves the idea of quantification over Possible Worlds. The translation of this version is:

$$(\exists w)\, Pw$$
$$(\forall w)(Pw \supset \neg Qw)$$
$$\overline{(\exists w)\, \neg Qw}$$

where: w is a variable for Possible Worlds and 'Pw' means 'P is true in world w'.

> ### Exercise
>
> Show that this Predicate argument is valid by constructing a deduction.

The validity of (M/PW) can be taken to show that the modal argument about Jones is valid. By transmuting a modal argument into talk about Possible Worlds, we end up with a method for validating it, without having to decide precisely what kind of modality is involved.

We can extend this method to arguments which mix modal and non-modal claims by the following expedient: treat the Actual World as a designated Possible World. That is, think of the Actual World as picked out by the designator w*. The claim that Jones is, in fact, married then comes out as:

Pw* (It is true in the Actual World that P).

On this understanding, it is easy to see why the following is valid.

Jones is married.
Therefore, it is possible that Jones is married.

This would be rendered as:

$$\frac{Pw^*}{(\exists w)\,Pw}$$

and is a straightforward example of $\exists I$.

16.6   A Note of Caution

It is clear that Possible World talk is extremely useful in connection with modality. Nonetheless, one must not get carried away. The use of Predicate in the above discussion is not all it seems. You may have noticed that I spoke of (M/PW) as a 'rewrite' of the original argument. I used this word because I did not want to say that (M/PW) translates (M). Strictly speaking, the Modal translation of (M) is the following:

$$\frac{\begin{array}{l}\Diamond P \\ \Box(P \supset \neg Q)\end{array}}{\Diamond \neg Q.}$$

The Predicate language was then used, not to give a further translation, but to provide us with *a way of talking about this translation*. Predicate is used as the *metalanguage* of modality. (See chapter 8 to remind yourself what this term means.) It is important to keep this in mind because we do not want any controversy about Possible World talk to infect the undoubtedly uncontroversial use made of modality in everyday reasoning.

The modal arguments we have discussed are very simple, and I have used them mainly to introduce you to the ways of thinking of Modal logicians. The full treatment of modality even within Sentential would require:

(1) a deeper investigation of Possible World talk and its relation to modal argumentation, and

(2) a discussion of how Possible Worlds are related to one another.

Work on (1) can be expected to shed light on the differences between kinds of modality. We would expect that the differences between modalities would show up somewhere in inference even though relatively simple arguments like (M) are valid whether the modality is epistemic or non-epistemic.

The second of these requirements is especially pressing if we are to deal with the following sort of argument.

>   It is possible that it is possible that Jones is married.
>   Therefore, it is possible that Jones is married.

Here we have a case of *iterated* modalities and people have different intuitions about which inferences involving them are valid.

Finally, and perhaps most important of all, no understanding of modality would be complete if it did not include an account of how it functions within Predicate. Remember, even though we used the Predicate idiom to talk *about* Possible Worlds, the modalities themselves were functioning only within Sentential. This is an advanced topic, guidance for which can be obtained from the Reading List. When you consult it you will find that a considerable amount of ink has been spilled over issues raised by the mixing of modality and quantification.

The Main Points of Chapter 16

1   An argument was presented which was intuitively valid, but whose validity seems to rest on such notions as 'possibility' and 'necessity'.

2   Two new symbols were introduced into Sentential. These symbols are called *modal operators*. They are:

$\square$ (it is necessarily the case that)
$\diamond$ (it is possibly the case that).

3   When modal operators play a crucial role in Sentential arguments, we can no longer use the truth-table method to decide validity. In an effort to find some method of evaluation we embarked on a discussion of the nature of modality.

4   There are two general kinds of modality: *epistemic* and *non-epistemic*. There are also many specific kinds of modality of which physical, practical and moral are instances.

5   Using Situations, a useful tool for discussing modality was introduced. This was the notion of Alternative Situations. When this is generalized into the more well-known notion of *Possible Worlds*, we can use some of the insights of Predicate to see why certain, relatively simple, modal arguments are valid.

6   For a complete treatment of modality, we need to see what happens when modal operators are introduced into Predicate, and we need to better understand the nature of, and relations between, Possible Worlds.

Chapter seventeen

Truth

17.0 Truth in Logic

Truth made its appearance very early on in the book. (Perhaps, I should say that 'true' made its appearance.) This was not merely fortuitous. Even before the use of the notion in truth tables, I needed it to characterize validity. It was said that in a valid argument it is not possible for the premises to be true and the conclusion false. In chapter 9, we discovered that we could work out whether an argument is valid without reference to truth. If we can deduce the conclusion of an argument from its premises using the rules, we can be sure that the argument is valid. And the rules can be stated in purely syntactical terms with no mention of truth. However, as our discussion of deduction showed, truth is never far away. The rules can be stated without mention of truth, but the fact that a deduction guarantees validity depends upon the rules being *truth*-preserving.

In earlier chapters, I relied on your common-sense grasp of the idea that sentences are true or false, and did not look any deeper. Almost the only general remark I made was that a sentence is true when it depicts reality correctly, and false otherwise. It was on this basis that I dispensed with pictures in favour of truth tables for Primitive and Sentential.

When we got to Predicate, things didn't seem to change much. Validity for Predicate was spoken of in terms of truth and possibility, just as it was for Sentential. However, there is an important difference between these languages in regard to the role of truth. It is a difference that has been only just below the surface in earlier chapters, and its time for comment has arrived.

In Sentential, the truth values of non-basic sentences depend on the truth values of their basic constituents. As a consequence, when it is said that an argument is valid, the use of 'true' and 'false' in the definition of validity is quite clear. Let me spell this out.

Take any valid Sentential argument. Such an argument could not possibly have true premises and a false conclusion. Given the truth-functional nature of Sentential, this comes to: *there is no assignment of truth values to the basic sentences in the argument which renders the premises true and the conclusion false.* Of course, it happens that there is an algorithm for assigning truth values to the basic sentences which allows us to decide whether the premises can be true and the conclusion false. This algorithm is the truth table method discussed in chapter 6. But what is at issue here is not the question of decision, so much as the use of truth in the definition of validity. What I am claiming is that so long as one understands the notion of truth as applied to basic sentences, the truth-functional nature of Sentential guarantees that we know what we are talking about when we say that non-basic sentences are true (or false). This, in turn, means that we know precisely what we are talking about when we say that a Sentential argument is valid.

In the case of Predicate, there is as yet no similar way of understanding the use of 'true' in the definition of validity. Take any valid Predicate argument. We know of this argument that it is not possible for its premises to be true and its conclusion false. But, we can hardly say: there is no assignment of truth values to its basic sentences which renders its premises true and its conclusion false. This is because Predicate sentences do not, in general, have their truth values fixed by the assignment of truth values to their basic sentence constituents. For example, the sentence:

$(\forall x)(Fx \supset Gx),$

is not made up of basic sentences. It is true, when it is, because of something to do with its quantifier and predicate, but not because of the truth values of these. Quantifiers and predicates do not have truth values.

Again, this is not a point about algorithms or the lack of them. It is a point about our understanding of the notion of truth as applied to the sentences of Predicate. What it shows is that we have no precise understanding of how the truth of a Predicate sentence depends on features of its construction. (The word 'feature' here is not very helpful, but that is the whole point.) What is needed is a more precise way of understanding how the truth of Predicate sentences depend on the way in which such sentences are built up out of constituents.

Understanding the application of 'true' to Predicate sentences is our goal. However, we will begin by discussing the notion of truth in a more general way. By seeing what is needed in order clearly to apply 'true' to sentences of any language, we will be in a better position to see how to accomplish this job for Predicate.

17.1   The Project of Defining Truth

In earlier chapters, I said that a sentence is true when it is appropriately related to reality. But saying that truth is a relation between sentences and reality is not saying anything very clear. It is certainly not like saying that parenthood is a relation between people. When one person is the parent of another, there is a definite physical relationship between them. The same hardly could be said about the relationship between a sentence and reality when the sentence is true. For example, the following sentence is true:

London is in England,

but it is not at all clear what relation this sentence has to what, for the want of a better word, I have called 'reality'.

The difference between these cases may not bother you, but it did bother a logician and philosopher named Alfred Tarski. It bothered Tarski because his philosophical beliefs led him to think that the concepts we use in science should be explicable in clear and precise ways. One sort of clarity comes when concepts can be understood in physical terms. The concept of *being a parent* is an example. But, as we have seen, truth is not like this. Yet, since he also recognized that you couldn't have science without mathematics and logic, and you couldn't have logic without truth, something had to be done to make the concept of truth clear.

Against this background, he proposed that we could safely use the concept of truth in logic if we could show how to *define* it. The sort of definition he had in mind would allow us to *replace* the use of 'true' as applied to specific languages by the concepts used in its definition. So long as these other concepts were clear and precise in the ways required by science, the definition would have shown truth to be equally secure.

The philosophical underpinnings of Tarski's project are interesting, but we do not have to adopt them in order to be interested in the project. We will investigate Tarski's proposals for defining truth because, as you will see, they are of direct relevance to our needs in regard to Sentential and Predicate. His view of whether the concepts used in the definitional project are scientifically clear in the ways he thought acceptable need not concern us here.

17.2 Definition

The project is that of defining truth, or, less dramatically, defining 'true'. It will be helpful to begin with a brief discussion of what it is to define any concept or word in the way that Tarski recommends. In particular, we must be clear about what we would count as success in any definitional project; we want to know what would constitute conditions of adequacy for any such definition.

Suppose you were asked to define 'classical'. This would be an almost impossible task, since so many different sorts of thing can be correctly called 'classical'. But actual success here is not what is at issue. What we want to know is what would *count* as success.

Two things we can say right away. Any successful definition will have to have the form of a one-place predicate, and the definition must not use the word 'classical' itself (or, perhaps, any term that is too close to it). The reason for the first requirement is that 'classical' is itself a one-place predicate, and any supposed definition had better share at least that feature. The second requirement is also a quite natural one. You would feel cheated if someone proposed a definition of 'classical' which used the very term it purported to define.

What we now know is that any definition of the predicate:

x is classical,

had better be of this form:

x is . . . ,

where what fills in the '. . .' is some form of words that does *not* include the word 'classical', or any too close relative of this word. Let us call these constraints on the definition *formal* constraints.

Let us see if we can say what would positively count as a filling for '. . .' in this case. Begin with a fairly common-sense thought that many are likely to have: a definition of 'classical' must enable someone who, at first, did not understand the term, to apply it. (Assuming, of course, that the terms of the definition were understood.) One way in which this thought might be taken is: everything that is correctly described as 'classical' can be correctly described as '. . .', and everything that is correctly described as '. . .' is also correctly described as 'classical'. If we define the *extension* of a predicate as the set of things which the predicate correctly describes, we could put the point this way: the extension of 'classical' matches the extension of '. . .'. What Tarski proposed is that this sort of matching of extensions is what we require in a definition.

It is important to understand precisely what this requirement comes to. Suppose it true that some friend of yours has a record collection, and that all his records are classical ones. You could, *in this case*, say that the extension of 'classical record' includes the extension of 'record in my friend's collection'. Yet it would hardly be acceptable to define 'classical record' as 'record in my friend's collection'. This is because there are bound to be more classical records than records in your friend's collection. A definition can only be adequate if it covers *all* the things in the extension of the term it seeks to define.

Suppose now that your friend has such an obsession about collecting records that you are willing to say that if it is in his collection, it is classical, *and* if it is classical, it is in his collection. If this were true, could we define classical as 'record in my friend's collection'? This is a tricky question. If what you are looking for is the essence of 'classical record', something which gives you insight into its nature, then defining it as 'record in my friend's collection' will seem insufficient. However, if your interest is in a definition which makes it easy to identify which are classical records (perhaps for buying and selling), then the above definition would certainly be adequate. If anyone asks you whether a certain record is classical, all you have to do is to check whether it is in your friend's collection. Of course, some of the hesitation you may have in accepting this definition is the implausibility of someone having a record collection as described, but this should not obscure the basic point. If two terms are related in such a way that the extension of one precisely and exhaustively matches that of the other, then there is a clear sense in which one can be used to define the other. I have admitted, and so does Tarski, that it is not the only sense of 'definition', but it is strong enough for our purposes in dealing with 'true'.

The matching extensions requirement on definitions is called the *material* condition of adequacy. Combined with the other two, we can now say that a definition is adequate if it meets the formal and material conditions.

17.3   The Material Adequacy Condition and 'True'

To test the material adequacy of a definition of 'classical' you have to think of actual and possible examples of things 'classical', and check whether they are '. . .', and vice versa. This requires you to be able to pick out things, and say of them that they are classical. Of course, this makes it impossible for you to tell whether the definition is adequate unless you already know how to apply the very term you are trying to define. Some would regard this as essentially paradoxical, but it isn't all that strange. After all, definitions are still useful things, even if the attempt at definition requires you to know how to apply the term being defined. A materially adequate definition might be useful for teaching the term to someone who doesn't yet know what the original term applies to, and we might learn a lot about our own use of a term by trying to define it.

What has just been said about 'classical' applies equally to 'true'. For the definition of 'true' to be correct, it must cover all and only sentences which are true. However, though correct, this way of stating the material condition of adequacy is not all that helpful. One of the first things Tarski did was to improve on it.

To appreciate his proposal, ask yourself: what would you have to know to be able to say whether any particular sentence is true? If you could say what this is, then you could require the definition of truth to deliver it; it would constitute your condition of adequacy. To begin with, we can think of sentences as sequences of signs, written or spoken. Here are three examples:

(a) Snow is white.
(b) Grass is green.
(c) Snow is green.

What is needed to tell us whether each of the above is in the extension of 'true'? The answers here are not difficult. The first string is in the extension of 'true' because snow is white, and the second because grass is green. In short, there are specific ways the world is, in virtue of which (a) and (b) are true, and we have to know what these are for each sentence in order to be able to classify the sentence as true. The third string is not in the extension of 'true', but even here we can say that we know this because we know that snow is not green. That is, there is a specific condition – a *truth condition* – associated with (c) which we need to know in order to be in a position to classify (c) as outside the extension of 'true'.

Encouraged by these examples, we should require our definition of 'true' to tell us what we need to know about any sentence of a language in order to certify it as true. Our definition must, for example, allow us to derive these sentences:

'Snow is white' is true if and only if snow is white.
'Grass is green' is true if and only if grass is green.
'Snow is green' is true if and only if snow is green.

If a definition of truth allowed us to work out these sorts of equivalences for absolutely any sentence, the definition would be materially adequate. It would give us what we need to apply 'true' to any sentence. Of course, such a definition would not tell us whether a given sentence was actually true. For that you have to do some looking around the world. But you wouldn't expect a definition of 'true' to do that. What you do expect is an account of what we would have to know to be able to apply 'true' to a specific sentence, and the above is a clear way of stating that requirement. There is, however, one small problem.

It was easy to work out the required truth conditions for (a), (b) and (c) because we think we know what these sentences mean. And we think this because they seem to be familiar sentences of English. But remember that (a)–(c) are just strings of signs. Suppose, for example, you were to come across a group of speakers who used a sentence which looked and sounded just like 'snow is white', but which simply did not mean what the English sentence does. This is perfectly possible. There could be a group of speakers, Martians if need be, who used just these letters to express a thought very different from the one we associate with 'snow is white'. Perhaps in their language, the sentence 'snow is white' means that rain is wet. For these speakers, it would simply not be the case that:

> 'snow is white' is true if and only if snow is white.

The sentence in quotes on the left of this equivalence is a name of their string of signs and, given that it means something different in their mouths than it does in ours, they would find it bizarre that we thought it true when snow is white. We could express what they would agree to this way:

> 'Snow is white' is true if and only if rain is wet.

This example shows that there is something crucial missing from the equivalences given above, viz. explicit mention of the language from which the quoted sentences come. From now on we have to write:

> 'snow is white' is true-in-English if and only if snow is white,

or:

> 'snow is white' is true-in-Martian if and only if rain is wet.

With this in mind, we can now formulate the adequacy condition in its most general (and well-known) form. We will say that a definition of 'true-in-L' is adequate if we can derive from it all instances of:

(T) *s* is true-in-L if and only if *p*,

where: L is the language under consideration,
          s is a place-holder for a name of a sentence of L,
          p is either the sentence named by *s* or a translation of it
          into the language of the truth definition.

In the trade, the above equivalence has come to be called *Convention T*. (The German version of Tarski's paper called it something like 'Criterion T', meaning the criterion of adequacy for truth. Somehow 'criterion' has become 'convention'.) The reason for the somewhat long-winded explanation of *p* is clear enough if you think again about the contrast between the English and Martian sentence 'snow is white'. The filling for *p* when *s* is the English sentence 'snow is white' is simply *snow is white*. When *s* is the Martian sentence 'snow is white' we have to fill in for *p* with an English sentence that translates the Martian one, viz. *rain is wet*.

With Convention T in place, we can now set about the task of defining 'true' for various languages. Remember, any definition will only count as adequate if it meets these conditions:

(i)   It is a one-place predicate of sentences which does not contain the notion of truth.

(ii)   It is possible to derive from the definition itself all instances of Convention T. That is, the definition must give us a way of finding out the truth condition for each and every sentence of the language under consideration.

17.4   Two Examples

A.   A Really Finite Language

Suppose we came across a language with only four sentences. In deference to its meagre resources, call this language F for 'finite'. We needn't bother about detailed description of these sentences; let us simply designate them as 1, 2, 3 and 4. Here is a truth definition.

x is true-in-F if and only if:

> x is 1 and it is cold or,
> x is 2 and it is wet or,
> x is 3 and it is cloudy or,
> x is 4 and it is windy.

In the box, we have a complex one-place predicate which does not contain the notion of truth, but from which we can derive the truth condition of any sentence of F. For example, suppose you want to derive the T-Convention sentence:

3 is true-in-F if and only if it is cloudy.

To derive a biconditional, we assume the left-hand side and derive the right-hand, and vice versa. Below is an informal derivation. (It could be made more precise, but it is really only to give you the idea, so I haven't bothered.)

1   Assume the left-hand side, i.e. that 3 is true-in-F.
2   By the definition, this means that the disjunction in the box is true.
3   But given that x is 3, it can only be true because its third disjunct is true.
4   Equally obviously, this disjunct can only be true if both its components are true.
5   We can thus conclude that it is cloudy.
6   So, if 3 is true-in-F then it is cloudy.

From right to left the derivation is even easier.

7   Assume that it is cloudy.
8   This makes the third disjunct in the box true, so what is in the box is true.
9   Hence, 3 is true-in-F.
10   So, if it is cloudy then 3 is true-in-F.
11   Putting the last lines of each half of the derivation together, we get the required biconditional.

What all this shows is that, for F, it is quite easy to define truth in a way which meets our intuitive requirements for definitions. The definition yields the right results though it does not itself contain the word 'true' or any equivalent. Admittedly, this is because F only contains four sentences, and what we must do now is to extend F. What I would encourage you to think now is that Tarski's method defined 'true-in-F' in virtue of the finiteness of F. This will make it all the more interesting when you see how his method can be extended to infinitary languages.

B.   A Simple Infinite Language

It is easy enough to convert F into a language with an infinite number of sentences. All we have to do is add some connectives (thereby creating the possibility of non-basic sentences), and allow sentences to be of any length (though any given sentence must be finitely long). I propose that we add the connectives '¬' and '&' since, as you saw in chapter 5, we can express any truth function using them. The new language will be called 'F+'. The most efficient way of referring to sentences is to use the code numbers, 1, 2, 3, 4 for the basic sentences as we did for F, and to use the connectives as names for themselves. Thus, the following are typical names of sentences of F+:

1 & 3

¬(2 & ¬3).

A truth definition for F+ must allow us to derive the correct truth condition for each and every one of the sentences of the language. Moreover, since there are an infinite number of such sentences, we cannot achieve this in the simple way we did for F. Here is a proposal.

x is true-in-F+ if and only if:

> x is 1 and it is cold or,
> x is 2 and it is wet or,
> x is 3 and it is cloudy or,
> x is 4 and it is windy or,
> x is ¬A and it is not the case that A is true-in-F+ or,
> x is A & B and A is true-in-F+ and B is true-in-F+.

In the definition, 'A' and 'B' are used as schematic letters which can be replaced by any sentence of F+. Do the contents of the box suffice to allow the derivation of all instances of Convention T? One example should suffice to show that the answer is 'Yes'.

> To derive: 1 & ¬2 is true-in-F+ if and only if it is cold and it is not the case that it is wet.

1 First assume that 1 and ¬2 is true-in-F+.
2 Since the sentence is of the form 'A & B', we appeal to the final disjunct to get: 1 is true-in-F+ and ¬2 is true-in-F+.
3 1 is true-in-F+ can be run through the definition again to get: it is cold.
4 Since B is ¬2, we appeal to the next to last disjunct to get: it is not the case that 2 is true-in-F+.
5 2 is true-in-F+ can be run through the definition again to get: it is wet.
6 When the items in the previous three steps are combined we get: it is cold and it is not the case that it is wet.

7   Hence, if 1 & ¬2 is true-in-F+ then it is cold and it is not the case that it is wet.

> **Exercise**
>
> Finish the derivation of the biconditional. That is, derive:
>
> > If it is cold and it is not the case that it is wet then 1 & ¬2 is true-in-F+

The above should convince you that what is in the box can be used to work out the truth conditions for any sentence of F+. However, there is a small snag. A close examination of the definition shows that it contains 'true-in-F+'. This violates our requirement that a definition must not use the very notion it purports to define. Here you must be wondering why I called this a 'small snag' instead of counting it as a reason to reject the definition outright. The reason is this.

The definition in the box uses 'true-in-F+' but it does so in an inessential way. If you reconsider the derivation given above, you will notice that 'true-in-F+' turns up in various steps, but that it drops out of consideration as the derivation proceeds. This is clear in, for example, step (3). We used the notion of 'true-in-F+' as applied to the conjunction, and then as applied to 1. But in step (3) it drops out in favour of the claim that it is cold – a claim that does not use 'true-in-F+'. In fact, it wouldn't really make much difference if instead of 'true-in-F+', I had written some nonsense word like 'glic' in the definition. You could then have considered that the definition in the box told you precisely under what conditions a sentence of F+ is glic, and we could have defined 'x is true-in-F+' as 'x is glic'. The extension of the complex predicate (the one that takes up six lines in the box) remains the same whether it contains the notion of 'true-in-F+' or 'glic'.

The original definition is called an *implicit* definition. Roughly, this means that it uses the notion it defines, but in an inessential way. Once you grasp some notion via an implicit definition, it is possible to convert the implicit definition into an *explicit* one, a definition that does not use the original notion at all. (Implicit definitions are also usually *recursive*, for the obvious reason that they define a notion by providing conditions to which appeal can be made in a recurring way. This is precisely what we did in the derivation.)

This topic is the subject of some rather advanced logical techniques. With those techniques, it is possible to lay down precise guidelines for implicit definitions, and to show how such definitions can be converted to explicit ones. In the present discussion, however, you can take my word for this, having seen, in outline, why 'true-in-F+' occurs inessentially in the above definition.

17.5 A Predicate Example

By now, you can see how Tarski sought to accomplish his aim. Truth can be defined for a finite language by little more than the listing of the truth conditions for each sentence. For an infinite language, you cannot hope to enumerate the truth condition of every sentence, but you can achieve the same result by saying something about each of the constructions used in the language. In particular, the truth definition for F+ told us how to work out the truth conditions for constructions using '¬' and '&'. By showing how the truth of non-basic sentences constructed with these connectives depends on the truth of their contained sentences, the definition delivers the wanted truth conditions for any sentence of F+. But, as we discussed at the beginning of the chapter, predicate–quantifier sentences do not depend for their truth on the truth values of their parts – the parts are not necessarily sentences. So, our next task will be to see how to define truth for a predicate–quantifier language which contains an infinite number of sentences. It is one of Tarski's lasting contributions that he showed how this could be done.

The details of a truth definition for a realistically rich predicate–quantifier language would occupy a great deal of space, but you don't need such a language to appreciate what Tarski did. We will construct a truth definition for a very simple language, P, which has the following elements:

(i)   variables: x_1, x_2,
(ii) predicates: Fx_1, Rx_1x_2,
(iii) quantifiers: ∃, ∀,
(iv) connectives: ¬, &.

The names of expressions of the language are formed by underlining the expressions themselves. For example, here is a name of a sentence of P:

$(\forall x_1)Fx_1$

This sentence is built up from a quantifier and a predicate neither of which can be said to be true-in-P, so we cannot implicitly define the truth of whole sentences in terms of the truth of their parts. Instead, we must sneak up on truth by first defining another notion, one which is more appropriate to predicates. That notion is called *satisfaction*.

The Satisfaction of Predicates

To illustrate how satisfaction is to be understood, we will think of the quantifiers of P as ranging over the very restricted domain of three persons: Tom, Dick and Harry.

Suppose you had to draw up lists using these three individuals as items. Each list would have three places in it, and each place could be taken by Tom, Dick or Harry. How many *different* lists could be constructed in this way? The answer is 27. (Three items and three places lead to the number 3^3, but the arithmetic is not important.) Some of these Lists (as I will now distinguish them) will assign the same individual to all three places, viz.:

List 1	List 2	List 3
Harry	Tom	Dick
Harry	Tom	Dick
Harry	Tom	Dick

Others will use two individuals, as in these samples:

List 4	List 5	List 6
Dick	Dick	Harry
Dick	Harry	Dick
Harry	Dick	Dick

And, of course, there will be Lists which have no repetitions:

List 8	List 9	List 10	List 11	List 12	List 13
Tom	Tom	Dick	Dick	Harry	Harry
Dick	Harry	Tom	Harry	Tom	Dick
Harry	Dick	Harry	Tom	Dick	Tom

These non-repetitive Lists present every item in the domain of quantification in every possible order.

What distinguishes one List from another is the order and identity of its elements. Remember that the above are only a sample of the full set of twenty-seven such Lists, though they will serve for the explanations which follow. (In the full account of even such a simple language as P, the domain of quantification could be infinite, so there could be an infinite number of different Lists each of which was infinitely long. However, you will get the idea even from our very restricted list of Lists.)

A List is said to *satisfy* a predicate when a chosen item in the List has the property specified by the predicate. Given that the predicate Fx_1 means 'x_1 is a parent', we can see that a List will satisfy this predicate if and only if the item chosen from the List is a parent. But how do we choose? To make everything determinate, we will assume that the subscript of the variable tells us which item to choose in a List. The expression:

List 10 (x_1),

will be understood to pick out the first item in List 10, viz. Dick, whereas the expression:

List 10 (x_2),

picks out the second item in List 10, viz. Tom. Using this notation, we can say precisely when any List (i.e. List N) satisfies the predicate Fx_1 as follows:

(I)   List N satisfies Fx_1 if and only if List $N(x_1)$ is a parent.

This can also be done for the two-place predicate Rx_1x_2:

(II)   List N satisfies Rx_1x_2 if and only if List N (x_1) is the father of List N (x_2).

For example, suppose that Harry is the father of Dick. This means that List 13 genuinely satisfies Rx_1x_2, whereas you can be sure that List 11 and List 2 do not. (If Harry is the father of Dick, then it cannot be that Dick is the father or Harry. And Tom is not the father of Tom.)

(I) and (II) lay down the satisfaction conditions for the predicates of P. These conditions tell you what is required for any given List (of the 27) to satisfy each of the predicates of P. We now have to turn our attention to the quantifiers and connectives.

The Satisfaction of Sentences with Connectives

Using 'A' and 'B' as schematic letters holding places for expressions of P, the satisfaction conditions for expressions with connectives are as follows:

(III)   List N satisfies $\neg\underline{A}$ if and only if List N does not satisfy $\underline{A}$.
(IV)   List N satisfies $\underline{A}\ \&\ \underline{B}$ if and only if List N satisfies $\underline{A}$ and List N satisfies $\underline{B}$.

Conditions (III) and (IV) are close copies of the conditions put in for '¬' and '&' in F+. Crucially, however, they are conditions on the notion of satisfaction rather than truth.

The Satisfaction of Quantified Sentences

The satisfaction conditions for quantified sentences are the ones that give the most trouble, so watch carefully.

> (V)   List N satisfies $(\exists x_i)\theta x_i$ if and only if some List N' which differs from List N in at most the ith place satisfies θx_i.

Here 'i' and 'θ' are used because in order to state the condition in the most general way we must avoid the use of specific numerical subscripts and specific predicates. After all, this condition is meant to explain satisfaction for any basic or non-basic predicate with variables that can be subscripted with '1' or '2'. That much should be clear, but what might not be is how (V) achieves its aim. It is easier to see what is going on in a specific case. Consider the sentence:

$$(\exists x_1)\ Fx_1,$$

and suppose that Dick is in fact a parent and Tom isn't. Does this mean that List 10 satisfies the sentence whereas List 8 does not? However tempting it is to say 'Yes', it would be a mistake. Because Dick is a parent, the above sentence is true regardless of what various Lists assign to the variable x_1. What we want to say is that, since *some* List has Dick in its initial place and satisfies the predicate, then all the other Lists might as well be counted as satisfying it too. And that is precisely what (V) says. If you read it carefully, you will see that it says of any List at all that it satisfies the sentence if and only if *some List satisfies the predicate in the sentence*. So, in virtue of List 10 satisfying the predicate Fx_1, we have the right to say that all Lists satisfy the whole sentence. Notice, they satisfy the whole *sentence* and not the predicate; we agreed that only List 10 does that. Also, notice that I required List N' to differ in 'at most' the ith place because I didn't want to rule List N out as a candidate for satisfying the predicate.

Predictably, the way to define satisfaction for a universally quantified sentence is:

> (VI)   List N satisfies $(\forall x_i)\theta x_i$ if and only if every List N' which differs from List N in at most the ith place satisfies θx_i.

The idea is that, if a universally quantified sentence is true, this must be because every item in the domain satisfies the predicate. Since the Lists are constructed so that every item is bound to turn up in each place of a List, we can say that a given List satisfies the sentence when every relevant List satisfies the predicate in the sentence.

Satisfaction Defined, and Then Truth

Putting (I)–(VI) together we can write out an implicit (recursive) definition of satisfaction in the following way using 'σ' as a variable for any sentence or predicate of P.

List N satisfies$_P$ σ if and only if:

- σ is Fx_i and List N (x_i) is a parent or,
- σ is Rx_ix_j and List N (x_i) is the father of List N (x_j) or,
- σ is ¬A and it is not the case that List N satisfies$_P$ A or,
- σ is A & B and List N satisfies$_P$ A and List N satisfies$_P$ B or,
- σ is (∃x_i)θx_i and some List N′ differing from List N in at most the ith place satisfies$_P$ θx_i or,
- σ is (∀x_i)θx_i and every List N′ differing from List N in at most the ith place satisfies$_P$ θx_i.

Having defined 'satisfies$_P$' ('satisfies-in-P'), we can now define 'true-in-P' as:

σ is true-in-P if and only if every List satisfies$_P$ σ.

It may not be obvious at first why this works, so begin by thinking about our original problem. What we wanted was a definition of truth for any *sentence* of P, but we were unable to treat P in the way we did F+ because the sentences of P contain parts that are not themselves sentences. These parts cannot be seen as true or false. However, the definition of satisfaction does apply to every predicate *and* sentence of P. Moreover, it was designed in such a way that the true sentences of P are satisfied by every List. For example, suppose that it is true that Tom is a parent. Then the sentence:

(∃x_1)Fx_1,

is true. The satisfaction condition for this sentence guarantees that any List satisfies it as long as some List satisfies its predicate. But we know that, since Tom is a parent, any of List 3, List 8 and List 9 satisfy the predicate. So, every List satisfies the sentence. You should be able to work out that, in any case in which we know that a sentence of P is true, it is satisfied by every List, and vice versa. Hence, we are justified in defining truth by means of the above definition of satisfaction.

The definition of satisfaction uses the notion of satisfaction, it is an implicit definition. However, as I remarked earlier, it is possible to convert this into an explicit definition using techniques from the more sophisticated branches of logic. We do not have to go into this, but it is important that it is possible. This is because satisfaction is a notion very close to truth, and we must be sure that such notions do not play an essential role in the final definition of truth.

The language P is a very restricted language, but it should be clear that a more complicated predicate–quantifier language is no more difficult to handle. First, each predicate must have its own satisfaction condition, so a more complicated language will have a longer definition. Also, if the language has designators in it, then these must be given special treatment. What you have to do is to give them a special status within Lists so that every List assigns the same item to its appropriate designator. This is merely a matter of making Lists more sophisticated, and getting the book-keeping right. Finally, the Lists that I used were for illustrative purposes only. As was mentioned earlier, the domain of quantification even for P is not going to be restricted to three individuals. What you have to do is to imagine that every item in a domain (possibly infinitely large) is ordered in just the way that Tom, Dick and Harry were ordered in Lists. The more usual term for these vast orderings is *sequences*, and I leave you to consult the more advanced texts on the Reading List to see how sequences are used.

17.6   Sentential and Predicate

The previous sections showed how to define truth for three languages: F, F+, and P. However, these languages differ from Sentential and Predicate in a fundamental way. For example, F+ is a language with basic sentences possessed of *fixed meaning*, whereas this is not so for Sentential. If I asked you under what conditions P_1 of Sentential is true, you would rightly be puzzled. The basic sentences of Sentential were used to mean different things on different occasions, so they cannot be given truth conditions in the way that we did for the basic sentences of F+. Similar considerations apply to the predicates of P and of Predicate. In the language P, 'Fx_1' means 'is a parent'. In Predicate, 'Fx_1' could mean 'is a parent' on one occasion and 'is round' on another.

The way forward requires a little general reflection on what we did when we defined truth for F+ and P. Consider the language P first. Our strategy was this: given that we know what the predicates of the language mean, we were able to define truth by organizing the domain of quantification so that we could say precisely when items in that domain satisfied the predicates and sentences of P. This organization was effected with Lists. Hence, when a domain of quantification is specified, it is easy enough to say when sentences of P are true. This is because we know what these sentences mean. The sentence:

$(\exists x_1)\, Fx_1,$

is true-in-P for any domain in which there is at least one parent. If the domain consisted entirely of books, the sentence would no longer be true.

In essence, then, we defined:

x is true-in-P relative to a domain D,

rather than simply:

x is true-in-P.

The specific, and purely illustrative, example was a domain consisting of Tom, Dick and Harry, but the definition of satisfaction itself did not restrict us to this domain. Indeed, you cannot tell which items are in the domain just by looking at the definition, though you can say this much: the domain D is the set of items from which Lists are constructed. This is why it is reasonable to say that our truth definition is relative to a choice of domain.

One presumes that if P were really a language spoken by some community, we could specify D so as to include any item they tended to speak of. That is, we could think of D as somehow part of their linguistic practice. In this case, our efforts at definition would really give us a definition of 'true-in-P'.

17.7   Truth Relative to (or in) a Structure

Given that Predicate (as opposed to P) does *not* come with fixed meanings for its predicates and a fixed domain, we could carry on the relativization so as to define:

(R)   x is true-in-Predicate relative to a domain D and an assignment of meanings to the predicates and designators of Predicate.

This is more the type of truth definition appropriate to a language like Predicate – a language which can be used for speaking about a variety of things, and whose symbols are not fixed in meaning. We will call the combination of a domain D and an assignment of meanings to predicates and designators a *structure*. What (R) does is define truth relative to a structure.

A brief return to Sentential should make the above clearer. Like Predicate, Sentential sentences are not fixed in meaning. For this reason, the definition of 'true-in-F+' is not wholly appropriate to Sentential. However, we could use the ideas in it to define a relativized notion of truth, viz. 'true-in-Sentential relative to an assignment of meanings to basic sentences'. For example, the sentence:

$$P_1 \lor P_2,$$

would be true-in-Sentential relative to assignments of meanings which rendered either of P_1 or P_2 true.

Of course, we don't really need to talk about *meanings* in an assignment. The truth of any sentence in Sentential is relative to the meanings of basic sentences, but this is because such meanings fix truth values. We could as well have said that $P_1 \lor P_2$ is true-in-Sentential relative to assignments which makes either P_1 true or P_2 true. We don't need to know what P_1 and P_2 are actually used to mean to say this.

So, truth-in-Sentential comes out as definable relative to an assignment of appropriate basic sentence truth values. But this is merely another way of saying 'relative to a row of a truth table'. Each row of a truth table for a sentence of Sentential is an assignment or *structure* relative to which the sentence is true or false.

The structures appropriate to Sentential are assignments of truth values to the basic sentences, whereas the structures appropriate to Predicate are domains plus assignment of meanings to predicates and designators. However, even though there is a different sort of structure appropriate to these different languages, the use of structures is the same. In each case, precise truth definitions can be provided for truth relative to a structure. The importance of this to our understanding of validity in Predicate can now be made clear.

At the beginning of this chapter, I pointed out that we had a precise understanding of the application of 'true' in the definition of validity for Sentential. A Sentential argument is valid when:

> any assignment of truth values to its basic sentence constituents which makes its premises true also makes its conclusion true.

We can now rephrase this in terms of our recently introduced notion of a structure:

> a Sentential argument is valid when every structure which makes its premises true also makes its conclusion true.

I am sure that you can see what is happening. Now that we have seen how to define precisely what it means for a Predicate sentence to be true in a structure, we can say:

a Predicate argument is valid when any structure which makes its premises true also makes its conclusion true.

NOTE I have said that a structure for Predicate is a domain and assignment of meanings to predicates and designators. This is true, but only the beginning. The notion of a structure in Sentential does not really require meanings, only truth values. Similarly, the notion of a structure in Predicate can be set out in a way that dispenses with this vague talk of meanings. Unfortunately, showing this requires some set theory and more space than I have here. Consult the advanced texts on the Reading List for details.

The Main Points of Chapter 17

1 A full understanding of validity requires a precise account of the notion of truth used in it. The recognition of this led us on a search for a definition of 'true' as applied to the sentences of Sentential and Predicate.

2 Using the conditions and method that Tarski laid out, we defined 'true' in its application to three sample languages. Two of them, F+ and P, resemble Sentential and Predicate, respectively. However, they differ in an important respect: key elements of Sentential and Predicate do not have fixed meanings. The basic sentences of Sentential and the predicates and designators of Predicate can have different meanings assigned to them in different contexts.

3 For this reason, one cannot define 'true' for Sentential and Predicate as we did for F+ and P. Truth must be understood as relative to an assignment of meanings.

4 In the case of Sentential, the assignment of meanings to basic sentences determines, in any given case, an assignment of truth values to basic sentences. Hence, truth in Sentential is relative to an assignment of basic sentence truth values. Any such assignment is called a *structure*. This means that each row of a truth table is a structure. Using this new way of describing the rows of a truth table, we can say that an argument is valid if every structure which makes its premises true also makes its conclusion true.

5   In the case of Predicate, truth is relative to the assignment of a domain for the quantifiers and meanings for the predicates and designators. Each such assignment is also called a structure, and the account of validity given in **4** can be repeated here. The function of the truth definition is to give us a precise idea of what it means to say that a Predicate sentence is true relative to (or in) a structure.

Appendix 1:
How to Learn Logic

It might seem strange to find an appendix to a book on logic with the above title. What has been going on for all the preceding pages if it wasn't aimed at instilling the subject? This is a fair question, and, in understanding the answer, you will be perfectly placed to take full advantage of what follows.

Introductory courses in logic figure centrally in philosophy and linguistics, as well as in computer science, because the concepts of logic are necessary for understanding thought and language. However, an adequate comprehension of logical concepts requires a mastery of various techniques. Amongst others, these include: constructing truth tables; evaluating formal arguments using truth tables; constructing deductions; and translating from natural language into formal language. Acquiring these techniques takes practice.

Skill in problem-solving is certainly important, but some logic courses over-emphasize it. In the main body of this book, I have tried to balance the theoretical and the practical – the understanding of what logic is about with a description of procedures that can de deployed. However, *descriptions* of procedures and techniques are often insufficient. To be good at logical problem-solving requires a more directed kind of instruction. 'How to Learn Logic' is intended for just this purpose. Whilst no substitute for reading the preceding chapters, it aims, by a mixture of focused explanation and exercises, to give you the confidence to solve logical problems. If you work through the Lessons which follow, doing the exercises and comparing your answers with those given, you should have no trouble with the practical side of the subject.

Note   Some answers to Exercises are worked out in each Lesson, but those marked with '*' are given at the end of this appendix.

A1.0   Sentential

Lesson 1: The Construction of Truth Tables

Stage One: basic knowledge

To employ Sentential effectively you must be able to construct truth tables for any sentences, or combination of sentences, thrown at you. In principle, this should not be difficult, since truth tables are constructed with the same recipe each time; as logician's say, there is an effective and mechanical procedure – an algorithm – for constructing them. However, in practice, there tends to be hesitation, since our minds are not naturally mechanical, and have to be trained to be so.

Think of the example of multiplication. We might not find it interesting or amusing to do, but we would not hesitate when asked how much is 3478 × 45. This is because we have been trained to recite certain basic facts – the multiplication table – and also trained to use a procedure for employing these facts. Knowing the product, e.g. of 5 × 8, is a small part of the getting the answer to the larger problem, but it is one long since committed to memory and requires no working out.

Analogously, constructing truth tables depends on training in regard to certain basic facts. These facts are the truth tables governing the five logical connectives: &, V, ⊃, ≡, ¬. You should know the facts recorded in these tables 'by heart'. The following EXERCISES should test that knowledge (and suggest how to instil it).

---

*Exercise 1

Given that the truth values of some sentence A are as listed below in the left-hand column, write out the column of values for ¬A.

A	¬A
T	
T	
F	
T	
F	
F	
T	
F	

Exercise 2

What is the truth value of P & Q, given that the value of P is T and the value of Q is F?

Answer

The answer is, of course, F. But this is a long-winded way of asking the question. More compactly, I could have asked simply what is T & F? (That is, what is the truth value of the conjunction of a sentence which is T with one which is F?) Using the truth values to stand in for sentences cuts out a certain amount of clutter, and the next EXERCISE uses this shorthand.

*Exercise 3

Below are all the rows of the truth tables for the two-place connectives (&, V, ⊃, ≡), though they are all jumbled up. (**Note:** they are written in the shorthand described above.) Give the resultant truth value in each case.

(a)	(b)	(c)	(d)
T ⊃ T	T & T	T V F	F ≡ T
F & T	F V T	T ≡ T	T V T
T ≡ F	F ≡ F	T & F	F & F
F V F	F ⊃ T	F ⊃ F	T ⊃ F

Suggestion

You should be able to give the required answers without hesitation – it should be second nature. However, if you found yourself pondering over each answer, make sixteen small cards with each of the above on one side, and the correct answer on the other. Test yourself on them whenever you get a chance, and you should come to know them as thoroughly as you do the multiplication table.

Stage Two: rows and columns

If you are now thoroughly familiar with the material in the EXERCISES above, you are ready for the next stage: constructing what can be thought of as the 'shell' of a truth table. In order to give more substance to this stage, we shall focus on the following sentence:

(1)   ((P & Q) ⊃ R) V ¬R.

But remember that what is described is intended as general – much of it figures in the construction of any truth table.

There are two tasks involved in constructing the shell: (i) you have to decide how many rows the table has; and (ii) you have to decide how many columns.

(i)   *Rows*

A truth table for a non-basic sentence aims to tell us what truth value the sentence has in every possible circumstance. So, there are as many rows as there are relevant possible circumstances. To calculate these, just count the number of different basic sentences contained in the target sentence (1). There are three, viz. P, Q, R. (**Note:** R occurs twice, but we are counting only the number of *different* basic sentences.) Having done this, use the following as a quick way to calculate how many rows you need:

> Number of rows = 2^n (where n = number of different basic sentences).

In respect of sentence (1), this is 2^3 (i.e. $2 \times 2 \times 2$) = 8. That is, there are eight different ways of assigning T/F to each of the three basic sentences.

In the completed shell, you must write these eight possibilities. The easiest way to do so without having to work it out each time, is to use the Half Again Method. Write half T and half F under the first basic sentence (P). Then write half as many again of T and F, alternately, under Q. Continue doing this and you will end up alternating T and F one at a time when you get to the last basic sentence (R). (Refer to the completed shell on the next page to see more clearly how this works.) Examine the rows to convince yourself that all eight distinct possibilities are included.

(ii)   *Columns*

Clearly we need to end up with a column giving the value of sentence (1) in each of eight possible circumstances (rows). This is the whole point of writing a truth table for a sentence. But what other columns do we need? The answer here is more practical than theoretical. You include various columns so as to make it easier to work out the final one. What is needed is a breakdown of the whole sentence into components whose truth values depends only on at most two other columns. In the case of sentence (1) such components are:

P & Q,

¬R,

(P & Q) ⊃ R.

The first of these depends only on P and Q, the second only on R and the third only on the column for components P & Q and R. With columns for each of these, it is easy to work out the column for the whole sentence as the resultant of the columns for (P & Q) ⊃ R and ¬R. (See column 7 below.) What one calls the truth table for sentence (1) is given by the column under the 'V' – what is called the main connective of the sentence. The shell for sentence (1) is:

1	2	3	4 5 7 6
P	Q	R	((P & Q) ⊃ R) V ¬R
T	T	T	
T	T	F	
T	F	T	
T	F	F	
F	T	T	
F	T	F	
F	F	T	
F	F	F	

The numbers are the columns discussed above: 1, 2 and 3 are already complete and they make up the appropriate rows of possible circumstances. Columns 4, 5 and 6 are for the truth values of the three component sentences of sentence (1). And column 7 is for the truth values of sentence (1) itself.

NOTE As shown in the completed shell, the columns for the component sentences are written under the appropriate connectives. This saves considerable space, but means that you have to keep your wits about you in deciding which column(s) to use – *and in which order*. For more detailed explanations of both (i) and (ii) see chapter 5, sections 5.5–5.9.

Stage Three: completing the job

All that remains is to fill in columns 4, 5, 6 and 7. Of course, column 7 could in theory be filled in immediately, and the truth table completed in this one step. However, this would require you to be able to just 'see' what truth value to assign to sentence (1) given each of the truth-value assignments to P, Q and R. This would be like being asked to give the answer to, say 43562 × 59812, without any calculation. Not being calculating prodigies, we need to do multiplication with pencil and paper, and the same applies to truth tables.

Column 4 is that of P & Q. Ignore the values under R, and work out the values using your knowledge of the truth table for '&'. (Remember: this was what you practised earlier in answering questions such as: T & F = ?)

Column 5 is the result of using column 4 and column 3 (the one for R). But be careful here. Since the connective involved is '⊃', the *order* in which you survey the truth values is crucial. You must first consider a value from column 4 and then the one in the same row from column 3. This is because the value of T ⊃ F is different from F ⊃ T.

Column 6 is also based on 3. It is governed by '¬' and requires only that you reverse the truth values of column 3.

Column 7, the truth table for the original sentence (1) is the result of using columns 5 and 6, though governed now by the 'V' which is the main connective of the sentence. Here is the completed truth table:

1	2	3		4 5 7 6
P	Q	R		((P & Q) ⊃ R) V ¬R
T	T	T		T T T F
T	T	F		T F T T
T	F	T		F T T F
T	F	F		F T T T
F	T	T		F T T F
F	T	F		F T T T
F	F	T		F T T F
F	F	F		F T T T

What does this table show? Interestingly, it shows that the truth value of sentence (1) is T in every row, i.e. in every possible assignment of truth values to the basic sentences P, Q and R. This means that sentence (1) is a tautology, but further discussion of this will figure in the next Lesson. For now what is important is that you be able to construct truth tables for any sentence. The guidance given above leaves nothing to chance, and all that remains is for you to familiarize yourself with the procedures by doing the following exercise.

*Exercise 4

Write out truth tables for the following sentences:

(a) P ∨ P
(b) ¬¬P
(c) ¬(P ⊃ Q)
(d) ¬(Q ⊃ P)
(e) ¬P ∨ Q
(f) P & ¬Q
(g) ¬(P & ¬Q)
(h) P ≡ ¬(Q ⊃ R)
(i) P ∨ (Q & R)
(j) (P ∨ Q) & R

Lesson 2: The Uses of Truth Tables

Being boring is usually a defect, but, exceptionally, in the case of truth tables this is not so. Having mastered the procedures of Lesson 1, you may well find that all interest has gone out of the task. However, that is just as it should be: truth-table construction is a purely mechanical process, therefore, its tediousness is a virtue. What is not boring – and is vital to understanding logical languages and inference – are the uses to which truth tables can be put.

(i) Sorting sentences

The truth-table example used in Lesson 1 showed that the sentence:

((P & Q) ⊃ R) ∨ ¬R,

has the value T in every row of its truth table. It is a *tautology*. This may have come as a surprise; just by looking, it is not obvious. But even if you suspected as much, the truth table is necessary to confirm it. A sentence which has F in every row is a *contradiction*, and one with at least one T and one F is *contingent*.

Exercise 1

Use truth tables to determine whether each of the following is a tautology, a contradiction or is contingent.

(a) P ⊃ (P ⊃ Q)
*(b) ¬P ⊃ P

*(c)   ¬¬P ⊃ P
*(d)   ((P ⊃ R) ⊃ Q) V R
*(e)   ¬(¬P V (¬Q V P))

Worked answer to (a)
The truth table for this sentence is in the third column:

P	Q	P ⊃ (P ⊃ Q)	
T	T	T	T
T	F	F	F
F	T	T	T
F	F	T	T

Since this has both Ts and Fs, the sentence (a) is contingent.

The compact sentence:

(1)   P V ¬P,

is clearly a tautology. What about this monster?

(2)   (((P & Q) ⊃ R) V ¬R) ≡ (P V ¬P).

To the left-hand side of the biconditional is the tautology described in Lesson 1; the right-hand side is the compact or 'standard' tautology. Clearly, since the left- and right-hand sides of the biconditional will always have the same truth value (in this case, T), the whole of the (2) above is a tautology. And there is an important lesson here: if two sentences have the same truth table then the biconditional sentence joining them will be a tautology. That is, if A and B have the same truth table values, then A ≡ B will be a tautology. When this latter fact is so, we say that A and B are *logically equivalent*.

*Exercise 2

Use truth tables to determine which of the following sentences are logically equivalent to which others.

(a)   ¬(P & ¬Q)
(b)   ¬P V Q
(c)   P & ¬Q
(d)   ¬(P ≡ Q)
(e)   ¬(P ⊃ Q)
(f)   ¬(P ⊃ Q) V ¬(Q ⊃ P)

> **Hint**
> Construct a single truth table with columns for each of the sentences and compare these columns.

(ii)   Testing arguments for validity

The main business of truth tables is testing validity. However, there is a small, though absolutely crucial, observation we must make before we can use them for this purpose. So far, all our efforts have been expended on constructing truth tables for sentences. But an argument is not a sentence – it is a structure involving sentences. In particular, it expresses a relationship between some sentences known as premises and a sentence identified as the conclusion. Arguments are valid or invalid; sentences are true or false. One must not confuse sentences and arguments. Yet what we have to do now is to extend the truth table method to arguments.

There are two ways to go about this: (a) the argument–sentence method; and (b) the direct inspection method.

(a)   Argument–sentences

Suppose we have the following (schematic) argument:

(3)   Premise1
Premise2
_____
Conclusion.

Using materials in this argument, we construct the following sentence:

(4)   (Premise1 & Premise2) $\supset$ Conclusion,

by conjoining the premises and making the resulting conjunction the antecedent of a conditional in which the conclusion is the consequent. This sentence is known as the *corresponding conditional* of the argument, or, more succinctly, as the *argument–sentence*.

There is an enormously useful relationship between sentence (4) and argument (3).

(5)   If the sentence is a tautology then the argument is valid (and vice versa).

Exercise 3

Explain why claim (5) is true.

Hint
See chapter 6, section 6.3.

(b)   Direct inspection

Consider this argument:

(6)   P ∨ Q

       ¬Q
       ———
       P

We can show that it is valid if we can show that all possible ways of making the premises jointly true also make the conclusion true. Relaxing the idea that truth tables are constructed only for sentences, imagine what happens if we treat the whole argument as apt for a truth table. What we do first is to count *collectively* the number of different basic sentences in the premises and conclusion. There are two in the above argument: P, Q. Then we construct a basic truth-table shell based on this. The result is:

1	2	
P	Q	
T	T	
T	F	
F	T	
F	F	

Next, we make sure that there are columns giving the truth values of each of the premises and the conclusion. Column 1 is the conclusion, but we need columns for each of the premises. The completed table is:

1	2	3	4
P	Q	P ∨ Q	¬Q
T	T	T	F
T	F	T	T
F	T	T	F
F	F	F	T

Finally – and this is the crucial step – we examine the table by first noting *all the rows* in which the premises are jointly true, and then making sure that the conclusion is also true *in each such row*. In the case of argument (6), the two premises are both T only in row 2. And in this row the conclusion is T. Since this shows that there is no possibility (row) in which the premises are true and the conclusion false, it shows the argument is valid.

NOTE   Some arguments will have many rows in which premises are jointly T, some will have very few or even none. The number of such rows makes absolutely no difference to the judgment of validity. All that matters is that *if there are any such rows, then the conclusion must be T in all of them.*

Exercise 4

Use truth tables to decide the validity of the following arguments. (You may use either method (a) or (b), but *in each case explain your answer*.)

(a)	(b)	(c)	*(d)
P	P ⊃ (Q & R)	(¬P & R) V Q	¬P ≡ R
P	¬Q	Q ⊃ ¬¬R	R ≡ Q
¬P		¬P	P ≡ Q
		¬R	

Worked answer to (a)
The truth table for P – the premise *and* conclusion – is simply:

P
—
T
F.

Given this, the premise is T only in the first row and the conclusion is also T there. So, the argument is valid.

(iii)   Consistency

Consistency in speech and opinion is generally praised, but it is not always understood. In logic, there is a simple and clear definition of this notion: to say a set of sentences is *consistent* means that it is *possible for all of them to be jointly true.* Note that consistency does not require actual truth. In this it resembles validity, but one must be careful here.

Consistency is a property of any set or list of sentences. These sentences may all be about the same subject matter, or they may be as unrelated to one another as you please. An argument is not, or is not merely, a list of sentences. It is a structured list in which, if it is valid, the initial part of the list (the premises) guarantee the truth of the conclusion. Given this, consistency and validity are notions that apply to quite different sorts of thing.

However, it is always possible to think of an argument structure as a mere list. And if you do some tinkering about with the conclusion of an argument, you get a list with a very interesting property. Here is one of the arguments that figured as an example above:

(6)   P ∨ Q
       ¬Q
       —————
       P.

Suppose we temporarily forget that this is an argument rather than a mere list of sentences, and suppose also we put a negation in front of the conclusion. This produces the list:

(7)   P ∨ Q
       ¬Q
       ¬P.

Is this list consistent? You may think this is a daft question, but recall what we know about argument (6) from which this list was generated. It was shown earlier to be valid. Hence, we have already shown that it is not possible for the premises to be true and the conclusion false. But the premises are the first two sentences on the above list. And if it is not possible for them to be true and the conclusion false, then it is not possible for them to be true and *the negation* of the conclusion also to be true. A statement is, after all, false when its negation is true. So, given that argument (6) is valid, we know that list (7) is not consistent – it is inconsistent.

Look at it the other way around: if list (7) were consistent, then it would be possible for its first two sentences to be true when its third was also true. But given the negation in the latter, this would mean that it was possible for P ∨ Q and ¬Q to be true whilst P was false. However, this would make argument (6) invalid – something we know it isn't. So, we must have been wrong when we assumed consistency: list (7) must in fact be inconsistent.

In moving from the question of validity to the question of consistency (of the list made from premises and the negation of the conclusion) don't forget that it is the *inconsistency* of the list which shows the validity of the original argument.

Given the connection between the notions of validity and inconsistency, it is unsurprising that truth tables can be used to test for the latter. One first constructs a truth table for the list of sentences whose consistency is in question, and then completes the test by seeing if there is a row of the table showing each member of the list to be T. The presence of at least one such row guarantees consistency, and its absence shows inconsistency

NOTE You must be careful about using truth tables to test for consistency. The same procedure for construction of truth tables is used, but what you need to look for in the finished table differs depending on which property you are seeking to uncover. Validity requires a search for rows where premises which are jointly T followed by a verification that, in each such case, the conclusion is also T. Consistency requires finding only a single row in which all items in the list are true.

Note too that the definition of consistency applies to lists containing even a single sentence, though it is perhaps more idiomatic to call a single sentence self-(in)consistent.

Exercise 5

Use truth tables to determine whether the following lists of sentences are consistent.

(a)	(b)	(c)	*(d)
P	R ⊃ Q	Q V (P & Q)	¬(¬P V ¬P)
¬P V Q	R ⊃ P	¬(P & Q)	¬P
	¬P		
	R		

Worked answer to (c)
There are two different basic sentences represented in the list. So, we need a four row truth table which has separate columns for the two non-basic sentences in (c). This is shown below.

P	Q	Q V (P & Q)	¬(P & Q)
T	T	T T	F
T	F	F F	T
F	T	T F	T
F	F	F F	T

In row 3, both of the sentences are true, so they are consistent with one another.

Lesson 3: Deduction – Introduction to the Rules of the Game

In order to have the confidence necessary to construct deductions, you have to feel comfortable with the rules of inference. And a quick look at them does not suffice. Think here about carpentry. Given a pile of wood and a set of tools, it is unlikely that as a novice you would be able to construct a table. Nor would it help much to be given descriptions of what the tools can be used to do. What is needed – and this is the point of carpentry classes – is a 'hands-on' facility with the way each tool works, and some idea of how they can together be used to transform the pile of wood into the desired table. As with the carpenter's tools, so it is with the rules of deduction.

NOTE   For the above reason, EXERCISE 1 in chapter 9 is of the greatest importance. If you haven't done so already, write out the ten rules on a sheet of paper, indicating how to keep score in using each of them. This sheet will be a handy reference for what follows in this Lesson and the next.

There are ten rules of inference and you are to assume that they suffice for constructing a deduction for any valid argument, and also that if you dropped any one of them, the remaining nine would not be up to this task. In other words, the ten rules are jointly sufficient and each necessary to proving validity. (The sufficiency of the set of ten rules and the necessity of each of them can itself be proved using techniques of mathematical logic which go beyond anything discussed in this book.) Knowing these facts may not actually get you started in proving any particular conclusion, but they certainly should give you confidence in the rules. For what you know is that mastery of them gives you a sure-fire instrument for proving the validity of any valid argument you come across.

Additionally – and more important practically – the rules come in pairs which are directly related to the connectives of Sentential. For each such connective, there is one rule showing how to eliminate the connective from some premise or premises, and another showing how to introduce it. In essence, elimination rules are 'break-down' rules and introduction rules are 'build-up' rules for each of the connectives, and this way of thinking can provide a useful clue for tackling any given deduction. Consider how you might approach the problem of constructing a deduction in the following case:

Example 1

  P & Q
  Q & R
  ———
  P & R

The conclusion contains '&' and so do each of the premises. You know that there are two rules applying to the '&', viz.

  I   CONJUNCTION ELIMINATION (&E)

  A & B   A & B
  ———   ———
  A   B

  II   CONJUNCTION INTRODUCTION (&I)

    A   A
    B   B
  ———   ———
  A & B   B & A

The first tells you how to break down a conjunction into components, and the second how to use certain items to build a conjunction. Moreover, the above are the only rules applying to conjunctions, and they clearly do not take you directly *from* conjunctive sentences *to* other conjunctive sentences. So what are you to do in respect of Example 1 – a case in which the premises and conclusion are all conjunctions? The best advice here (and it will prove to be of general use) is:

  Look first at the conclusion and determine what you would need to get it.

Here the conclusion is P & R, and this could be constructed, using the build-up rule II (&I), if only you had P and R as separate lines in the proof. But, of course, having got this far, it is easy to see that you can get P and R as separate lines by applying the break-down rule I (&E) to each of the premises. Putting it all together, we get:

  (1) P & Q
  (2) Q & R
  (3) P
  (4) R
  (5) P & R

Lines 3 and 4 are the result of breaking down the premises in line 1 and 2 respectively, and line 5 results from building a conjunction from those two lines.

NOTE   The sequence of five lines given above is not strictly speaking a deduction answering to the demands of Example 1. This is because it is not clear, merely by inspection, what justifies each line and how the truth-dependencies are transmitted from line to line. In short, the above sequence is missing its explicit score-keeping. Here is the proper deduction:

1	(1)	P & Q	Premise
2	(2)	Q & R	Premise
1	(3)	P	1, &E
2	(4)	R	2, &E
1,2	(5)	P & R	3,4 &I

Each premises depends for its truth on itself – a premise is simply a given. Line 3 comes from the premise in line 1 by &E (and so depends for its truth on it). Similarly for line 4 and premise 2. And finally line 5 comes from lines 3 and 4 by &I and so it depends on both premises. (One adds up the truth dependencies of lines 3 and 4.)

What is absolutely crucial is that one be able to read the final line as confirming the sought after deduction. In this case, line 5 is the required conclusion *and* it depends for its truth on lines 1 and 2. But this is just what we set out to show, since lines 1 and 2 are the premises of Example 1.

If all of the inference rules were as simple as those governing conjunction, then constructing deductions would be very simple indeed. Unfortunately, they are not. Nor is this because logicians are a perverse lot who have intentionally chosen difficult rules. What causes the trouble is the simple but crucial fact that we need a sufficiently strong set of rules which are also truth-preserving: any rule for eliminating or introducing a connective must not lead us from true premises to a possibly false conclusion. Thus, if we had a rule for the conditional like the following (marked to show it would be a rotten apple indeed):

$$\text{\Large\Apple} \quad \frac{A \supset B}{A}$$

it is easy enough to see how quickly we could get into trouble. This convenient but crazy rule would allow us to conclude that it was truly going to rain merely from the truth of the premise:

If it is going to rain, we had better take an umbrella.

Only someone thoroughly confused about the meaning of 'if' could ever make such a mistake, and we can scarcely build deductions on such absurd foundations.

The need for the rules of inference governing each connective to be truth-preserving, combined with the need to make them strong enough to handle any possible valid argument, results in certain of them being difficult customers.

Given that it is usually best to begin gently, I have already discussed the two straightforward rules governing '&', and I shall continue with this policy. As you will see from the reference list of rules you should have prepared (or from chapter 9), the following five rules are no more complicated than those governing conjunction:

Elimination Rules

$$(\neg E) \quad \frac{\neg\neg A}{A}$$

$$(\supset E) \quad \begin{array}{c} A \supset B \\ \underline{A} \\ B \end{array}$$

$$(\equiv E) \quad \frac{A \equiv B}{(A \supset B) \ \& \ (B \supset A)}$$

Introduction Rules

$$(\equiv I) \quad \frac{(A \supset B) \ \& \ (B \supset A)}{A \equiv B}$$

$$(VI) \quad \frac{A}{A \lor B} \qquad \frac{A}{B \lor A}$$

The score-keeping procedures for all of the above are no more demanding than those for conjunction elimination and introduction. There are two elements to score-keeping: first, to *justify* a line in a deduction, write down to the right of each line the name of the rule used and the line (or lines) to which the rule appeals. Second, to indicate *truth dependencies*, write to the left of each line the line (or lines) which guarantee its truth.

Both of these score-keeping procedures are direct and simple. Clearly, if you want to justify your entitlement to a given step in a deduction, you must cite one of the ten rules. Similarly, if someone were to ask of a given step in a proof: 'On what does this line depend for its truth?', this information is shown by numbers on the left-hand side of the deduction sequence. Moreover, the seven rules given above make the tabulation of truth dependencies easy. As Example 1 showed, you need only note two things. First, premises depend for truth on themselves. And, second, the truth dependencies of any given line come from the lines used in the application of the relevant rule. Thus, in Example 1 (see Note box above), line 3 comes from 1 by &E. So, line 3 depends on whatever line 1 does. In this case, line 1 is a premise, so it depends on itself. Put simply: if you use a line or lines in applying a rule, then the truth dependencies of those lines follow through to the new line.

---

*Exercise 1

Below are three deductions which show their correct truth dependencies. Fill in on the right of each line the appropriate justification.

(a)			(b)			(c)		
1	(1)	$P \equiv Q$	1	(1)	$P \supset \neg\neg Q$	1	(1)	P
2	(2)	$\neg\neg Q$	2	(2)	$R \,\&\, \neg\neg P$	2	(2)	$P \supset (Q \,\&$
1	(3)	$(P \supset Q) \,\&$	2	(3)	$\neg\neg P$			$\neg\neg R)$
		$(Q \supset P)$	2	(4)	P	1,2	(3)	$Q \,\&\, \neg\neg R$
1	(4)	$Q \supset P$	1,2	(5)	$\neg\neg Q$	1,2	(4)	$\neg\neg R$
2	(5)	Q	1,2	(6)	Q	1,2	(5)	R
1,2	(6)	P	1,2	(7)	$Q \lor R$			

Hint

First look at the last line. The truth dependencies of that line show which lines are premises in the deduction. Also, once you have identified these premises, try to do the deduction yourself even before you attempt to justify each line of the above.

Exercise 2

Below are three deductions each of whose lines is justified appropriately. Fill in correct truth dependencies on the left-hand side of each line.

(a)
(1)	¬¬P	Premise
(2)	P ⊃ ¬¬Q	Premise
(3)	P	1 ¬E
(4)	¬¬Q	2,3 ⊃E
(5)	Q	4 ¬E

*(c)
(1)	P ⊃ Q	Premise
(2)	R ⊃ (Q ⊃ P)	Premise
(3)	R	Premise
(4)	Q ⊃ P	2,3 ⊃E
(5)	(P ⊃ Q) & (Q ⊃ P)	1, 4 &I
(6)	P ≡ Q	5 ≡I

*(b)
(1)	P & Q	Premise
(2)	Q	1 &E
(3)	Q ∨ R	2 VI

Worked answer to (a)
(1) and (2) are dependent on themselves since each is a premise; (3) comes from (1) so is dependent on it; (4) comes from (2) and (3), so is dependent on whatever they are, namely (1) and (2). (5) has the same dependencies as (4), namely, (1) and (2).

Exercise 3

Construct deductions for each of the arguments below.

(a)
P ≡ (Q ∨ R)
Q
_____
P

*(b)
P & (Q & R)
_____
Q & (P & R)

(c)
P ⊃ (Q ⊃ (R ⊃ S)))
P
Q & R
_____
S

Worked answer to (a)
The conclusion is a single letter which is only located in the first premise, so somehow you have to get it out of there. Now the first premise is an equivalence which, if broken down by ≡E, reveals:

(P ⊃ (Q ∨ R)) & ((Q ∨ R) ⊃ P).

The second premise and the right-hand side of the above offer some hope of getting the needed conclusion P by ⊃E, but the second premise is Q and you need Q ∨ R. This is no problem, though, as you can always get Q ∨ R from Q by VI. Putting it all together, here is the deduction:

1	(1)	P ≡ (Q ∨ R)	Premise
2	(2)	Q	Premise
1	(3)	(P ⊃ (Q ∨ R)) & ((Q ∨ R) ⊃ P)	1 ≡E
1	(4)	(Q ∨ R) ⊃ P	3 &E
2	(5)	Q ∨ R	2 ∨I
1,2	(6)	P	4,5 ⊃E

Lesson 4: Deduction – The More Difficult Rules

The remaining three rules present most of the problems. Because they can be difficult to understand, there is a reluctance to reach for them in planning a deduction. But of course many deductions can only be constructed with their help. In this Lesson you will get practice with each of them separately. This should give you the confidence to use them in any circumstances.

(i)   Conditional Introduction

One reason often given for not buying lottery tickets is that winning might not be a blessing. Let us suppose, for example, that you have a friend who wants to buy a ticket and that you want to dissuade him by showing that:

(1)   If he wins the lottery, his life will be ruined.

This conclusion is a conditional and it would be translated into Sentential as:

P ⊃ Q.

Forget for the moment any of the apparatus of Sentential. How would one go about convincing someone of the truth of the (1)?
   Typically, you would begin by saying:

(2)   Suppose that you did win the jackpot in this week's lottery.

Then you would use various background features of your friend's life to argue from this assumption to the truth of:

(3)   Your life would be ruined.

Of course, there might be lots of disagreement about these background features, and whether they did show conclusively that his life would be ruined. It is not easy to convince someone that he or she would be worse off in acquiring £10 million. However, insofar as you do manage it, we can describe your reasoning this way: you used the supposition (2), together with a set of agreed truths about your friend, to demonstrate (3). Having done this – and this is the crucial step – you and your friend would be right to think that you had thereby proved the truth of the original conditional claim (1).

On what would the truth of this depend? What makes it true that *if your friend wins the lottery, his life will be ruined*? Well, clearly, the background facts about your friend that you and he share functioned as premises in your reasoning. Hence, the conclusion you reached certainly does depend for its truth on them. What about the supposition you made about your friend actually winning the lottery? Is the truth of (1) dependent on the actual truth of (2)? Certainly not. The whole point about (2) was that it was a supposition or assumption, allowing you to get started. Making such an assumption and then using it, together with the background premises, to reach (3), in no way commits you to taking (2) to be actually true. The most natural way of expressing this is to say that, having assumed (2), it is *discharged* when you eventually conclude (1). That is part of the point of the word 'if' in your final conclusion: what you wanted to show was that IF he won, his life would be ruined. The interim assumption (2) was made, as we say, only for the 'sake of the argument'.

Against the background of this discussion, look at the rule for:

Conditional Introduction ($\supset$I)

Given that you can show:

$$\frac{A}{B}$$

(That is, you can deduce B from A.)

you have the right to assert:

$$A \supset B$$

This rule encapsulates exactly the kind of reasoning used about the purchase of the lottery ticket, though the rule is stated in a more general, and yet precise, way. In the first stage of the rule, a deduction from A to B is constructed. (This is like showing 'Your life will be ruined' follows from 'You win the lottery.') In the second, the conditional $A \supset B$ is asserted. (In the example, 'If you win the lottery then your life will be ruined.')

The tricky part of using this rule comes in the score-keeping. In justifying any line using Conditional Introduction, you cite on the right-hand side the line number of A and the line number of B together of course with the abbreviation '⊃I'. That is straightforward. But, in contrast to the rules already discussed, with Conditional Introduction there is a *decrease* in truth dependencies cited on the left. This is a reflection of the point discussed above: the use of A in the proof of B is discharged when you conclude A ⊃ B. And this means that A ⊃ B does not depend for its truth on A, or on whatever A itself depends. In effect, A is dropped, having done its work 'for the sake of the argument'. (It is easy to see this in terms of our example: the final 'If you win the lottery then your life will be ruined' does not depend for its truth on 'You win the lottery.' Indeed, the later might (probably will) be false.) Of course, the final conditional does still depend for its truth on any *other* lines used to establish the valid transition from A to B. (Just as the conditional conclusion about the lottery depends for its truth on whatever facts you use to convince your friend.)

Exercise 1

Construct deductions for the arguments below using the seven rules of Lesson 3 and Conditional Introduction.

*(a)
Q ⊃ R
P ≡ R
───────
¬¬Q ⊃ P

(b)
P ⊃ (Q & S)
Q ⊃ R
───────
P ⊃ R

(c)
P ⊃ Q
P ⊃ R
───────
P ⊃ (Q & R)

Worked answer to (b)

1	(1)	P ⊃ (Q & S)	Premise
2	(2)	Q ⊃ R	Premise
3	(3)	P	Assumption
1,3	(4)	Q & S	1,3 ⊃E

1,3	(5)	Q	4 &E
1,2,3	(6)	R	2,5 ⊃E
1,2	(7)	P ⊃ R	3,6 ⊃I

Notice how the assumption was discharged in the move from (6) to (7) as we formed the conditional with that assumption as antecedent.

(ii)   Negation Introduction

Three people are standing by a tennis court hoping for their Sunday morning doubles match. The fourth person – Oliver – hasn't shown up and they have done all the warming up they can stand. One of them says: 'Oliver might be late because he didn't realize that the clocks were put forward last night.' To this, another responds:

> Well, suppose that you are right. Still, it only takes him ten minutes to get here from his house and he always arrives for our matches twenty minutes early. He would be at most forty minutes late. And we have been waiting an hour already. So, you can't be right about the reason for his not being here.

The key to Negation Introduction is contained in this familiar kind of reasoning. A supposition is made about the reason for Oliver's being late. From this supposition someone derives a conclusion which is absurd because it is, or is near to being, a contradiction. One then concludes that the *negation* of the original supposition must be true. In the case above, it would look roughly like this:

(a)   *Suppose:* The reason for Oliver's being late is his ignorance of the clock-change.

(b)   From this and certain other premises which are considered plausible *deduce*:

Oliver would be here now.

(c)   This contradicts the obvious fact that Oliver is not here.

(d)   *Therefore*, the clock-change is not the reason for his being late.

The conclusion of this piece of reasoning is the negation of the supposition made in (a). What the reasoning has done is to introduce the negation. Familiar as an explicit form of argument for more than two thousand years, this reasoning has been variously called *indirect proof* (you suppose the opposite of what you want to conclude) or *reductio ad absurdum* (the supposition is shown to imply a contradiction – something it would be absurd to regard as true.)

As with the Conditional Introduction, this kind of reasoning ends with the discharging of its original assumption. The conclusion in the above does not depend for its truth on the truth of the supposition (a). It is assumed solely for the sake of the argument. Here is the rule in its full glory:

Negation Introduction (¬I)

If you can show that:

> A
> _____
> B & ¬B

then you have the right to conclude:

> ¬A

In justification, you cite – on the right of ¬A – the line in which you assume A and the line in which you formally derive the contradiction B & ¬B, as well as the rule: ¬I. Since the conclusion does not depend on the supposition A, you drop this from the truth dependencies listed to the left of the line in which you conclude ¬A.

Exercise 2

Construct deductions for the arguments below using the seven rules of Lesson 3 and Negation Introduction.

(a)
P ⊃ Q
P ⊃ ¬Q
_____
¬P

(b)
¬P ⊃ (Q & P)
_____
P

*(c)
P
_____
¬(¬P & Q)

Worked answer to (b)

1	(1)	¬P ⊃ (Q & P)	Premise
2	(2)	¬P	Assumption
1,2	(3)	Q & P	1,2 ⊃ E
1,2	(4)	P	3 &E
1,2	(5)	P & ¬P	2,4 &I
1	(6)	¬¬P	2,5 ¬I
1	(7)	P	6 ¬E

Unable to see how to get a single letter conclusion from the premise by any of the seven rules, we tried assuming the negation of the desired conclusion. This gave us the chance for the contradiction at line (5), and the negation of the assumption by ¬I. Then we used ¬E to get the conclusion. Note how the assumption is discharged as the negation is introduced at line (6).

(iii)   Disjunction Elimination

You have to book a ferry to France for the weekend. As this means getting to the Dover road from central London on a Friday evening, you decide to book for as late as possible in the evening. Why? Here is the reasoning:

> One gets to the Dover road either by taking the Blackwall Tunnel or going over Shooters Hill. Suppose one takes the Tunnel. They are rebuilding the Commercial Road – the main route to the Blackwall Tunnel – and with the Friday traffic, this will ensure a terrible delay and no chance of getting to Dover for an early evening ferry. Suppose one heads for Shooters Hill? They have closed a relief road halfway up the hill which guarantees that the tailbacks will be severe, so no chance of getting to Dover for an early evening ferry. Either way there is no chance to catch the early ferry, so there is no chance. Better book the later one.

This common form of reasoning captures the essence of conjunction elimination. Starting out with a disjunction – A ∨ B – you derive some claim, C, by assuming in turn each side of the disjunction. This then entitles you to count C as following from the original disjunction itself. As was said in the everyday argument above: either way we can't get there early, so we can't get there early. Here is the formal statement of the rule:

Disjunction Elimination

Given you can show that:

$$\frac{A}{C} \quad \frac{B}{C}$$

You have the right to conclude that:

$$\frac{A \lor B}{C}$$

The full justification of a line got from this rule requires that you write:

> the line number of A ∨ B;
> the line numbers where A is assumed and C is deduced;
> line numbers where B is assumed and C is deduced.

That makes five line numbers, plus of course the abbreviation of the rule: VE. On the left, the final conclusion C depends for its truth on whatever previous lines you used, except of course those in which you assumed A and B. This is because those two assumptions were used simply for the sake of the argument, and are discharged as you reach the conclusion.

The trickiest part of all this is the fact that, in using this rule, you reach the conclusion C *three* times: once as a result of assuming A, once as a result of assuming B, and finally without these assumptions. But this should be clear enough if you keep in mind my earlier example. Applied to the reasoning about the trip to Dover, you concluded three times that you cannot make the early ferry: once on the assumption that you go by the Blackwall Tunnel, once on the assumption that you take Shooters Hill, and finally without these assumptions. It is only in this final statement of the conclusion that it is shown genuinely to follow from the initial disjunction.

Exercise 3

Construct deductions for the arguments below using the seven rules of Lesson 3 and Disjunction Elimination.

(a)

$$\frac{P \lor (Q \& R)}{(P \lor Q) \& (P \lor R)}$$

*(b)

R ∨ Q

Q ⊃ S

R ⊃ ¬¬S

S

(c)

(P ∨ Q) & (P ∨ R)

P ∨ (Q & R)

Worked answer to (a)

1	(1)	P ∨ (Q & R)	Premise
2	(2)	P	Assumption
2	(3)	P ∨ Q	2 VI
2	(4)	P ∨ R	2 VI
2	(5)	(P ∨ Q) & (P ∨ R)	3,4 &I
6	(6)	Q & R	Assumption
6	(7)	Q	6 &E
6	(8)	P ∨ Q	7 VI
6	(9)	R	6 &E
6	(10)	P ∨ R	9 VI
6	(11)	(P ∨ Q) & (P ∨ R)	8,10 &I
1	(12)	(P ∨ Q) & (P ∨ R)	1,2,5,6,11 VE

Here we assume each side of the disjunction of (1) in lines (2) and (6). From each of these we deduce the conclusion. This work done, we have the right to assert the conclusion again at line (12) by VE, but this time as dependent for its truth just on line (1).

NOTE *A warning about assumptions* If you make an assumption – something you are free to do at any stage in any proof – you must be able to discharge it on reaching the intended conclusion. If you fail to do this, then the assumption will figure on the left of your conclusion, and would be a clear sign that you have not finished. Remember, a deduction only counts as correct if (i) every line can be justified by one of the ten rules; (ii) the desired conclusion is the last line; and (iii) the conclusion depends for its truth only on the premises. (It might not depend on all the premises. That doesn't matter in respect of validity, though it does show that the unused premise is irrelevant.)

This is not merely a technical point: if you were allowed to have undischarged assumptions, you could deduce any conclusion in one step simply by assuming it. This would make deduction easy, but worthless.

Since the only way to discharge an assumption is by one of the three rules just discussed, you must plan your deductive moves carefully. Don't make an assumption unless you have a fairly clear idea of what you need to get to in order to discharge it. Your aim might be to get a conditional (⊃I), or contradiction and, hence, a negation of the assumption (¬I), or a conclusion depending on both sides of the disjunction (VE). Each of these will allow you to discharge your assumption at the end.

Lesson 5: Deduction: Putting all the Rules to Work

Having mastered the seven straightforward break-down and build-up rules, and practised with the other three individually, you should be ready to put them together with confidence. Several pieces of advice before you start.

1.   Begin with the conclusion

It cannot be said too often how important it is to look long and hard at the conclusion in order to give yourself some idea of a good strategic line for constructing the deduction. Indeed it is sometimes a good idea to treat the conclusion as a premise in order to see what you can prove from it. You might find that the conclusion is provably equivalent to some other sentence – one that is easier to prove from the initial premises.

2.   An eye on assumptions

If it is not obvious how you can reach the conclusion by straightforward breaking down and building up of the premises, you will probably have to make some further assumptions with a view to using the three rules that work from such assumptions.

3.   Trial and error

Be prepared to make a number of forays which turn out to be dead-ends. Have plenty of scratch paper to hand, since it is always a mistake to think you will see your way clear to constructing a deduction without making false moves.

Exercise 1

Construct deductions showing that each of the following arguments is valid.

    (a) $\neg(\neg P \lor \neg Q) \vdash P$
    (b) $P \supset Q \vdash (R \lor P) \supset (R \lor Q)$
   *(c) $P \supset Q \vdash \neg Q \supset \neg P$
    (d) $(P \supset Q) \supset P \vdash P$
   *(e) $P \supset Q \vdash \neg P \lor Q$
    (f) $P \lor (\neg Q \lor R), \neg P \& Q \vdash R$

Worked answer to (a)

The conclusion is a single letter and none of the elimination rules are applicable so as to yield a single letter. So, certain assumptions will have to be made. Most likely to lead somewhere is negation introduction, so it would be sensible to start by assuming the negation of the conclusion, viz. ¬P. But what can be done with this? The aim will be to get a contradiction, yet it might not be obvious how. Look hard at the premise: it is a negation of a disjunction. As mentioned above, there are no elimination rules applying directly to such a sentence. Still, consider disjunction introduction. If we are careful about what we disjoin with our assumption, ¬P, we can get an unnegated disjunction (¬P ∨ ¬Q), and this can be conjoined with the premise to give us the needed contradiction. The deduction in full is:

1	(1)	$\neg(\neg P \lor \neg Q)$	Premise
2	(2)	$\neg P$	Assumption
2	(3)	$\neg P \lor \neg Q$	2 ∨I
1,2	(4)	$(\neg P \lor \neg Q) \& \neg(\neg P \lor \neg Q)$	1,3 &I
1	(5)	$\neg\neg P$	2,4 ¬I
1	(6)	P	5 ¬E

Worked answer to (b)

Whenever a conclusion is a conditional, it is sensible to assume the antecedent of it. This gives you an extra premise, and sets your goal as the consequent. (For if you reach the goal, you can get the original conditional conclusion in one step by conditional introduction.) The antecedent in this case is a disjunction and so is the consequent. This should set two thoughts going. First, you can deduce something from a disjunction if you can deduce it from the assumption of each side. And, second, given that you need eventually to get a disjunction, you need only one side of it; disjunction introduction will do the rest. Here then is where we have got to in this informal survey:

Assume R ∨ P. You need now to get R ∨ Q. If you assume R, then R ∨ Q follows immediately by VI. What about the assumption of P – the other side of the disjunction? Here you can see that P and the first premise will give you Q. But with Q, you can also get R ∨ Q by VI. Since R ∨ Q follows from the assumption of each side of R ∨ P, it follows from R ∨ P itself (plus any other premises used). A single application of ⊃I finishes the deduction:

1	(1)	P ⊃ Q	Premise
2	(2)	R ∨ P	Assumption
3	(3)	R	Assumption
3	(4)	R ∨ Q	3 VI
5	(5)	P	Assumption
1,5	(6)	Q	1,5 ⊃E
1,5	(7)	R ∨ Q	6 VI
1,2	(8)	R ∨ Q	2,3,4,5,7 VE
1	(9)	(R ∨ P) ⊃ (R ∨ Q)	2,8 ⊃I

Lesson 6: Translation

Unlike the construction of truth tables, there can be no mechanical procedure for translating from a natural language like English into Sentential. Hence, practice is crucial. The exercises below are organized in a way which should help you to achieve the necessary level of competence.

Being clear about the translation of basic sentences is crucial. You must translate only *complete* English sentences by basic sentences of Sentential. Be careful about cases where there seems to be a connective such as 'and' or 'or' but there isn't. The EXERCISE below, and the remarks which follow it, should make this advice clear.

Exercise 1

Translate each of the following into Sentential. State fully and precisely which English sentence is translated by which Sentential sentence.

(a)   Vanessa and Dorothy are in the History Department.
(b)   Vanessa and Dorothy figured out the answer.
(c)   Aqua regia, or a mixture of hydrochloric and sulphuric acids, will dissolve gold.
(d)   Paris and London are capital cities.

(e)   A variegated leaf is green and white.
(f)   Vanessa and Dorothy lifted the picnic hamper.
(g)   Paris and London are 259 miles apart.
(h)   Oil and water do not mix.

Some answers and suggestions

(a)   Suppose we agree that:

P – Vanessa is in the History Department.
Q – Dorothy is in the History Department.

Does (a) then mean the same thing as: P & Q? The answer seems clearly 'Yes'. But let's look at (b).

(b)   Suppose that:

P – Vanessa figured out the answer.
Q – Dorothy figured out the answer.

Does (b) mean the same as: P & Q? The answer here is not so clear. It may mean this – each of them may have been separately set a problem to which they figured out the answer. Or perhaps they worked together on the problem, so that 'Vanessa and Dorothy' is really a way of pointing to a team effort. If the latter is the case, the translation of (b) by P & Q is not very accurate. What about (f)?

(f)   Here we begin by supposing that:

P – Vanessa lifted the picnic hamper.
Q – Dorothy lifted the picnic hamper.

The translation of (f) by P & Q seems wrong. Anyone hearing it would think that each of them lifted the hamper, whereas the original sentence implies that they did this as a joint effort. (Though, I can imagine someone suggesting that even if they lifted the hamper together – one on each handle – it is in some sense true that Vanessa lifted it and true that Dorothy lifted it. This, however, seems a very strained interpretation. It is as if, having said that I lifted something with both hands, someone commented: 'So your left hand lifted it and your right hand lifted it.')

The moral of (a), (b) and (f) is that 'and' is a slippery customer. Sometimes it is a straightforward sentence connective, and sometimes a way of fusing two subject terms. Moreover, these different interpretations depend on knowing, not just about logic, but about the way things are in the world. Being in a

History Department is a property of people individually, solving problems may or may not be the result of individual effort, and the lifting of a single object is most plausibly a joint effort. Still, don't worry too much if you are uncertain in a given case. The aim of this EXERCISE is to make you aware of certain problems. Faced with a real case of argument – outside a textbook – you could make further inquiries to settle any doubts.

(c) shows a use of the 'or' which is not properly a disjunctive sentence connective. Aqua regia is that mixture of acids, and the 'or' functions something like the phrase 'that is to say'.

(d) and (g) make a nice contrast. The first sentence has 'and' as a straightforward sentence connective. But, if we treated the second in this way we would get the following piece of nonsense:

London is 259 miles apart and Paris is 259 miles apart.

This is why it is so important to write out the full interpretation of each basic sentence. When you do so, you will be able to see straightaway whether you have got a genuine connective or some other use of a connective word.

The remaining examples are left to the reader.

There are lots of ways of expressing conditionality in English. However, in Sentential, there is only one: $\supset$. Thus, translation of conditionality always involves re-expression into straightforward 'if ... then' form, and this can be surprisingly difficult. (It is surprising because when speaking we usually have no trouble at all with the different forms of conditionality, yet we can lose our grip when translation is at issue.) The following EXERCISE, by focusing on a single, well-known, kind of conditionality, should make clear how the different sorts are to be translated into Sentential.

Exercise 2

The law is clear enough: in the United Kingdom, the minimum drinking age is eighteen. However, the owner of the University Tavern wants to convey this to his customers in more colloquial terms, so he sets out to put up a sign behind the bar. Below are some of the options he considers. Translate all of them into Sentential and then say which of them correctly expresses the law?

(a) If you are over eighteen, you will be served here.

(b) If you are served here, you are over eighteen.

*(c) You will be served here only if you are over eighteen.

*(d) You will not be served here unless you are over eighteen.

*(e) You will be served here if you are over eighteen.

*(f) Only if you are over eighteen will you be served here.

*(g) You will be served here unless you are not over eighteen.

*(h) You will be served here provided that you are over eighteen.

*(i) Unless you are not over eighteen, you will be served here.

*(j) If you are not over eighteen, you will not be served here.

Some suggestions and answers

Let us agree right away that the basic sentences for this Exercise are:

P – you are over eighteen.
Q – you will be served here.

This makes the translation of (a) easy, namely:

$P \supset Q$.

Does this correctly capture the legal situation? Not really. There may, of course, be lots of reasons why someone is not served in a pub other than being underage. (The customer is drunk, the staff have walked off, the roof has fallen in, there has been a fire, there is no drink left, etc.) Anyone seeing (a), and being over eighteen, would have the right to insist on being served regardless of these sorts of circumstance. Failure to serve such a person would falsify (a).

(b) is better. It would be translated as:

$Q \supset P$,

and it captures the law whilst still allowing that there could be other reasons to refuse service.

Given these two cases, you should try to translate the remainder, having one eye to whether they are equivalent to the unsatisfactory (a) or the acceptable (b). It might help too to keep in mind that $P \supset Q$ is logically equivalent to:

$\neg Q \supset \neg P$,
$\neg P \vee Q$.

(These were established by truth tables in earlier **Exercises**.)

*Exercise 3

Translate each of the following into Sentential, indicating the meaning of each basic sentence you use.

(1)   Jennifer will be seeing her friends in England next year, but only if Kim gets some work or Jennifer wins the lottery.
(2)   Clouds yield rain if and only if glaciation takes place.
(3)   It would be a strange old world if we all thought alike.
(4)   Serpents and white whales inhabit that distant ocean but no living man has seen either.
(5)   We can have an Indian takeaway, or fish and chips if the chip shop is still open.
(6)   If we organize tennis, it is either raining or one of us is busy.
(7)   The Athenian youths will be saved if Theseus turns up and if the ball of string guiding him is long enough.
(8)   When it rains in the Far East, it pours.
(9)   The contract will be ready on time or the legal department will have a lot of explaining to do.
(10)   Ted and Alice are not speaking to Bob or Carol.

Lesson 7: The Strategy Applied

The material in the previous five lessons should have honed your skills in:

(i)   employing truth tables to probe sentences and evaluate arguments in Sentential,
(ii)   constructing Sentential deductions,
(iii) translating from English into Sentential.

At this point, then, you can be let loose on arguments in natural language. You should now find it a simple matter first to translate such arguments into Sentential and then evaluate them by truth tables. Moreover, in the case of valid arguments, you should be able to confirm their truth-table validity by constructing deductions.

There are no skills additional to those listed above needed for dealing with natural language argumentation. But before you begin the exercise below, a few words of advice.

It is reasonable to approach each argument as if it were an exercise in sentence-by-sentence translation, but take care to note how the language of one sentence can depend on others. Any premise (or conclusion) is bound to make more sense if it is understood as part the complete discourse of the argument. For example, the sentence:

She hadn't either,

is not intelligible except as following, say:

Keith and Miranda went to Sicily. Keith had never travelled there before,

Also, once you have completed the translation you will apply the methods of logic as if you were simply doing an exercise in Sentential. But if you get a result too much at variance with your initial thoughts about the original argument, be prepared to re-examine your translation.

Exercise 1

Evaluate each of the following arguments using truth tables. For any that you find to be valid, construct a deduction as further confirmation of validity.

*(a) If today is Tuesday, there will be a logic class. Therefore, if today is Tuesday and the rain has stopped, there will be a logic class.

*(b) Michael will come to dinner if and only if David doesn't. If David doesn't come to dinner, then James will send an apology. James will send an apology. Therefore, Michael will come to dinner.

*(c) Either Helen will get home before seven or Dora will worry. If Dora does not worry then Helen will get home before seven. Dora worries. Therefore, Helen does not get home before seven.

*(d) It is not the case that Maria keeps her cake and eats it too. In fact, she either keeps her cake or eats it. Therefore, Maria keeps her cake if and only if she doesn't eat it.

*(e) If Mrs Sorel was asleep and her son was in France then the Rolls could not have been driven that night. However, if the Rolls was not driven that night, it would not now be dented. As any fool can see, it is dented. Therefore, if Mrs Sorel was asleep her son was not in France.

(f) If Professor Grote publishes his new book, he will lose his academic reputation. He will however become Dean unless he doesn't lose his academic reputation. Therefore, if Professor Grote publishes his new book, he will become Dean.

A1.1   Predicate

Lesson 8: Predicates and Sentences

Predicates are the descriptive ingredients in sentences. They work by expressing either properties of things or relations among them. Here are some natural language predicates:

> . . . is blue,
> . . . is plastic,
> . . . won,
> . . . is the sister of . . .,
> . . . bought . . .,
> . . . is ten miles to the north of. . . .

In each case, if we want to use the predicate to describe some specific object or objects, we have to put designators of the object(s) in the gaps shown by '. . .'. If there is one gap, then the predicate is said to express a property (e.g. the property of being blue); and if more than one, it is said to express a relation (e.g. being the sister of).

What if someone were to ask whether, for example:

> (1)   . . . is the sister of . . .,

is true? The answer would be a short and sharp rejection of the question as foolish; given the gaps in it, it makes no sense at all to wonder whether it is true. One could put the point this way: (1) is a predicate, not a sentence, and only sentences are truth-evaluable.

The distinction between predicates and sentences is fairly obvious in connection with natural-language examples, though exactly the same distinction figures in the formal language of Predicate. Of course, in Predicate we use variables to indicate the appropriate gaps, since this gives us more flexibility and precision. Yet even though variables look distinctly less 'gappy' than '. . .', the distinction between predicates and sentences is just as real.

Consider the predicate:

> (1)   Rxy (where 'R' means 'is the sister of').

Suppose someone asked whether it is true. The expression 'Rxy' is not a sentence – it is a predicate – and it makes no sense at all to wonder whether a predicate is true or false. To be sure, the predicate 'Rxy' can be *true of* a pair of items – it is in fact true of, for example, Virginia Woolf and Vanessa Bell, though it is not true of Virginia Woolf and

Vita Sackville West. (One could also say that the pair consisting of Virginia Woolf and Vanessa Bell *satisfies* the predicate 'Rxy'.) However, on its own a predicate, containing as it does variables, is just not fit for making a true/false claim.

NOTE   Basic sentences in Sentential are treated as indestructible atoms out of which the premises and conclusions of Sentential arguments are fashioned. Sentential methods of testing validity probe the argument structures created by the connectives, without at the same time probing into the basic sentences themselves. Indeed, Sentential says nothing about them except that they are either true or false and that their truth values contribute to the truth values of the non-basic sentences in which they figure. In Predicate, however, we have a language which takes even basic sentences seriously. Designators, predicates, variables and quantifiers are the key elements which allow us to investigate what is usually called 'sub-sentential' structure.

Predicates are the building blocks of sentences. For example, if we fill the gaps in (1) by designators, we can construct various sentences such as:

(2)   Virginia is the sister of Vanessa.
(3)   Virginia is the sister of Vita.

Designating Virginia, Vanessa and Vita as 'a', 'b' and 'c', sentences (2) and (3) could be rendered into the Predicate language as:

(2′)   Rab,
(3′)   Rac.

Replacing the variables in a predicate is not the only way to transform it into a sentence. Consider:

(4) $(\exists x)\,(\exists y)\, Rxy.$

This means (roughly):

(4′)   Someone is the sister of someone.

The variables in the predicate 'Rxy' have been, as one says, *bound* by quantifiers, and this transforms it into a sentence – an expression apt for saying something true. The claim in (4′) is of course general – it is not about this or that designated pair of human beings – but it is obviously (if unadventurously) true.

Some students find the idea of a quantifier binding a variable a technical notion too far. But there really isn't anything fundamentally technical about it. Suppose you overhear part of a remark, viz.:

(5)   ... he is over-tired. ...

Clearly, you are not in a position even to begin to decide whether (5) is true. To get into such a position, one thing you might do is ask who is being talked about – which particular being is in fact designated by the use of 'he' in this (part of a) sentence. But you might get a surprise. On asking to whom 'he' refers, you might be told: no one specifically. What was said was:

(6)   Anyone who drives a taxi sixty hours a week, he is over-tired.

This latter sentence employs a universally quantified phrase 'anyone who drives a taxi sixty hours a week' and we can hear it as attaching to, or binding, the pronoun 'he'. Put together, the quantifier phrase, the pronoun it binds and the predicate containing the pronoun ('is over-tired') produce the general sentence (6).

Essentially, a sentence is a predicate which has no loose ends – no variables that are not bound (i.e. *free*). Remember, for all their apparent mathematical pedigree, Predicate variables are just a place-holders or gaps. These loose ends – free variables – can be tidied up either by replacing one or more of them by designators or by binding them with quantifiers.

Or by a combination of both. (As will now be explained.)

Consider this expression:

(7)   Rax.

Here one of the variables has been replaced by a designator (of Virginia). But there is another variable free, so the result is still a predicate and not a sentence. In fact, (7) functions as a *one-place* predicate, which can be rendered in the familiar mixture of Predicate and English as:

(7′)   Virginia is the sister of x.

As we know from the earlier example, if the 'x' in (7) were replaced by a designator of Vanessa, the result would be the sentence:

(8)   Rab
       (Virginia is the sister of Vanessa.)

But if someone was keen on asserting a general sentence, (7) could be transformed into:

(9)   (∃x) Rax,

by binding 'x' with an existential quantifier. (9) says that Virginia is the sister of someone, and we know this to be true.

NOTE   At the risk of emphasizing the obvious, I want to stress three things.

First, a sentence is an expression apt for saying something true or *false*; (8) and (9) happen to be true, but they would be sentences even if they weren't.

Second, a general sentence like (9) is not merely an indirect or disguised way of referring to a specific individual. In saying that Virginia is the sister of someone, we have a sentence which is made true (as a matter of fact) by the existence of either Vanessa Bell or George Duckworth. But (9) does not specifically refer to either – its truth is of a general kind.

Third, talk of procedures for turning predicates into sentences – i.e. replacing variables by designators or binding them with quantifiers – should not mislead you. In the normal course of events you don't start with a predicate and turn it into a sentence. You just make assertions with sentences and these contain predicates.

---

*Exercise 1

Which of the following are sentences and which are predicates? (Assuming that a, b and c are designators.)

  (a)   Fx
  (b)   Saxy
  (c)   Fb
  (d)   (∀x) Fx
  (e)   Rax
  (f)   (∀x) Fy
  (g)   (∃x) Rcx
  (h)   (∃x) (∀y) Ryx
  (i)   (∀y) Ryx

*Exercise 2

Highlight all the free variables in the expressions in EXERCISE 1. (**Note:** be especially thoughtful about expression (f), which is not a misprint.)

*Exercise 3

How many different sentences can you construct from the predicate:

Rxy,

assuming that you have available the designators a, b as well as the quantifiers?

Lesson 9: Non-basic Predicates

As we said in the previous Lesson, predicates are the descriptive element in any sentence. For the moment, let us leave on one side discussion of sentences whilst refining our understanding of predication. The task in this Lesson will be to understand how descriptions can come to be more complex. In effect, we shall be taking the message of the last Lesson a little further (and deeper). We begin with the important distinction between *basic* and *non-basic* predicates. Focus on the following three predicate expressions:

(1) Fx,
(2) (∃y) Rxy,
(3) Fx ⊃ Gx.

The first is a basic *one-place* predicate, the second and third are also one-place predicates but they are more complicated.

A basic predicate is an upper-case letter followed by those variables needed to display the relevant 'gaps' in the predicate. Thus, if 'F' is intended as 'is plastic' then the full predicate expression is 'Fx'. This is because 'is plastic' has only one 'gap' in it – it would take only one designator to transform 'F' into a sentence ('a is plastic'). The letter 'R' (intended as 'is the sister of') is properly written as 'Rxy'. This is because it would take two gap-filling designators to turn it into a sentence ('a is the sister of b').

In contrast, (2) and (3) are *non-basic* predicates constructed from basic ones. (2) comes by quantifying one of the variable places in a two-place predicate, thereby creating a new one-place predicate. (That is, leaving only one gap to be filled.) (3) uses a connective to transform two predicates – each of which is one-place and basic – into a non-basic predicate (which is still one-place). The transforming elements in (2) and (3) – quantification and the use of connectives – are the two fundamental devices for transforming basic into non-basic predicates. If you understand what is going on in them, the whole of Predicate should become clearer. For that reason, let us dwell a little more on (2) and (3).

In natural language there is a real, even if less formal, distinction between certain basic and non-basic predicates. For example, it is difficult to see how the predicate 'is the sister of' could be broken down into simpler predicates. You could try to analyse the predicate expressing sisterhood as: having the same parents and being female. But this is not a simplification in any real sense, since it relies on yet another two-place predicate, viz. 'x is the parent of y'. However, taking sisterhood to be a basic *relation* between certain pairs of individuals, there is a *property* of individuals – expressed as the predicate: 'is the sister of someone' – which is familiar enough. It is a property which is true of no men, but is true of many – though far from all – women. Moreover, the predicate expressing this property somehow seems to involve the two-place predicate 'is the sister of' as well as another ingredient, and it is at this point that (2) comes into its own. For it captures precisely the otherwise vague idea that 'is someone's sister' *involves* the predicate 'is the sister of'; you can actually see a two-place predicate contained in (2). And you can see how the quantification of one of these places transforms the basic two-place predicate into a non-basic one-place predicate.

The non-basic predicate in (3) does not correspond to any very natural-sounding English language expression. Nonetheless, it is clear enough that (3) is built out of basic predicates. Suppose for example that we took 'Fx' to be 'x is a dog' and 'Gx' to be 'x is a mammal'. Then the predicate in (3) would be true of those things that were *if dogs then mammals*. As noted, this sounds a bit strange, but it more than makes up for it by giving Predicate a precise way to make certain claims. To see this, we shall return briefly to sentences.

Look around the room you are in, asking yourself *which things is predicate (3) true of*. Guessing a little about your room's contents, this predicate is true of:

> the chair you are sitting on,
> the table in front of you,
> the lamp you are reading by,
> the pen you have to hand.

This is because the kind of conditional in question is the material conditional ($\supset$), and we know that anything which falsifies the antecedent makes it true. That is, in this case, all non-dogs make it true. What would *falsify* predicate (3)? You would have to find a dog (making the antecedent true) which was not a mammal (making the consequent false). But, of course, there aren't any dogs that are not mammals. So, (3) is in fact a predicate true of everything unrestrictedly. And this gives us a simple way to capture the thought that every dog is a mammal. To do so, we merely universally quantify the predicate:

(3)   Fx ⊃ Gx.

This gives us the sentence:

(3′)   (∀x) (Fx ⊃ Gx).

This says that everything in the universe – absolutely everything – is, if a dog, then a mammal. And this is the way to say, in the Predicate language, exactly what is intended by the English sentence: 'All dogs are mammals.'

As noted, the translation of 'Fx ⊃ Gx' into English sounds awkward; there is no natural predicate in English corresponding to it in the way that 'x is the sister of y' corresponds to 'Rxy'. The awkwardness of *direct* translation between the predicates of English and those of Predicate is in fact quite important. It has been a central aim of this book to get students of logic to think of Predicate – at least initially – as independent of natural languages such as English. Your aim should be to learn how Predicate expressions relate directly to the objects, properties and relations which make up the world. If you can understand, for example, 'Fx ⊃ Gx' as applying or not applying to certain objects (given the properties relevant to 'F' and 'G'), then you will be well on your way both to understanding Predicate logic and to using it later to display English-language argument forms.

*Exercise 1

Which of the predicates below is true of which objects? (Use the key provided for interpretation, and refer to the letters below the objects as an aid to answering.)

Key
Fx – x is round
Gx – x is black
Hx – x is grey

Predicates
(a) Gx
(b) Hx
(c) Fx & Gx
(d) Fx ⊃ Gx
(e) Fx ∨ ¬Gx
(f) Gx ⊃ Fx
(g) Fx ≡ Gx

Objects

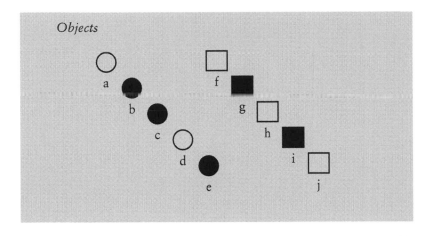

*Exercise 2

On the next page is a picture of some points and connections. Which points satisfy the predicates given? (Use the key provided for interpretation of the predicates. Use the designators of the points in the diagram to give your answers.)

Key
Rxy – x is directly connected to y. (This means connected by a single line. Also, we assume that no point is connected to itself.)
Sxyz – x is connected by y to z. (That is, connected via some intermediary point.)

Predicates
(a) Rxy
(b) Sxyz
(c) (∃x) Rxy
(d) (∃y) Rxy
(e) (∃y) Sxyz
(f) (∃y) (∃z) Sxyz
(g) (∀y) ¬ Rxy
(h) (∃y) ¬ Rxy

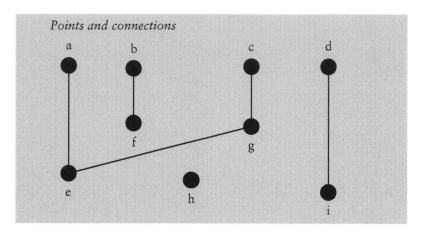

Points and connections

Exercise 3

Here is a part of a family tree:

   (i)   Person a has only one sister, whom we designate b.
   (ii) Person a's mother (designated c) has only one sister, desig-
        nated d.
   (iii) d has a son (designated e) and a daughter (designated f).

Using the predicates as interpreted (below), write ten true sentences about this family (try to include at least four with quantifiers).

    R_1xy – x is the mother of y
    R_2xy – x is the aunt of y
    R_3xy – x is the cousin of y

Hint
Given (i) and (ii) we can see that d is the aunt of a and b. So, some of the possible true sentences are:

    R_2da, R_2db, $(\exists x)\, R_2xa$, $(\exists x)\,(\exists y)\, R_2xy$.

Lesson 10: More Complicated Predicates

Consider the non-basic predicate:

   (1) $Gx\ \&\ (\exists y)\,(Fy\ \&\ Rxy)$.

This is more intricate than previous examples – it employs both connectives and a quantifier. Still, if you don't try to render it too directly into

English, it shouldn't be difficult to get the measure of it. Assuming the key given, let us see how it apply to the objects shown below.

Key
Fx – x is a circle
Gx – x is a square
Rxy – x is to the right of y

Objects

(**Note:** I have provided designators to make it easier to keep track of the objects.)

(1) is a predicate with a single free variable ('x'), so we know that the whole must say something like:

x is . . . .

The difficult part is to fill in the dots. First, and temporarily, ignore the quantifier. This gives us the predicate:

(2)   Gx & (Fy & Rxy).

This is of course two-place – it is true of whatever fills the gaps signalled by 'x' and 'y'. In particular, it holds when *x is a square* and *y is a circle* and *x is to the right of y*. Of which objects does this relationship hold? You answer this by looking for things which are squares (a, d, e), and things which are circles (b, c, f) and then finally seeing which of the first are to the right of the second. Here is a complete list of the pairs of things which meet all three conditions:

(i)   d,b,
(ii)   d,c,
(iii) e,b,
(iv) e,c.

Why pairs? Remember that (2) is a two-place predicate: it is true of pairs of things which meet the conditions laid down in the basic predicates of which (2) is constructed.

Of course, our original predicate:

(1)   Gx & (∃y) (Fy & Rxy),

is not a two-place predicate, and we cannot go on ignoring the quantifier. But now it is easy to see the contribution that the quantifier makes: it binds 'y' in 'Fy' and in 'Rxy'. The effect of this is to change our search for pairs of objects meeting the three conditions, into a search for single objects meeting the condition which we can now render as:

(3)   . . . is a square to the right of some circle.

Finding these objects is straightforward. Look at the pairs we listed above. The first item in each is a square which is to the right of a specific, designated circle. So, each of these items fit the bill – they are each squares to the right of some (i.e. at least one) circle. Of course, the first item in pair (i) is the same as that in pair (ii), and similarly for pairs (iii) and (iv). So, eliminating this redundancy, the objects which satisfy predicate (1) are d and e.

The non-basic predicate in (1) is built up by using both connectives and quantifiers. Therefore, the easiest strategy in this case is to separate these two building up processes. Summarizing, we first found out what satisfied the non-basic predicate you get by ignoring the quantifiers, and then found out what satisfied the original – the predicate with the quantifier restored.

---

*Exercise 1

Here is a list of predicates. Say: (i) how many free variables they have; and (ii) using the key provided, try to express them as best as you can in English.

Key
Hx – x is human
Mxy – x is married to y
Lxy – x lies to y

Predicates
(a)   (Hx & Hy) & Mxy
(b)   (Hx & Hy) ⊃ Mxy
(c)   (Hy & Hx) & Lxy
(d)   Hx ⊃ Lxx
(e)   Mxy ⊃ (Hx & Hy)
(f)   (Hx & Hy) ⊃ Lxy
(g)   (Hy & Hx) & (Mxy ⊃ Lxy)
(h)   (Hx & Hy) & (Mxy ⊃ Myx)

Here is yet another predicate:

(4)   Gx & (∀y) (Fy & Rxy).

The key, as above, is:

Fx – x is a circle,
Gx – x is a square,
Rxy – x is to the right of y.

To which of the objects below does it apply?

Objects

a   b   c   d   e   f   g

The predicate got by dropping the quantifier is:

(5)   Gx & (Fy & Rxy),

and this is precisely the same as (3) above. Applied to our new set of objects, this predicate is true of the following pairs:

(i)   d,b,
(ii)   d,c,
(iii)   e,b,
(iv)   e,c,
(v)   g,b,
(vi)   g,c,
(vii) g,f,

Each of these pairs has a square as the first item and a circle as the second, and the first is to the right of the second. Let's see what happens when we restore the quantifier so as to get the original predicate:

(4)   Gx & (∀y) (Fy & Rxy).

Be very careful here. The quantifier is universal (unlike that in (1) above which was existential). The only way to interpret this predicate with its universal quantifier is as demanding that:

x is a square and every object is a circle which x is to the right of.

But this is absurd. In the sequence of objects above, it is clearly false that every object is a circle. (Nor could it be true of any square that it is to the right of every object. How could an object be to the right of itself?) Hence, there are no objects in the above sequence which satisfy the predicate. Indeed, it will not be possible to find any sequence containing objects that satisfy it. How could there be objects which were both squares and circles?

What has gone wrong here? You might have expected that (4) was satisfied by squares that were to the right of *every* circle. This expectation would be natural enough given that the first example of a predicate in this Lesson, viz.

(1)   Gx & (∃y) (Fy & Rxy),

was true of squares to the right of *some* circles. But instead we ended up with a bizarre predicate, unlikely to be true of any object at all.

The problem here is the too potent mix of a universal quantifier and the '&'. When you say:

(∀x) (x is . . . & x is __),

you are in effect demanding that every object satisfy both '. . .' and '__'. There may be some situation in which something this strong is true, but it is unlikely to be common. Remember that the universal quantifier ranges over everything in the universe. The restricted Situations (and sequences of objects) in this book are sort of 'cut-down' universes, serving merely as manageable examples. But the quantifiers are unrestricted. Any conjunctive claim made with the universal quantifier is thus very strong indeed. In the case of (4) it is just too strong to have a hope of ever being true.

To get around the problem here, recall the way in which the '⊃' figured in:

Fx ⊃ Gx.

This predicate is very weak. It is trivially satisfied by the myriad objects that simply fail to be F. However, as noted in the previous Lesson, when it is bound by the powerful universal quantifier, we get a claim of just about the right strength. The sentence:

(∀x) (Fx ⊃ Gx),

is true precisely when anything that is actually an F is also a G. The same strategy applies to (4). What is wrong with it is very simply fixed: the connective '&' is the main connective within the scope of the universal quantifier and we must change it to '⊃'. This gives us:

(6)   Gx & (∀y) (Fy ⊃ Rxy).

Using the technique adopted before, let us imagine this without its quantifier. We get:

(7)   Gx & (Fy ⊃ Rxy).

Which objects in the above sequence fit this predicate? We are looking for pairs of objects of which the first is a square and the second is:

> if a circle, then the first item in the pair (the square) is to its right.

Here is a complete list of those pairs:

(i)	a,a	a,d	a,e	a,g		
(ii)	d,a	d,b	d,c	d,d	d,e	d,g
(iii)	e,a	e,b	e,c	e,d	e,e	e,g
(iv)	g,a	g,b	g,c	g,d	g,e	g,f	g,g

There are rather a lot of them, so I have arranged them in four rows. Studying these pairs will repay the effort. Each row contains those pairs whose *first member is one of the squares*. (After all, 'Gx' is the first conjunct, so we must always select a square as the first object in any pair for there to be any hope of finding objects which match the whole predicate.) The second member of each pair either trivially satisfies 'Fy ⊃ Rxy' by failing to be F (a circle), or is a circle with the relevant square on its right. (Note, by the way, that the pair consisting of a square written twice does actually satisfy the whole predicate precisely because such a square is definitely not a circle, i.e is not F.)

What happens when we put the quantifier back in? With the quantifier binding the 'y' variable, the whole expression is a non-basic, one-place predicate. To remind you, it is:

(6)   Gx & (∀y) (Fy ⊃ Rxy).

We then have to find objects which are squares and to the right of everything if it is a circle. The circles are b, c and f. Row (i) shows that the square, a, is not to the right of the three; neither are squares d and e, as you can see by consulting rows (ii) and (iii). But square g is shown in row (iv) to be to the right of the circles b, c and f. So, only object g in the sequence fits the predicate in (6). It is the only square which is to the right of everything if a circle.

*Exercise 2

Say which objects (labelled below with designators) satisfy which predicates (interpreted by the key).

Key
Fx – x is a circle
Gx – x is a square
Rxy – x is in y

Predicates
(a)   Fx & (∀y) (Gy ⊃ Rxy)
(b)   Fx & (∃y) (Gy & Rxy)
(c)   (∃x) (Gx & Ryx)
(d)   (∀y) (Fx & (Gy ⊃ Rxy))
(e)   (∃y) (Fx & (Gy & Rxy))
(f)   (∃y) (Fy & Ryx)

Objects

Lesson 11: Predicates and Identity

Very few basic predicates are true of everything. This is unsurprising. Try to imagine some property which you would be happy to attribute to every object in the universe. (Some might suggest that every object is material, but even this is controversial.) However, there is a basic two-place predicate which is so important to the language of Predicate that we have a special symbol for it. Moreover, this predicate truly describes a relationship that every object has to itself. The predicate is called *identity*, and it is written this way:

(1)   x = y.

(The negation of an identity claim is either: '¬ (x = y)'; or, more compactly: 'x ≠ y'.)

Since there is no object in the universe to which this predicate doesn't apply, the following is a true, universally quantified sentence:

(?) (∀x) (x = x),

asserting that everything is self-identical. (In another variation: everything is one and the same as itself.) Yet, for obvious reasons, no two objects can ever be identical. So, if x and y are replaced by designators of objects which are numerically distinct – one is here and the other there – then the claim that x = y is always false.

The identity predicate strikes many as either too promiscuous or too restrictive to be taken seriously. Normally, a helpful description is one which is true of certain objects, and not others. That a thing can be characterized as an animal is interesting to us, in part, because we then can rule out the possibility that it is vegetable or mineral. However, the identity predicate is either a trivially true relation that an object has to itself, or a virtual logical falsehood when asserted of two distinct objects. Even so, identity is useful. It has an indirect role, allowing the construction of various predicates which are themselves important. Some idea of these can be gleaned from the Exercises below (in which you are guided through some of the answers).

---

*Exercise 1

Indicate which objects satisfy each of the predicates shown below? (Use the key provided to guide your interpretation.)

Key
Fx – x is a circle
Gx – x is a square

Objects

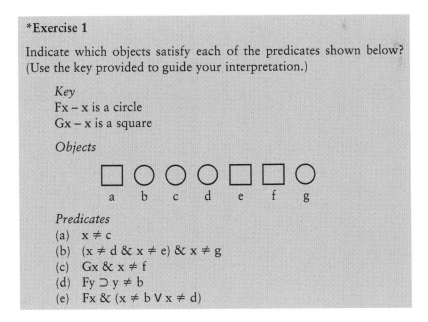

Predicates
(a) x ≠ c
(b) (x ≠ d & x ≠ e) & x ≠ g
(c) Gx & x ≠ f
(d) Fy ⊃ y ≠ b
(e) Fx & (x ≠ b ∨ x ≠ d)

Exercise 2

Which objects satisfy the following predicates? (The key is as for EXERCISE 1.)

(a)   Gx & Gy
(b)   (Gx & Gy) & x ≠ y

Objects

d   e   f

Answer to EXERCISE 2

There is only a single square, and in (a) there are two predicates of squareness, each with alphabetically different variables. This might confuse someone into thinking that (a) could only be satisfied by two different squares. But this would be wrong, and it is vital to understand why. Variables are gaps. Predicate (a) in essence says: '. . . is a square, . . . is a square'. That is, it repetitiously requires squareness, and is hence perfectly satisfied by the solitary square d. However, predicate (b) requires three things: a square, a square, and an assurance that the first square is distinct from (non-identical to) the second. In the given sequence of objects, no such assurance is possible. Hence, the third conjunct and, thus, predicate (b) are not satisfied by any of the objects shown.

Exercise 3

Using the key given in EXERCISE 1, say which of the sequences below contain objects satisfying the following predicates:

(a)   (∀y) ((Gy & Gz) ⊃ y = z)
(b)   (∀y) (Fy ⊃ x = y)

Sequences
(i)

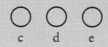

c   d   e

(ii)

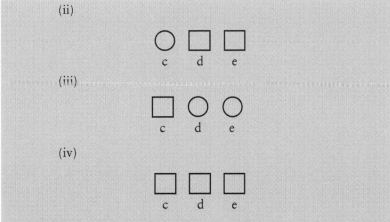

(iii)

(iv)

Answer to EXERCISE 3

(a) Put into a sort of Predicate–English, this says:

> every y, if y is a square and z is a square then y is identical to z.
> Or, a little more idiomatically, we might say that it is true of
> squares which are identical to everything if a square.

Sequence (i) has no squares, so the predicate applies to c, d, e
trivially.

Sequence (ii) has two squares. Suppose one thought that the middle square d was a candidate for satisfying the predicate – a candidate to fill the 'z' gap. Since there is a second square, e, it would have
to be identical to d. After all, the universal quantifier demands that it
be identical to all squares. But this is absurd. Since the same logic can
be repeated if we start with e, this shows that neither d nor e satisfy
predicate (a). What about the circle c? Not being a square, this
makes the antecedent false, even though the other conjunct might
well be true. So, c does trivially satisfy the predicate.

Sequence (iii) has just one square, here designated as c. Of this
square, it is certainly true that it is self-identical. And it is also true
that d and e (circles) are not squares, and, hence, that they trivially
satisfy the conditional predicate in (a). Hence, each of c, d and e
satisfy predicate (a).

Sequence (iv) has three squares and it should be easy to see
that none of them satisfy the predicate. This is for the same reason as
was offered in connection with Sequence (ii). The presence of three
distinct squares makes the needed identity of every square with z
impossible.

NOTE   The explanation of this predicate may seem convoluted, but it repays careful study. Indeed, such study would reveal a pattern to the sequences: any sequence with no squares or at most one square will completely satisfy predicate (a). But this means that predicate (a) is true of each member of a sequence of objects, amongst which at most one is a square.

(b) Against the background of the discussion of (a), this second case should present no difficulties. What this predicate demands is an object (not necessarily a circle) which is identical to all things if they are circles. Clearly, (i) and (iii) have too many circles. But since (b) does not require that x be a circle, even object c in (iii) is ruled out. For it is certainly not an object identical to all the circles. Sequence (ii) is trickier. There is only one circle, c, and it is clearly identical to all the circles. But d and e – squares – are definitely not objects identical to all the circles because they are not identical to c. Finally, all the objects in (iv) satisfy (b) trivially. They are certainly objects identical to all things if circles, since there are no circles.

Lesson 12: Back to Sentences

Having investigated the structure of predicates in some depth, it is time to return wholeheartedly to sentences. Predicates are ways of describing objects, or pairs of objects, or threesomes of objects, etc. One can say that some object or objects *satisfy* or fit a predicate. Put the other way around, one can say that a predicate is *true of* some object or objects. In contrast, sentences are not true or false of objects; they are just true or false. This very fact licenses a way of speaking which is revealing.

Suppose that 'Rxy' means 'x is the sister of y'. This is a two-place predicate. If we replace the second variable by a designator of, say Virginia, we get 'Rxa'. This can be read as: 'x is Virginia's sister', and the replacement of the variable has changed a two-place into a one-place predicate. What if we now replace the last remaining variable by a designator of, say Vanessa? We get the sentence: 'Vanessa is Virginia's sister'. The first replacement took us from a two-place to a one-place predicate, the second from a one-place predicate to a sentence. There is, however, nothing to prevent our describing this last move as from a one-place predicate to a *zero-place* predicate. But in doing so we have discovered that we can describe sentences as zero-place predicates.

The idea of a zero-place predicate might seem strange. But it is a useful way of thinking about the relationship between predicates and sentences. It also means that, in working on the structure of complicated non-basic predicates, we have thereby done most of the work needed to appreciate the sentences of Predicate. The movement from predicates of one order to another, effected by quantification and variable replacement, can now be seamlessly extended in the move from predicates back to sentences. The following two Exercises show this clearly.

Exercise 1

Which objects in the sequence below satisfy predicate (a)?

(a)   Gx ⊃ (∃y) (Fy & Rxy)

Key
Fx – x is a circle
Gx – x is a square
Rxy – x is to the right of y

Sequence

a   b   c   d

Answer
The predicate is true of any object which, if a square, is to the right of some circle. This is true of a, b and d trivially, because they are not squares. And it is true of c because it is a square and there is in fact at least one circle it is to the right of. So, the one-place predicate above is satisfied by a, b, c and d.

Exercise 2

Does the sentence.

(∀x) (Gx ⊃ (∃y) (Fy & Rxy)),

truly describe the sequence in Exercise 1?

Answer
This sentence is merely the universal quantification of the predicate in Exercise 1. It requires that every square is to the right of some circle. You can see that it is true just by comparing it to the sequence shown. Or, you can notice that, in Exercise 1, the predicate there was satisfied by each and every object in it. But the one-place predicate in **Exercise 1** – true of each object – becomes a zero-place predicate (i.e. a sentence) in Exercise 2 which is, of course, now merely true.

*Exercise 3

Below are some one-place predicates. Taking into account the key provided, turn each of them into a quantified sentence plausibly regarded as true. (Be careful about quantifier scope.)

(a) $(F_1x \supset H_2x)$
(b) $(F_2x \ \& \ H_1x)$
(c) $(F_1z \supset \neg F_2z)$
(d) $(H_1x \ \& \ H_2x)$
(e) $(H_2y \ \& \ \neg F_2y)$
(f) $(F_1x \ \& \ F_2x) \supset H_2x$
(g) $F_1x \supset (H_1x \lor F_2x)$
(h) $Gx \supset (\exists y) (H_1y \ \& \ Ryx)$
(i) $Gx \ \& \ (\exists y) (F_1y \ \& \ Ryx)$
(j) $F_1x \supset (\exists y) (Gy \ \& \ \neg Rxy)$
(k) $(\exists x) (Gy \supset ((F_1x \lor H_2x \lor H_1x) \ \& \ Rxy))$

Key
F_1x – x is a tiger
F_2x – x is tame
Gx – x is a zoo
H_1x – x is a mammal
H_2x – x is striped
Rxy – x is in y

*Exercise 4

Using the key provided, say which of the following are true sentences (as applied to the Situation below).

Key
Fx – x is a point
Rxy – x is directly connected to y, i.e. connected by a single line. (You should also assume that a point *is* directly connected to itself.)

Sentences
(a) $(\exists x) (Fx \ \& \ (\forall y) (Fy \supset Rxy)$
(b) $(\forall x) (Fx \supset Rxx)$
(c) $(\forall x) (Fx \supset Rxb)$
(d) $(\forall x) ((Fx \ \& \ x \neq a) \supset Rxb)$

(e)   (∃x) (∃y) (((Fx & Fy) & Rxy) & x ≠ y)
(f)   (∀x) (Fx ⊃ ¬Rxa)
(g)   (∀x) ((Fx & x ≠ a) ⊃ ¬Rxa)

Situation

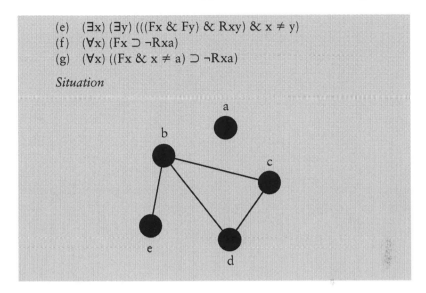

Lesson 13: Translation

In the first four Lessons, we distinguished first between sentences and predicates, and then between basic and non-basic predicates. Though these Lessons were mainly aimed at firming up your grasp of Predicate, they can now be put to use in helping us translate from natural language to Predicate. For any sentence of natural language is bound to contain a predicate. And if you can figure out how to find this predicate (or predicates), you will have done most of the hard work of translation.

NOTE   Incidentally, it is the fundamental role of predicates that led me to call the formal language 'Predicate'. Alternative names you might find are 'Quantifier' and 'First-order'. The first of these emphasizes the importance of quantification, but it should be noted that many of the ideas of predicate make their appearance before we get to the quantifiers. Predicate wouldn't be as powerful as it is without quantification, but the quantifiers need predicates to so much as make sense, so 'Predicate' seemed more appropriate.

The name 'First-order' is intended to capture the fact that the variables used in Predicate are place-holders for designators. Also, recall that designators are intended as labels for particular persons, places and things. What Predicate doesn't have is a type of variable which stands for predicates themselves. Such a variable would be 'second-order', and it would allow second-order quantification which seems to be found in sentences such as:

Plastic has some good properties.

Taking the 'some' to range unspecifically over properties is not something we can do in First-order or Predicate languages. However, since there are deep problems for logical systems attendant on what can seem a simple move from first- to second-order quantification, this book has stuck to the first-order variety.

If a sentence contains no quantifiers (or implicit quantification), then the job of translation is quite easy: simply find those expressions which designate objects – expressions like proper names, demonstratives, pronouns and definite descriptions. Then replace these with variables and examine the frame that is left over. For example, suppose you are asked to translate:

(1)   Aaron spent his vacation working in his father's office.

Underlining the designating expressions, we get:

(1′)   <u>Aaron</u> spent <u>his vacation</u> working in <u>his father's office</u>.

Then replacing each referring expression we get:

(1″)   x spent y working in z.

This is a little less 'natural' than 'is the sister of', but it is a perfectly good example of a three-place predicate. Choosing 'Sxyz' as the translation (this is the easy part) and appropriate designators, the final translation is:

(2)   Sabc.

More complexity could be introduced by trying to translate the two definite descriptions: 'his vacation' and 'his father's office'. But since translating the descriptive designators here would bring in quantification, I have taken the simplest way out in regard to (2). (Note that these are definite descriptions even though they do not begin with 'the', because the possessive serves just as well to mark out uniqueness. One could understand 'Aaron's vacation' as a version of 'the vacation of Aaron'.)

Sentences with quantifiers – and hence more complicated predicates – require a bit more effort. One piece of advice about quantified sentences is blindingly obvious but is sometimes overlooked: decide first how many quantifiers the sentence has. In the logician's favoured terminology, decide if a sentence is *singularly general* (one quantifier and hence will require one type of variable) or *multiply general* (has at least two quantifiers and hence will require at least two types of variable). If the sentence is singularly general, then you can be sure it will involve one or more basic predicates, possibly made into a non-basic predicate with Sentential connectives. There are four sentences, extensively used in formulations of Aristotle's logic, which mark out the central cases of singularly general sentences. It is important that you understand how they are constructed and are ready to use them in translation. With predicate translations to the right, these sentences-forms are as follows:

All Fs are Gs	$(\forall x)\ (Fx \supset Gx)$
Some Fs are Gs	$(\exists x)\ (Fx\ \&\ Gx)$
No Fs are Gs	$(\forall x)\ (Fx \supset \neg Gx)$
Some Fs are not Gs	$(\exists x)\ (Fx\ \&\ \neg Gx)$

In cases where you have more than one quantifier, you must first decide what kinds of thing are at issue and, if appropriate, what relation(s) among them are being asserted. I say 'if appropriate' because it is possible to have multiple generality with and without relations. Thus, compare these sentences:

(3) Some are talented and some are hard-working, but no one is content.

(4) Every cloud has a silver lining.

(3) has three quantifiers in it, but there are no asserted relations between the various categories which are quantified. It would be translated (leaving implicit the fact that we are dealing with persons) as:

(3′) $(\exists x)\ (\exists y)\ (Fx\ \&\ Gy)\ \&\ (\forall x)\ \neg\ Hx.$

Note that the scopes of the first quantifiers end after 'Gy', so that we can re-use the variable 'x' without interfering with the 'x' in 'Fx'. Also, nothing in this sentence rules out the possibility that some one individual is both talented and hard-working, though it clearly allows that there may be different individuals satisfying these predicates.

Sentence (4) also has more than one quantifier: the obvious universal 'every cloud', and the subtle existential 'a silver lining' (some silver lining). But unlike (3), this sentence asserts a relationship between things which are clouds and things which are silver linings, namely that the first *has* the second. Its translation (treating 'silver lining' as a unitary predicate) would be:

(4′) $(\forall x)\ (Fx \supset (\exists y)\ (Gy\ \&\ Rxy)).$

One final piece of advice before some practice: sentences sometimes have both designating expressions and quantifiers (and can be singly or multiply general). Watch out for these, of which the following is an example:

(5)   Everyone who liked anyone liked Harry.

The translation of this is:

(5′) $(\forall x)\,(\exists y)\,(Rxy \supset Rxa)$.

The 'anyone' in (5) sounds universal, but it is clearly intended existentially; clearly Harry is not being characterized as so hard to like that you have to like *everyone* to like him. The translation says of everyone and someone that if the first likes the second, then the first likes Harry.

Keeping the various categories of unquantified and quantified sentences in mind should be helpful in getting you started in translation, but nothing can replace practice. The following long EXERCISE (with some worked out answers) should help.

---

*Exercise

Below are a number of sentences. Decide what kind of sentence each is, i.e. quantified, unquantified or mixed, multiply or singly quantified, relational or not. Then translate them into Predicate, noting any alternative translations you think possible.

(1)   Some pilots are dare-devils.
(2)   Some roses are not red.
(3)   Oswald shot Kennedy and then Oswald was shot by Jack Ruby.
(4)   If anyone is honest, then Jennifer is.
(5)   Every train is faster than any bicycle.
(6)   Apples are not vegetables.
(7)   Some mushrooms are edible only when cooked.
(8)   Not every philosopher understands every existentialist.
(9)   No one who throws stones should live in a glass house.
(10)   If you all behave yourselves, someone will get a reward.
(11)   Serpents and white whales inhabit that distant ocean, but no living man has ever seen either.
(12)   Who dares wins.
(13)   Fisher can beat anyone in chess.
(14)   Each rider was cautious.
(15)   Monet gardened in Giverny.
(16)   Monet painted waterlilies.
(17)   Everyone picked a card.
(18)   No cards were hearts.

(19)   If anyone loses, coach Thomas will not be happy.
(20)   If everyone loses, coach Thomas will not be happy.
(21)   Anyone who is an athlete is fit.
(22)   If coach Thomas is happy, then someone won.
(23)   Some lawyers are honest.
(24)   Aaron ate at least two chocolates.
(25)   The quickest way home is blocked.
(26)   Rachel helped Sarah with some maths problems.
(27)   Any setback is annoying.
(28)   Gloria gave Johnnie a present.
(29)   Round pegs do not fit into square holes.
(30)   Rob bought a ticket to a basketball game.
(31)   Any train is faster than any bicycle.
(32)   Nelson won the Battle of Trafalgar.
(33)   All logicians are truth-tellers unless they are not truth-tellers.
(34)   All apples and pears are tasty when ripe.
(35)   Any cat is friendly if hungry.

Some comments and hints

(3)   Watch out for order in the relational predicate you choose: 'shot' and 'shot by' are converse.

(7)   Be careful about where the conditional comes, since this is basically an existentially quantified sentence, and you don't want a conditional as the main connective.

(9)   Treat the 'a' of 'a glass house' as an existential quantifier, as well as the plural 'stones'.

(10)   No guarantee that the persons who behave include the person rewarded. Also, 'behave yourself' is not a thing that one person does to himself.

(11)   Clearest if you treat 'that distant ocean' as a designating expression. Also, interesting to compare the Predicate formulation of this with the Sentential one you were asked to do in Lesson 6.

(12)   Clearly a universally quantified sentence.

(16)   Plural 'waterlillies' mandates an existential quantifier.

(19)–(20)   Be careful with quantifier scope: coach Thomas has a much higher standard in (19) than in (20).

(25)   To do justice to this one, treat 'quickest' as 'quicker than any other'.

(33)   Make sure that this one does not come out as a straight contradiction.

(34)   It says 'and' but you don't want to quantify over things which are both apples and pears. There aren't any such things.

Lesson 14: Deductions in Predicate

As explained in chapter 14, Predicate inferences are not evaluable by truth tables. Indeed, no mechanical and effective method of evaluation can be devised for Predicate arguments. That is, there can be no general method which, after a finite number of steps, delivers a yes/no verdict on the question of validity. This makes deduction especially important. For, even though one cannot use it generally to decide whether arguments are valid or invalid, it is sufficient to demonstrate that a valid argument is indeed valid.

Having worked through the Lessons on Sentential rules of inference, you should find Predicate deduction quite easy. One simply co-opts the ten Sentential rules of inference, supplementing them with rules for quantification. There are four such rules because, following the pattern in Sentential, we need introduction and elimination rules for both the universal and existential quantifiers. These rules are discussed at some length in chapter 14, but, before getting down to work with them, it is worth stressing some of my earlier advice.

In a typical case you will begin with quantified premises aiming to derive a quantified conclusion. In outline, what you do in such a case is first use quantifier elimination rules to get non-quantified sentences. Then you use the ten rules to derive a sentence which is appropriately close to the conclusion. Finally, you convert this sentence into the conclusion by re-introducing the requisite quantifiers. Here is an example:

Example

> No Olympic winners are poor athletes and some poor athletes are brilliant students. So, some brilliant students are not Olympic winners.

The translation of each premise (numbered here for later reference) and the conclusion is:

(1) $(\forall x)\,(Fx \supset \neg Gx)$
(2) $(\exists x)\,(Gx\ \&\ Hx)$
_____
$(\exists x)\,(Hx\ \&\ \neg Fx)$.

The basic strategy of the proof is to strip away the universal quantifiers from each of the two premises to get:

(3) $Fa \supset \neg Ga$
(4) $Ga\ \&\ Ha$

Then to use Sentential rules on (3) and (4) – ordinary non-quantified sentences which could be thought of as Ps and Qs – to get to a result which is 'close' to the conclusion of the original argument. (We need a result which, save for the absence of the quantifier, is the requisite conclusion.) A deduction beginning with (3) and (4) above as premises and giving the desired result is:

1	(3)	Fa ⊃ ¬Ga	
2	(4)	Ga & Ha	
5	(5)	Fa	Assumption
1,5	(6)	¬Ga	3,5 ⊃E
2	(7)	Ga	4 &E
1,2,5	(8)	Ga & ¬Ga	6,7 &I
1,2	(9)	¬Fa	5,8 ¬I
2	(10)	Ha	4 &E
1,2	(11)	Ha & ¬Fa	9,10 &I

Here we began with two unquantified sentences derived from the original premises and thus marked as dependent on them for truth. (More will be said about this derivation shortly.) We then assumed 'Fa' as part of deriving 'Fa' by the *reductio* rule, ¬I (in line 9). Breaking down the conjunction in line 4 gives us the sentence we need to conjoin with '¬Fa' to get the final line. Note that, if we could quantify the final line we would have completed the deduction of the original conclusion. *There is, however, a problem.*

Dropping and then later adding quantifiers to what are essentially Sentential inferences makes Predicate deduction sound very easy indeed. But of course you cannot just drop and add quantifiers without regard to truth preservation. We need rules which are above reproach in guaranteeing truth. In line 11 above, some one individual thing – a – has been shown to be both a brilliant student and not an Olympic winner. This follows validly from lines (3) and (4). But did we have the right to assume that the same individual can figure in the quantifier-dropping moves that led to these lines? The first premise of the original argument is universal, so it is reasonable to think it applies to everything, including a. But the second premise is existential: it says that some (at least one) individual is a poor athlete and brilliant student. How do we know that this individual is the same as that derived from dropping the quantifier in (1)? Finally, there must be some story about the quantifiers we are allowed to add to line 11. We certainly cannot simply move from that quite specific conclusion to the claim that *every* brilliant student is not an Olympic winner, though in this case the conclusion only requires an existential quantifier.

In sum, whilst rules permitting us to drop or add quantifiers are what we want, we have to hedge these rules about with restrictions so that we don't go astray in regard to truth. And it is these restrictions on the quantifier rules which make Predicate deduction seem complicated.

The restrictions needed for the quantifier rules are given in full detail in chapter 14, and the reasons for them are discussed at length. You should now go to that chapter and work through those explanations. (Pay special attention to the *replacement convention*, and the notion of an *arbitrary designator*.) In most cases they are commonsensical, but because they must protect against invalidity when the rules are used in any combination, they can appear quite formidable. The finished, correct deduction for our Example illustrates some of these points. Here it is:

1	(1)	(∀x) (Fx ⊃ ¬Gx)	Premise
2	(2)	(∃x) (Gx & Hx)	Premise
1	(3)	Ff ⊃ ¬Gf	1 ∀E
4	(4)	Gf & Hf	Assumption
5	(5)	Ff	Assumption
1,5	(6)	¬Gf	3,5 ⊃E
4	(7)	Gf	4 &E
1,4,5	(8)	Gf & ¬Gf	6,7 &I
1,4	(9)	¬Ff	5,8 ¬I
4	(10)	Hf	4 &E
1,4	(11)	Hf & ¬Ff	9,10 &I
1,4	(12)	(∃x) (Hx & ¬Fx)	11 ∃I
1,2	(13)	(∃x) (Hx & ¬Fx)	2,4,12 ∃E

Compare the difference between this and the part-deduction given earlier. First of all, we introduce an arbitrary designator in lines 3 and 4. In line 4 it is required by our eventual use of ∃E, and in line 3 the same arbitrary designator is used in anticipation of later steps. After all, we want our messing about in lines 3–11 to use the same sentences and this requires us to use the same designator. The rule of ∃E says that, having made a quantifier-dropping assumption, you can only discharge it when you get to some conclusion not containing the designator used in that assumption. That is what we have at line 12. And having correctly got to 12, we have the right to insist that the original existential-dropping inference was allowable. That is what is asserted at line 13. Note that you may think it extra unnecessary work to repeat the sentences at 12 and 13, but these lines are really quite different. Just examine the dependencies on their left to appreciate this.

Exercise 1

Translate the following single-premise arguments into Predicate and construct deductions to show them valid.

   *(a) Some tigers are tame creatures. So, some tame creatures are tigers.

   (b)   No logicians are weightlifters. So, no weightlifters are logicians.

   *(c) Some writers are happy. So, some writers are not unhappy.

   (d)   Some students are not hard-workers. So, some non-hard-workers are students.

   (e)   All cricket balls are spherical. So, no cricket balls are non-spherical.
        (**Hint:** be careful about the negations in the conclusion.)

Answers to (b) and (e)

   (b)

1	(1)	(∀x) (Fx ⊃ ¬Gx)	Premise
1	(2)	Ff ⊃ ¬Gf	1 ∀E
3	(3)	Gf	Assumption
4	(4)	Ff	Assumption
1,4	(5)	¬Gf	2,4 ⊃E
1,3,4	(6)	Gf & ¬Gf	3,5 &I
1,3	(7)	¬Ff	4,6 ¬I
1	(8)	Gf ⊃ ¬Ff	3,7 ⊃I
1	(9)	(∀x) (Gx ⊃ ¬Fx)	8 ∀I

Here, after dropping the universal quantifier in favour of an arbitrary name, we assume the antecedent of the conclusion, as well as Ff. The latter, when negated by *reductio*, will be the consequent of a conditional which, when universally quantified, is the conclusion.

   (e)

1	(1)	(∀x) (Fx ⊃ Gx)	Premise
1	(2)	Ff ⊃ Gf	1 ∀E
3	(3)	Ff	Assumption
4	(4)	¬Gf	Assumption
1,3	(5)	Gf	2,3 ⊃E
1,3,4	(6)	Gf & ¬Gf	4,5 &I
1,3	(7)	¬¬Gf	4,6 ¬I
1	(8)	Ff ⊃ ¬¬Gf	3,7 ⊃I
1	(9)	(∀x) (Fx ⊃ ¬¬Gx)	8 ∀I

Note first the double negation in the conclusion. One negation comes from the form of the sentence: 'No F is G' (i.e. $(\forall x)$ $(Fx \supset \neg Gx)$; the other from the fact that 'non-spherical' is the negation of 'spherical'.

After quantifier-dropping, deduction involves assuming the antecedent of the conclusion and the sentence, which, when negated, is the consequent we are looking for. This is because, when we get this consequent, we can introduce the conditional and then add the universal quantifier to get the conclusion.

In both of the above deductions, the adding of the universal quantifier at the end was to a sentence with an arbitrary designator. In effect, 'f' could be anything – it comes after all from a universally quantified sentence – so the final step in each deduction is truth preserving.

Exercise 2

Construct deductions showing that each of the following Predicate arguments is valid.

(a) $(\forall x)$ $(Rax \supset \neg Rxb)$
      $(\exists x)$ Rxb
      _____
      $(\exists x)$ $\neg$ Rax

(b) $(\exists x)$ $(\forall y)$ $(Fx$ & $(Fy \supset Rxy))$
      _____
      $(\exists x)$ $(Fx$ & $Rxx)$

(c) $(\forall x)$ $(Fx \supset (\forall y)$ $(Gy \supset Rxy))$
      $(\exists x)$ Fx
      _____
      $(\forall y)$ $(\exists x)$ $(Fx$ & $(Gy \supset Rxy))$

Answers to (a) and (c)

(a)

1	(1)	$(\forall x)$ $(Rax \supset \neg Rxb)$	Premise
2	(2)	$(\exists x)$ Rxb	Premise
1	(3)	$Raf \supset \neg Rfb$	1 $\forall$E
4	(4)	Rfb	Assumption
5	(5)	Raf	Assumption
1,5	(6)	$\neg Rfb$	3,5 $\supset$E
1,4,5	(7)	Rfb & $\neg Rfb$	4,6 &I
1,4	(8)	$\neg Raf$	5,7 $\neg$I
1,4	(9)	$(\exists x)$ $\neg$ Rax	8 $\exists$I
1,2	(10)	$(\exists x)$ $\neg$ Rax	2,4,9 $\exists$E

Here we assume a sentence which is the one we would get if we dropped the existential quantifier in favour of an arbitrary name. The aim is to get a useful conclusion not containing this name or dependent on another line in which it occurs. Aiming for line 8, we assume the opposite and use ¬I to get it. This is not the 'useful conclusion' because it contains 'f'. However, in the next line, we get rid of 'f' (legally) by existential introduction. So, line 9 follows from the assumption at line 4 and does not contain 'f'. This allows us to assert line 10, but now dependent on line 2 and not on line 4 (plus of course line 1).

(c)

1	(1)	$(\forall x)\,(Fx \supset (\forall y)\,(Gy \supset Rxy))$	Premise
2	(2)	$(\exists x)\,Fx$	Premise
3	(3)	Ff_1	Assumption
1	(4)	$Ff_1 \supset (\forall y)\,(Gy \supset Rf_1 y)$	1 $\forall$E
1,3	(5)	$(\forall y)\,(Gy \supset Rf_1 y)$	3,4 $\supset$E
1,3	(6)	$Gf_2 \supset Rf_1 f_2$	5 $\forall$E
1,3	(7)	$Ff_1 \;\&\; (Gf_2 \supset Rf_1 f_2)$	1 &I
1,3	(8)	$(\exists x)\,(Fx \;\&\; (Gf_2 \supset Rxf_2))$	7 $\exists$I
1,2	(9)	$(\exists x)\,(Fx \;\&\; (Gf_2 \supset Rxf_2))$	2,3,8 $\exists$E
1,2	(10)	$(\forall y)\,(\exists x)\,(Fx \;\&\; (Gy \supset Rxy))$	9 $\forall$I

The assumption at line 3 is part of the application of $\exists$E. We complete this by deriving 8 from the assumption and line 1. Then we can assert 9 dependent only on the original two premises. One more step of $\forall$I completes the deduction. (Notice that this last step is with respect to a different arbitrary name from the one assumed to be 'F' in line 3.)

Exercise 3

Below are two arguments whose validity can seem surprising. (They are freely adapted from Lewis Carroll's *Symbolic Logic*.) Construct deductions to show them valid.

   *(a)   Everyone who is sane can do logic. No one who is insane is fit to serve on a jury, but none of my friends can do logic. Therefore, none of my friends is fit to serve on a jury.

   (b)   Anyone who is sensitive is likely to be neurotic. All profound scholars are great lovers of music. Only profound scholars can be dons at Oxford. No-one insensitive is a great lover of music. Therefore, all Oxford dons are likely to be neurotic.

Answer to (b)

The translation of the basic predicates should be clear enough from the premises listed in lines 1–4 below.

1	(1)	$(\forall x)\,(F_1 x \supset G_1 x)$	Premise
2	(2)	$(\forall x)\,(F_2 x \supset G_2 x)$	Premise
3	(3)	$(\forall x)\,(F_3 x \supset F_2 x)$	Premise
4	(4)	$(\forall x)\,(\neg F_1 x \supset \neg G_2 x)$	Premise
1	(5)	$F_1 f \supset G_1 f$	1 $\forall$E
2	(6)	$F_2 f \supset G_2 f$	2 $\forall$E
3	(7)	$F_3 f \supset F_2 f$	3 $\forall$E
4	(8)	$\neg F_1 f \supset \neg G_2 f$	4 $\forall$E
9	(9)	$F_3 f$	Assumption
3,9	(10)	$F_2 f$	7,9 $\supset$E
2,3,9	(11)	$G_2 F$	6,10 $\supset$E
12	(12)	$\neg F_1 f$	Assumption
4,12	(13)	$\neg G_2 f$	8,12 $\supset$E
2,3,4,9,12	(14)	$G_2 f\ \&\ \neg G_2 f$	11,13 &I
2,3,4,9	(15)	$\neg\neg F_1 f$	12,14 $\neg$I
2,3,4,9	(16)	$F_1 f$	15 $\neg$E
1,2,3,4,9	(17)	$G_1 f$	5,16 $\supset$E
1,2,3,4	(18)	$F_3 f \supset G_1 f$	9,17 $\supset$I
1,2,3,4	(19)	$(\forall x)\,(F_3 x \supset G_1 x)$	18 $\forall$I

Long though it may be, this is actually quite an easy proof. After dropping all the universal quantifiers (using an arbitrary designator), the antecedent of the unquantified conclusion is assumed at 9. Chains of $\supset$E and one strategic use of $\neg$I result in the necessary consequent of the unquantified conclusion at 17. The rest is straightforward.

Exercise 4

*(a)   Martha can solve every exercise in this book. Anyone who can do that is a first-class student. Therefore, Martha is a first-class student.

(b)   Some philosophers are worshipped by every philosopher. Therefore, some philosophers worship themselves.

(c) Whichever side scored a goal won. James's side scored a goal. Therefore, James's side won.

Answer to (b)

1	(1)	$(\exists x) (Fx \ \& \ (\forall y) (Fy \supset Rxy)$	Premise
2	(2)	Ff & $(\forall y) (Fy \supset Rfy)$	Assumption
2	(3)	$(\forall y) (Fy \supset Rfy)$	2 &E
2	(4)	Ff $\supset$ Rff	3 ∀E
2	(5)	Ff	2 &E
2	(6)	Rff	4,5 ⊃E
2	(7)	Ff & Rff	5,6 &I
2	(8)	$(\exists x) (Fx \ \& \ Rxx)$	7 ∃I
1	(9)	$(\exists x) (Fx \ \& \ Rxx)$	1,2,8 ∃E

The assumption needed for ∃E was made at line 2. This eventually led, by fairly obvious means, to 7 which, when existentially generalized, left behind all traces of the 'f' from the assumption. That done, we had the right to treat the sentence in 8 as deduced from the premise alone (line 9).

Exercise 5

The argument below is a good advertisement for the power of Predicate. Deceptively simple, and intuitively valid, it can come as a surprise that it is possible to construct a deduction for it.

> All horses are animals. Therefore the head of a horse is the head of an animal.

Suggestion

The most straightforward translation of this argument is:

$(\forall x) (Fx \supset Gx)$

$(\forall x) (\forall y) ((Fx \ \& \ Ryx) \supset (Gx \ \& \ Ryx))$

where: Fx – x is a horse, Gx – x is an animal, Rxy – x is a head of y.

The best way to proceed with this deduction is to begin by assuming the negation of the conclusion. This will result in a sentence which is equivalent to: $(\exists x) (\exists y) ((Fx \ \& \ Ryx) \ \& \ \neg(Gx \ \& \ Ryx))$. (In English: there is a head of a horse which is *not* a head of an animal.) Of course, you have to use your ingenuity to prove that the negation of the conclusion leads to this double existential. (You need two run-throughs of the deduction leading from ¬(∀x) to (∃x)¬. See chapter 14, section 14.6 for help on these quantifier equivalences.) Once you have the double existential sentence, it is not difficult to deduce a contradiction from it. This will entitle you to assert the original con-clusion by ¬I and ¬E.

Answers to Exercises
Marked '*' in Lessons 1–14

LESSON 1

Exercise 1: F,F,T,F,T,T,F,T.

Exercise 3: (a) T,F,F,F; (b) T,T,T,T; (c) T,T,F,T; (d) F,T,F,F.

Exercise 4 (answers are given in column under each label in the slightly compacted tables below)

P		(a) P V P	(b) ¬ ¬P
T		T	T F
F		F	F T

P	Q	(c) ¬(P ⊃ Q)	(d) ¬(Q ⊃ P)	(e) ¬P V Q	(f) P & ¬Q	(g) ¬(P & ¬Q)
T	T	F T	F T	F T	F F	T F
T	F	T F	F T	F F	T T	F T
F	T	F T	T F	T T	F F	T F
F	F	F T	F T	T T	F T	T T

P	Q	R	(h) P ≡ ¬(Q ⊃ R)	(i) P V (Q & R)	(j) (P V Q) & R
T	T	T	F F T	T T	T T
T	T	F	T T F	T F	T F
T	F	T	F F T	T F	T T
T	F	F	F F T	T F	T F
F	T	T	T F T	T T	T T
F	T	F	F T F	F F	T F
F	F	T	T F T	F F	F F
F	F	F	T F T	F F	F F

LESSON 2

Exercise 1: (b) contingent;   (c) tautology;   (d) contingent;   (e) contradiction.

Exercise 2: (a) is equivalent to (b);   (c) is equivalent to (e);   (d) is equivalent to (f).

Exercise 4

(d)

P	Q	R	¬P ≡ R		R ≡ Q	P ≡ Q
T	T	T	F	F	T	T
T	T	F	F	T	F	T
T	F	T	F	F	F	F
T	F	F	F	T	T	F
F	T	T	T	T	T	F
F	T	F	T	F	F	F
F	F	T	T	T	F	T
F	F	F	T	F	T	T

The premises are jointly true in row 4. The conclusion is false in that row, so the argument is invalid.

Arguments (b) and (c) are left to the reader.

Exercise 5

(d)

P	¬P	¬(¬P V ¬P)	
T	F	T	F
F	T	F	T

The sentences whose truth tables are shown in columns two and three are inconsistent since there is no row where they are both true.

Items (a) and (b) are left for the reader.

LESSON 3

Exercise 1

(a)   (1)Premise/   (2)Premise/   (3)1 ≡ E/   (4)3 &E/   (5)2 ¬E/ (6)4,5 ⊃E.
(b)   (1)Premise/   (2)Premise/   (3)2 &E/   (4)3 ¬E/   (5)1,4 ⊃E/ (6)5 ¬E/ (7)6 VI.
(c)   (1)Premise/ (2)Premise/ (3)1,2 ⊃E/ (4)3 &E/ (5)4 ¬E.

Exercise 2

 (b) 1 (1)/ 1 (2)/ 1 (3).
 (c) 1 (1)/ 2 (2)/ 3 (3)/ 2,3 (4)/ 1,2,3 (5)/ 1,2,3 (6).

Exercise 3

 (b)

1	(1)	P & (Q & R)	Premise
1	(2)	P	1 &E
1	(3)	Q & R	1 &E
1	(4)	R	1 &E
1	(5)	P & R	2,4 &I
1	(6)	Q	3 &E
1	(7)	Q & (P & R)	5,6 &I

Argument (c) is left for the reader.

LESSON 4

Exercise 1

 (a)

1	(1)	$Q \supset R$	Premise
2	(2)	$P \equiv R$	Premise
2	(3)	$(P \supset R)$ & $(R \supset P)$	2 $\equiv$E
4	(4)	$\neg\neg Q$	Assumption
4	(5)	Q	4 $\neg$E
1,4	(6)	R	1,5 $\supset$E
2	(7)	$R \supset P$	3 &E
1,2,4	(8)	P	6,7 $\supset$E
1,2	(9)	$\neg\neg Q \supset P$	4,8 $\supset$I

(c) is left to the reader.

Exercise 2

 (c)

1	(1)	P	Premise
2	(2)	$\neg\neg(\neg P$ & $Q)$	Assumption
2	(3)	$\neg P$ & Q	2, $\neg$E
2	(4)	$\neg P$	3 &E
1,2	(5)	P & $\neg P$	1,4 &I
1	(6)	$\neg\neg\neg(\neg P$ & $Q)$	2,5 $\neg$I
1	(7)	$\neg(\neg P$ & $Q)$	6 $\neg$E

(a) is left to the reader.

Exercise 3

(b)

1	(1)	R V Q	Premise
2	(2)	Q ⊃ S	Premise
3	(3)	R ⊃ ¬¬S	Premise
4	(4)	R	Assumption
3,4	(5)	¬¬S	3,4 ⊃E
3,4	(6)	S	5 ¬E
7	(7)	Q	Assumption
2,7	(8)	S	2,7 ⊃E
1,2,3	(9)	S	1,4,6,7,8 VE

Exercise (c) is left for the reader. (**Hint:** you will have to use two applications of VE, one as a part of the other.)

LESSON 5

Exercise 1

(c)

1	(1)	P ⊃ Q	Premise
2	(2)	¬Q	Assumption
3	(3)	P	Assumption
1,3	(4)	Q	1,3 ⊃E
1,2,3	(5)	Q & ¬Q	2,4 &I
1,2	(6)	¬P	3,5 ¬I
1	(7)	¬Q ⊃ ¬P	2,6 ⊃I

Note: the assumption of ¬Q was part of ⊃I. But this means that ¬P is our new goal, so the assumption of P makes sense as part of ¬I.

(e)

1	(1)	P ⊃ Q	Premise
2	(2)	¬(P V ¬P)	Assumption
3	(3	P	Assumption
3	(4)	P V ¬P	3 VI
2,3	(5)	(P V ¬P) & ¬(P V ¬P)	2,4 &I
2	(6)	¬P	3,5 ¬I
2	(7)	¬P V P	6 VI
2	(8)	(P V ¬P) & ¬(P V ¬P)	2,7 &I
	(9)	¬¬(P V ¬P)	2,8 ¬I
	(10)	P V ¬P	9 ¬E
11	(11)	P	Assumption
1,11	(12)	Q	1,11 ⊃E

1,11	(13)	¬P ∨ Q	12 VI
14	(14)	¬P	Assumption
14	(15)	¬P ∨ Q	14 VI
1	(16)	¬P ∨ Q	10,11,13,14,15 VE

Note: in lines 2–10 we deduced the tautology P ∨ ¬P, from no premises, by using ¬I (see chapter 9, section 9.4). This allowed us to get the needed conclusion by VE in a fairly straightforward way in lines 11–16.

LESSON 6

Exercise 2

(c)	Q ⊃ P	correct, i.e. captures the law
(d)	¬Q ∨ P	correct – equivalent to (c)
(e)	P ⊃ Q	incorrect
(f)	Q ⊃ P	correct
(g)	Q ∨ ¬P	incorrect – equivalent to P ⊃ Q
(h)	P ⊃ Q	incorrect
(i)	Q ∨ ¬P	incorrect – equivalent to P ⊃ Q
(j)	¬P ⊃ ¬Q	correct – equivalent to Q ⊃ P

Exercise 3

(1)	P ⊃ (Q ∨ R)	P – Jennifer will be seeing her friends in England next year; Q – Kim gets some work; R – Jennifer wins the lottery.
(2)	P ≡ Q	P – Clouds yield rain; Q – Glaciation takes place.
(3)	P ⊃ Q	P – We all thought alike; Q – It would be a strange old world.
(4)	(P & Q) & (R & S)	P – Serpents inhabit that distant ocean; Q – White whales inhabit that distant ocean; R – No living man has seen a serpent; S – No living man has seen a white whale.
(5)	P ∨ (Q ⊃ R)	P – We can have an Indian take-away; Q – The chip shop is still open; R – We can have fish and chips.
(6)	P ⊃ (Q ∨ R)	P – We organize tennis; Q – It is raining; R – One of us is busy.

(7)   P ⊃ (Q ⊃ R)   P – Theseus turns up; Q – The ball of string guiding him is long enough; R – The Athenian youths will be saved (or: (P & Q) ⊃ R).

(8)   P ⊃ Q   P – It rains in the Far East; Q – It pours.

(9)   P ∨ Q   P – The contract will be ready on time; Q – the legal department will have a lot of explaining to do.

(10)   (¬P & ¬Q) & (¬R & ¬S)   P – Ted is speaking to Bob; Q – Ted is speaking to Carol; R – Alice is speaking to Bob; S – Alice is speaking to Carol.

LESSON 7

Exercise

(a) Valid, deduction below:

1	(1) P ⊃ Q	Premise
2	(2) P & R	Assumption
2	(3) P	2 &E
1,2	(4) Q	1,3 ⊃E
1	(5) (P & R) ⊃ Q	2,4 ⊃I

(b) P ≡ ¬Q, ¬Q ⊃ R, R ∴ P/Invalid.

(c) P ∨ Q, ¬Q ⊃ P, Q ∴ ¬P/Invalid.

(d) Valid, deduction below:

1	(1) ¬(P & Q)	Premise
2	(2) P ∨ Q	Premise
3	(3) P	Assumption
4	(4) Q	Assumption
3,4	(5) P & Q	3,4 &I
1,3,4	(6) (P & Q) & ¬(P & Q)	1,5 &I
1,3	(7) ¬Q	4,6 ¬I
1	(8) P ⊃ ¬Q	3,7 ⊃I
9	(9) ¬Q	Assumption
10	(10) P	Assumption
9,10	(11) P & ¬Q	9,10 &I
9,10	(12) P	11 &E

10	(13) ¬Q ⊃ P	9,12 ⊃I
14	(14) Q	Assumption
15	(15) ¬P	Assumption
16	(16) ¬Q	Assumption
14,15	(17) ¬P & Q	14,15 &I
14,15	(18) Q	17 &E
14,15,16	(19) Q & ¬Q	16,18 &I
14,16	(20) ¬¬P	15,19 ¬I
14,16	(21) P	20 ¬E
14	(22) ¬Q ⊃ P	16,21 ⊃I
2	(23) ¬Q ⊃ P	2,10,13,14,22 VE
1,2	(24) (P ⊃ ¬Q) & (¬Q ⊃ P)	8,23 &I
1,2	(25) P ≡ ¬Q	24 ≡I

(e) Valid, deduction below:

1	(1) (P & Q) ⊃ ¬R	Premise
2	(2) ¬R ⊃ ¬S	Premise
3	(3) S	Premise
4	(4) P	Assumption
5	(5) Q	Assumption
4,5	(6) P & Q	4,5 &I
1,4,5	(7) ¬R	1,6 ⊃E
1,2,4,5	(8) ¬S	2,7 ⊃E
1,2,3,4,5	(9) S & ¬S	3,8 &I
1,2,3,4	(10) ¬Q	5,9 ¬I
1,2,3	(11) P ⊃ ¬Q	4,10 ⊃I

LESSON 8

Exercise 1
Predicates: (a); (b); (e); (f) – see answer to next EXERCISE; (i). The remainder are sentences.

Exercise 2
Free variables are underlined below.

(a) F<u>x</u>; (b) Sa<u>xy</u>; (e) Ra<u>x</u>; (f) (∀x) F<u>y</u>; (i) (∀y) Ry<u>x</u>. **Note:** (f) is strictly speaking well-formed by most accounts of Predicate, but the quantifier might as well not be there. Having a letter not matching any in the predicate, it is otiose. (f) might as well just be 'Fy'.

Exercise 3
There are twenty possible sentences. To find them, first try all combina-

tions of the two quantifiers (e.g. (∀x) (∀y) Rxy); then all the combinations of a quantifier and the two designators (e.g. (∀x) Rxa); then all the combinations of designators only (e.g. Rab).

LESSON 9

Exercise 1

(a) b,c,e,g,i;   (b) a,d,f,h,j;   (c) b,c,e;   (d) b,c,e,f,g,h,i,j;
(e) a,b,c,d,e,f,h,j; (f) a,b,c,d,e,f,h,j; (g) b,c,e,f,h,j.

Exercise 2

(a)   ae, ea, bf, fb, cg, gc, di, id, ge, eg;
(b)   aeg, cge, egc, gea;
(c)   all except h;
(d)   all except h;
(e)   ag, ga, ec, ce;
(f)   a, c, g, e;
(g)   h;
(h)   all including h.

LESSON 10

Exercise 1

(i)   all have two free variables except (d).
(ii)
   (a) pairs of human beings the first of which is married to the second;
   (b) pairs of things which, if human, the first is married to the second;
   (c) pairs of human beings the first of which lies to the second. (**Note:** these pairs include, e.g. (a,a), if it is true that 'a lies to a');
   (d) things which if human, lie to themselves;
   (e) pairs of things which, if married to each other, are both human beings;
   (f) pairs of things which, if human, then the first lies to the second;
   (g) pairs of human beings and if the first is married to the second, the first lies to the second;
   (h) pairs of human beings and if the first is married to the second, then the second is married to the first.

Exercise 2

(a)   no objects are circles in all squares;
(b)   a and e are circles in at least one square;
(c)   a and e are items in at least one square;
(d)   this is the same predicate as (a), albeit with the quantifier to the front.
(e)   this is the same predicate as (b), albeit with the quantifier moved to the front.
(f)   b and f are things with some circle in them.

LESSON 11

Exercise 1

(a) a,b,d,e,f,g;   (b) a,b,c,f;   (c) a,e;   (d) a,c,d,e,f,g;   (e) b,c,d,g.

LESSON 12

Exercise 3

(a) $(\forall x)$ $(F_1x \supset H_2x)$/Every tiger is striped.
(b) $(\exists x)$ $(F_2x \ \& \ H_1x)$/Some tame thing is a mammal.
(c) $(\forall z)$ $(F_1z \supset \neg F_2z)$/No tiger is tame.
(d) $(\exists x)$ $(H_1x \ \& \ H_2x)$/Some mammal is striped.
(e) $(\exists y)$ $(H_2y \ \& \ \neg F_2y)$/Some striped thing is not tame.
(f) $(\forall x)$ $((F_1x \ \& \ F_2x) \supset H_2x)$/Every tame tiger is striped.
(g) $(\forall x)$ $(F_1x \supset (H_1x \lor F_2x))$/Every tiger is a mammal or tame.
(h) $(\forall x)$ $(Gx \supset (\exists y) (H_1y \ \& \ Ryx))$/Every zoo has a mammal in it.
(i) $(\exists x)$ $(Gx \ \& \ (\exists y) (F_1y \ \& \ Ryx))$/At least one zoo has at least one tiger in it.
(j) $(\forall x)$ $((F_1x \supset (\exists y) (Gy \ \& \ \neg Rxy))$/Every tiger is not in at least one zoo.
(k) $(\forall y)$ $(\exists x)$ $(Gy \supset ((F_1x \lor H_2x \lor H_1x) \ \& \ Rxy))$/Every zoo has either some tiger, some striped thing or some mammal in it.

Exercise 4

(a)   False/(In English: there is a point connected to every point.)
(b)   True/Every point is connected to itself.
(c)   False/Every point is connected to b.
(d)   True/Every point other than a is connected to b.
(e)   True/There are at least two distinct connected points.

(f)   False/No point is connected to a.

(g)   False/a is connected to itself.

LESSON 13

Exercise

Note: key to predicates and designators will only be given in cases where confusion is likely.

(1)   (∃x) (Fx & Gx)

(2)   (∃x) (Fx & ¬Gx)

(3)   Rab & Rca   [c – Ruby]

(4)   (∃x) Hx ⊃ Ha

(5)   (∀x) (Fx ⊃ (∀y) (Gy ⊃ Rxy))

(6)   (∀x) (Fx ⊃ ¬Gx)

(7)   (∃x) (Fx & (Gx ⊃ Hx))   [Gx – x is edible, Hx – x is cooked]

(8)   ¬(∀x) (Fx ⊃ (∀y) (Gy ⊃ Rxy))
       [Or: (∃x) (Fx & (∃y) (Gy & ¬Rxy))]

(9)   (∀x) ((Fx & (∃y) (Gy & R_1xy)) ⊃ (∀z) (Hz ⊃ ¬R_2xz))
       [Fx – x is a person, Gy – y is a stone, Hz – z is a glass house, R_1xy – x throws y, R_2xy – x should live in y]

(10)   (∀x) (Fx) ⊃ (∃x) (Gx)

(11)   (∃x) (∃y) ((Fx & Gy & R_1xa & R_1ya) & (∀z) (Hz ⊃ ¬R_2zx & ¬R_2zy))   [R_1xy – x inhabits y, R_2xy – x has seen y. Note that some liberties have been taken with parentheses.]

(12)   (∀x) (Fx ⊃ Gx)

(13)   (∀x) Rax

(14)   (∀x) (Fx ⊃ Gx)

(15)   Rab

(16)   (∃x) (Fx & Rax)

(17)   (∀x) (Fx ⊃ (∃y) (Gy & Rxy))   [Fx – x is a person, Gy – y is a card, Rxy – x picked y]

(18)   (∀x) (Fx ⊃ ¬Gx)

(19)   (∃x) Fx ⊃ ¬Ga

(20)   (∀x) Fx ⊃ ¬Ga

(21)   (∀x) (Fx ⊃ Gx)

(22)   Ga ⊃ (∃x) Fx

(23)   (∃x) (Fx & Gx)

(24)   (∃x) (∃y) (Fx & Fy & x ≠ y & Rax & Ray)   [Liberties taken with parentheses.]

(25) (∀x) ((Fx & ((∀y) (Fy & x ≠ y) ⊃ Rxy)) ⊃ Gx)   [Fx – x is a way home, Gx – x is blocked, Rxy – x is quicker than y]

(26) (∃x) (Fx & Rabx)

(27) (∀x) (Fx ⊃ Gx)

(28) (∃x) (Fx & Rabx)

(29) (∀x) (∀y) ((F₁x & F₂x & G₁y & G₂y) ⊃ ¬Rxy)   [Some liberties taken with parentheses.]

(30) (∃x) (∃y) ((Fx & Gy) & Raxy)

(31) (∀x) (Fx ⊃ (∀y) (Gy ⊃ Rxy))

(32) Rab

(33) (∀x) (Fx ⊃ (Gx ⊃ ¬Gx))

(34) (∀x) ((Fx ∨ Gx) ⊃ (H₁x ⊃ H₂x))   [Fx – x is an apple, Gx – x is a pear, H₁x – x is ripe, H₂x – x is tasty]

(35) (∀x) (Fx ⊃ (Gx ⊃ Hx))   [Gx – x is hungry, Hx – x is friendly]

LESSON 14

Exercise 1

(a)

1	(1)	(∃x) (Fx & Gx)	Premise
2	(2)	Ff & Gf	Assumption
2	(3)	Gf	2 &E
2	(4)	Ff	2 &E
2	(5)	Gf & Ff	3,4 &I
2	(6)	(∃x) (Gx & Fx)	5 ∃I
1	(7)	(∃x) (Gx & Fx)	1,2,6 ∃E

(c) Premise is the same as (a) except that ¬¬Gx replaces Gx. The deduction is of almost the same form as for (a) except that you have to drop the double negation from your assumption before introducing the existential quantifier and finishing as in lines 6 and 7 of (a).

Exercise 2

(b)

1	(1)	(∃x) (∀y) (Fx & (Fy ⊃ Rxy))	Premise
2	(2)	(∀y) (Ff & (Fy ⊃ Rfy))	Assumption
2	(3)	Ff & (Ff ⊃ Rff)	2, ∀E
2	(4)	Ff	3 &E
2	(5)	Ff ⊃ Rff	3 &E
2	(6)	Rff	4,5 ⊃E
2	(7)	Ff & Rff	4,6 &I

2	(8)	(∃x) (Fx & Rxx)	7 ∃I
1	(9)	(∃x) (Fx & Rxx)	1,2,8 ∃E

Exercise 3

(a)

1	(1)	(∀x) (F₁x ⊃ G₁x)	Premise
2	(2)	(∀x) (¬F₁x ⊃ ¬G₂x)	Premise
3	(3)	(∀x) (F₂x ⊃ ¬G₁x)	Premise
1	(4)	F₁f ⊃ G₁f	1 ∀E
2	(5)	¬F₁f ⊃ ¬G₂f	2 ∀E
3	(6)	F₂f ⊃ ¬G₁f	3 ∀E
7	(7)	F₂f	Assumption
3,7	(8)	¬G₁f	6,7 ⊃E
9	(9)	F₁f	Assumption
1,9	(10)	G₁f	4,9 ⊃E
1,3,7,9	(11)	G₁f & ¬G₁f	8,10 &I
1,3,7	(12)	¬F₁f	9,11 ¬I
1,2,3,7	(13)	¬G₂f	5,12 ⊃E
1,2,3	(14)	F₂f ⊃ ¬G₂f	7,13 ⊃I
1,2,3	(15)	(∀x) (F₂x ⊃ ¬G₂x)	14 ∀I

Exercise 4

(a)

1	(1)	(∀x) (Fx ⊃ Rax)	Premise
2	(2)	(∀x) (∀y) (Fy ⊃ (Rxy ⊃ Gy))	Premise
1	(3)	Ff ⊃ Raf	1 ∀E
2	(4)	(∀y) ((Ff ⊃ Ryf) ⊃ Gy)	2 ∀E
2	(5)	(Ff ⊃ Raf) ⊃ Ga	4 ∀E
1,2	(6)	Ga	3,5 ⊃E

Appendix 2:
Truth Trees

A2.0   Introduction

In chapter 6 you were introduced to truth tables, and, in chapters 8, 9 and 14, to deduction. Truth tables afford a quick and effective method for testing Sentential arguments, but they have no role with respect to Predicate. Deduction is an alternative method in Sentential – one which is more challenging practically, though no less effective. For Predicate arguments, deduction was the only method described, though it is not there an effective method for answering questions about validity. That is, one can construct deductions for valid arguments in Predicate, but cannot use the deductive method to demonstrate invalidity. (It can be shown that there can be no effective procedure for Predicate.)

In this Appendix, yet another method will be given. Known as the *truth tree* method (or, sometimes, as the method of *semantic tableaux*), it can seem a cross between semantic (truth-invoking) and syntactic (deductive) methods. Many find it both compact to use and theoretically interesting. It is particularly 'user-friendly' in connection with Predicate, though it doesn't alter the theoretical fact of non-effectiveness mentioned above.

The key idea behind this method were already present in chapter 6, where we discussed the relationship between consistency and validity. Suppose that we are presented with a valid argument (in Sentential or Predicate):

(a)   Premise 1
      Premise 2
      ─────────
      Conclusion.

If we negate the conclusion, we produce a list of sentences as follows:

(b)   Premise 1
      Premise 2
      ¬Conclusion.

Is this list consistent? From the fact that the original argument is valid, we know that it is not possible for the premises to be jointly true when the conclusion false. But this means that it is not possible for the premises to be jointly true when the *negation* of the conclusion is true. In short, list (b) must be inconsistent.

The truth tree method exploits this fact by asking us to write down conditions which make each of the premises and the negation of the conclusion true. If we do so, *but fail to find a consistent set of conditions*, then we can conclude that the original argument was valid. The reason that this method is more compact than truth tables is that we only need to write down *truth* conditions, not conditions for truth or falsity. Resemblances to deduction will be apparent as the details of the method are presented below, as will be the important differences between the use of trees in Sentential and Predicate.

A2.1   Sentential

Details are best appreciated by doing an example.

Example

$$P \supset (Q \lor R)$$
$$\neg Q \& P$$
$$\overline{}$$
R.

To test this argument, we first make a list consisting of the premises and the negation of the conclusion:

(1) $P \supset (Q \lor R)$
(2) $\neg Q \& P$
(3) $\neg R$.

(**Note:** the line numbers are for ease of reference, and are not an essential feature of the method.)

Next, we continue this list by writing down the truth conditions for each of (1)–(3). This is the crucial idea behind the method. A truth condition for a sentence A is a complete list of those components of A which would make it true. Look at (2) above. Since it is a conjunction, its truth would require the truth of *both* $\neg Q$ and P. We show this by writing the latter sentences below (1)–(3) in the list:

```
(1)   P ⊃ (Q ∨ R)
(2)   ¬Q & P      ✓
(3)   ¬R
      ------------------
(4)   ¬Q
(5)   P.
```

Note that we also check (2) to show that we have indeed written its truth conditions, and I have put in a dotted line to mark off the original list from those items we add.

> *The object is to continue writing truth conditions for (1)–(3) until we have completed the task, and then to see whether the set (or sets) we have written is consistent or not.*

The truth conditions for (3) are transparent: a basic sentence (or its negation) is its own truth condition. Since (3) is already in the list, we can check it to get:

```
(1)   P ⊃ (Q ∨ R)
(2)   ¬Q & P      ✓
(3)   ¬R          ✓
      ------------------
(4)   ¬Q
(5)   P.
```

Not much of a 'tree' yet, but things will now change. What are the truth conditions for (1)? As a material conditional – and calling on your hours of practice with truth tables – you know that if the antecedent is false, it is true; or if the consequent is true, it is true. That is, a conditional comes out true if either of these possibilities (or both) obtains. This is wholly unlike the truth conditions for (2). There truth required the joint truth of both sides.

To represent the 'either … or' nature of (1)'s truth conditions, we make our growing list fork in the following way:

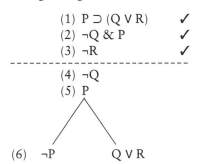

```
(1) P ⊃ (Q ∨ R)    ✓
(2) ¬Q & P         ✓
(3) ¬R             ✓
    --------------------------
(4) ¬Q
(5) P
```

(6)   ¬P   Q ∨ R

In effect, this fork, or branching, creates two lists: one with lines (1)–(5) and ¬P, and one with lines (1)–(5) and Q ∨ R. This is just how it should be since each list gives the truth conditions of the original sentences. The fork is necessitated by the fact that (1) has alternative truth conditions, and (2) doesn't. The fork saves us having to write out two separate lists. Note that we have now checked (1).

We are almost finished, but some inspection of our creation will best prepare us for the final stage. What can you say about the consistency of the list containing (1)–(5) and ¬P (i.e. the left branch)? At (5) it contains P and at (6) it contains ¬P. But P & ¬P is what we recognize as the 'standard' contradiction. So this list is obviously inconsistent, which we show by putting a cross at the bottom of the branch:

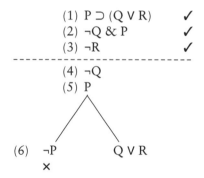

The effect of this is to condemn the left branch of the tree as inconsistent, thereby closing it. It need not be considered further.

What about the right branch? Is it consistent? Well, we have checked all the original items on our list, but we still cannot tell whether it is consistent. This is because the right branch contains a non-basic sentence whose truth conditions are not yet listed, namely Q ∨ R. Looking back up through the branch, one cannot find any standard contradictions, but who knows what the truth conditions for Q ∨ R might reveal.

The truth conditions for a disjunction, like those for the conditional, are branching conditions. This is pretty much what you would expect, since Q ∨ R is true when *either* Q is true, *or* R is true. What we do now is to write these conditions under the branch in the tree containing Q ∨ R. (Incidentally, some prefer to speak of 'paths', rather than branches. I have stuck to the latter because I find it odd to speak of a path through a tree. But then these are more tree-roots than trees.)

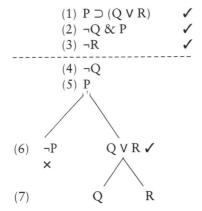

Note that we have now checked the non-basic Q V R. The last step is now the inspection for consistency of the two remaining open branches. The one ending in Q also contains ¬Q, so it is inconsistent, and the one ending in R also contains ¬R, so it too is inconsistent. Putting crosses below these gives us the following completed tree:

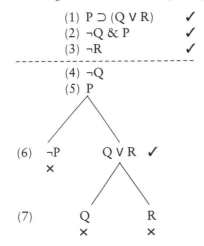

What it shows us is that all branches are closed: there is no way of assigning consistent truth conditions to the list of sentences (1)–(3). But, since this list contains the premises of our original argument and the negation of the conclusion, we know now that that argument was valid. (Remember: a tree with all branches *closed* shows *inconsistency* and this leads to a verdict of *valid* for the argument which generated the list.)

As with truth tables, the explanation of the method is more involved than its use in specific cases. In succinct form, the truth tree method consists in the following:

(1) List the premises of the argument and the negation of the conclusion.
(2) Write down all the truth conditions of the sentences in (1), checking them as you do so, and branching as necessary. If any branch has a non-basic sentence, write its truth conditions in that branch, and put a check next to it. Close (by marking with a cross) any lists which contain a basic sentence and its negation.
(3) When all the sentences are checked, and no list contains an unchecked non-basic sentence, see if you have an open list. If you do, the argument is invalid. If all lists are closed, the argument is valid.

AN IMPORTANT NOTE   When constructing a tree, you must put down the truth conditions of the sentences in your original list *under every open branch*. (That is, the truth conditions of every sentence above the dotted line.) But if you have a non-basic sentence somewhere lower down in a branch, its truth conditions need be added only to that branch.

In order to apply this method with a minimum of fuss, you must be able to write down unhesitatingly the truth conditions of sentences using any of the connectives of Sentential. Our Example showed what was involved for some of these, but you should study and then memorize the procedures given below. Note that these include procedures for dealing both with sentences and their negations.

Truth Table Extension Procedures

Conjunction	Disjunction	Conditional	Equivalence
A & B A B	A ∨ B ⟋⟍ A B	A ⊃ B ⟋⟍ ¬A B	A ≡ B ⟋⟍ A ¬A B ¬B
¬(A & B) ⟋⟍ ¬A ¬B	¬(A ∨ B) ¬A ¬B	¬(A ⊃ B) A ¬B	¬(A ≡ B) ⟋⟍ A ¬A ¬B B

Finally, we must add one further rule to make sure that we don't get caught out when constructing truth trees by a sentence of the form: ¬¬A. The rule of Double Negation is very obvious:

¬¬A
Λ.

You should now go back to some of the EXERCISES requiring truth table testing of validity and see if you can get the same answers using truth trees.

A2.2   Predicate

The truth-tree method can be adapted to Predicate, but the adaptation will require both care and caution. As to care: writing down the truth conditions of quantified sentences is not going to be straightforward. For example, it is possible to think of a universally quantified sentence such as:

($\forall$x) Fx,

as an infinite conjunction:

Fa & Fb & ...,

each of which is part of the truth condition of the original sentence. But clearly, it is just not possible to list *all* of these in constructing a tree.

As to caution: remember what was said in chapter 14 (section 14.7) about mechanical and effective methods in Predicate. Logicians, using the sophisticated machinery of mathematical logic, have proven that there can be no such test for validity in Predicate. Hence, you should expect that even the truth-tree method will fail to give us a completely general decision procedure for validity. Throwing caution to the winds for now, let us see how to carefully adapt truth trees to Predicate.

Extension Rules for the Quantifiers

As noted above, the full set of truth conditions for a universally quantified sentence are infinite. If we tried to check the sentence:

($\forall$x) Fx,

by writing down its truth conditions, we would begin this way:

```
(∀x) Fx
- - - - - - -
Fa
Fb
Fc

 .

 .

 .
```

But we would never get far enough – have a complete enough list – to justify putting a check-mark next to the original sentence. What about an existentially quantified sentence? Here the problem takes a slightly different shape, though the end result is just as inconclusive. An existentially quantified sentence:

(∃x) Fx,

is an infinite disjunction. If we tried to write its truth conditions we would get:

```
       (∃x) Fx
      - - - - - - -
      /  |   \
Fa  Fb  Fc  Fd   . . .
```

where the number of branches was infinite. As before, this rules out any hope of being able to check the quantified sentence above the line.

Definite extension rules for quantified sentences (such as those for the connectives of Sentential) are thus out of the question. But we need not despair of the truth tree method. Instead of insisting that we write down *the* truth conditions for sentences, we can relax the requirement to this:

Write down *some* truth conditions.

By picking the right truth conditions, it may be possible to show that the branches in a tree close, and that the set of sentences which generated the tree is inconsistent. After all, if a tree has inconsistent branches, then they aren't going to become consistent by getting longer. And if we can show that some appropriate set of sentences is inconsistent, this will constitute a proof of the validity of the argument which generated the set. For the underlying idea of truth trees is the same for Predicate as for Sentential:

If the set of sentences consisting of the premises and the negation of the conclusion is inconsistent, then the original argument is valid.

Here are some examples:

Example 1

Everything is green.
—————————
Albert is green.

Translation

(∀x) Fx
—————
Fa.

The set of sentences for truth tree construction, and the completed truth tree are shown below.

(∀x) Fx
¬Fa   ✓
- - - - - - - - - -
Fa.
✗

In this Example, we chose to extend the tree by writing the truth condition 'Fa' for the first premise. We chose the designator 'a' because it offered us some hope of causing an inconsistent collision with the second premise. And it did. The tree closed immediately we took this step, and, even if we were to add 'Fb' or other truth conditions for the first premise, the tree would remain closed.

Example 2

Every wallaby is a marsupial
There are wallabies.
—————————————
There are marsupials.

Translation

(∀y) (Fy ⊃ Gy)
(∃x) Fx
—————
(∃y) Gy.

Sentences to be tested

(∀y) (Fy ⊃ Gy)
(∃x) Fx
¬(∃y) Gy.

Here we have two problems. First, we haven't said anything about extension rules for negated quantified sentences. How are we to write the truth conditions for the third sentence in this list? Second, we know that we must be careful about inferences where existentially and universally quantified sentences are both present. We certainly don't want to have procedures which allow the move from 'some ...' to 'every ...'. The restrictions used in the deductive rules blocked this possibility, so one would expect something similar in the truth-tree rules.

The first problem is easily solved by recalling the quantifier equivalences:

(i) $\neg(\forall x)$ Fx is equivalent to $(\exists x) \neg$ Fx,
(ii) $\neg(\exists x)$ Fx is equivalent to $(\forall x) \neg$ Fx.

Using the second of these, we extend the tree in the following way:

$(\forall y) (Fy \supset Gy)$
$(\exists x)$ Fx
$\neg(\exists y)$ Gy   ✓
- - - - - - - - - - - - - - - - -
$(\forall y) \neg$ Gy.

We have the right to check the third sentence because what we have written is in fact *the* truth condition for it, and not merely part of it.

The second problem requires only a simple expedient: in writing down a truth condition for an existentially quantified sentence you must use a designator that has *not* been used in the branch of the tree where you are proposing an extension. This stops you from using a designator got from some other sentence whose truth condition figured higher up in the branch. If you did re-use a designator in dealing with the existential, you might well be presuming something illicit about the designated item. In the deductive rules, we took care over this by using arbitrary names and putting restrictions on their introduction in assumptions. Here we don't have assumptions, so the conventions about arbitrary names wouldn't be in place. But we are in effect achieving a kind of arbitrariness by requiring the use of a fresh new designator each time you write the truth conditions for an existential.

Taking all of this on board leads to:

(∀y) (Fy ⊃ Gy)
(∃x) Fx
¬(∃y) Gy   ✓

(∀y) ¬ Gy
Fa.

Note here that we cannot check the second premise. 'Fa' is a truth condition of it, but only one of an infinite variety, so we have no right to think we have written *the* truth condition.

The next stage is easy: write a truth condition for the first premise. Since this is universal, it is true of everything, so we have a completely free choice of designator. But, given that we want to close branches as part of proving validity, the most sensible choice would be 'a'. (To repeat: this is not illicit since the premise is universal. Only existential claims require the selection of a previously unused designator.) The result is:

(∀y) (Fy ⊃ Gy)
(∃x) Fx
¬(∃y) Gy   ✓

(∀y) ¬ Gy
Fa
Fa ⊃ Ga.

There are two more steps. First, the newly introduced conditional at the bottom of the tree needs to be checked. We cannot claim that that conditional is *the* truth condition of the first premise, but we can at least write the truth condition of the conditional itself. Second, we need to write a truth condition for the sentence just below the line. It is not one of the original premises, but it is a non-basic Predicate sentence for which we haven't yet written any truth condition. Remember that what we are trying to do is to put down enough truth conditions to show that all branches close. The result of these two steps is:

(∀y) (Fy ⊃ Gy)
(∃x) Fx
¬(∃y) Gy   ✓

(∀y) ¬ Gy
Fa
Fa ⊃ Ga   ✓

         ╱‾‾‾‾╲
    ¬Fa   Ga
     ×   ¬Ga
               ×

The left branch closes because it contains Fa and ¬Fa, and the right branch closes because it contains Ga and ¬Ga. Because there are no open branches left to work on, the tree is finished and shows the original argument to be valid (the premises and the negation of the conclusion are inconsistent). Of course, there are still truth conditions for the quantified sentences which we haven't written, but these won't change what we have now discovered about validity.

The extension rules for the quantifiers were given informally whilst constructing the above tree, so we need to take just a little more care in stating them. Using the schematic letters as we did in chapter 14, the rules are given below.

Quantifier Rules

(1)

$$(\forall v)\ \Phi v$$
$$\Phi t$$

where t is a designator that replaces each occurrence of v in Φv. (This is the replacement convention of chapter 14.)

(2)

$$(\exists v)\ \Phi v$$
$$\Phi t$$

where t is a designator not appearing in the branch above, and the replacement convention holds.

Quantifier Negation Rules

(3)

$$\neg(\forall v)\ \Phi v$$
$$(\exists v)\ \neg\Phi v.$$

(4)

$$\neg(\exists v)\ \Phi v$$
$$(\forall v)\ \neg\Phi v.$$

The four rules, when added to those given for Sentential, suffice to prove that any valid argument of Predicate can be shown to be valid by the tree method. (All valid arguments will result in trees which close.) Or almost. For we have at this point left out of account those valid arguments containing identity claims.

In chapter 15, we introduced some extra deductive apparatus for identity, and the complete tree method will involve some more exten-sion rules. In particular, we need to recognize that:

$$a \neq a,$$

is not a formal contradiction, but comes pretty close to it. After all, we agreed that:

$$(\forall x) (x = x),$$

is logically true. (You can prove this using the rules of inference of chapter 14. See section 14.6.) In short, any branch containing 'a ≠ a' can be closed. If now we add a rule allowing us to substitute identicals for identicals as part of extending a tree, then we will have what is needed to handle all valid arguments in the Predicate language with identity. (The formal statement of these rules is left to the reader.)

The tree method works only for all *valid* arguments. However, as was noted earlier, no effective and mechanical decision procedure can be devised for Predicate, and this means that there will be invalid arguments which are undetectable as such by the tree method. How so? Well, remember that in Sentential, when you finished a tree you had only to look at the branches: if all were closed, the argument was valid; if there was still one open, it was invalid. Though we don't have the heavyweight materials to prove this, it is a fact that trees in Sentential will have a finite number of branches and each branch will be of finite length. This finiteness is what ensures the surveyability of a tree, and is effectively the reason why the truth tree method is an algorithm in Sentential. In Predicate, however, there are cases where a branch is not yet closed, but is also not yet finished. That is, it can happen that writing down more and more truth conditions for a quantified sentence produces a longer, still unclosed, branch. It would of course be nice if we could look at the branch and pronounce it 'open' (hence showing the invalidity of the argument). But until we have written down *all* the relevant truth conditions, we cannot be sure the branch won't suddenly close. And, sadly, the truth conditions for quantified sentences lend themselves to producing, in certain cases, infinitely long branches which clearly cannot be surveyed in a finite amount of time.

You should now go back to chapter 14 and try to prove valid by the truth tree method those arguments which were shown valid by deduction. Compare the ease of using these different methods in each case.

Appendix 3:
Alternative Notations

A3.0 Alternative Logical Connectives and Quantifiers

The following table lists common alternatives to the basic logical symbols used in this book.

Symbol used here	Alternatives
¬P	~P, −P, $\overline{P}$
P & Q	$P \wedge Q$, $P \cdot Q$, PQ
P ⊃ Q	$P \rightarrow Q$
P ≡ Q	$P \leftrightarrow Q$
(∀x)	(x), Πx
(∃x)	(Ex), Σx

Note: the quantifier symbols come from the first letters of 'All' and 'Exist'. However, so that they are not confused with predicate letters, logicians originally suggested that the universal be the upside-down 'A' and the existential, the backwards 'E'. This was of course easy when type was set with individual pieces of metal put into a block. But nowadays, word processors and computerized typesetting machines require special symbols for the quantifiers, so the original benefit of using letter-shaped pieces of metal is lost. That is why some books just give up and use '(Ex)' for the existential. (Given that there are only two quantifier symbols, it is possible to use a variable on its own for one of them, so long as you have some way of marking the other. That is why the universal is sometimes '(x)'.)

A3.1 Parentheses and Grouping

On occasion in this book – and when it helped make a sentence clearer – parentheses were dropped, even though they were strictly speaking needed. However, it is possible to adopt certain conventions so as to eliminate parentheses still further. (Some logicians obviously feel that they clutter up their sentences.) A brief survey of the alternatives is given below, though I think that, in contemporary philosophical writing, most logical formalism tends to be written with (nearly) full parenthetical markings.

(a)   If we agree to think of the symbols as having an order of precedence, then we can change:

P ⊃ (Q ∨ R),

into:

P ⊃ Q ∨ R,

without re-introducing ambiguity. One simply says that '⊃' always has scope over '∨' unless parentheses are used to say otherwise. If this is done with the other connectives, most parentheses become redundant (except when you have multiple uses of the same connective).

(b)   If you think about it, you don't always need both the left and right parentheses. Thus, if we assume that left parentheses go to the end of a sentence, then:

P ⊃ (Q ⊃ (R & S)),

would be understood unambiguously if written:

P ⊃ (Q ⊃ (R & S.

So as to deal with cases where parentheses might not act this way, we could use dots written after a connective (in ones, twos, threes, etc.) in place of parentheses. Thus, we could write the above this way:

P ⊃: Q ⊃. R & S,

where dot(s) give a connective scope that goes to the end of the sentence unless they encounter dots of a higher power (i.e. more of them). In the above, the double dots which follow the first conditional carry on past the single dot and take in the remainder of the sentence. This makes the first conditional the main connective of the sentence.

(c)   Both of the methods above minimize the need for parentheses but don't remove it. More radical in this respect is the Polish notation, so-called because of its development by the important school of logic that existed in Poland. First one defines Polish connectives this way:

Np   ¬P
Kpq   P & Q
Apq   P ∨ Q
Cpq   P ⊃ Q

Epq   P ≡ Q

This now suffices to eliminate the need for parentheses since, for example, we can represent:

(1)   P ∨ (Q & ¬R)

as:

ApKqNr.

Compare this to the representation of:

(2)   (P ∨ Q) & ¬R,

namely:

KApqNr.

The order of the upper case letters, and the need for them to be followed by one or two complete sentences, gives us all we need if we are faced by (1) or (2). The Polish notation is clever, but is not easy to read. (Though this has been disputed by those who think we are predisposed to parentheses by familiarity and haven't given the alternative a fair trial.)

Answers to Exercises
Marked '*' in Chapters 1–17

CHAPTER 2

Exercise 2

(iii) The following is one of several suggested ways of carrying out the task. The argument is valid (and someone in the Middle Ages was burnt at the stake for propounding it).

(1) If God is omnipotent, there is nothing he cannot do.
(2) If God can build a mountain he cannot move, or he cannot build a mountain he cannot move, there is something he cannot do.

God is not omnipotent.

CHAPTER 4

Exercise 2

(a) Tiny was called 'Tiny' because of his size.
(c) The name 'Theodore' means the same as 'Dorothy'.

Exercise 3

(i)

P	Q	Q V P
T	T	T
T	F	T
F	T	T
F	F	F

Exercise 4

P	Q	Q ⊃ P
T	T	T
T	F	T
Γ	T	F
F	F	T

CHAPTER 5

Exercise 1
(a) Not wf; (b) not wf; (c) not wf; (d) wf; (e) not wf.

Exercise 2
(a) Scope is whole sentence; (b) scope is (P_3 & P_4).

Exercise 6

(a)

P_1	P_2	P_3
T	T	T
T	T	F
T	F	T
T	F	F
F	T	T
F	T	F
F	F	T
F	F	F

(c)

P_1
T
F

Exercise 7

(i)   Final answer is in fourth column below.

P₁	Q₁	Q₂	P₁ ⊃ ¬(Q₁ & Q₂)		
T	T	T	F	F	T
T	T	F	T	T	F
T	F	T	T	T	F
T	F	F	T	T	F
F	T	T	T	F	T
F	T	F	T	T	F
F	F	T	T	T	F
F	F	F	T	T	F

(iii)   Final answer in fourth column below.

P₁	Q₁	Q₂	P₁ ≡ (Q₁ V Q₂)	
T	T	T	T	T
T	T	F	T	T
T	F	T	T	T
T	F	F	F	F
F	T	T	F	T
F	T	F	F	T
F	F	T	F	T
F	F	F	T	F

Exercise 8

(a)   ¬(¬P₁ & ¬P₂); ¬(P₁ & ¬P₂) & ¬(P₂ & ¬P₁).
(b)   Only pair (i) is functionally complete.

CHAPTER 6

Exercise 1

(a)   Premises are jointly true in first and third rows (see below) and conclusion is also true in those rows. Thus, the argument is valid.

P	Q	P V Q	P ⊃ Q
T	T	T	T
T	F	T	F
F	T	T	T
F	F	F	T

(c)   Premises are jointly true only in fifth row (see below) and conclusion is also true in that row. So, the argument is valid.

P	Q_1	Q_2	P V (Q_1 & Q_2)		¬P	Q_1 V P
T	T	T	T	T	F	T
T	T	F	T	F	F	T
T	F	T	T	F	F	T
T	F	F	T	F	F	T
F	T	T	T	T	T	T
F	T	F	F	F	T	T
F	F	T	F	F	T	F
F	F	F	F	F	T	F

(e)   Premise is only true in last row and conclusion is also true in that row. Thus, the argument is valid.

P	Q	¬(P V Q)		¬Q
T	T	F	T	F
T	F	F	T	T
F	T	F	T	F
F	F	T	F	T

Exercise 2
(a) contingent;   (b) contingent;   (c) tautology;   (d) tautology;
(e) contradiction.

Exercise 3
(a) is equivalent to (i);   (b) is equivalent to (g);   (c) is equivalent to (e);   (d) is equivalent to (j);   (f) is equivalent to (h).

Exercise 4
(a) inconsistent;   (b) consistent;   (c) consistent.

CHAPTER 7

Exercise
Note: displaying answers to this exercise is problematic because, in order to appreciate which answer is correct, translations for basic sentences must be shown. Therefore, below you will find basic sentences in English (underlined) and connectives in Sentential. It is left to you to choose your favourite basic Ps and Qs, but note exactly what counts as a basic sentence in each case.

(a)   I will take my holiday abroad this year V the weather improves.

[Acceptable variations: ¬I will take my holiday abroad this year ⊃ the weather improves; ¬the weather improves ⊃ I will take my holiday abroad this year.]

(b)   ¬(<u>love would persuade him to help with the project</u> V <u>money would persuade him to help with the project</u>)

[Acceptable variation: ¬<u>love would persuade him to help with the project</u> & ¬<u>money would persuade him to help with the project</u>.]

(c)   <u>Greek is a difficult language to learn</u> & <u>Greek is a worthwhile language to learn</u>.

(d)   ¬<u>You do play</u> ⊃ ¬<u>you can win</u>.

(e)   (<u>Smith comes to dinner</u> & ¬<u>Jones comes to dinner</u>) ⊃ <u>we can all travel in the same car</u>.

(f)   ¬(<u>Robert can be travelling to London</u> & <u>Robert can be dining in Paris</u>).

(g)   ¬<u>You work hard</u> ⊃ ¬<u>you can succeed</u>.

[Acceptable variation: <u>you can succeed</u> ⊃ <u>you work hard</u>.]

(h)   (<u>The fuel holds out</u> & (<u>we get a following wind</u> V <u>we get a calm sea</u>)) ⊃ <u>we will be in harbour today</u>.

(i)   <u>The trains are running</u> ⊃ <u>I'll be there</u>.

(j)   ¬<u>Smoking is healthy</u>.

CHAPTER 8

Exercise

(1)
Translation key: P – Mark went to the restaurant around the corner.
Q – Mark went to Mexico.

Argument: $\underline{P}$

P V Q.

Truth table (below) shows the premise true in rows 1 and 2, but the conclusion is also true in these rows, so the argument is valid.

P	Q	P V Q
T	T	T
T	F	T
F	T	T
F	F	F

(3)
Translation key: P – I finish this book by Christmas.
Q – The book will be published before 1987.
(Note the way 'until' works with the negation
in the first sentence, so that we have to change
it to 'before' when we drop the negation.)
R – I will forfeit my advance on royalties.

Argument: ¬P ⊃ ¬Q
¬Q ⊃ R
¬R

P.

Truth table (below) shows the premises jointly true only in the second
row. Since the conclusion is also true in that row, the argument is
valid.

P	Q	R	¬P ⊃ ¬Q	¬Q ⊃ R	¬R
T	T	T	F T F	T	F
T	T	F	F T F	T	T
T	F	T	F T T	T	F
T	F	F	F T T	F	T
F	T	T	T F F	T	F
F	T	F	T F F	T	T
F	F	T	T T T	T	F
F	F	F	T T T	F	T

(5)
Translation: P – The Americans have been able to solve the
problems of the arms race.
Q – The Soviets have been able to solve the
problems of the arms race.
R – We face certain annihilation.

Argument: ¬(P V Q)
¬P ⊃ R

¬Q ⊃ R.

The truth table (below) shows the premises jointly true only in row 7
and the conclusion is also true there. So, the argument is valid.

P	Q	R	¬(P V Q)		¬P ⊃ R		¬Q ⊃ R	
T	T	T	F	T	F	T	F	T
T	T	F	F	T	F	T	F	T
T	F	T	F	T	F	T	T	T
T	F	F	F	T	F	T	T	F
F	T	T	F	T	T	T	F	T
F	T	F	F	T	T	F	F	T
F	F	T	T	F	T	T	T	T
F	F	F	T	F	T	F	T	F

(7)

Translation: P – Emily gets a bicycle for her birthday.
Q – Emily gets a dress for her birthday.
R – Emily will be happy.

Argument: ¬R V P (or: R ⊃ P; or: ¬P ⊃ ¬R)

Q ⊃ ¬R.

The truth table (below) shows the premise true in rows 1–4, 6 and 8. In those rows the conclusion is true everywhere except row 1. But this is enough to make the argument invalid, since the conclusion must be true in *every* row where the premises are jointly true. (**Note:** the invalidity of this argument can seem surprising. But what must be remembered is that the conclusion doesn't rule out her getting a bicycle too. Therefore, the conclusion can be false (she gets a dress and is happy) whilst the premise is true because she gets a bicycle.)

P	Q	R	¬R V P		Q ⊃ ¬R
T	T	T	F	T	F
T	T	F	T	T	T
T	F	T	F	T	T
T	F	F	T	T	T
F	T	T	F	F	F
F	T	F	T	T	T
F	F	T	F	F	T
F	F	F	T	T	T

CHAPTER 9

Exercise 2
Note: the left-side number and line number are shown here separated by a backslash.

(a)   1(1)/ 2(2)/ 3(3)/ 1,3(4)/ 1,2,3(5)/ 1,2(6).

(b)   1(1)/ 2(2)/ 2(3)/ 4(4)/ 4(5)/ 1(6).

(c)   1(1)/ 2(2)/ 3(3)/ 1,3(4)/ 1,2,3(5)/ 1,2(6).

(d)   1(1)/ 2(2)/ 3(3)/ 4(4)/ 1,4(5)/ 1,4(6)/ 1,2,4(7)/ 1,2,3,4(8)/ 1,2,3(9)

Exercise 3
Note: the line number and right-side justification are shown here separated by a backslash.

(a)   (1) Premise/ (2) Assumption/ (3) Assumption/ (4) 2,3 &I/ (5) 1,4 &I/ (6) 3,5 ¬I/ (7) 6 ¬E/ (8) 2,7 ⊃I.

(b)   (1) Premise/ (2) Assumption/ (3) 2 &E/ (4) 1,3 ⊃E/ (5) 2 &E/ (6) 4,5 &I/ (7) 2,6 ¬I.

(c)   (1) Premise/ (2) Premise/ (3) Premise/ (4) Assumption/ (5) 1,4 ⊃E/ (6) Assumption/ (7) 2,6 ⊃E/ (8) Assumption/ (9) 3,8 ⊃E / (10) 5,6,7,8,9 VE/ (11) 4,10 ⊃I.

(d)   (1) Premise/ (2) Assumption/ (3) Assumption/ (4) 1,3 ⊃E/ (5) 4 VI/ (6) 2,5 &I/ (7) 3,6 ¬I/ (8) 7 VI/ (9) 2,8 &I/ (10) 2,9 ¬I/ (11) 10 ¬E.

Exercise 4

(a)

1	(1)	
1	(2)	1 &E
1	(3)	1 &E
1	(4)	2,3 &I

(b)

1	(1)	
2	(2)	
3	(3)	
4	(4)	Assumption
1,4	(5)	1,4 ⊃E
1,2,4	(6)	2,5 ⊃E
1,2,3,4	(7)	3,6 &I
1,2,3	(8)	4,7 ¬I

(c)

1	(1)	
2	(2)	
3	(3)	Assumption
1,3	(4)	1,3 ⊃E
1,2,3	(5)	2,4 &I
1,2	(6)	3,5 ¬I

Exercise 6

(a)
Translation of argument: ¬(P V Q) ⊢ ¬P & ¬Q

1	(1)	¬(P V Q)	Premise
2	(2)	P	Assumption
2	(3)	P V Q	2 V I
1,2	(4)	(P V Q) & ¬(P V Q)	1,3 &I
1	(5)	¬P	2,4 ¬I
6	(6)	Q	Assumption
6	(7)	P V Q	6 V I
1,6	(8)	(P V Q) & ¬(P V Q)	1,7 &I
1	(9)	¬Q	6,8 ¬I
1	(10)	¬P & ¬Q	5,9 &I

(b)
Translation of argument: ¬P ⊃ Q ⊢ P V Q

1	(1)	¬P ⊃ Q	Premise
2	(2)	¬(P V Q)	Assumption

Here insert the same ten steps from deduction (a) above, changing only line numbers. This continues:

2	(11)	¬P & ¬Q	6,10 &I
2	(12)	¬P	11 &E
1,2	(13)	Q	1,12 ⊃E
2	(14)	¬Q	11 &E
1,2	(15)	Q & ¬Q	13,14 &I
1	(16)	¬¬(P V Q)	2,15 ¬I
1	(17)	P V Q	16 ¬E

(c)
Translation of argument: (P ⊃ Q) & (R ⊃ S), ¬Q & ¬S ⊢ ¬P & ¬R

1	(1)	(P ⊃ Q) & (R ⊃ S)	Premise
2	(2)	¬Q & ¬S	Premise
3	(3)	P	Assumption
2	(4)	¬Q	2 &E
1	(5)	P ⊃ Q	1 &E
1,3	(6)	Q	3,5 ⊃ E
1,2,3	(7)	Q & ¬Q	4,6 &I
1,2	(8)	¬P	3,7 ¬I
9	(9)	R	Assumption
2	(10)	¬S	2 &E

1	(11) R ⊃ S	1 &E
1,9	(12) S	9,11 ⊃E
1,2,9	(13) S & ¬S	10,12 &I
1,2	(14) ¬R	9,13 ¬I
1,2	(15) ¬P & ¬R	8,14 &I

(d)
Translation of argument: ¬P & ¬Q ⊢ ¬(P V Q)

1	(1) ¬P & ¬Q	Premise
2	(2) P V Q	Assumption
3	(3) P	Assumption
1	(4) ¬P	1 &E
1,3	(5) P & ¬P	3,4 &I
3	(6) ¬(¬P & ¬Q)	1,5 ¬I
7	(7) Q	Assumption
1	(8) ¬Q	1 &E
1,7	(9) Q & ¬Q	7,8 &I
7	(10) ¬(¬P & ¬Q)	1,9 ¬I
2	(11) ¬(¬P & ¬Q)	2,3,6,7,10 VE
1,2	(12) (¬P & ¬Q) & ¬(¬P & ¬Q)	1,11 &I
1	(13) ¬(P V Q)	2,12 ¬I

(This is a difficult proof which would repay study.)

(e)
Translation of argument: P V Q, Q ⊃ (¬R & S) ⊢ ¬P ⊃ ¬R

1	(1) P V Q	Premise
2	(2) Q ⊃ (¬R & S)	Premise
3	(3) ¬P	Assumption
4	(4) P	Assumption
5	(5) ¬Q	Assumption
4,5	(6) P & ¬Q	4,5 &I
4,5	(7) P	6 &E
3,4,5	(8) P & ¬P	3,7 &I
3,4	(9) ¬¬Q	5,8 ¬I
3,4	(10) Q	9 ¬E
11	(11) Q	Assumption
1,3	(12) Q	1,4,10,11,11 VE
1,2,3	(13) ¬R & S	2,12 ⊃E
1,2,3	(14) ¬R	13 &E
1,2	(15) ¬P ⊃ ¬R	3,14 ⊃I

(**Note:** we had to make a little circular move in lines 4–7 in order to make the assumption at line 5 one of the premises for line 8. This makes it more transparent that we are discharging line 5.

(g)
Translation of the argument: $P \lor Q$, $Q \supset R_1$, $P \supset (R_2 \lor R_3)$, $\neg R_1 \& \neg R_3 \vdash R_2$

1	(1)	$P \lor Q$	Premise
2	(2)	$Q \supset R_1$	Premise
3	(3)	$P \supset (R_2 \lor R_3)$	Premise
4	(4)	$\neg R_1 \& \neg R_3$	Premise
5	(5)	Q	Assumption
2,5	(6)	R_1	2,5 $\supset$E
4	(7)	$\neg R_1$	4 &E
2,4,5	(8)	$R_1 \& \neg R_1$	6,7 &I
2,4	(9)	$\neg Q$	5,8 $\neg$I
10	(10)	$\neg P$	Assumption
2,4,10	(11)	$\neg P \& \neg Q$	9,10 &I

Here insert the steps of the proof given in (d) above.

2,4,10	(23)	$\neg(P \lor Q)$	12,22 $\neg$I
1,2,4,10	(24)	$(P \lor Q) \& \neg(P \lor Q)$	1,2,3 &I
1,2,4	(25)	$\neg\neg P$	10,24 $\neg$I
1,2,4	(26)	P	25 $\neg$E
1,2,3,4	(27)	$R_2 \lor R_3$	3,26 $\supset$E
28	(28)	$\neg R_2$	Assumption
4	(29)	$\neg R_3$	4 &E
4,28	(30)	$\neg R_2 \& \neg R_3$	28,29 &I

Here insert again the steps of the proof (allowing for letter changes) of (d) above.

4,28	(42)	$\neg(R_2 \lor R_3)$	31,41 $\neg$I
1,2,3,4,28	(43)	$(R_2 \lor R_3) \& \neg(R_2 \lor R_3)$	27,42 &I
1,2,3,4	(44)	$\neg\neg R_2$	28,43 $\neg$I
1,2,3,4	(45)	R_2	44 $\neg$E

Exercise 7

(a)

1	(1)	$P \& \neg P$	Assumption
	(2)	$\neg(P \& \neg P)$	1,1 $\neg$I

(c)

1	(1)	P	Assumption
1	(2)	P ∨ P	1 VI
	(3)	P ⊃ (P ∨ P)	1,3 ⊃I
4	(4)	P ∨ P	Assumption
5	(5)	P	Assumption
4	(6)	P	4,5,5,5,5 VE
	(7)	(P ∨ P) ⊃ P	4,6 ⊃I
	(8)	(P ⊃ (P ∨ P)) & ((P ∨ P) ⊃ P)	3,7 &I
	(9)	P ≡ (P ∨ P)	8 ≡I

CHAPTER 12

Exercises 1 and 2

(a) (∀y) (Fy) ∨ Gy – first two 'y's are bound, third is free.

(b) (∃x) ((Fx & Gx) ∨ Fy) – first three 'x's are bound, 'y' is free.

(c) (∀x₁) (Gx₁ ⊃ Gx₂) ⊃ Fx₁ – first two 'x₁'s are bound, 'x₂' and final 'x₁' are free.

(d) (∃y) Fy & Gy – first two 'y's are bound, last is free.

(e) (∀x) (((Fx ∨ Gy) ∨ Hy) ⊃ F₂x) – all 'x's are bound, 'y's are free.

Exercise 3

(i)
(a) Every square is in at least one (some) triangle.
(b) At least one (some) circle is to the left of at least one (some) triangle.
(c) There is some triangle in every square.
(d) Every circle is in every square.

Exercise 5

(a) Fa ∨ Fb; (Fa ∨ Ga) & (Fb ∨ Gb).
(b) Re-read carefully section 12.5 for the answer.

Exercise 7

(∀x) (((Hx & (x ≠ a)) ⊃ (∃y) (Fy & Rxy)), where Hx – x is a child, 'a' designates Mary, Fx – x is ice-cream, Rxy – x has y. This does *not* entail that Mary does not have an ice-cream, merely that everyone else does. This seems right since one could imagine Mary having an ice-cream and someone setting out to make sure that everyone else has one too.

Exercise 9

(a) $(\exists x)\,(\exists y)\,(\exists z)\,((Fx\ \&\ Fy\ \&\ Fz)\ \&\ x \neq y\ \&\ y \neq z\ \&\ x \neq z)$.
(Some liberties taken here with parentheses.)

(b) $(\forall x)\,(\forall y)\,((Gx\ \&\ Gy) \supset x = y)$.

Exercise 10

(a) $(\exists x)\,(\exists y)\,((H_1 x\ \&\ H_1 y)\ \&\ x \neq y\ \&\ (\forall z)\,((H_1 z) \supset (z = x \lor z = y)))$.

CHAPTER 13

Exercise 1
Potentially designating expressions are indicated by underlining.

(a)   <u>Byron</u> died in <u>Greece</u>.
(b)   <u>This book</u> is not meant to be read in one sitting.
(c)   <u>John</u> ran <u>himself</u> down.
(d)   <u>My favourite stories</u> are those by <u>Balzac</u>.
(e)   <u>This</u> will serve as a table.

Exercise 2

(a)   x and y spent the whole day on the beach (Rxy).
      x and y spent the whole day on z (Sxyz).
(b)   x shared with y (Rxy).
      x shared with Jim (Fx).
(c)   x came around the bend without braking (Fx).
      x came around y without braking (Rxy).
(d)   The road marked x goes to y (Rxy).
      x marked y goes to z (Sxyz).
(e)   x sat impassively in y smoking z (Sxyz).
      x sat impassively in y smoking his pipe (Rxy).

Exercise 3

(a) $(\exists x)\,(Fx\ \&\ \neg Gx)$ (Fx – x is a person, Gx – x is employed).

(b) $(\forall x)\,(Fx \supset Hx)$ (Fx – x is a violin, Hx – x is hand-crafted).

(c) $(\forall x)\,(Fx \supset Gx)$ (Fx – x is an apple, Gx – x is seeded).

(d) $(\exists x)\,(Fx\ \&\ Hx)$ (Fx – x is an apple, Hx – x is eaten).

(e) $(\forall x)\,(Fx \supset Gx)$ (Fx – x is a train, Gx – x will do).

(f) $(\forall x)\,(Rax \supset Hx)$ (Rxy – x said y, 'a' designates the speaker, Hx – x is to no avail). (**Note:**

this last predicate is an idiom and there isn't really a negative quantifier in 'no avail'.)

(g)   (∀x) (Fx ⊃ Gx)   (Fx – x is a dodo, Gx – x is extinct). (**Note:** you might think that '¬(∃x) Fx' would be better. But Predicate quantifiers are intended as timeless; if there were once dodos, saying that they are extinct means that they can no longer be found.)

(h)   (∃x) (Rxa & Hx)   (Rxy – x is in y, 'a' is the text, Hx – x is misleading).

Exercise 4

(a)   ¬(∀x) (¬Hx ⊃ Fx)   (Hx – x is honest, Fx – x is a politician.) (**Note:** it could be argued that the English sentence entails that there is a dishonest politician, or indeed that they all are. Context plays an important role in understanding 'only', but the minimally correct translation is the one given.)

(b)   (∀x) (Fx ⊃ ¬Gx)   (Fx – x is a whale, Gx – x is a fish).

(c)   (∃x) (Gx & ¬Hx)   (Gx – x glisters (glistens), Hx – x is gold). (Be careful: this proverb does *not* mean: nothing which glisters is gold.)

(d)   (∀x) (Fx ⊃ Gx)   (Fx – x is talented, Gx – x is lucky).

(e)   (∀x) (Fx ⊃ ¬Gx)   (Fx – x is an apple, Gx – x was edible).

Exercise 5

(a)   (∃x) (Fx & (∀y) (Gy ⊃ Ryx));
or: (∀y) (Gy ⊃ (∃x) (Fx & Ryx))   (Fx – x is a Vermeer, Gx – x is a person, Rxy – x likes y). (**Note:** both readings could be conveyed by the English sentence.)

(d)   (∀x) Fx ⊃ (∃x) Gx   (Fx – x is a person who stands up, Gx – x gets wet). (**Note:** one can use the same variable here because the first quantifier has only the antecedent of the conditional in its scope.)

(f)   (∀y) (Gy ⊃ (∃x) (Fx & Rxy));   (Fx – x is a person, Gy – y
or: (∃x) (Fx & (∀y) (Gy ⊃ Rxy))   is a time, Rxy – x is late
at y).

CHAPTER 14

Exercise 1

(a)

1	(1)	(∀x) Fx	Premise
1	(2)	Fa	1 ∀E
1	(3)	(∃x) Fx	2 ∃I

(d)

1	(1)	(∀x) (Fx ⊃ Gx)	Premise
2	(2)	(∃x) Fx	Premise
3	(3)	Ff	Assumption
1	(4)	Ff ⊃ Gf	1 ∀E
1,3	(5)	Gf	3,4 ⊃E
1,3	(6)	(∃x) Gx	5 ∃I
1,2	(7)	(∃x) Gx	2,3,6 ∃E

Exercise 2

(b)
Translation
(∀x) (Fx ⊃ ¬Gx)
(∃x) (Fx & Hx)

(∃x) (Hx & ¬Gx).

Deduction

1	(1)	(∀x) (Fx ⊃ ¬Gx)	Premise
2	(2)	(∃x) (Fx & Hx)	Premise
3	(3)	Ff & Hf	Assumption
1	(4)	Ff ⊃ ¬Gf	1 ∀E
3	(5)	Ff	3 &E
1,3	(6)	¬Gf	4,5 ⊃E
3	(7)	Hf	3 &E
1,3	(8)	Hf & ¬Gf	6,7 &I
1,3	(9)	(∃x) (Hx & ¬Gx)	8 ∃I
1,2	(10)	(∃x) (Hx & ¬Gx)	2,3,9 ∃E

(d)
Translation
S_1abc
$(\forall x)(\forall y)(S_1axy \supset S_2axy)$

S_2abc

(where S_1xyz – x borrowed y from z, S_2xyz – x returned y to z, 'a' is Nigel, 'b' is *War and Peace*, 'c' is Inga.)

1	(1)	S_1abc	Premise
2	(2)	$(\forall x)(\forall y)(S_1axy \supset S_2axy)$	Premise
2	(3)	$(\forall y)(S_1aby \supset S_2aby)$	2 $\forall$E
2	(4)	$S_1abc \supset S_2abc$	3 $\forall$E
1,2	(5)	S_2abc	1,4 $\supset$E

Exercise 3

(a)
1	(1)	$(\forall y) Fy$	Assumption
1	(2)	Ff	1 $\forall$E
1	(3)	$(\forall x) Fx$	2 $\forall$I
	(4)	$(\forall y) Fy \supset (\forall x) Fx$	1,3 $\supset$I
5	(5)	$(\forall x) Fx$	Assumption
5	(6)	Ff	5 $\forall$E
5	(7)	$(\forall y) Fy$	6 $\forall$I
	(8)	$(\forall x) Fx \supset (\forall y) Fy$	5,7 $\supset$I
	(9)	$((\forall y) Fy \supset (\forall x) Fx)$ & $((\forall x) Fx \supset (\forall y) Fy)$	4,8 &I
	(10)	$(\forall y) Fy \equiv (\forall x) Fx$	9 $\equiv$I

(c)
1	(1)	$(\forall x)(Fx \supset (\forall y)(Gy \supset Rxy))$	Premise
1	(2)	$Ff_1 \supset (\forall y)(Gy \supset Rf_1y)$	1 $\forall$E
3	(3)	Ff_1 & Gf_2	Assumption
3	(4)	Ff_1	3 &E
1,3	(5)	$(\forall y)(Gy \supset Rf_1y)$	2,4 $\supset$E
1,3	(6)	$Gf_2 \supset Rf_1f_2$	5 $\forall$E
3	(7)	Gf_2	3 &E
1,3	(8)	Rf_1f_2	6,7 $\supset$E
1	(9)	$(Ff_1$ & $Gf_2) \supset Rf_1f_2$	4,8 $\supset$I
1	(10)	$(\forall y)(Ff_1$ & $Gy) \supset Rf_1y$	9 $\forall$I
1	(11)	$(\forall x)(\forall y)((Fx$ & $Gy) \supset Rxy)$	10 $\forall$I
	(12)	$[(\forall x)(Fx \supset (\forall y)(Gy \supset Rxy))] \supset [(\forall x)(\forall y)((Fx$ & $Gy) \supset Rxy)]$	1,11 $\supset$I

Reading List

1 On the experimental investigation of how we think deductively:
> J. Evans, *The Psychology of Deductive Reasoning*. London: Routledge & Kegan Paul, 1982.

2 A good general introduction to the linguistics of natural language:
> N. Smith and D. Wilson, *Modern Linguistics*. Harmondsworth: Penguin Books, 1979.

3 On the fascinating history of logic:
> W. Kneale and M. Kneale, *The Development of Logic*. Oxford: Oxford University Press, 1961.

4 For demonstrations of soundness, completeness and the discussion of decision procedures (and more):
> G. Hunter, *Metalogic*. Berkeley, CA: University of California Press, 1971.
> E. Mendelson, *Introduction to Mathematical Logic*. Princeton, NJ: Princeton University Press, 1964.
> D. Prawitz, *Natural Deduction*. Stockholm: Almquist & Wicksell, 1965.
> N. Tennant, *Natural Logic*. Edinburgh: Edinburgh University Press, 1978.

5 For more detailed discussions of adjectives, definite descriptions, names, pronouns, quantifiers and discussions of the logical treatment of natural language constructions not considered in this book:
> D. Davidson and G. Harman, *The Logic of Grammar*. Encino, CA: Dickenson Publishing Co., 1975.
> M. Davies, *Meaning, Quantification, Necessity*. London: Routledge & Kegan Paul, 1981.
> D. Dowty, R. Wall and S. Peters, *Introduction to Montague Semantics*. Dordrecht: D. Reidel, 1981.
> M. Platts, *Ways of Meaning*. London: Routledge & Kegan Paul, 1979.

6 On modal logic:
> G. Hughes and M. Cresswell, *An Introduction to Modal Logic*. London: Methuen, 1968.
> See also M. Davies mentioned under 5 above.

7 On truth definition:
   A. Tarski, *Logic, Semantics and Metamathematics*, translated by J. Woodger. Oxford: Oxford University Press, 1956.

8 On artificial intelligence:
   E. Charniak and D. McDermott, *Introduction to Artificial Intelligence*. Reading, MA: Addison-Wesley, 1985.

Index

Printed in Poland
by Amazon Fulfillment
Poland Sp. z o.o., Wrocław